Kaplan Publishing are constantly fi ways to make a difference to your s exciting online resources really do different to students looking for exam success.

This book comes with free EN-gage online resources so that you can study anytime, anywhere.

cher190188!

Having purchased this book, you have access to the following online study materials:

CONTENT	ACCA (including FFA,FAB,FMA)		AAT		FIA (excluding FFA,FAB,FMA)	
	Text	Kit	Text	Kit	Text	Kit
iPaper version of the book	✓	✓	✓	✓	✓	✓
Interactive electronic version of the book	✓					
Fixed tests / progress tests with instant answers	✓		✓			
Mock assessments online			✓	✓		
Material updates	✓	✓	✓	✓	✓	✓
Latest official ACCA exam questions		✓				
Extra question assistance using the signpost icon*		✓				
Timed questions with an online tutor debrief using the clock icon*		✓				
Interim assessment including questions and answers		✓			✓	
Technical articles	✓	✓			✓	✓

* Excludes F1, F2, F3, FFA, FAB, FMA

How to access your online resources

Kaplan Financial students will already have a Kaplan EN-gage account and these extra resources will be available to you online. You do not need to register again, as this process was completed when you enrolled. If you are having problems accessing online materials, please ask your course administrator.

If you are already a registered Kaplan EN-gage user go to www.EN-gage.co.uk and log in. Select the 'add a book' feature and enter the ISBN number of this book and the unique pass key at the bottom of this card. Then click 'finished' or 'add another book'. You may add as many books as you have purchased from this screen.

If you purchased through Kaplan Flexible Learning or via the Kaplan Publishing website you will automatically receive an e-mail invitation to Kaplan EN-gage online. Please register your details using this email to gain access to your content. If you do not receive the e-mail or book content, please contact Kaplan Flexible Learning.

If you are a new Kaplan EN-gage user register at www.EN-gage.co.uk and click on the link contained in the email we sent you to activate your account. Then select the 'add a book' feature, enter the ISBN number of this book and the unique pass key at the bottom of this card. Then click 'finished' or 'add another book'.

EN-gage

Your Code and Information

This code can only be used once for the registration of one book online. This registration and your online content will expire when the final sittings for the examinations covered by this book have taken place. Please allow one hour from the time you submit your book details for us to process your request.

Please scratch the film to access your EN-gage code.

Please be aware that this code is case-sensitive and you will need to include the dashes within the passcode, but not when entering the ISBN. For further technical support, please visit www.EN-gage.co.uk

KAPLAN PUBLISHING

Financial Performance

Qualifications and Credit Framework

Level 4 Diploma in Accounting

British Library Cataloguing-in-Publication Data

A catalogue record for this book is available from the British Library.

Published by
Kaplan Publishing UK
Unit 2, The Business Centre
Molly Millars Lane
Wokingham
Berkshire
RG41 2QZ

ISBN 978 0 85732 605 8

Printed and bound in Great Britain

We are grateful to the Association of Accounting Technicians for permission to reproduce past assessment materials and example tasks based on the new syllabus. The solutions to past answers and similar activities in the style of the new syllabus have been prepared by Kaplan Publishing.

CONTENTS

Introduction			v
Unit guide			vii
The assessment			xxv
Study skills			xxvii
Terminology			xxxi

STUDY TEXT AND WORKBOOK

Chapter		*Study text*	*Workbook Activities Answers*
1	The business environment	1	–
2	Collection of cost information	23	489
3	Accounting for overheads	51	489
4	Cost management	119	493
5	Time series, sampling and index numbers	145	495
6	Standard costing and variance analysis	197	497
7	Investigating and reporting variances	275	510
8	Performance indicators	345	528

Practice Assessment	559
Practice Assessment Answers	575
Glossary	583
Index	I.1

INTRODUCTION

HOW TO USE THESE MATERIALS

These Kaplan Publishing learning materials have been carefully designed to make your learning experience as easy as possible and to give you the best chance of success in your AAT assessments.

They contain a number of features to help you in the study process.

The sections on the Unit Guide, the Assessment and Study Skills should be read before you commence your studies.

They are designed to familiarise you with the nature and content of the assessment and to give you tips on how best to approach your studies.

STUDY TEXT

This study text has been specially prepared for the revised AAT qualification introduced in July 2010.

It is written in a practical and interactive style:

- key terms and concepts are clearly defined
- all topics are illustrated with practical examples with clearly worked solutions based on sample tasks provided by the AAT in the new examining style
- frequent activities throughout the chapters ensure that what you have learnt is regularly reinforced
- 'pitfalls' and 'examination tips' help you avoid commonly made mistakes and help you focus on what is required to perform well in your examination.
- practice workbook activities can be completed at the end of each chapter

WORKBOOK

The workbook comprises:

Practice activities at the end of each chapter with solutions at the end of this text, to reinforce the work covered in each chapter.

The questions are divided into their relevant chapters and students may either attempt these questions as they work through the textbook, or leave some or all of these until they have completed the textbook as a final revision of what they have studied.

ICONS

The study chapters include the following icons throughout.

They are designed to assist you in your studies by identifying key definitions and the points at which you can test yourself on the knowledge gained.

Definition

These sections explain important areas of Knowledge which must be understood and reproduced in an assessment

Example

The illustrative examples can be used to help develop an understanding of topics before attempting the activity exercises

Activity

These are exercises which give the opportunity to assess your understanding of all the assessment areas.

UNIT GUIDE

Financial Performance is divided into two units but for the purposes of assessment these units will be combined.

Principles of Managing Financial Performance (Knowledge)

3 credits

Measuring Financial Performance (Skills)

4 credits

Purpose of the units

The creation of these two core units at level four recognises the more complex costing and management accounting units.

Learning objectives

The "Principles of Managing Financial Performance (Knowledge)" unit is about understanding the principles of managing financial performance. Learners will have the knowledge to be able to use a range of techniques to analyse information on expenditure. They will be able to make judgements to support decision making, planning and control by managers.

The "Measuring Financial Performance (Skills)" is about measuring financial performance. Learners will have the skills to collect and analyse information, monitor performance, and present reports to management.

In order for learners to be successful in the two financial performance units they will need to be able to explain, define, describe, calculate and analyse a range of fundamental concepts and techniques. Many of the concepts and techniques are interrelated and learners will need to understand how the concepts and techniques interrelate. They may also be required to explain and describe these relationships.

The Financial Performance unit requires candidates to have a detailed understanding of the fundamental management accounting concepts and techniques in order to demonstrate competence in the learning outcomes. Learners will also need to be able to define and explain the following fundamental concepts (for the knowledge standards) and apply their knowledge to questions which may require the calculation or application of one or more of these fundamental concepts or techniques (for the skills standards).

On completion of these units the learner will be able to:

Learning Outcomes and Assessment criteria

Each unit consists of two learning outcomes, each comprising of a number of assessment criteria

Principles of Managing Financial Performance (Knowledge)

1 Demonstrate an accurate understanding of the internal and external factors that affect organisations

2 Be aware of the cost accounting techniques needed in monitoring financial performance

3 Understand the techniques necessary for measuring performance and managing costs

Measuring Financial Performance (Skills)

1 Collate information from various sources and prepare routine cost reports

2 Make suggestions for improving financial performance by monitoring and analysing information

3 Prepare performance reports for management

Knowledge

To perform this unit effectively you will need to know and understand the following:

		Chapter
1	Demonstrate an accurate understanding of the internal and external factors that affect organisations	
1.1	Explain the purpose and structure of reporting systems within the organisation	1
1.2	Describe the contribution of an organisation's functional specialists to cost reduction and value enhancement	8
1.3	Explain the organisations external environment	1
1.4	Identify costs correctly (materials, labour and expenses) and the sources of information about these costs, including: • Government statistics • Professional or trade associations • Quotations • Price lists	1
2	Be aware of the cost accounting techniques needed in monitoring financial performance	
2.1	Explain the types of cost centres, profit centres and investment centres	2
2.2	Describe the use of standard units of inputs and outputs	6
2.3	Recognise the difference between standard, marginal and absorption costing in terms of cost recording, cost reporting and cost behaviour	2,3
2.4	Explain the use of variance analysis in labour, materials and overhead costing	6
2.5	Accurately identify fixed, variable, semi-variable and stepped costs and explain their use in cost recording, cost reporting and cost analysis	2

		Chapter
3	Understand the techniques necessary for measuring performance and managing costs	
3.1	Identify the relevant performance and quality measures to use to monitor financial performance	8
3.2	Explain the principles of discounted cash flow	4
3.3	Identify appropriate performance indicators to use for: • Efficiency • Effectiveness • Productivity • Cost per unit • Balanced scorecard • Benchmarking • Control ratios (efficiency, capacity, activity) • Scenario planning ('what if' analysis)	8
3.4	Explain the use and purpose of techniques: • Indexing • Sampling • Time series (e.g. moving averages, linear regression and seasonal trends)	5
3.5	Identify the correct ratios used to monitor financial performance	8
3.6	Describe a range of cost management techniques and recognise when these should be used: • Life cycle costing • Target costing (including value engineering) • Activity based costing	3,4

Skills

To perform this unit effectively you will need to be able to do the following.

		Chapter
1	Collate information from various sources and prepare routine cost reports	
1.1	Obtain income and expenditure information from different units within the organisation and consolidate in an appropriate form	2
1.2	Reconcile income and expenditure information collected from various departments or information systems within the organisation	2
1.3	Account for transactions between the separate units of the organisation, in accordance with the organisation's procedures	2
1.4	Identify other valid relevant information from internal and external sources	1
1.5	Prepare routine cost reports	8
1.6	Analyse routine cost reports and compare with budget and standard costs to accurately identify any differences and the implications of these	7
1.7	Correctly identify variances and prepare relevant reports for management	6,7
2	Make suggestions for improving financial performance by monitoring and analysing information	
2.1	Compare results over time using methods that allow for changing price levels	5
2.2	Monitor and analyse current and forecast trends in prices and market conditions on a regular basis	5
2.3	Compare trends with previous data and identify potential implications	5
2.4	Consult relevant staff in the organisation about the analysis of trends and variances	5,7

		Chapter
2.5	Calculate ratios, performance indicators and measures of value added in accordance with the organisation's procedures	8
2.6	Prepare relevant performance indicators	8
2.7	Interpret the results of relevant performance indicators, indentify potential improvements and estimate the value of such improvements	8
2.8	Identify ways to reduce costs and enhance values, consulting specialists where necessary	8
2.9	Prepare estimates of capital investment projects using discounted cash flow techniques	4
3	Prepare performance reports for management	
3.1	Prepare reports in the most appropriate format and present them to management within the required timescales	8
3.2	Prepare exception reports to identify matters which require further investigation	8
3.3	Make specific recommendations to management in a clear and appropriate form	8

Delivery guidance

The AAT have provided delivery guidance giving further details of the way in which the unit will be assessed.

1 Cost classification, Cost recording, Cost reporting and Cost behaviour

(a) Production costing and the elements of direct and indirect costs, cost classification into materials, labour, and overhead,

(b) Cost classification by behaviour (fixed, variable, stepped fixed and semi variable) relevant range for fixed costs.

(c) Calculation of variable and fixed costs using the high low method of cost estimation

(d) Prime cost, full production cost, marginal product cost,

(e) High low method of fixed and variable cost estimation

(f) Explain the types of cost centres, profit centres and investment centres

The High Low method of cost estimation

A fundamental cost technique is the high low method which can be used to estimate the fixed and variable elements of any cost. The technique could be assessed as a simple split of fixed and variable costs or where the fixed costs step up above a certain level of activity.

Example 1 – costs are either fixed or variable

Volume of production	12,000 units	15,000 units
Total Cost	£510,000	£525,000

In the above example total costs have been provided for tow activity levels, 12,000 and 15,000. The total costs include a fixed element and a variable element. The variable element can be calculated by taking the difference between the two cost levels and dividing this by the difference between the two activity levels. This is because the only difference in the two cost levels must be the variable costs.

Therefore the variable cost per unit must be 15,000/3,000 = £5 per unit ((£525,000 less £510,000)/(15,000 less 12,000))

Example 2 – costs are fixed with a step up at an activity level of 27,000 units. The variable cost per unit is constant

Volume of production	25,000 units	29,000 units
Cost	£418,750	£458,750

In the above example fixed costs step up at 27,000 units. In order to calculate the fixed and variable elements further information is required. Tasks will either state the fixed cost at the lower or higher level of output, the variable cost per unit or the stepped fixed cost increase. Then the other elements can be calculated.

For example, in this case the fixed costs step up by £25,000 at an output level of 27,000 units. Therefore the difference in cost between the £458,750 and the £418,750 consists of the fixed cost of £25,000 and the variable cost per unit multiplied by 4,000 units. So £40,000 = fixed costs of £25,000 plus 4,000 units x VC/unit. Therefore the variable cost per unit is £3.75

2 Marginal costing and Absorption costing

(a) Absorption costing – definition, explanation and calculation of an overhead absorption rate, calculation of under and over absorption, explanation of the advantages and disadvantages of absorption costing – link with financial accounting requirements and price setting model.

(b) Marginal costing – definition, explanation and calculation of the marginal cost, explanation of the advantages and disadvantages of marginal costing, marginal costing and decision making, see link with contribution theory below.

(c) Marginal costing v Absorption costing – explain the differences between the treatment of costs, calculation of profit and effects of changing inventory levels. Preparation of an absorption costing income statement, a marginal costing income statement, calculation of the changes in profit when inventory levels change and a reconciliation between the marginal costing profit and the absorption costing profit.

(d) Absorption Costing v Marginal Costing in decision making. Learners need to understand how absorption costing and marginal costing can be used in tasks which measure performance and which consider ways of enhancing value. Absorption Costing may be relevant for measuring the performance of a business and it may also be appropriate to use absorption costing principles in enhancing value. A product may be re-engineered in order to reduce production costs and it would be perfectly appropriate to consider the full absorption cost of the redesigned product. Lifecycle Costing needs to consider both fixed and variable costs. However, it may be inappropriate to use absorption costing in certain circumstances. For example, if the business is considering contracting out the manufacture of a product, selling surplus capacity or other limiting factor decisions, then marginal costing is the appropriate method as fixed costs will not change as a result of the decision. However, Learners need to understand that certain fixed costs may well change when a decision is made and the marginal (incremental) cost may in these circumstances include both variable and fixed components.

(e) Practical limitations of cost classification, non linear behaviour

(f) Absorption Costing v Marginal Costing could feature in Standard Costing questions relating to performance measurement or as a stand-alone task

(g) Contribution analysis - Learners must be able to deal with tasks requiring the analysis of a situation by considering the contribution of a product or business. This is an area where many students struggle. Often the fundamental concept of Contribution is not understood and students include fixed cost in their calculations.

(h) Break even analysis and margin of safety - Learners must be able to deal with calculations of break even analysis and the margin of safety. The information may be given so that calculations can be undertaken by calculating contribution per unit, or by calculating the Contribution to Sales Ratio.

3 Standard Costing and Variance Analysis

(1) Explain how standard costs can be established, the different types of standard (ideal, target, normal, basic) and how the type of standard can affect the behaviour of the budget holder and workforce.

(2) Explain the role of standard costing in the planning, decision making and control process. Standard costing variances aid budgetary control systems by breaking down the simple variance identified in a budgetary control system into components based upon an expected outcome (the standard). Standard costing is a method of analysing a variance from a budget when standard costs are used in creating the budget.

(3) Extract relevant data from the question in order to calculate various requirements. Learners may be required to calculate any of the following

- (a) Standard quantity of inputs (materials, labour, overheads)
- (b) Standard cost for given production volumes
- (c) Actual quantity of inputs (materials, labour, overheads)
- (d) Actual costs for given production volumes

(4) Explain and calculate the following variances (or elements of the calculation)

- (a) Raw materials total, price, usage
- (b) Labour total, rate, efficiency
- (c) Labour idle time variance
- (d) Fixed overhead expenditure variance
- (e) Fixed overhead volume, capacity and efficiency.

(5) Prepare an operating statement under both absorption costing principles and marginal costing principles.

(6) Prepare a reconciliation of the budgeted material cost with the actual material cost using the material cost variances

(7) Prepare a reconciliation of the budgeted labour cost with the actual labour cost using the labour cost variances

(8) Prepare a reconciliation of budgeted fixed overheads with actual fixed overheads using fixed overhead variances.

(9) Prepare journal entries for the posting of variances.

(10) Break down variances using index numbers to isolate controllable and non- controllable parts. Break down variances, using additional information, into controllable and non-controllable variances. Further subdivision of variances using index numbers may be assessed as a small part of a larger task and will not feature as a substantial proportion of a question. Learners will not be required to use changes in exchange rates to subdivide variances.

- (a) Prepare reports giving possible reasons for the variances, showing an understanding of the interrelationship between the variances. This will normally feature in one of the longer written tasks. Often Learners will be provided with a schedule of variances, additional narrative and the following requirement.

Using this information, prepare a report to the Managing Director to cover an analysis of each variance by:

- Identifying the sign of those variances where the sign has not been shown
- Explaining what the variance means
- Providing one possible reason for each variance
- Explaining any links between the variances
- Providing an action which could have been taken

(11) Comment on additional information provided by the budget holder as to reasons for the variance. For example, the production manager may say that the quality of raw materials or the old, poorly maintained machines or unskilled staff have caused the adverse raw material usage variance, when the raw materials price variance was adverse, implying that the material was of better than expected quality. This may not be the case - it could be that the buyer bought an inferior material but still paid more than the standard. It may be that an independent assessment of the quality of the material needs to be made.

(12) Explain how standards are developed and appreciate the concepts of Ideal standard, attainable (expected) standard and basic standard. Explain how the chosen standard may affect the behaviour on managers and staff.

(13) Explain the difference between controllable and non controllable variances, apply index numbers to variances in order to explain how general rising prices can cause variances, and adjust variances for changes in prices.

4 Performance indicators and "what if" analysis

(a) **Calculate performance indicators**

Learners will be asked to calculate a range of performance indicators. Some, such as the return on capital employed or the current ratio, are applicable to many organisations, whilst others might be unique to a particular type of organisation. For example, if the task relates to a hotel, learners might be given data and asked to calculate the cost per room night, the percentage occupancy and the average discount given to customers.

The following is a list of the type of performance indicators learners might be asked to calculate.

(1) Financial (Profitability, Liquidity, Efficiency and Gearing)

(a) Gross Profit Margin, = Gross Profit / Sales Revenue x 100%

(b) Profit Margin, = Profit/ Sales Revenue x 100%

(c) Administration costs as a percentage of revenue, any cost as a percentage of revenue = Cost/ Sales Revenue x 100%

(d) Current ratio = current assets/current liabilities

This can be expressed as a number only or as a number:1, for example if current assets are £10,000 and current liabilities are £8,000 the ratio is 1.25 or 1.25:1. In question students should just use 1.25 as their answer.

(e) Quick ratio = (current assets less inventory)/ current liabilities and again should be expressed as a single number in assessments.

(f) Trade cycles (receivable days = receivables/revenue x 365, inventory days = inventory/ cost of sales x 365, payable days = payables / cost of sales x 365)

(g) Gearing ratio,

The gearing ratio can be calculated as either Total debt/ (Total debt plus Equity) x 100% or

Total debt/ Total equity x 100%. Total debt must include both long term and short term debt. Both computer marked and human marked tasks will allow both calculations.

(h) Value added = Revenue less the cost of materials used and bought in services

(2) Efficiency, Capacity and Activity ratios

(a) Labour efficiency ratio = standard hours for actual production/actual hours worked (expressed as a percentage).

(b) Capacity ratio = actual hours worked/ budgeted hours (expressed as a percentage).

(c) Labour activity ratio = standard hours for actual production/ budgeted hours, or actual output / budgeted output (expressed as a percentage).

(3) Indicators to measure efficiency, effectiveness and productivity

(a) Measures of efficiency include ROCE or RONA, Profit Margin and efficiency ratio for labour

ROCE = Return / Capital employed, in tasks return will be equal to the profit in the income statement. This ratio is always expressed as a percentage.

RONA = Return / Net assets, return will be equal to the profit in the income statement. This ratio is always expressed as a percentage.

(b) Effectiveness measures include percentage of production free from defects, delivery times to customer, number of coaches, buses or trains on time, percentage of learners passing exams first time, number of times a class is cancelled, percentage of parcels delivered within the agreed time. Average waiting times.

(c) Productivity measures are likely to be measured in units of output, or related to output in some way. Examples include number of, say, vehicles manufactured per week, operations undertaken per day, passengers transported per month, units produced per worker per day, rooms cleaned per hour or meals served per sitting.

(4) Indicators to measure quality of service and cost of quality

(a) The number of defects/units returned/warranty claims/customer complaints, the cost of inspection/ repairs/re-working,

(b) Prevention costs, appraisal costs, internal failure costs, external failure costs

(5) Learners may be asked to compare given indicators with performance indicators that they have calculated. They may have to undertake a benchmarking exercise and need to understand the purpose of benchmarking

(6) Learners need to recognise that a business has to select key performance indicators and monitor these in order to manage the business. The balanced scorecard is an approach often used and learners need to understand the concept of a balanced scorecard and may be asked to prepare one from given performance indicators.

(7) Tasks may require the calculation of specific performance indicators. If this is the case the calculation of the indicator will either be obvious or the formula for the indicator will be provided. For example, if the task is based on a hotel the occupancy rate calculation should be obvious given the number of rooms sold in the month divided by the total number of room nights available in the month. If the indicator is more complicated the formula will be given.

(b) **Comment on the information generated from the calculation of the performance indicator**

Learners need to be able to explain what the ratios are designed to show and analyse the ratio.

(c) **Understand the interrelationships and limitations of the performance indicator**

Learners need to be able to explain, describe the limitations of the ratios and the interrelationships. Learners may also be required to apply their understanding of the interrelationship in order to make recommendations to management.

(d) **Prepare estimates of capital investment projects using discounted cash flow techniques**

Learners need to be able to explain, describe and calculate discounted cash flow calculations of net present value, net present cost and net terminal cost and make recommendations to management.

(e) **"What if" analysis**

After having prepared performance indicators, Learners may be faced with taking or recommending action. They may be asked to do one or more of the following:

- Show what the results would have been if benchmark data had been achieved.
- Forecast the performance indicators for the next period based upon a set of assumptions.
- Re-calculate the performance indicators, taking account of given changes to the business, or perhaps select changes which will maximise given indicators.

- Work backwards through a ratio. For example, they may be asked, "What would the revenue need to have been for the asset turnover to be 3 times if the total assets are £950,000?" the answer is £2,850,000 or 3 x £950,000, or "What would the profit need to have been for the ROCE to be 25% if the net assets are £450,000? The answer is £112,500". This is simple equation manipulation.
- Given several options, learners may be asked to evaluate and recommend a course of action. This could be to improve a key performance indicator like ROCE. They might also be asked to comment on options which cause an improvement in one indicator with a deterioration of another.
- Calculate indicators for 2 years and explain changes in performance
- Compare two businesses and comment on their relative performance.
- Identify potential improvements and estimate the value of them
- Suggest ways of improving the performance of a poorly performing business.
- Make recommendations.
- Make calculations and recommendations to management for any of the following scenarios
  - Make or buy decision – learners may be required to prepare workings and key ratios to aid the assessment of outsourcing manufacture
  - Limiting factor decision making – learners may have to adjust figures and recalculate ratios if a resource constraint limits production.
  - Break – even analysis and margin of safety – learners need to be able to calculate and comment on measures of risk, particularly where a business changes or proposes to change the fixed cost and variable costs of production.
  - Closure of a business segment, transferring production overseas – learners may have to prepare calculations and make recommendations to management regarding the closure of a business segment

- Mechanisation – learners may be required to provide calculations and make recommendations to management regarding changing the production process from a labour intensive one to a machine intensive one. They may also be required to bring in break-even analysis in order to demonstrate the changing risk in the business.

With scenario planning or "what if" analysis, learners have to understand how elements of the income statement and statement of financial position are linked. For example, a 10% increase in sales volume will lead to a 10% increase in variable costs as more units are produced but no increase in fixed costs, assuming that capacity exists (fixed costs are fixed over the relevant range). A 10% increase in sales price, however, will not lead to any changes in costs. The increase in sales will change the profit and, if no dividends are paid, this will increase the net assets of the business. The change in sales will therefore affect several ratios.

(f) **Key performance indicators and the behaviour of managers**

Learners need to understand that the way in which business unit managers are assessed can have a great influence on the decisions they make. The use of key performance indicators such as ROCE can lead to a lack of goal congruence where managers make decisions which improve performance in certain indicators but which may not be best for the organisation as a whole.

For example, a manager may not be prepared to invest in new machinery if the increase in the net asset position will reduce the ROCE, even though the investment may reduce other costs, lead to zero defects or increase customer satisfaction.

(g) **Cost management**

(a) Lifecycle costing and how it can be used to aid cost management. Learners may be required to calculate lifecycle costs for different options. Lifecycle cost calculations may require the use of discounted cash flow techniques.

(b) The concepts behind target costing (including value analysis/engineering). Learners may be required to explain target costing and prepare a target cost from information in the task. Learners may also have to analyse information provided from functional specialists like designers, engineers and marketing professionals.

(c) Activity based costing and how it can be applied to an organisation. Learners may be given information and asked to calculate the absorption rates under activity based costing and comment on its applicability.

(d) The principles of Total Quality Management. Learners may be provided with information about the various costs incurred to prevent faulty production and costs incurred to rectify faulty production and settle warranty claims. Learners may then be asked to calculate the cost of quality. Whilst the general theory is that organisations should plan to have zero defects, learners should be aware that there may be commercial justifications for allowing some defects, perhaps because of expensive quality assurance systems.

(e) Product lifecycle and how costs change throughout the life of a product. Concepts of economies of scale, mechanisation, a switch from variable to fixed costs may be assessed.

(f) Understanding of the planning, decision making and control stages in management accounting and how cost management techniques can aid the stages.

(h) **Basic statistical methods:**

The learners must be able to explain the use and purpose of indexing, sampling and time series (e.g. moving averages, linear regression and seasonal trends).

Index numbers – learners must be able to calculate index numbers and use them to forecast costs and prices and also to subdivide variances. Learners must also be able to interpret indices and compare them with methods of securing contracts to reduce the risk of rising prices.

Moving averages – learners must be able to calculate moving averages and seasonal variations and use calculations to extrapolate a forecast of sales or costs.

Seasonal variations – **l**earners need to understand types of variation from the trend and may be required to identify the seasonal variation or use the seasonal variation and a given trend to forecast sales volume, prices or cost information.

Regression analysis

Learners will **not** be required to derive the regression equation $y = a + bx$ but they may be given the equation and asked to use it to calculate a and b, given y and x, for several points, or to calculate y and x, given a and b. The equation could then be used to predict prices, demand and costs.

THE ASSESSMENT

The format of the assessment

The assessment will be divided into two sections.

Section 1:

Expect to see 6 tasks in section 1 covering the core topics of standard costing, forecasting, and variance analysis.

There will be five mainly computational tasks and one extended written task (on variances in the practice assessment).

Section 2:

Expect to see 4 tasks in section 2 covering performance indicators, what if analysis and cost management techniques.

There will be three mainly computational tasks and one extended written task (on performance indicators in the practice assessment).

Learners will normally be assessed by computer based assessment (CBA), which will include extended writing tasks, and will be required to demonstrate competence in both sections of the assessment.

For the purpose of assessment the competency level for AAT assessment is set at 70 per cent.

Time allowed

The time allowed for this assessment is **150 minutes.**

STUDY SKILLS

Preparing to study

Devise a study plan

Determine which times of the week you will study.

Split these times into sessions of at least one hour for study of new material. Any shorter periods could be used for revision or practice.

Put the times you plan to study onto a study plan for the weeks from now until the assessment and set yourself targets for each period of study – in your sessions make sure you cover the whole course, activities and the associated questions in the workbook at the back of the manual.

If you are studying more than one unit at a time, try to vary your subjects as this can help to keep you interested and see subjects as part of wider knowledge.

When working through your course, compare your progress with your plan and, if necessary, re-plan your work (perhaps including extra sessions) or, if you are ahead, do some extra revision / practice questions.

Effective studying

Active reading

You are not expected to learn the text by rote, rather, you must understand what you are reading and be able to use it to pass the assessment and develop good practice.

A good technique is to use SQ3Rs – Survey, Question, Read, Recall, Review:

1 **Survey the chapter**

Look at the headings and read the introduction, knowledge, skills and content, so as to get an overview of what the chapter deals with.

2 **Question**

Whilst undertaking the survey ask yourself the questions you hope the chapter will answer for you.

3 Read

Read through the chapter thoroughly working through the activities and, at the end, making sure that you can meet the learning objectives highlighted on the first page.

4 Recall

At the end of each section and at the end of the chapter, try to recall the main ideas of the section / chapter without referring to the text. This is best done after short break of a couple of minutes after the reading stage.

5 Review

Check that your recall notes are correct.

You may also find it helpful to re-read the chapter to try and see the topic(s) it deals with as a whole.

Note taking

Taking notes is a useful way of learning, but do not simply copy out the text. The notes must:

- be in your own words
- be concise
- cover the key points
- well organised
- be modified as you study further chapters in this text or in related ones.

Trying to summarise a chapter without referring to the text can be a useful way of determining which areas you know and which you don't.

Three ways of taking notes

1 Summarise the key points of a chapter

2 Make linear notes

A list of headings, subdivided with sub-headings listing the key points.

If you use linear notes, you can use different colours to highlight key points and keep topic areas together.

Use plenty of space to make your notes easy to use.

3 Try a diagrammatic form

The most common of which is a mind map.

To make a mind map, put the main heading in the centre of the paper and put a circle around it.]

Draw lines radiating from this to the main sub-headings which again have circles around them.

Continue the process from the sub-headings to sub-sub-headings.

Highlighting and underlining

You may find it useful to underline or highlight key points in your study text – but do be selective.

You may also wish to make notes in the margins.

Revision phase

Kaplan has produced material specifically designed for your final examination preparation for this unit.

These include pocket revision notes and a bank of revision questions specifically in the style of the new syllabus.

Further guidance on how to approach the final stage of your studies is given in these materials.

Further reading

In addition to this text, you should also read the “Student section” of the “Accounting Technician” magazine every month to keep abreast of any guidance from the examiners.

TERMINOLOGY

There are different terms used to mean the same thing – you will need to be aware of both sets of terminology.

UK GAAP	IAS
Profit and Loss	Income Statement
Sales	Revenue
Balance Sheet	Statement of Financial Position
Fixed Assets	Non-Current Assets
Stock	Inventory
Trade Debtors	Trade Receivables
Trade Creditors	Trade Payables
Capital	Equity
Profit	Retained Earnings

The business environment

1

Introduction

This chapter provides general background information to the context of management accounting which is essential background knowledge and should be useful in answering Financial Performance examinations.

KNOWLEDGE
Explain the purpose and structure of reporting systems within the organisation (1.1)
Explain the organisations external environment and the specific external costs (1.3)
Identify costs correctly and the sources of information about these costs (1.4)
SKILLS
Reconcile income and expenditure information collected from various departments or information systems (1.2)

CONTENT	
1	The business environment
2	Management information systems (MIS)
3	The role of the cost and management accountant
4	General factors affecting forecasts
5	SWOT analysis

1 The business environment

1.1 Management accounting vs financial accounting

Accountants have to provide **information** to very diverse groups. The specific needs of each determine whether these can best be served by the financial accounting or the management accounting function of the business organisation. The main **differences between financial accounting and management accounting** are as follows:

- Financial accounting provides information to users who are **external** to the business, such as the shareholders of a company; management accounting is usually concerned with **internal** users of accounting information such as the managers of the business.
- Financial accounting draws up financial statements, the formats of which are governed by law and accounting standards for limited companies; management accounting reports can be in any format which suits the user and may differ considerably from one company to another.
- Financial accounting reports on **past** transactions; management accounting records historic transactions, compares actual figures to budget figures and hence makes **predictions for the future**.

Management accounting information can take many different forms as it is designed specifically to be of use to the managers of the business.

1.2 Cost accounting

Cost accounting is normally a large part of the management accounting role. It is primarily concerned with ascertainment of costs and it was developed to a great extent within a manufacturing context where costs can be difficult to isolate and analyse. In such a business there are two things which the financial accountant's profit and loss account will not disclose:

- the amount of profit attributable to each unit of a product or service;
- the amount of cost and/or revenue attributable to each manager.

The information provided by the cost accountant will be part of the **management information system** (MIS) of the business (often the major part).

Activity 1

Required

Tick the correct boxes.

	Management accounts	*Financial accounts*
These accounts are prepared yearly		
These accounts are for internal use		
These accounts have a standardised format		
These accounts estimate the future		
These accounts are prepared monthly		
These accounts are for external use		
These accounts are for the shareholders		

2 Management information systems (MIS)

Definition

A management information system (MIS) is a system using formalised procedures to provide managers at all levels with appropriate information from all relevant sources (internal and external to the business) for the purposes of planning and controlling the activities for which they are responsible.

An MIS has been defined as 'a system in which defined data are collected, processed and communicated to assist those responsible for the use of resources'.

2.1 Type of management information system

Each MIS will be determined by:

- the type of organisation or business;
- the products or services offered;
- the principal markets;
- the principal objectives;
- the organisation structure and reporting relationships;
- the principal users of information; and the use to which the information is put.

The information systems will operate within **different levels**, from the board of directors down to shop-floor supervisors, and within different functions (for example, production, marketing and finance).

The manner in which information is presented should depend on the recipient; so that the recipient obtains the maximum value from the information he is being given. It may be appropriate to present shop-floor supervisors with diagrams or bar charts that they can easily understand, while experienced financial managers should perhaps be presented with detailed tables of figures that they can themselves manipulate (e.g. with a spreadsheet program) to reach their own conclusions.

2.2 Why is management information needed?

Information is mainly needed:

- to assist management in **planning** the most effective use of resources, such as labour and materials;
- to assist management in **decision-making** (i.e. choosing between alternative courses of action), for example whether to make a product or purchase it from an outside supplier;
- to aid management in **controlling** day-to-day operations, for example by comparing actual results with those planned.

A manager will use resources in the light of the information that is relevant and available to him. The problem facing the chairman of a large group might be to decide how much funds to allocate to a particular activity, whereas a supervisor in the machine shop might be deciding which machine to use and which operators should be asked to operate it to produce a particular job.

Information is necessary at each level to **guide decisions** and, in due course, to **measure the effectiveness** of the action taken.

2.3 Requirements of management information

A successful business needs management capable of making decisions. In turn, a successful business manager must have the responsibility and authority to make those decisions. Irrespective of whether these decisions may dictate the future long-term policy or conduct of the business or simply its day to day routine operation, management must be equipped with **adequate and timely information**.

Management information may be of two types, as follows:

- information about the past results of the type of action envisaged – **historical information**;
- information about the future effects of decisions – **forecast information**.

2.4 Types of information

Three basic types of information have been identified:

(a) **Scorekeeping** – The accumulation of data to enable both internal and external parties to evaluate organisational performance and position. This embraces internal reporting for use in planning and controlling non-routine operations. To some extent this also embraces external reporting to shareholders, government and other external parties.

(b) **Attention-directing** –The reporting and the interpretation of information which helps managers to focus on operational problems, imperfections, inefficiencies and opportunities. This aspect of accounting assists managers with the provision of important data about the operations enabling timely decision making, whether on a long-term or a short-term basis.

(c) **Problem-solving** – This *ad hoc* aspect of accounting involves the concise quantification of the relative merits of possible courses of action, often with recommendations as to the best procedure. In this it is seen that the cost accountant is a very vital part of the management team.

2.5 Attributes of information

Since management at all levels must perform a certain amount of planning, decision-making and control, it is vital that the manager has the necessary information to perform his tasks. There are four fundamental attributes of information:

(a) **Relevance to the scope of responsibility**. A production manager will primarily be concerned with information about stocks, production levels, production performance and machine loads within his department. He will not be interested in the shortcomings of other departments unless they specifically affect his area.

(b) **Relevance to any particular decision**. This is a difficult one. Management have to be able to identify the decisions that need to be made.

This requires information that directs attention to specific problems. However, having identified the decisions, the information that enables the right decisions to be made needs to be acquired.

(c) **Production in time**. This is an area of great conflict for manager and accountant. Two of the most desirable attributes of the accountant's work are accuracy and timeliness. Of course, information to satisfy the requirements already outlined must be accurate, but to be of use in the business it must be presented quickly. A beautiful, well written, superbly accurate report, covering and analysing all the facets of a particular problem and all the possible solutions and their consequences is useless if it cannot be prepared in time for the decision to be taken, or is delivered after the problem has been resolved.

(d) **Value.** This may be assessed by the resulting cost and benefit in the planned course of action. If a change takes place then the value is represented by the benefit in changing. The information also has a cost and the cost of obtaining information must be compared with the potential benefit arising from it.

For management information to be useful it must be provided to the appropriate manager must be relevant, timely and cost effective.

2.6 The accounting information system

The major objective of most commercial organisations is to **make profits**. Consequently, the accounting system is a most important information system. It provides the basis for the process of budgetary planning and control and linking together the other information systems within the organisation, e.g. production, personnel, etc.

The purpose of an MIS is to determine and provide as efficiently, effectively and economically as possible, **what management need to know**. Since most of the information within any business is handled by the accounts department, the cost accountant is in a very important position.

Activity 2

A management information system can only be used by managers.

(Tick one box.)

True	
False	

Activity 3

A system providing managers at all levels with the information that they need to carry out their roles is:

A A transaction processing system

B A management information system

C A decision support system

D An executive information system

Activity 4

The attributes of valuable information do not include:

A Relevant

B Timely

C Costly

D Reliable

3 The role of the cost and management accountant

3.1 The accountant's skills

The chief role of the accountant was traditionally **'stewardship'**. He began as the custodian of the firm's assets and the faithful recorder of their movement. Because profit is the net increase in asset values, stewardship gradually developed so that the emphasis fell on the **calculation of the organisation's profit**.

Stewardship involves the careful, effective and efficient use of assets, and so the management accountant is concerned with the pursuit of efficiency and of productivity in the use of the firm's resources, as well as with the generation of profits.

3.2 The functions of a management accountant

The management accountant helps managers to answer the following questions:

- **Score keeping** – How well have we done? The management accountant records, aggregates and presents costs so that we can see where profit has been made.
- **Control** – Did we do as well as we thought we would? Comparing actual results with the budget helps to identify where operations are not running according to plan. Investigation of the causes and subsequent action achieves effective control of the business.
- **Planning** – How well will we do next year? Primarily through preparation of a short-term annual budget, but also through long range strategic planning, planning enables all departments involved to be organised and avoids lack of goal congruence, i.e. individual managers seeking good results for their department but with a bad overall effect on the company.
- **Co-ordinating** – How can we overcome any identified problems so we can do even better next year? Bottlenecks and delays pinpointed by the questions above can be analysed and new strategies put in place to overcome them.
- **Decision-making** – How can we make the right decisions as new problems and opportunities come along?
- **Motivation** – How can we make sure that managers and staff are kept motivated to achieve the objectives of the organisation as measured by accounting information?

Management accounts will therefore serve a variety of purposes and it should be of no surprise that they take a variety of forms. There is no set format; management accounts should include information relevant to their purpose.

4 General factors affecting forecasts

4.1 Forecasting and long-range planning

Long-range plans are often based on estimates of the future from extrapolations of the past to find trends, a method which can be fairly accurate in the short term. However, using data and relationships derived from past behaviour is limited in that such data cannot forecast something which has never happened before, nor can it accurately forecast very far ahead.

If a company were to rely solely on forecasting rather than long-range planning, it would need to operate in a very predictable environment. Planning is an attempt to control outcomes whereas forecasting is a more passive attempt to predict outcomes, making educated guesses about the future.

Long-range planning is concerned with deciding which courses of action the organisation should take for the future. Corporate long-range planning does not attempt to minimise risks as, usually, the greater the risk the higher the return, but it helps to ensure that the organisation takes the right kind of risks with the best possible knowledge of the consequences.

4.2 Forecasting economic change

Forecasting changes in the external economy is an area fraught with problems and there are various conflicting views on the appropriate model to use. However, it is still essential for a company to be aware of likely trends in, for example, gross domestic product per capita. To this end, many large organisations have their own models or adapt the findings of other models to reflect their requirements. Whatever the applicability of the models for forecasting the likely effects on a particular organisation, it would be foolish to ignore trends in consumer incomes and expenditure, and sources of long-term finance.

4.3 External sources of information for assessing economic change

- The Government's National Statistics (available on the internet).
- Government reports on particular industries.
- Reports prepared by international bodies, such as the UN, OECD and EU.
- Commercial publications dealing with economic matters of particular industries.

- Publications by trade associations and professional organisations.
- Bank reviews.
- Stockbroker reports.
- Statistics from advertising agencies.
- Special sampling surveys
- Price lists and quotations from suppliers and competitors.

Management must monitor a wide range of external sources of information so that their decisions on managing costs and setting prices fit in with the prevailing environment.

In principle, data can either be **primary** data, gathered for the purpose in hand, or **secondary** data, gathered for another purpose but used by the business for the purpose in hand. There is an inherent limitation in using published statistics for a secondary purpose, since the statistics were not expressly gathered for the purpose they are being put to by the business.

4.4 General economic environment

As a result of government intervention the plans of companies can require revision. The government's task is to keep the economy in balance and this may well result in a stop-go type of policy, particularly towards the end of the life of a parliament. Management must therefore be prepared to rethink drastically and immediately should the situation arise.

The effective business can act in the manner of a detective and by keeping track of party political publications try to predict likely governmental changes and when they will occur. Remember that policies can change drastically with a change of government.

4.5 Social and environmental responsibility

Regularly in the media there are examples of companies that are considered to lack social responsibility because they fail to protect the area surrounding their factories from the hazards of their product or because they treat their staff or members of the public shabbily. Society today is far more socially aware and will not accept hazards which can be avoided. This developing awareness has resulted in changes in the attitudes of companies.

Awareness of the activities of pressure groups can be of critical importance to business planning. Often items that start off as aspects of consumer pressure can lead to legislative controls.

4.6 Indicators

Indicators of likely change in the wider environment can be identified. Thus for example problems which are occurring currently may indicate major changes, such as late payment from a customer highlighting possible trading difficulties or potential bankruptcy. Current political changes within a country may indicate future problems for the supply of raw materials and availability of markets.

The degree of influence that suppliers, markets etc have on the organisation will determine the priority which should be given to these indicators in the planning process.

4.7 The importance of trends

It is important to be able to identify trends in market competition. Increasing competition can provide the threat of likely takeover or the need to merge with another organisation in order to obtain from larger production units any economies of scale available. It is also important to realise that increasing competition, perhaps even within the context of a diminishing market, may present an opportunity. An efficient organisation should be capable of successfully competing, and where organisations go into liquidation this will free sections of the market previously served by the liquidated enterprises.

5 SWOT analysis

5.1 Introduction

Before any long-term planning or a decision can be made, four factors have to be taken into consideration: the organisation's **strengths** and **weaknesses**, and the **opportunities** and **threats** presented to the organisation by its environment (SWOT analysis)

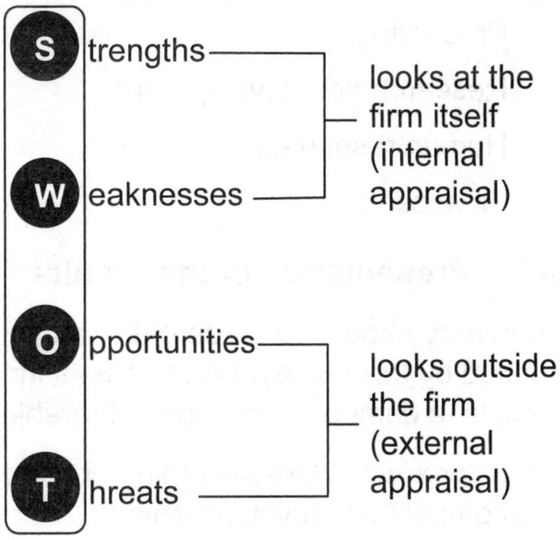

- Internal appraisal is the assessment of the strengths and weaknesses of an organisation.
- External appraisal is the assessment of opportunities and threats.

5.2 Internal appraisal – strengths and weaknesses

The objective is to ascertain the company's strengths and areas where improvements can be made, and to forecast what the results may be if the company continues as it is, in the light of information at present available to it. The review should be organised and co-ordinated throughout the company and carried out in a way that motivates management to face up to the true issues and think constructively and not defensively.

5.3 Elements of the review

Such a review should include the following.

(a) A comprehensive review of the company's results.

(b) An investigation to ascertain the strengths of the company (the areas in which it has exclusive skills or does well as compared with competitive standards) and areas where significant improvements are needed. The word 'improvements' is used instead of 'weaknesses' because people are reluctant to confess to weaknesses and are likely to make a better contribution if they are asked to suggest how they think improvements can be made.

(c) Comparisons with competitors, and other industries where useful. It is this feature which gives the internal appraisal its alternative title of 'competitive audit'.

The main areas considered in a strengths and weaknesses survey would include the following:

- Products
- Marketing
- Distribution
- Production
- Research and development
- Human resources
- Finance

5.4 Presentation of the results

A summary should be made of the major strengths and weaknesses revealed by this survey. Weaknesses indicate areas of 'vulnerability'; for example, a company could be vulnerable to adverse conditions if:

- its products were becoming obsolete, and could be replaced by competitors' developments;
- it were short of liquid resources;

- particular markets (for example, overseas) ceased to be available;
- the strength of competition were augmented by amalgamations or mergers;
- selling prices were being forced below an economic level.

The company's current strengths may relate to similar areas, and should be highlighted as a means by which the company can increase its profits.

5.5 Need for continuous reviews

The absence of an objective analysis of the organisation's strengths and weaknesses may result in the selection of a strategy which is totally inadequate or inappropriate. Circumstances change rapidly and it is therefore necessary to see the process of internal appraisal as a continuous monitoring of critical aspects of the business. A single snapshot of the organisation is only relevant for one point in time and consequently continual review is essential.

Activity 5

Required

Tick the correct box to identify which of the issues below is a strength, weakness, opportunity or threat.

	S	W	O	T
A growing overdraft				
A well trained workforce				
A new competitor entering the market				
A new piece of software is developed				

Activity 6

SWOT stands for strengths, weaknesses, opportunities and _________.

5.6 External appraisal – opportunities and threats (PEST analysis)

Definition

External analysis is often referred to as PEST analysis because it focuses on Politics (Government), Economics, Social policy and Technology. To this we have added competition.

5.7 Politics (Government)

Environmental legislation, concerning the control of pollution and health hazards, can affect the future plans of a company. The banning of the use of a particular substance (e.g. asbestos) will initially represent a threat to the manufacturers and to suppliers of goods that use it, but it will also present an opportunity for the development of new replacement products.

Full use needs to be made of government grants and tax concessions available in the industry. Plans for the levels and directions of government spending must be monitored carefully for business opportunities and threats.

5.8 Economics

General economic conditions and trends are critical to the success of an organisation. Wages, price changes by suppliers and competitors, and government policies affect both the costs of producing products or offering services and the market conditions under which they are sold.

Common economic indicators measure national income and national product, savings, investment, prices, wages, productivity, employment, government activities, and international transactions. All these factors vary over time, and managers can usefully devote part of their organisation's time and resources to forecasting the economy and anticipating changes.

5.9 Social aspects

Changes in demographic variables – such as age, sex, family size, income, occupation, education, nationality and social class – can have major effects upon the organisation.

People's attitudes and values are an important consideration and are reflected in their lifestyles. In recent years, change rather than stability has become the norm for lifestyle in the UK. For example, families account for a shrinking proportion of UK households and fewer of these families include married couples; households consisting of single adults and one-parent families are becoming more numerous.

Other lifestyle changes include a trend towards better education. Smaller cars, oven-ready meals and paid household help are only a few examples of new consumption patterns. Physical fitness has experienced a big surge in popularity, and other home-centred activities – notably satellite TV, video recorders and DVD players – are more and more prevalent.

All these factors will have an effect, favourable or adverse, upon businesses in the consumer sector.

5.10 Technology

The level of technology in a particular industry determines to a large extent what products and services will be produced, what equipment will be used and how operations will be managed.

Technological development begins with basic research, when a scientist discovers some new phenomenon; other researchers then examine the breakthrough for its potential. If further development leads to a workable prototype and engineering refinements make commercial exploitation practical, then the technology is finally put to use and may be widely adopted.

5.11 Competitors

The degree of competition between organisations already operating within the market is likely to be based on:

- whether there is a dominant organisation(s) – generally the most stable markets have dominant organisations;
- whether the market is growing or declining – generally when markets are entering a 'maturity' phase and firms are trying to establish themselves as market leaders, competitive rivalry will be high;
- whether the product or service can be differentiated between competitors – generally if products and services can be clearly differentiated then competitive rivalry will be lower;
- whether the economy is in recession or booming – generally as an economy goes into recession competitive rivalry will intensify in an attempt to 'survive'.

The 'degree' of competition will be reduced by the effectiveness of any barriers to entry. Typical barriers to entry are as follows:

(a) **Financial or capital requirement of entry.** The amount of capital required may not be the major barrier to entry but rather the availability and cost of raising finance.

(b) **The patterns of distribution or access to distribution channels.** The soft drinks industry in the UK for example, was traditionally dominated by two companies because brewers such as Bass and Whitbread owned the soft drinks companies and the distribution outlets (i.e. the public houses).This pattern of distribution, however, has been forced to change with government legislation now restricting the number of public houses that can be owned by brewers.

(c) **Government legislation** and changes in such legislation obviously have a major effect on barriers to entry. Deregulation and privatisation has meant that extensive barriers to entry have now been lowered in an attempt to make markets contestable.

There are other barriers to entry such as advertising, patents and trade secrets, but it is not possible to state which are the most important. What is important is the recognition that barriers to entry have a major impact on the threat of potential entry.

Activity 7

Required

Tick the correct box to identify which of the issues below is a political, economic, social or technological issue.

	P	E	S	T
More of the population are moving into the countryside				
A new prime-minister is elected				
Interest rates are rising				
A computer virus has been released by a hacker				

Activity 8

External information sources do not include:

A Government reports

B Industry journals

C Management accounts

D Supplier price lists

Activity 9

An external appraisal is done using a:

SWOT ☐

PEST ☐

(Tick the appropriate box)

Activity 10

Barriers to entry do not include:

A High investment costs

B Access to distribution channels

C Government legislation

D The power of customers

Activity 11

An external analysis covers:

A Competition

B A highly skilled workforce

C Sound finances

D Competent managers

6 Summary

The cost accountant is mainly concerned with the proper recording and analysis of costs incurred in a business in a manner that will enable management to control current operations and to plan and make decisions for the future.

Effective communication with the workforce and management is vital.

This chapter also considered internal and external information which affects forecasts, and then looked at SWOT and PEST analysis which are ways of assessing the company's strategic location in the business environment it is operating in.

Answers to chapter activities

Activity 1

	Management accounts	*Financial accounts*
These accounts are prepared yearly		√
These accounts are for internal use	√	
These accounts have a standardised format		√
These accounts estimate the future	√	
These accounts are prepared monthly	√	
These accounts are for external use		√
These accounts are for the shareholders		√

Activity 2

True	
False	√

Activity 3

B A management information system is a system providing managers at all levels with the information that they need to carry out their roles.

Activity 4

C Costly. Information should be relevant, timely, cost-effective, reliable and understandable.

Activity 5

	S	W	O	T
A growing overdraft		√		
A well trained workforce	√			
A new competitor entering the market				√
A new piece of software is developed			√	

Activity 6

SWOT stands for strengths, weaknesses, opportunities and threats.

Activity 7

	P	E	S	T
More of the population are moving into the countryside			√	
A new prime-minister is elected	√			
Interest rates are rising		√		
A computer virus has been released by a hacker				√

Activity 8

C Management accounts are an internal source of information.

Activity 9

A PEST is an external analysis. A SWOT is an internal analysis.

Activity 10

D The power of a customer does not prevent entry into an industry.

Activity 11

A The workforce, managers and finances are all internal factors.

Collection of cost information 2

Introduction

This chapter is concerned with the classification of costs by behaviour. Much of the information here has been met in Basic Costing and Costs and Revenues so should be considered to be revision of relevant areas.

Some costs change when activity levels change, whilst others do not. The ability to isolate cost elements by behaviour is essential to management who are concerned with predicting future costs as part of the planning and decision making processes. It will also be necessary to enable a marginal costing approach to be taken, as covered in the next chapter.

KNOWLEDGE

Explain the types of cost centres, profit centres and investment centres (2.1)

Accurately identify fixed, variable, semi-variable and stepped costs and explain their use in cost recording, cost reporting and cost analysis (2.5)

SKILLS

Obtain income and expenditure information from different units within an organisation and consolidate in an appropriate form (1.1)

Identify information from internal and external cost reports (1.4)

Reconcile income and expenditure information collected from various departments or information systems within the organisation (1.2)

Account for transactions between the separate units of the organisation, in accordance with the organisation's procedures (1.3)

CONTENTS

1 Cost accounting
2 The cost accounting department
3 Cost units
4 Cost centres
5 Cost classification
6 Cost behaviour
7 Cost estimation
8 The high/low method

1 Cost accounting

1.1 The need for cost accounting

Historically, financial accounts have reflected the transactions of a business entity in its relationships with the outside world: customers, suppliers, employees, shareholders and other investors. To this end, financial accounting has been geared up to the preparation of annual and other periodic accounts, with the emphasis upon statutory requirements.

A typical income statement has the following general layout.

Example

Income statement for the period ended…

	£
Revenue	500,000
Cost of sales	(370,000)
Gross profit	130,000
Expenses	(80,000)
Operating profit	50,000

Typically the income statement will include a subjective analysis of expenses according to category either by function (distribution/administrative) or by nature (materials/staff costs/depreciation).Despite some recent changes, financial accounts do not readily disclose:

(a) profit performance by individual products, services or activity; but more importantly

(b) the responsibility of individual managers for performance.

Thus financial accounts can only provide 'scorekeeping' statistical information, rather than information that will form the basis of decision-making or control. The provision of this additional detail is one of the functions of cost accounting: cost-finding.

Definition

Cost-finding means taking the transactions which make up the financial accounts and analysing them to turn data into information which will be more helpful to the managers of the business. This will be an 'objective' analysis, matching the expenses to the purposes for which they were incurred. This analysis may be done on a purely memorandum basis, the results being reconciled with the financial records, or it may be sometimes incorporated into the general bookkeeping system of the company.

Whichever procedure is adopted, cost accounting has two important effects on business documentation:

(a) Additional internal documents will be needed to identify which products or departments are affected by various transactions.

(b) Additional data regarding transactions will be needed to assist accurate classification and analysis.

Example

Assume that the income statement illustrated above related to a company marketing four different products during a particular month. For management a more detailed analysis is required.

Solution

From his analysis of the source documents (purchase invoices, payrolls, petty cash vouchers and so on), the cost accountant is able to provide the following detailed report.

	Product A	*Product B*	*Product C*	*Product D*	*Total*
Revenue					
Quantity	315,000	32,500	80,500	28,100	–
Price per unit	£0.50	£2.50	£1.50	£5.00	–
Amount	£157,500	£81,250	£120,750	£140,500	£500,000
	£	£	£	£	£
Costs					
Materials	50,000	40,000	75,000	85,000	250,000
Wages	40,000	30,000	20,000	30,000	120,000
Expenses	22,000	25,500	17,500	15,000	80,000
Total	112,000	95,500	112,500	130,000	450,000
Operating profit/(loss)	45,500	(14,250)	8,250	10,500	50,000

From this 'product income statement', the managers of the business can see that the total profit of £50,000 resulted from profits on products A, C and D, offset by a loss on product B, and that product A alone yielded 91% of the company total.

We do not know at this stage whether the information will lead them to take any decision to change things for the future, because we do not know whether the above result is in accordance with a deliberate plan or not. Nor can we be sure without further information whether it would be a good thing to discontinue product B since such a decision might involve some further analysis of the costs incurred, and some forecasts of future developments.

Both comparisons against plan and the preparation of special analyses for decision purposes fall within the scope of the cost accounting function.

2 The cost accounting department

2.1 Data required for reports

A company's requirements for historical information include three main types of data:

(a) Data from the normal financial accounts of the business: the statement of financial position and profit and income statement with their supporting notes and schedules, and the statement of cash flows.

(b) Data obtained by analysing the accounts of the business, identifying items with cost units and cost centres: in other words the work of the cost accounting department (details of stockholdings would come from this source).

(c) Data derived immediately from source documents without evaluation, such as statistics on labour efficiency, material usage, sickness, absenteeism and machine breakdowns.

In addition, most reports will include comparisons with budgets, standards, targets or estimates, and the explanations of variances based on detailed investigation and close knowledge of the data used in budget preparation.

2.2 Organisation

The accounts department, therefore, comprises a financial accounting segment, a costing segment and a budgetary control segment. The extent to which these are separate departments within the organisation depends on the number and diversity of the transactions to be handled and on the management organisation of the business, including the extent of divisional autonomy. All these factors affect the required number of accounting staff and the consequent need for specialisation of effort.

2.3 Cost recording

The cost department is responsible for maintaining the cost accounting records. To be effective these records should:

(a) analyse production, administration and marketing costs to facilitate cost and profit computations, inventory valuations, forecast and budget data and decision-making data;

(b) enable the production of periodic performance statements which are necessary for management control purposes;

(c) permit analysis of:

  (i) past costs for profit measurement and inventory valuation;

  (ii) present costs for control purposes;

  (iii) future costs – forecasts, targets, budgets and decision-making.

2.4 Cost accountant and other managers

Because his job is to interpret physical facts into money values, the cost accountant is in an excellent position to ensure that all types of report are integrated and are prepared on a consistent basis. Although inevitably other departments will wish to report on their own activities, the cost accountant should maintain close liaison and build a good relationship with them so that:

(a) the information he provides can assist them in interpreting the results of their own activities;

(b) there is no conflict on questions of fact between reports prepared by, for example, the sales manager or the production manager and the information emerging from the costing system.

2.5 Cost accounting and computers

Whilst records can be maintained manually, computer-based data concerning sales and production quantities, inventory levels, costs, etc will assist the cost accounting function in the following ways:

(a) Reports and cost accounts can be prepared quickly.

(b) Information for decision-making will be more plentiful and be available more speedily than would be the case with manual data.

(c) Large volumes of data can be stored and manipulated with ease.

2.6 The benefits of cost accounting

The benefits of cost accounting can be identified as:

(a) disclosure of profitable and non-profitable activities (as might appear in the product profit and loss account already illustrated). This data could also be modified to identify locations which are unprofitable;

(b) identification of waste and inefficiency, particularly in relation to usage of materials and labour;

(c) analysis of movements in profit;

(d) assistance in the determination of selling prices;

(e) valuation of inventory (there are auditing and taxation implications here);

(f) development of planning and control information;

(g) evaluation of the cost effect of policy decisions.

3 Cost units

3.1 Cost units

Definition

A cost unit is a quantitative unit of product or service in relation to which costs are ascertained.

Example

Have a look at the costing income statement illustrated earlier. This showed the sales quantity of various products (A-D) and the total cost of those sales under the headings materials, wages and expenses.

Further additional calculations could be made from that example.

Solution

Calculation of cost per unit for the month ended ... 20X0

	Product A	*Product B*	*Product C*	*Product D*
	£	£	£	£
Materials	0.16	1.23	0.93	3.02
Wages	0.13	0.92	0.25	1.07
Expenses	0.07	0.78	0.22	0.53
Total cost per unit	0.36	2.93	1.40	4.62

We have taken the total costs attributable to each product in a month (any other period could have been used) and arrived at the average cost per unit of each product, rounded to the nearest penny, by dividing the totals by the numbers of units involved. The 'cost unit' in this instance is the unit of product sold.

The cost unit might have been a piece, a pack, a kilogram, a litre or any other measure appropriate to what was being produced.

3.2 Average unit costs

In practice the business would probably have produced more units than it sold in the period, the unsold quantity being taken into inventory. In such a case, the costs of production would have been collected and divided by the number of units produced to give the average unit cost. This would have been applied to the number of units sold to give the cost of sales, and to the number of units remaining to give the costs of the residual inventory.

This average unit cost approach is used whenever production is continuous and leads to uniform product units, as in the case of many chemical plants, food processors or extractive operations such as mining and quarrying.

3.3 Job costs

Some businesses, however, undertake special jobs for their customers. A workshop making tools and jigs does this; and so on a much larger scale does the contractor building bridges or putting up a factory. In such cases, costs are first analysed between the various jobs or contracts, and then the costs of the jobs

invoiced will be gathered together into the periodic summary income statement. For such businesses, in other words, the 'cost unit' is the job or contract.

3.4 Batch costs

In the manufacture of mechanical or electrical components, such products are customarily made in batches of say 1,000 or 10,000 items, according to the circumstances of the case. In this type of business, the cost of each batch is determined and the batch is the primary 'cost unit'. Thereafter it is possible, if desired, to calculate the average cost per item in the batch.

3.5 Non-manufacturing cost units

The above examples have concentrated on cost units for production or manufacturing processes. Examples of cost units for service industries, or non-manufacturing activities within a business are as follows:

Service industry/activity	*Cost unit*
Accountants	Chargeable hour
College	Student enrolled
Hotel	Bed-night
Hospital	Patient-day
Transport department	kg-mile
Credit control department	Customer account
Selling	Calls made
Maintenance department	Man-hours

Note that some of these are in fact composite cost units, where a cost is considered to be dependent upon two main factors. For example, if the manager of a chain of hotels wanted to compare costs between two of the hotels, calculating costs per bed would not take account of the differing levels of occupation of the beds of the two hotels. Thus the cost can be calculated per bed-night (i.e. the cost of one bed per night of occupation).

A cost unit is a quantitative unit of product or service in relation to which costs are ascertained; the purpose of product costing is to arrive at the cost of the cost unit appropriate to the business concerned.

4 Cost centres

Definition

A cost centre is a location, function or item(s) of equipment in respect of which costs may be accumulated and related to cost units for control purposes.

A cost centre therefore is used as an initial collection point for costs; once the total cost of operating the cost centre for a period has been ascertained, it can be related to the cost units that have passed through the cost centre.

The location, function or item of equipment referred to in the definition can be directly related to production, to a service department or to a business.

4.1 Examples of cost centres

Production	Assembly line Packing machine
Service department	Stores Canteen Quality control
Service	Tax department (accountants) Ward (hospital) Faculty (college)

4.2 Responsibility for cost centres

Control can only be exercised by people, and for every cost somebody must be responsible; so whether a cost centre is impersonal or personal there must always be a manager in whose sphere of responsibility that cost centre is included.

4.3 Profit centres

Definition

A profit centre is a location, function or item(s) of equipment in respect of which costs and revenues may be ascertained for the purposes of control of the resulting profit.

Thus, while the paint shop in a factory might be treated as a cost centre (to monitor the costs incurred there), a large company might treat its French operations as a profit centre (since they generate both costs and revenues).

4.4 Investment centres

Definition

An investment centre is a location, function or item(s) of equipment in respect of which costs and revenues and investments may be ascertained for the purposes of control of the resulting profit.

A large company might treat one of its divisions as an investment centre since it generates both costs and revenues, and has the ability to make investments in assets, such as buying a fleet of sales vehicles or a new photocopier.

Activity 1

A location or function for which costs and revenues are ascertained for the purpose of controlling the resultant profit is a:

A Cost centre

B Revenue centre

C Profit centre

D Investment centre

5 Cost classification

5.1 Types of cost classification

Costs can be classified (collected into logical groups) in many ways. The particular classification selected will depend upon the purpose for which the resulting analysed data will be used.

Purpose	Classification
Cost control	By nature – materials, labour, overheads, etc.
Cost accounts	By relationship to cost units – direct/ indirect costs, etc.
Budgeting, contribution analysis	By behaviour – fixed/variable costs.
Decision-making	Relevant and non-relevant costs.
Responsibility accounting	Controllable and uncontrollable costs.

You will come across these classifications in more detail as you work through this study text. At this stage, we will revise the basic classification terms used in cost accounting.

5.2 Direct and indirect costs

For cost accounting purposes, the costs of the business will be classified in quite a different way from the analysis required by a financial accountant for the income statement in published accounts.

The basic classification of costs in cost accounting may be illustrated as follows.

Example

	£	£
Direct costs		
Direct materials		250,000
Direct labour		120,000
Direct expenses		10,000
Prime cost (= total of direct costs)		380,000
Indirect production costs		25,000
Production cost		405,000
Indirect non-production costs		
Administration overhead	20,000	
Selling and distribution overhead	25,000	
		45,000
Total cost		450,000

5.3 Direct costs

Definition

Direct costs are costs which can be related directly to one cost unit. Direct costs comprise direct materials, direct labour and direct expenses.

For example, considering a cost unit of a chair, direct costs will include the cost of wood and screws used (direct material cost) and the cost of manufacturing labour hours per chair (direct labour cost).

In a service context, the direct costs relating to, say, a student enrolled at a college would include the costs of books provided, individual tuition and marking costs.

5.4 Indirect costs

Definition

Indirect costs cannot be identified directly with a cost unit and are often referred to as *overheads.*

For inventory valuation purposes a distinction needs to be made between overheads incurred in the production process (factory costs, e.g. factory rent and rates, power etc) and non-production costs.

Non-production costs are indirect costs involved in converting finished goods into revenue, comprising:

(a) administrative overhead costs (e.g. executive salaries and office costs); and

(b) marketing, selling and distribution overhead costs.

Non-production costs are not included in inventory valuation since they are not costs of making a product, but costs of selling it. Inventory on hand at the end of a period is valued at total production cost only, including production overheads (in a total absorption costing system).We shall return to this point in the next chapter.

Considering the cost unit of a chair, the salaries of the sales representatives who promote and sell the chairs to retail outlets would be a selling overhead.

Indirect costs associated with a college would include premises running costs, lecturers' salaries and administrative staff costs.

Overhead costs can always be identified with cost centres; and because cost centres are the responsibility of particular functional managers one will find overheads classified according to the main functional divisions of the business.

5.5 Full production cost

Full production cost is the total of all costs (direct and indirect) that were incurred in the production of a unit. This means that selling costs, etc are excluded. In the example above, the full production cost was £405,000.

5.6 Marginal cost

The marginal cost of a product is the total of all variable costs. (Often the words marginal and variable are substituted for each other because they mean the same thing.)

Activity 2

The total of all direct costs is:

A Marginal cost

B Absorption cost

C Prime cost

D Standard cost

6 Cost behaviour

6.1 The nature of costs

We mentioned earlier the need for cost classification by behaviour for budgeting purposes. In order to make predictions of future cost levels, we must determine the basis of the charge.

As an example, consider the cost of direct materials expected next month. The charge would depend on the amount used and the cost per unit. The amount used would depend, in turn, on the production anticipated for the period.

In order to derive this cost therefore we must make an estimate such as the following:

(a)	Production levels	10,000 units
(b)	Usage of materials per unit:	
	Material A	2 kg
	Material B	1 kg
	Material C	0.2 kg
(c)	Costs of materials:	
	Material A	30 pence per kg
	Material B	25 pence per kg
	Material C	50 pence per kg

Estimate of next month's material cost

		£
Material A	20,000 kg @ 30p/kg	6,000
Material B	10,000 kg @ 25p/kg	2,500
Material C	2,000 kg @ 50p/kg	1,000
Total estimated material cost		9,500

6.2 Variable costs

We have set up a simple mathematical model which will, for any level of production, usage and cost of materials, enable the total level of cost in a future period to be predicted. The direct materials example was perhaps the easiest to use and, in practice, we may wish to deal with other variables which affect the cost such as wastage rates thus producing a slightly more complex model.

Direct labour costs may tend to vary due to changes in productivity and other factors in addition to the more obvious variables such as grade and rate of payment. A certain amount of estimation will still be required; if payment is on a production related basis we would expect a cost which, like materials, will vary in line with the volume of production.

At this stage, therefore, we have come to the rule-of-thumb guide that direct material, labour and expenses will probably vary roughly in line with anticipated production levels or the level of activity. We call such costs **variable** costs.

6.3 Fixed costs

This will not be the case with all costs. If we take the cost of rent and rates, for example, the charge is not determined on the basis of the intensity of usage of the premises but rather on the basis of time. Costs that are unaffected by the volume of production are called **fixed costs**. Rent and rates are an example. Labour paid on a time basis would also fall under this heading. How then can we predict the cost of such expenses for next month? Well, there is no difficulty in doing this as all we have to do is consult our rental agreement and the rates notice and we can forecast with complete certainty what these costs will be for the month.

6.4 Classification of costs by behaviour

The above example illustrates the need for cost behaviour classification. For cost prediction purposes, we must make a distinction between costs which vary with production or activity levels (variable costs) and those which do not (fixed costs). There also exists a type of cost which moves in sympathy with production levels but contains an element which does not, such as an electricity charge which contains a minimum standing charge plus an element which relates to the usage of the period. Such a cost would be described as semi-variable or mixed.

Definition

Variable costs are those that vary (usually assumed in direct proportion) with changes in level of activity of the cost centre to which they relate (e.g. output volume), for example the raw material used in a product. It should be noted that the variable cost per unit may not remain constant over a wide range. It may be possible, for example, to obtain discounts for large purchases of material, reducing the cost per unit.

Fixed costs are those that accrue with the passage of time and are not affected by changes in activity level; they are therefore also known as period costs, for example rent of premises.

Stepped costs are fixed over a range of output and then suddenly increase in one big jump, for example a staffing level of up to 20 people may only require one supervisor but, if the staff level is more than 20, an extra supervisor will be needed.

Semi-variable (mixed) costs contain both a fixed and a variable element. When output is nil, the fixed element is incurred, but they also increase, like variable costs, as output increases. An example is telephone charges where there is a fixed rental to which is added the charge for calls made. These are also sometimes known as semi-fixed costs.

6.5 Graphical illustrations

Various cost behaviour patterns are illustrated in the graphs below.

(a) **Variable cost:** direct materials, the purchase price per unit being constant

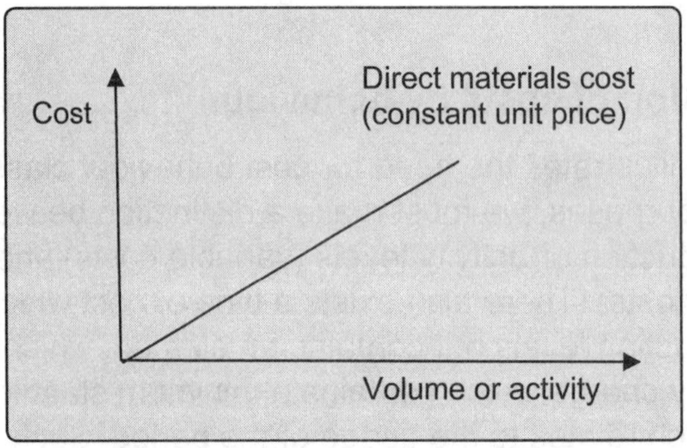

(b) **Fixed cost:** rent of factory payable under a long-term lease

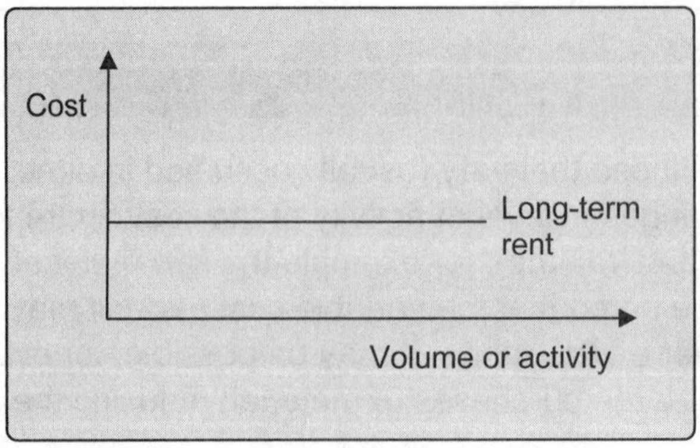

(c) **Stepped costs**

(i) Canteen cost where additional assistants are required as increases in activity result in larger numbers of factory personnel

(ii) Rent of premises, additional accommodation eventually being required

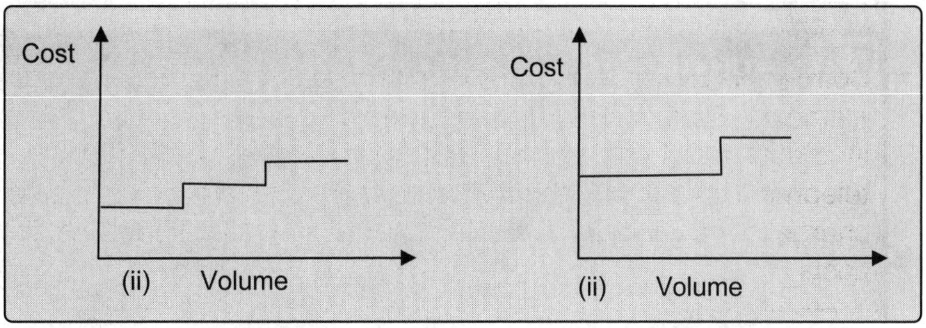

(d) **Semi-variable costs**

(i) Direct materials cost (trade discount at higher levels of activity)

(ii) Salesmen's remuneration with added commission from a certain level of activity

(iii) Electricity charges comprising a fixed standing charge and variable unit charge

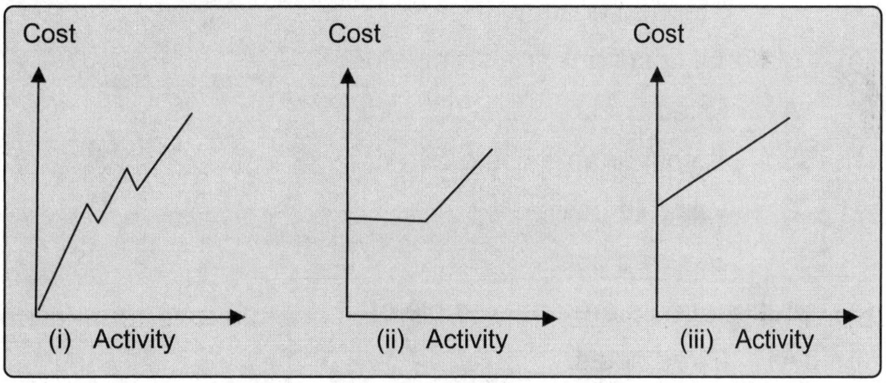

6.6 Practical limitations of cost classification

As you can see from the graphs above, costs may not be totally fixed or totally variable. In the real world costs often act in more complex ways than we have seen so far.

For example, discounts may be given to customers that order goods in large volumes causing the cost line to fragment not unlike the graph above for semi-variable costs (i).

Production in large quantities can bring economies of scale to a business whereby the cost graph may not be a linear variable cost but a curved one that becomes less steep at higher volumes.

The common approach that we take in order to keep it simple is as follows:

(a) Treat as variable those costs which change by regular steps.

(b) Treat as fixed those costs which only change at wide intervals of activity; this recognises that review will be required if there is a permanent change in the normal level of activity.

Activity 3

Required

(a) Electricity charges are an example of:

A Fixed costs

B Semi-variable costs

C Variable costs

D Stepped costs

(b) Rents paid are an example of:

A Fixed costs

B Semi-variable costs

C Variable costs

D Stepped costs

(c) Material costs are an example of:

A Fixed costs

B Semi-variable costs

C Variable costs

D Stepped costs

(d) Labour costs are an example of:

A Fixed costs

B Semi-variable costs

C Variable costs

D Stepped costs

(e) Supervisors salaries that increase occasionally due to increases in volume are best described as:

A Fixed costs

B Semi-variable costs

C Variable costs

D Stepped costs

Activity 4

The rent of premises where at certain levels of activity extra premises will have to be rented is an example of a:

A Fixed cost

B Variable cost

C Stepped cost

D Mixed cost

7 Cost estimation

7.1 Introduction

As we have seen, some costs may have both fixed and variable elements. These will need to be identified for budgeting purposes.

If it is not easy to do this directly (as it is in the case of the telephone cost, where the bill clearly shows the fixed charge and rate per unit), then an analysis of past cost and volume data will need to be carried out.

7.2 Methods of cost estimation

It is assumed that there is a linear relationship, i.e.:

Total cost = Fixed cost + (Variable cost per unit × Units produced)

and that the total fixed cost and the variable cost per unit are constant at all levels of production unless told otherwise.

Possible techniques include the high/low method and linear regression.

8 The high/low method

8.1 Introduction

This is a simple method of estimating future costs from past results. It takes the costs for the highest and lowest activity levels, and assumes that a linear relationship covers the range in between.

Example

Widgets are produced by a process that incurs both fixed and variable costs.

Total costs have been recorded for the process for each of the last six months as follows.

Month	*Output (units)*	*Total cost* £
1	4,500	33,750
2	3,500	30,500
3	5,100	34,130
4	6,200	38,600
5	5,700	38,000
6	4,100	31,900

(a) What is the estimated fixed cost element and estimated variable cost per unit?

(b) What would be the estimated total cost at the budgeted activity level for month 7 of 6,000 units?

Solution

Select the months with the highest and lowest output levels as follows.

	Output (units)	*Total cost* £
Lowest output	3,500	30,500
Highest output	6,200	38,600
Increase	2,700	8,100

For an increase of 2,700 units, cost has increased by £8,100. If we assume that the fixed cost element remains constant, this cost increase must represent a change in variable costs only.

Assuming a straight-line relationship, then the variable cost per unit =

$$\frac{£8,100}{2,700} = £3 \text{ per unit}$$

Note that the factor determining which values to choose is the total cost at the highest output level and the total cost at the lowest output level. These are not necessarily the highest and lowest costs. The high/low observations are always based on the independent variable (in this case, output).

We can now substitute back into either of the two output levels to obtain the fixed cost.

At the 3,500 units level:

	£
Total cost	30,500
Variable cost (3,500 × £3)	(10,500)
Fixed costs	20,000

As a check on the accuracy of the calculations, at the 6,200 units level:

	£
Total costs	38,600
Variable cost (6,200 × £3)	(18,600)
Fixed costs	20,000

(a) Therefore the estimated fixed cost element is £20,000 and the estimated variable cost is £3 per unit.

(b) At an output level of 6,000 units the total estimated cost would be:

	£
Variable cost (6,000 × £3)	18,000
Fixed cost	20,000
Total cost	38,000

The high-low method can involve the use of a stepped cost.

Example

A company has achieved the following output levels and total costs:

Volume of production (units)	190	240
Total cost	£150,000	£210,000

Total cost includes a fixed element which steps up by £25,000 at an activity level of 200 units.

The variable cost per unit is constant.

The variable cost per unit is £ ______

Solution

£210,000 – £150,000 = £60,000 of which £25,000 is the step up. Therefore only £35,000 is the total variable cost.

Change in output = 240 – 190 = 50 units.

Variable cost per unit = £35,000 / 50 units = £700

8.2 Advantages of the high-low method

- Simple to operate.
- Easy to understand.

8.3 Disadvantages of the high-low method

The problem with the high-low method is that it could give a completely inaccurate result. This is because we are only considering two sets of data, and ignoring all of the others. It is possible that the points we have chosen are completely unrepresentative of the rest of the data. This is a distinct possibility since we have chosen the two points at the extreme ends of the activity range. At these levels it is more likely that operating conditions will be atypical compared with more normal output. One way around this problem is to choose the 'next to highest' and 'next to lowest' figures, but this destroys some of the simplicity of the model.

Activity 5

Production

Given below are the production quantities and production overhead costs for each of the last six months:

Month	*Production quantity (units)*	*Production overheads* £
January	10,000	58,000
February	9,000	50,000
March	12,000	65,000
April	11,000	62,000
May	8,000	45,000
June	9,500	52,000

Production in July is anticipated to be 10,500 units. What should be the cost of the budgeted production overhead for July?

Production

Use the high/low method.

	Production quantity (units)	*Production overheads* £
Highest	12,000	
Lowest	8,000	
Increase in activity and overheads		

Variable cost = £ / units

= £ per unit

Substituting at 12,000 unit level:

	£
Variable cost 12,000 × £	
Total cost	65,000
Fixed cost	

At a production level of 10,500 units:

	£
Variable cost 10,500 × £	
Fixed cost	
Total cost	

Activity 6

A company has achieved the following output levels and total costs:

Volume of production (units)	198,000	203,000
Total cost	£150,000	£192,000

Total cost includes a fixed element which steps up by £35,000 at an activity level of 200,000 units.

The variable cost per unit is constant.

The variable cost per unit is £ [ ]

9 Summary

Much of cost accounting is about gathering information about current costs and making predictions about future costs. Some costs, direct costs, can be allocated directly to a cost unit whereas other costs, indirect costs or overheads, are allocated initially to a cost centre.

Costs can also be usefully classified according to their behaviour. This is particularly useful when budgeting costs for future periods or for making decisions about activity levels. Costs can be classified as variable, fixed, stepped or semi-variable.

For semi-variable costs the fixed element and the variable element will need to be identified for forecasting purposes. This can be done using the high/low method.

Answers to chapter activities

Activity 1

C A profit centre is a location or function for which costs and revenues are ascertained for the purpose of controlling the resultant profit.

Activity 2

C Prime cost is the total of all direct costs.

Activity 3

(a) B Electricity costs usually have a standing charge (fixed cost) and the usage (variable cost).

(b) A (Rent is usually a fixed cost unless there is mention of having to rent further space when it becomes a stepped cost.)

(c) C Materials are a variable cost.

(d) C Labour is a variable cost usually.

(e) D Supervisors salaries can be a fixed cost but there is mention here of extra supervisors being required therefore it will actually be a stepped cost.

Activity 4

C An example of a stepped cost is the rent of premises where at certain levels of activity extra premises will have to be rented.

Activity 5

Production

Use the high/low method.

	Production quantity (units)	*Production overheads* £
Highest	12,000	65,000
Lowest	8,000	45,000
Increase in activity	4,000	20,000

Variable cost = $\frac{£20,000}{4,000 \text{ units}}$

= £5 per unit

Substituting at 12,000 unit level:

	£
Variable cost 12,000 × £5	60,000
Total cost	65,000
Fixed cost	5,000

At a production level of 10,500 units:

	£
Variable cost 10,500 × £5	52,500
Fixed cost	5,000
Total cost	57,500

Activity 6

£192,000 – £150,000 = £42,000 of which £35,000 is the step up. Therefore only £7,000 is the total variable cost.

Change in output = 203,000 – 198,000 = 5,000 units.

Variable cost per unit = £7,000 / 5,000 units = £1.40

10 Test your knowledge

Workbook Activity 7

You work as an accounting technician for Eastoft Feeds and Fertilisers Ltd.

You use a computer model for forecasting the quarterly costs on your various product lines. The software includes a regression analysis program which builds a simple linear cost model. After inputting data for product 'EF 3', values for the quarterly fixed cost and marginal cost per unit are determined and the cost model is y = 25,000 + 35x, where x is the quarterly production volume (in tonnes) and y is the total quarterly cost (in £).

The following is the estimated volume of output for the quarters ended March, June, September and December 20XY.

Product 'EF3'

Quarter ended	*Volume (tonnes)*
March	15,000
June	12,000
September	16,000
December	14,000

Task

Estimate the fixed cost, variable cost and total cost for each quarter of 20XY and complete the table below.

Product 'EF3'

Quarter ended	*Volume tonnes*	*Fixed cost* £	*Variable cost* £	*Total cost* £
March				
June				
September				
December				

Accounting for overheads 3

Introduction

Overhead is the general term used to describe costs which are not direct costs of production. They are also known as indirect costs and they may be indirect production costs or indirect non-production costs. When a management accountant is trying to ascertain the cost of a product or service, there are two possible approaches available for dealing with overheads.

Firstly, apportionment and allocation of all production overheads may be used to arrive at a 'full' cost per unit. This is known as absorption costing and is considered first. Remember that as well as the indirect production cost there are indirect non-production costs. These non-production costs are never included in the cost of the product, or inventory or cost of sales.

Alternatively, one can use only direct costs to arrive at the cost per unit and leave indirect costs as a general overhead not related to units of output. This approach is generally known as marginal costing and will be dealt with later in the chapter.

KNOWLEDGE

Recognise the differences between standard, marginal and absorption costing (2.3))

Describe and recognise when activity based costing should be used (3.6)

SKILLS

Account for transactions between the separate units of the organisation (1.3)

Prepare routine cost reports (1.5)

CONTENTS

1 Allocation, apportionment and absorption of overheads
2 Activity-based costing (ABC)
3 Absorption costing and marginal costing
4 Contribution
5 CVP analysis
6 Breakeven analysis
7 Limiting factor analysis

1 Allocation, apportionment and absorption of overheads

1.1 Introduction

We have already identified two types of costs that make up the full production cost of a unit:

(a) Direct costs are those that can be uniquely identified with an individual cost unit (e.g. direct materials, direct labour, direct expenses).

(b) Indirect costs (overheads) are costs incurred in production but not easily 'traced' to individual units, e.g. machine power (variable), factory rent (fixed), telephone (semi-variable).

The problem we are considering here is how to divide indirect production costs between cost units, in order to prepare a 'standard' total cost per unit for budgeting, inventory valuation and pricing purposes.

The method used to divide production overheads between production units is made up of three processes: allocation, apportionment and absorption.

Step 1 Identify the indirect cost with a cost centre

This can be done in two ways depending on the nature of the cost.

(a) **Allocation**

Definition

Where the indirect cost is borne entirely by one cost centre, the entire cost is allocated to that cost centre.

(b) **Apportionment**

Definition

Where the indirect cost is shared by more than one cost centre, the cost is apportioned or shared between the cost centres.

Step 2 Identify the indirect costs of the cost centre calculated in Step 1 with the cost units produced by that centre.

This is called absorption.

Definition

Absorption is the technique of relating a cost centre's indirect costs to the units produced by the cost centre.

We shall now look at each of these in more detail.

1.2 Cost allocation

Certain cost items will be incurred entirely by one cost centre. Allocation deals with this type of cost and simply allots it to the cost centre which has incurred the cost.

Cost centre	*Allocated cost*
Canteen	Spaghetti
	Tea bags
	Chef's wages
Packing department	Cardboard String

1.3 Cost apportionment (primary)

More frequently, however, the benefit of an item of cost will be shared by a number of cost centres. The overhead will be split or apportioned between the relevant cost centres on an 'equitable' basis.

The rent of buildings, for example, can relate to the total floor space occupied by a number of different departments and it is usual to allot the rental charge to those departments in proportion to the floor space they occupy.

Nature of cost	*Possible bases of apportionment*
Rent and rates	Floor area occupied by various departments
Lighting and heating	Cubic capacity of locations or metered usage
Insurance of inventory	Value of inventory in various locations

Example

A general cost in a manufacturing company is factory rental. Annual rental costs are £80,000. How should this cost be apportioned between production departments and service departments?

Rental costs are usually apportioned between departments on the basis of the floor space taken up by each department. For example, suppose that three departments have floor space of 10,000 square metres, 15,000 square metres and 25,000 square metres, and annual rental costs are £80,000. If we apportion rental costs between the departments on the basis of their floor space, the apportionment would be as follows.

Annual rental	£80,000
Total floor space (10,000 + 15,000 + 25,000)	50,000 square metres
Apportionment rate (£80,000/50,000)	£1.60/square metre

	£
Apportion to department with 10,000 square metres	16,000
Apportion to department with 15,000 square metres	24,000
Apportion to department with 25,000 square metres	40,000
	80,000

Example

The costs of heating and lighting might also be apportioned on the basis of floor space. Alternatively, since heating relates to volume rather than floor space, it could be argued that the costs should be apportioned on the volume of space taken up by each department. Yet another view is that electricity costs relate more to the consumption of electrical power by machines, therefore the apportionment of these costs should be on the basis of the number and power of the machines in each department.

A reasonable argument could be made for any of these bases of apportionment.

1.4 Cost apportionment (secondary)

After completing the allocation and primary apportionment stages, you should have assigned all costs to cost centres.

Some cost centres, however, will not have production units passing through them; these cost centres are called service departments (e.g. quality control department, works canteen). Before the final stage of absorption into cost units can be carried out, it is necessary to perform a further type of apportionment whereby the total costs of the service cost centres are reassigned to production cost centres. This is known as secondary apportionment. This should be done on a fair basis to reflect the benefit derived from the service centre.

The following example is an illustration of primary and secondary apportionment.

Example

Overhead Analysis Sheet			**Period Ending……………….**		
	Total	**Production**		**Service**	
		Assembly	*Finishing*	*Stores*	*Canteen*
	£	£	£	£	£
Overheads allocated directly to cost centres	133,000	49,000	36,000	27,000	21,000
Overheads to be apportioned					
Rent (Apportionment basis: ………………………..)	76,000	26,000	24,000	15,000	11,000
Equipment depreciation (Apportionment basis: ………………………..)	15,000	8,000	1,000	5,000	1,000
Total overhead	224,000	83,000	61,000	47,000	33,000
Apportioning of stores (Apportionment basis: ………………………..)		31,000	16,000	(47,000)	
Apportioning of canteen (Apportionment basis: ………………………..)		14,000	19,000		(33,000)
		128,000	96,000	–	–

Activity 1

A fair basis for apportioning the factory rental cost between the various cost centres in the business would be:

A Building insurance

B Machine value

C Floor area

D Number of staff

1.5 Absorption

Having collected all indirect costs in the production cost centres via overhead allocation and apportionment, the cost has to be spread over the output of the production cost centre.

The allotment of accumulated overhead costs to cost units is called overhead absorption. The absorption rate is normally calculated at the start of the period and therefore based on budgeted quantities. Various methods of absorption exist and the one most fitting should be chosen.

The following are the most common methods you will encounter.

(a) **Rate per unit**

The simple unit rate is obtained by dividing total budgeted overheads by the number of units budgeted to be produced. However, where more than one product is produced, this is an unsatisfactory basis for absorbing overheads as it will not reflect the relative demands of each product on the production departments through which they pass.

(b) **Alternative bases of absorption**

There are a number of bases commonly used as an alternative to the simple unit rate:

- rate per direct labour hour;
- rate per machine hour;
- percentage of material cost;
- percentage of wage cost;
- percentage of total direct cost (prime cost).

It is important to appreciate, however, that whichever method or combination of methods is used, the result will only be an approximate estimate of what that product actually costs.

In practice, many businesses use a 'direct labour hour rate' or 'machine hour rate' in preference to a rate based on a percentage of direct materials cost, direct wages or prime cost, as it may be possible to associate some overheads either with labour time or with machine time.

It may be possible to analyse the total overhead apportioned to each production department into fixed and variable elements. In this case a variable overhead rate per unit and a fixed overhead rate per unit can be calculated.

The absorption rates will normally be calculated at the beginning of a period and hence be based on budgeted costs and production levels. This can lead to problems when actual costs and volumes are not the same as budgeted leading to over- or under-absorption.

Example

For the year ended 31 December 20X4 the planned overhead for the Machining Cost Centre at Cuecraft Ltd was:

Overhead	£132,000
Volume of activity	15,000 machine hours

In January 20X4 the cost centre incurred £12,000 of overhead and 1,350 machine hours were worked.

Task

Calculate the pre-determined overhead rate per machine hour and the overhead under or over-recovered in the month.

Solution

Absorption rate, based on the budget:

$$\frac{\text{Planned overhead}}{\text{Machine hours}} = \frac{£132,000}{15,000 \text{ machine hours}} = £8.80 \text{ per machine hour}$$

	£
Overhead absorbed	
1,350 machine hours at £8.80	11,880
Overhead incurred	12,000
Under-absorption	120

Here, the amount of overhead actually charged to production are £11,880, which is less than actual expenditure. We therefore have under-absorption of overhead.

Under-recovery of overheads is shown as a separate item in the costing income statement. Since production has been charged with fewer overheads than the amount of overheads incurred, an adjustment to profit for under-absorption is downwards. In other words, under-absorption is a 'loss' item.

Example

The following example covers all stages of overhead allocation, apportionment and absorption summarised above. Work through it carefully to ensure you have fully understood this area.

SB Limited has two production departments (Assembly and Finishing) and two service departments (Maintenance and Canteen).The following costs are expected to be incurred during the next time period.

	£
Indirect materials	20,000
Rent	15,000
Electricity	10,000
Machine depreciation	5,000
Building depreciation	10,000
Direct labour	55,000

The following information is available.

	Assembly	*Finishing*	*Maintenance*	*Canteen*
Area (square metres)	1,000	2,000	0,500	0,500
Kw hours consumed	1,000	4,000	Nil	5,000
Machine value	£45,000	£35,000	£11,000	£9,000
Number of staff	0,020	0,030	0,010	0,004
Indirect materials				
consumed	7,000	8,000	3,000	2,000
Direct labour hours	10,000	2,000	0,500	0,200
Machine hours	1,000	5,000	–	–

The maintenance department spends 60% of its time servicing equipment for the assembly department and 40% of its time servicing equipment for the finishing department. The canteen equipment is serviced by outside specialist contractors.

(a) Calculate the total overheads in each cost centre.

(b) Reapportion the service centre costs to production cost centres.

(c) Calculate appropriate absorption rates for each production department.

(d) One of SB Ltd's products is the JK. Production details for each unit of JK are:

	Assembly	*Finishing*
Direct labour hours	4	1
Machine hours	0.5	2.5

How much overhead should be absorbed into each unit of JK?

Solution

(a)

Overhead	*Total*	*Basis of apportionment (note)*	*Assembly*	*Finishing*	*Maintenance*	*Canteen*
	£		£	£	£	£
Indirect materials	20,000	Allocate (i)	7,000	8,000	3,000	2,000
Rent	15,000	Area (ii)	3,750	7,500	1,875	1,875
Electricity	10,000	Kw hours (iii)	1,000	4,000	–	5,000
Machine depreciation	5,000	Machine value (iv)	2,250	1,750	0,550	0,450
Building depreciation	10,000	Area (v)	2,500	5,000	1,250	1,250
Direct labour	55,000	– (vi)	–	–	–	–
Total	60,000		16,500	26,250	6,675	10,575

Notes

(i) We are given the amount of indirect materials used by each cost centre. This allows us to allocate the cost straight to each cost centre.

(ii) Rent is something that is shared by the whole factory and therefore the cost must be apportioned between the cost centres. The first thing to decide is what basis to use. Since rent is related to area, floor space would be a sensible basis to use (the bigger the area of a cost centre the more rent will be apportioned to it). The apportionment is carried out as follows.

- Calculate the total floor area for the factory.
- For each cost centre calculate what fraction of the total floor area this represents.
- Multiply this fraction by £15,000.

In the present case this would be as follows:

Total floor area =1,000 + 2,000 + 500 + 500 = 4,000 square metres.

Assembly is 1,000 square metres, i.e. 1,000/4,000 of the total area. Assembly is apportioned £15,000 × 1,000/4,000 = £3,750.

Similarly, finishing is apportioned £15,000 × 2,000/4,000 = £7,500 and Maintenance and Canteen are apportioned £15,000 × 500/4,000 = £1,875 each.

(iii) The most appropriate basis for apportioning the electricity between the cost centres will be the Kw hours consumed since these are a measure of the amount of electricity used.

The total Kw hours consumed = 1,000 + 4,000 + 0 + 5,000 = 10,000.

Assembly will be apportioned £10,000 × 1,000/10,000 = £1,000 etc.

(iv) Machine depreciation will be based on the value of the machinery and again needs to be apportioned between the cost centres.

The total machine value is £45,000 + £35,000 + £11,000 + £9,000 = £100,000.

This results in Assembly being apportioned £5,000 × 45/100 = £2,250 etc.

(v) Since the whole building is being depreciated, building depreciation should be related to the area of each cost centre. It does not matter that we have already used area once. There is no restriction against using it again if it is the most appropriate basis for apportioning this cost.

(vi) You may have thought that using number of employees was a good way to share out the direct wages bill, but remember that we are only interested here in overheads. Direct wages will already be included in the costs of the products that are made by the company. (Similarly direct materials are ignored for overheads.) If the question had included indirect labour then that would be included as an overhead and could be apportioned using the number of people working in each cost centre.

(b) A suitable basis for sharing out canteen costs is the number of employees. A suitable basis for sharing out the maintenance costs is the time spent servicing equipment.

First re-apportion canteen costs since the canteen provides services for maintenance but maintenance do not work for the canteen. Then re-apportion the maintenance work, which include a share of the canteen

Overhead	*Basis*	*Assembly*	*Finishing*	*Maintenance*	*Canteen*
		£	£	£	£
Total from above		16,500	26,250	6,675	10,575
Canteen	Personnel 20:30:10	3,525	5,288	1,762	(10,575)
Sub-total		20,025	31,538	8,437	
Maintenance	Time 60:40	5,062	3,375	(8,437)	
Total		25,087	34,913		

Total overhead = £60,000

(c) The assembly department seems to be labour based, therefore overhead is absorbed on the basis of labour hours:

$$\text{Overhead absorption rate } \frac{£25{,}087}{10{,}000 \text{ hours}} = £2.51 \text{ per direct labour hour}$$

The finishing department seems to be machine based, therefore overhead is absorbed on the basis of machine hours:

$$\text{Overhead absorption rate } \frac{£34{,}913}{5{,}000 \text{ hours}} = £6.98 \text{ per machine hour}$$

(d) Overhead absorbed per unit of JK:

(£2.51 × 4 hours) + (£6.98 × 2.5 hours) = £27.49

Activity 2

Which basis of absorbing factory overheads has traditionally been the most common?

A Labour hours

B Machine hours

C Units of output

D Units of inventory

Activity 3

Lorus Limited

Lorus Limited makes cupboards. This involves three production departments (Sawing, Assembly and Finishing) together with two service departments (Maintenance and Materials Handling).

Last year 4,000 cupboards were made.

Costs incurred:

	Sawing	*Assembly*	*Finishing*
	£	£	£
Materials	120,000	80,000	20,000
Wages	50,000	25,000	40,000
Overheads	75,000	50,000	20,000

Materials Handling wages:	£9,000
Maintenance wages:	£20,000

The benefits derived from the service departments are estimated to be as follows:

	Sawing	*Assembly*	*Finishing*	*Handing materials*
	%	%	%	%
Maintenance	30	40	20	10
Materials Handling	50	20	30	

Required

(a) Prepare a memorandum to the managing director, copied to each production head, showing the overheads allotted to each production department.

(b) Calculate the unit cost of a cupboard.

Lorus Limited

(a) **Memorandum re overheads**

MEMORANDUM

To:

CC:

From:

Date:

Subject:

	Sawing	*Assembly*	*Finishing*	*MH*	*Maintenance*
	£	£	£	£	£
Overhead					
Apportion maintenance wages					
Apportion materials handling wages					
	———	———	———	———	———
Total allotted				–	–
	———	———	———	———	———

Note: Service department overhead has been apportioned to production departments on the basis of percentage estimates of relative benefit, as specified.

(b) 4,000 cupboards were produced with the following costs incurred:

	Sawing	*Assembly*	*Finishing*	*Total*	*Unit cost*
	£	£	£	£	£
Materials					
Wages					
Overheads					
	———	———	———	———	———
	———	———	———	———	———

The unit cost of a cupboard is £______________.

Activity 4

Sandsend Engineers Ltd specialise in agricultural engineering. The business is divided into three cost centres: machining, fabrication and outside contract work.

The budgeted overhead for the quarter ended 31 March 2003 shows:

Cost centre	*Machining*	*Fabrication*	*Outside contracts*	*Total*
	£	£	£	£
Allocated overhead	21,000	25,500	19,500	66,000
Apportioned overhead	15,000	16,100	9,100	40,200
	36,000	41,600	28,600	106,200
Budgeted machine hours	4,000	5,200		
Budgeted labour hours			1,950	

In early January, the company receives an order for a replacement door on a grain silo for a local farmer. The specification of costs includes:

Direct material	£3,100
Direct labour rate per hour	£7.50

Machine hours and labour hours per cost centre:

Machining	12 hours
Fabrication	8 hours
Outside contracts	6 hours

The business has a pricing policy based on full absorption costing principles. It adds 10% to production costs to cover for administration, selling and distribution. It then plans for profit based on 25% of the selling price or contract price.

Task

Determine, using absorption costing principles, the contract price of the replacement grain silo door. (Calculate to the nearest '£'.)

Overhead recovery rates for each cost centre:

Machining = £ ____________ per machine hour

Fabrication = £ ____________ per machine hour

Outside contract work = £ ____________ per direct labour hr

Production cost of contract:

	£
Direct material	
Direct labour:	
Machining	
Fabrication	
Outside work	
Overheads:	
Machining	
Fabrication	
Outside work	
Production cost	
Add 10% for admin, selling and distribution	
Selling price/contract price	

Activity 5

Roberts and Ranson are partners trading as licensed accounting technicians. They employ one other fully qualified technician and two trainees, together with a general administration assistant.

The budgeted salaries for the year comprise:

	£
Roberts	30,000
Ranson	30,000
Qualified senior	18,500
Trainee (1)	10,500
Trainee (2)	12,000
Administrator	14,500*
	115,500

*The administrator's salary is to be treated as overhead.

The budgeted overheads include:

	£
Building occupancy costs	9,100
Telephone, postage, stationery	4,700
Other overheads	11,200
	25,000

The total forecast labour hours for the year include:

	Hours
Partners	3,760
Qualified senior	1,880
Trainees (split equally)	3,760
	9,400

Clients' work is priced on full absorption costing principles. Overhead is recovered on labour hours. The labour charge-out rates for partners, the qualified senior and the trainees are based on their budgeted salaries divided by their labour hours.

The business accepts a new client, the White Rose Hotel, and the senior partner estimates, having met with the client, that the hours required on the work will be:

	Hours	
Partners	5	
Qualified senior	12	
Trainees	6	(3 hours each)
	23	

The pricing policy is based on adding an element for profit which will yield a 30% profit margin on the price charged to the client.

Task

Determine the estimated fees chargeable to the White Rose Hotel based on the partner's notes.

Overhead recovery rate:

Overheads	£
Building occupancy	
Telephone, postage and stationery	
Other overheads	
Administrator's salary	
	–––––
	–––––
Labour hours	
Overhead rate per labour hour	
	–––––
Partners' labour charge-out rate	
Qualified senior	
Trainee (1)	
Trainee (2)	
White Rose Hotel estimated fees:	
	£
Direct labour:	
Partners	
Qualified senior	
Trainee (1)	
Trainee (2)	
	–––––
Overheads:	
	–––––
Total cost	
	–––––
Thus charge to client	
	–––––

Activity 6

Refer again to the scenario in Activity 4 – Sandsend Engineers Ltd.

The actual overhead incurred during the quarter ended 31 March 2003 was:

	£
Machining	37,800
Fabrication	42,000
Outside work	29,100
	108,900

Overhead is recovered on machine hours in machining and fabrication, and labour hours on outside work.

The actual level of activity in the quarter was:

Machining	4,250 machine hours
Fabrication	5,300 machine hours
Outside work	1,975 labour hours

Task

(a) Calculate the overhead recovered in each cost centre for the period.

(b) Post both the actual overhead incurred and the overhead recovered to the overhead control ledger account for the period, showing the under or over recovery transferred to the income statement.

Task

(a) **Sandsend Engineers Ltd overhead recovered:**

	£
Machining	
Fabrication	
Outside work	
	______
	______

(b)

Overhead control account			
	£		£
Actual:		*Recovered in work-in-progress*	
Machining		Machining	
Fabrication		Fabrication	
Outside work		Outside work	
Over-recovered – I.S (bal)			
	______		______
	______		______

2 Activity-based costing (ABC)

2.1 Criticisms of absorption costs

Historically a direct labour rate for absorption of all fixed overheads was a very common method, as production tended to be highly labour-intensive. Such items as rent would be apportioned using the area involved, but the absorption rate would usually be labour hours. It was reasonable to assume that the more labour time spent on a product, the more production resources in general were being used. Thus the product should be charged with a higher share of the overheads.

However, nowadays, production is far more mechanised. This has two impacts as follows:

(a) A higher proportion of the overhead is accounted for by machine-related costs (power, depreciation, maintenance, etc).

(b) The amount of labour time spent upon a unit is far less representative of its final significance in the use of production resources.

To take a simple example, Product A may use 9 machine hours and 1 labour hour, whilst Product B requires 1 machine hour and 4 labour hours. The traditional approach would charge B with four times as much production overhead (including machine costs) as A, even though it takes half the time overall.

In this example, one solution would be to use machine hours as a basis. However, this still tries to relate all overhead costs, whatever their nature, to usage of machines. This would not necessarily be appropriate for, say, costs of receiving and checking materials going into the production process. This will be more likely to depend upon the number of times an order of material is received into stores for a particular product.

2.2 Activity-based costing (ABC) approach

Professors Robin Cooper and Robert Kaplan at the Harvard Business School have developed a costing system called activity-based costing (ABC) which avoids the problems experienced by traditional costing methods. If management are keen to control costs, then it is vital that they should know the activities that cause costs to arise.

(a) **Cost drivers**

Those activities that are the significant determinants of cost are known as cost-drivers. For example, if production-scheduling cost is driven by the number of production set-ups, then that number is the cost-driver for the cost of production-scheduling. The cost-drivers represent the bases for charging costs in the ABC system, with a separate cost centre established for each cost-driver.

(b) **Cost pools**

Where several costs are 'driven' by the same activity (e.g. engine oil, machine breakdown and repairs) then these costs are put into 'cost pools' and the total of the cost pool is absorbed by, say, machine hours.

2.3 Mechanics of ABC

The mechanics of operating an ABC system are similar to a traditional costing system. The significant cost drivers need to be ascertained and a cost centre is established for each cost driver. Costs are allocated to products by dividing the cost centre costs by the number of transactions undertaken.

For example, in Plant Y a set up of a production run would be a cost driver. The cost of the engineers who do the set ups would be a cost centre. If the cost of the engineers is say £280,000 and the number of sets ups is 500, then the charging out rate is $\frac{280{,}000}{500}$ = £560. A product which has a number of small production runs will thus have a greater proportion of these costs relative to the quantity of the product produced, than a product with large production runs.

Other overheads will be allocated to products in a different way; which way depends upon the cost drivers which have been ascertained.

Example

Plant Y produces about one hundred products. Its largest selling product is Product A; its smallest is Product B. Relevant data is given below.

	Product A	*Product B*	*Total products*
Units produced pa	50,000	1,000	500,000
Material cost per unit	£1.00	£1.00	
Direct labour per unit	15 minutes	15 minutes	
Machine time per unit	1 hour	1 hour	
Number of set ups p.a.	24	2	500
Number of purchase orders for materials	36	6	2,800
Number of times material handled	200	15	12,000
Direct labour cost per hour			£5

Overhead costs

	£
Set up	280,000
Purchasing	145,000
Materials handling	130,000
Machines	660,000
	1,215,000

Total machine hours are 600,000 hours.

Traditional costing (absorbing overheads on machine hours):

Unit cost	*A*	*B*
	£	£
Material cost	1.00	1.00
Labour cost	1.25	1.25
Overhead per machine hour		
$\frac{1,215,000}{600,000} = 2.025$	2.025	2.025
	4.275	4.275

The above costings imply that we are indifferent between producing Product A and Product B.

Using an ABC approach would show:

Step 1 Calculate the direct material and labour costs as for the traditional approach.

Unit cost	*A*	*B*
	£	£
Material cost	1.00	1.00
Labour cost	1.25	1.25
	2.25	2.25

Step 2 Calculate the overheads that will be charged to each product by:

(a) Calculating the overhead cost per cost driver for each type of overhead (e.g. cost per set-up).

(b) Charge cost to each unit by calculating the unit cost accordingly.

	A	*B*
Overheads:	£	£
Set up		
$\frac{280,000}{500} = £560$ per set up		
$\frac{560 \times 24}{50,000}$	0.27	
$\frac{560 \times 2}{1,000}$		1.12

Purchasing:

$\frac{145,000}{2,800}$ = £51.79 per purchase order		
$\frac{36 \times 51.79}{50,000}$	0.04	
$\frac{6 \times 51.79}{1,000}$		0.31
Materials handling:		
$\frac{130,000}{12,000}$ = 10.83 per time		
$\frac{200 \times 10.83}{50,000}$	0.04	
$\frac{15 \times 10.83}{1,000}$		0.16
Machines:		
$\frac{660,000}{600,000}$ = £1.10 per machine hour	1.10	1.10
	1.45	2.69
Add: Direct material and labour costs	2.25	2.25
	£3.70	£4.94

Commonsense would lead us to conclude that ABC is a more accurate representation of the relative real costs of the two products.

What must be considered, however, is whether the benefits of this approach outweigh the costs of implementing and applying the system.

The following example again contrasts a traditional product costing system with an ABC system and shows that an ABC system produces much more accurate product costs.

Example

Mayes plc has a single production centre and has provided the following budgeted information for the next period.

	Product A	*Product B*	*Product C*	*Total*
Production and sales (units)	40,000	25,000	10,000	75,000
Direct material cost	£25	£20	£18	£1,680,000
Direct labour hours	3	4	2	240,000
Machine hours	2	4	3	210,000
Number of production runs	5	10	25	40
Number of component receipts	15	25	120	160
Number of production orders	15	10	25	50

Direct labour is paid £8 per hour.

Overhead costs in the period are expected to be as follows:

	£
Set-up	140,000
Machine	900,000
Goods inwards	280,000
Packing	200,000
Engineering	180,000
	————
	1,700,000
	————

What are the unit costs of each product using:

(a) the traditional approach?

(b) the ABC method?

Solution

(a) A traditional costing approach would cost each product as follows:

	Product A	*Product B*	*Product C*
	£	£	£
Direct materials	25.00	20.00	18.00
Direct labour (@ £8 per hour)	24.00	32.00	16.00
Overhead (@ £7.08 per hour – see below)	21.24	28.32	14.16
	———	———	———
Total cost	70.24	80.32	48.16
	———	———	———

Overhead recovery rate = $\frac{£1,700,000}{240,000}$ = £7.08 per direct labour hour

(b) An ABC system needs to investigate the cost determinants for the indirect overheads not driven by production volume. Assume that these are as follows.

Cost	*Cost driver*
Set-up	Number of production runs
Goods inwards	Number of receipts
Packing	Number of production orders
Engineering	Number of production orders

The machine overhead of £900,000 is likely to be related primarily to production volume, so it will be recovered on the basis of machine hours used = $\frac{£900,000}{210,000}$ = £4.29 per machine hour (after rounding)

The cost per activity for each of the other cost centres is as follows.

Set-up cost $\frac{£140,000}{40}$ = £3,500 per production run

Goods inwards $\frac{£280,000}{160}$ = £1,750 per component receipt

Packing $\frac{£200,000}{50}$ = £4,000 per production order

Engineering $\frac{£180,000}{50}$ = £3,600 per production order

An ABC approach would allocate overheads to each of the product groups as follows:

	Product A	*Product B*	*Product C*
	£	£	£
Set-up costs			
5 × £3,500	17,500		
10 × £3,500		35,000	
25 × £3,500			87,500
Machine costs (rounded down)			
(2 × 40,000) × £4.29	343,000		
(4 × 25,000) × £4.29		429,000	
(3 × 10,000) × £4.29			128,000
Goods inwards costs			
15 × £1,750	26,250		
25 × £1,750		43,750	
120 × £1,750			210,000
Packing costs			
15 × £4,000	60,000		
10 × £4,000		40,000	
25 × £4,000			100,000
Engineering costs			
15 × £3,600	54,000		
10 × £3,600		36,000	
25 × £3,600			90,000
Total overhead	500,750	583,750	615,500
Average overhead per unit			
£500,750/40,000	£12.52		
£583,750/25,000		£23.35	
£615,500/10,000			£61.55
This compares to the traditional overhead absorption of:			
	£21.24	£28.32	£14.16

It can be seen that product C is significantly under-costed under the traditional system, while products A and B are over-costed. This situation arises because the large proportion of costs driven by product C is not picked up under the traditional costing system. Since it is the cost-drivers identified in the ABC system which generate the costs in the first place, the ABC system will produce a more accurate final analysis.

Activity 7

Products X and Y

Calculate the unit cost of products X and Y, where products X and Y are sole output of the business:

	Product X	*Product Y*
Units produced	45,000	5,000
Material cost per unit	£1.50	£4.00
Direct labour per unit	£7.00	£3.50
Direct labour time per unit	1 hr	30 mins
Number of set ups	30	10
Number of purchase orders for materials	70	10
Overhead costs:		£
Set up		20,000
Purchasing		16,000
Labour supervision		23,750

Products X and Y

	X £	*Y* £
Material cost		
Labour cost		
Direct costs		
Overhead cost:		
Set-up		
Purchasing		
Labour supervision		
Total unit cost		

Activity 8

Which method of costing gives a more accurate product cost?

A Activity based costing

B Total absorption costing

C Marginal costing

D Standard costing

Activity 9

The accounting technician and the planning engineer have recently analysed the value adding processes and identified various activities, cost drivers within those activities and current volumes of production and decide to apply the ABC methodology.

Budgeted plans 2003

	Activity	*Cost pool* £	*Cost driver volume*
(1)	Process set up	260,000	200 set ups
(2)	Material procurement	74,000	50 purchase orders
(3)	Maintenance	64,000	12 maintenance plans
(4)	Material handling	120,000	2,500 material movements
(5)	Quality costs	80,000	200 inspections
(6)	Order processing	30,000	1,000 customers
		628,000	

The company plan to produce 1,000 tonnes per month which will require the following approximate activity demand:

17 set ups

4 purchase orders

1 maintenance plan

210 material movements

16 inspections

80 customers

Task

(a) Calculate the cost driver rates.

(b) Determine the amount of overhead to be recovered per tonne of product.

(a) **Cost driver rates:**

Activity	*Cost pool*	*Cost driver volume*	*Cost driver rate*
	£		
Process set up			
Material procurement			
Maintenance			
Material handling			
Quality costs			
Order processing			

(b) Using the ABC method, the following overhead would be recovered for each 1,000 tonnes of output:

				£
	set ups	×		
	purchase orders	×		
	maintenance plan	×		
	material movements	×		
	inspections	×		
	customers	×		
				______
				______

Thus the overhead cost per tonne of product would be:

£ ____________ per tonne.

Activity 10 (June 2002)

Data

Drampton plc has recently taken over Little Ltd, a small company making mainframe and desktop computers. Little appears to make all of its profits from mainframe computers. Drampton's finance director tells you that Little's fixed overheads are currently charged to production using standard labour hours and gives you their standard cost of making mainframe and desktop computers. These are shown below.

Little Ltd: Standard cost per computer

Model	*Mainframe*	*Desktop*
Annual budgeted volume	5	5,000
Unit standard cost	£	£
Material and labour	50,000	500
Fixed overhead	4,000	40
Standard cost per computer	54,000	540

The finance director asks for your help and suggests you reclassify the fixed overheads between the two models using activity-based costing. You are given the following information:

- Budgeted total annual fixed overheads

	£
Set-up costs	10,000
Rent and power – production time	120,000
Rent – stores area	50,000
Salaries of store issue staff	40,000
Total	

- Every time Little makes a mainframe computer, it has to stop making desktop computers and rearrange the factory layout. The cost of this is shown as set-up costs. If the company did not make any mainframe computers, these costs would be eliminated.

- Cost drivers

	Mainframe	*Desktop*	*Total*
Number of set-ups	5	0	5
Number of weeks of production	10	40	50
Floor area of stores (square metres)	400	400	800
Number of issues of stock	2,000	8,000	10,000

Task

Use the cost drivers to:

(a) reallocate Little's budgeted total fixed annual overheads between mainframe and desktop production;

(b) show the revised *unit* fixed overheads for each of the two types of computers.

(a) **Allocation of overheads**

		Mainframe		*Desktop*
		£		£
Set up costs				
Rent and power – prod'n				
Rent – stores				
Salaries – store issue staff				
		———		———
Total				
		———		———

(b) **Fixed overheads per unit**

Number of computers		
Fixed overhead per computer		

3 Absorption costing and marginal costing

3.1 Introduction

We have discussed the idea of the collection of costs initially in cost centres and then attributing them to the cost units passing through those cost centres. But should all costs eventually be attributed to (absorbed by) cost units?

Two points should be noted regarding the absorption of costs into cost units:

- **Production/selling costs** – in a manufacturing context, we have already seen that inventory of finished goods will never include an element of selling costs. The inventory will be valued at production costs only (including overheads). However, for pricing or profitability purposes, the cost of units sold may well include a selling cost element.

- **Fixed/variable costs** – whether or not all production costs will be absorbed into cost units for inventory valuation will depend upon the particular system being used.
  - (i) A total absorption costing (TAC) system absorbs all production costs (direct or indirect, fixed or variable) into cost units.
  - (ii) A marginal costing (MC) system only absorbs variable production costs (direct and indirect) into cost units. Fixed costs are treated as period costs, and deducted as a 'lump sum' from the profits of the period concerned.

3.2 The main difference between absorption and marginal costing

The main difference between absorption and marginal costing is that under absorption costing the fixed production overheads are absorbed into the production cost of the units produced. They are thus treated as part of the cost per unit and are shown as part of the cost of sales.

Because the absorption rate for these costs is determined from the budgeted figures for output and the cost of the fixed overheads, there may be a difference between the amount absorbed into the units produced (which is based on the budgeted amounts) and the amount that should have been absorbed into the units produced if it had been based on the actual amounts. This may result in an over- or under-absorption of the production overheads which has to be corrected by an entry in the profit statement.

Example

A business has the following actual results (there are no opening or closing inventory)

Units produces and sold	5,000 (units)
Sales price per unit	£15
Direct materials (£4 per unit)	£20,000
Direct labour (£3 per unit)	£15,000
Variable production costs (£1 per unit)	£5,000
Fixed production costs incurred	£12,000
Admin and selling costs	£8,000

The budgeted production was 4,800 units.

Budgeted fixed overheads were £14,400.

Task

Prepare operating statements under absorption and marginal costing.

Solution

	Absorption		*Marginal*	
	£	£	£	£
Revenue (5,000 × £15)		75,000		75,000
Less cost of sales				
Materials	20,000		20,000	
Labour	15,000		15,000	
Variable overhead	5,000		5,000	
Fixed overhead absorbed (W2)	15,000			
		55,000		40,000
		20,000		35,000
Over-absorbed overhead (W3)		3,000		–
		23,000		
Fixed production costs		–		12,000
Admin and selling costs		8,000		8,000
		15,000		15,000

Workings

1 Calculate the fixed production overhead absorption rate

= £14,400/4,800 = £3 per unit

2 Calculate the fixed production overhead absorbed into production under absorption costing

= actual units produced × absorption rate = 5,000 × £3 = £15,000

3 Calculate the over absorbed fixed overhead

Actual overhead	12,000
Absorbed overhead	15,000
Overabsorbed	3,000

The overhead was over absorbed by £3,000 and this amount has to be added back to profit in the absorption statement to restore the figure to the actual amount.

3.3 The effect of changes in stock levels

The above example illustrated the difference between the two types of accounting but note that the profit figure at the end of the period was the same under both systems.

However if inventory levels change in the period, the two systems will give a different figure for profit. This occurs because if inventory is carried forward under absorption costing, the inventory value will include some of the overheads incurred in the period. This effectively carries those overheads forward into the next period which reduces the overheads charged to profit in the first period thereby increasing the reported profit.

In the example above, if there had been no opening inventory but 500 units of inventory at the end of the period, the absorption statement would carry forward the production cost of this inventory to the next period including the fixed overhead element. The marginal statement would also carry forward the production cost of the inventory but there would be no fixed cost element.

Example

Consider the previous example with the business manufacturing 5,000 units, selling 4,500 units and carrying forward 500 units of inventory to the next period. All other facts are the same.

Task

Prepare operating statements under absorption and marginal costing.

Solution

	Absorption		*Marginal*	
	£	£	£	£
Revenue (4,500 × £15)		67,500		67,500
Less cost of sales				
Materials	20,000		20,000	
Labour	15,000		15,000	
Variable overhead	5,000		5,000	
Fixed overhead absorbed	15,000			
Less:	55,000		40,000	
closing inventory (W1)	(5,500)		(4,000)	
		49,500		36,000
		18,000		31,500
Over-absorbed overhead		3,000		–
		21,000		
Fixed production costs		–		12,000
Admin and selling costs		8,000		8,000
		13,000		11,500

Working

Value of closing inventory

	Absorption	*Marginal*
	£	£
Cost per unit		
Materials	4	4
Labour	3	3
Variable overhead	1	1
Fixed overhead	3	Nil
Unit cost	11	8
Cost of 500 units	5,500 (500 × £11)	4,000 (500 × £8)

Example

Solution

(a) **Marginal costing**

Cost of production (per unit)

	£
Direct materials	10
Direct labour	5
Variable production overheads	8
Total variable cost	23

	Month 1		*Month 2*		*Month 3*	
	£	£	£	£	£	£
Revenue @ £30		150,000		255,000		285,000
Opening inventory	–		34,500		46,000	
Cost of production @ £23	149,500		207,000		230,000	
	149,500		241,500		276,000	
Closing inventory (W) £23	(34,500)		(46,000)		(57,500)	
Variable cost of sales		(115,000)		(195,500)		(218,500)
Contribution		35,000		59,500		66,500
Fixed costs		(27,000)		(27,000)		(27,000)
Profit		8,000		32,500		39,500

Working

	Month 1 (units)	*Month 2* (units)	*Month 3* (units)
Opening inventory	–	1,500	2,000
Production	6,500	9,000	10,000
Sales	(5,000)	(8,500)	(9,500)
Closing inventory	1,500	2,000	2,500

(b) **Absorption costing**

Fixed costs are allocated to units of production based on the budgeted rate of activity, i.e. 9,000 units per month. Therefore the fixed cost per unit is £3 (£27,000/9,000).

Cost of production (per unit)

	£
Direct materials	10
Direct labour	5
Variable production overheads	8
Fixed production costs	3
Total cost	26

However, actual production levels are not known until the end of the period, by which time each product has been charged with standard fixed costs per unit.

So an adjustment for over or under absorption of overheads has to be made at the end of each period, as follows.

Month 1 (9,000 – 6,500) × £3 = £7,500 under absorbed.

Month 2 Production is equal to budget, so no adjustment necessary.

Month 3 (9,000 – 10,000) × £3 = £3,000 over absorbed.

	Month 1		*Month 2*		*Month 3*	
	£	£	£	£	£	£
Revenue @ £30		150,000		255,000		285,000
Opening inventory	–		39,000		52,000	
Cost of production @ £26	169,000		234,000		260,000	
	169,000		273,000		312,000	
Closing inventory @ £26	(39,000)		(52,000)		(65,000)	
Fully absorbed cost of sales		(130,000)		(221,000)		(247,000)
Gross profit		20,000		34,000		38,000
(Under)/ overabsorption		(7,500)		–		3,000
Profit		12,500		34,000		41,000

Notice that the profit figure under both methods would have been the same if there had been no change in inventory levels in each month.

Example

Let us assume that Tivoli has the same budgeted monthly output for the new product but it sells everything it produces every month.

Direct materials	£10 per unit
Direct labour	£5 per unit
Variable production overheads	£8 per unit
Fixed production costs	£27,000 per month
Budgeted output	9,000 units per month
Sales price	£30 per unit

	Month 1	*Month 2*	*Month 3*
Production and sales	5,000	8,000	10,000

Produce an income statement for each of the three months under (a) marginal costing and (b) absorption costing.

Solution

(a) **Marginal costing**

Unit cost of production (10 + 5 + 8) £23

	Month 1	*Month 2*	*Month 3*
	£	£	£
Revenue @ £30	150,000	240,000	300,000
Variable cost of sales @ £23	(115,000)	(184,000)	(230,000)
Contribution	35,000	56,000	70,000
Fixed costs	(27,000)	(27,000)	(27,000)
Marginal costing profit	8,000	29,000	43,000

(b) **Absorption costing**

Fixed cost to be absorbed per unit is at £27,000/9,000 = £3. Unit cost of production is still £26 therefore.

Adjustment for over/under absorption

Month 1	(9,000 – 5,000) × £3 =	£12,000 under absorbed
Month 2	(9,000 – 8,000) × £3 =	£3,000 under absorbed
Month 3	(9,000 – 10,000) × £3 =	£3,000 over absorbed

	Month 1	*Month 2*	*Month 3*
	£	£	£
Revenue @ £30	150,000	240,000	300,000
Variable cost of sales @ £26	(130,000)	(208,000)	(260,000)
Gross profit	20,000	32,000	40,000
(Under)/over absorption	(12,000)	(3,000)	3,000
Absorption costing profit	8,000	29,000	43,000

In this example, inventory levels remained constant at zero, therefore marginal costing profit and absorption costing profit were the same. The only reason for differences in profit under the two methods is any increase or decrease in inventory levels and the fixed overhead absorbed in those units of inventory.

Activity 11

Which gives the higher closing inventory valuation:

Marginal costing ☐

Absorption costing ☐

4 Contribution

Definition

Remember, contribution is defined as the **difference between selling price and the variable cost of producing and selling that item**. This is in contrast to profit per unit, which is the difference between selling price and the total absorption cost of producing and selling that item, which includes an element of fixed cost.

We need to decide between courses of action and **which course of action will be most beneficial**, looking at the revenues and costs under each alternative.

Fixed costs, by definition, are unavoidable and do not change with the level of production. Therefore, in any decision which is connected with varying the level of production, **fixed costs are not a relevant cost** as they do not change regardless of which course of action is taken.

Example

Katie Limited is currently producing decorated mirrors. Each mirror sells at £10 each and has a variable cost of production of £8 per unit. Current production is 900 units per period. Fixed costs are expected to be £900 for the coming period, and therefore are charged at £1 per unit to production.

Katie has been approached to supply a new customer with 100 mirrors but at a discounted price of £8.25 per mirror.

Should she accept the order?

Solution

If we look at profit per unit, then the decision would be to reject the order, as we would not sell for £8.25 per unit something which has cost us (£8 + £1) = £9 to produce.

However, if we look at total profits generated by the business before and after the acceptance of project, we find the following.

		Reject	*Accept*
		£	£
Revenue	(900 @ £10)	9,000	9,000
	(100 @ £8.25)		825
			9,825
Variable costs	(900/1,000 @ £8)	(7,200)	(8,000)
Fixed costs		(900)	(900)
Profit		900	925

Therefore we can see that profits are improved by accepting the contract. Whilst revenue is increasing by £825, costs only increase by £800 as **fixed costs do not change**.

We could have derived the same answer by looking at contribution generated by the contract. Remember contribution is calculated as selling price – variable cost. On a per unit basis for the contract, this is £8.25 – £8 = £0.25 contribution on each extra unit sold. As we sell 100 units more, this generates a total increase in contribution, and thus profit, of £25 (100 × £0.25).We should accept the project; the use of **contribution analysis** enables us to determine this quickly.

Activity 12

Roger Morton

Roger makes a single product, the Morton. During 20X9 he plans to make and sell 10,000 Mortons and accordingly has estimated the cost of each to be £50 (see below). Each Morton sells for £75.

	£
Materials	12
Labour	24
Variable overheads	10
Fixed overheads	4
Total cost	50

Required

(a) Calculate the total fixed overhead.

(b) Calculate the contribution earned by each Morton.

(c) Calculate the total profit if Roger sells 2,000 Mortons.

(a) Total fixed overhead

Fixed overhead per unit based on planned output.

= £__________

(b) Contribution per unit

Selling price per unit – Variable cost per unit

= £__________

(c) Profit

Contribution – Fixed costs

= £__________

5 Cost-volume-profit (CVP) analysis

5.1 Introduction

How many units do we need to sell to make a profit? By how much will profit fall if price is lowered by £1? What will happen to our profits if we rent an extra factory but find that we can operate at only half capacity?

All of the above are **realistic business questions**. One solution would be to set up a model of the business on a PC and feed in the various pieces of information. Packages such as Lotus 1-2-3 and Microsoft Excel mean that this is an easy option.

But we have to appreciate that the PC is simply performing **cost-volume-profit (CVP) analysis** by another route. We can do this without a PC.

5.2 Approach to CVP

- Costs are assumed to be either **fixed** or **variable**, or at least **separable into these elements**.
- Economies or diseconomies of scale are ignored; this ensures that **the variable cost per unit is constant**.
- We look at the effect a change in volume has on **contribution** (not profit).
- Contribution per unit = selling price per unit – total variable cost per unit.

6 Breakeven analysis

Definition

Breakeven point

The breakeven point is the volume of sales at which neither a profit nor a loss is made.

Calculations are made easier, however, if we think in terms of contribution rather than profit. Breakeven is then the volume of sales at which total contribution (contribution per unit multiplied by number of units sold) is equal to fixed costs.

Note that fixed costs here are total fixed costs, i.e. fixed production and fixed selling costs.

The breakeven point can then be found using the following formula.

$$\text{Breakeven point} = \frac{\text{Fixed cost}}{\text{Contribution/unit}}$$

Example

Breakeven point

Rachel's product, the 'Steadyarm', sells for £50. It has a variable cost of £30 per unit. Rachel's total fixed costs are £40,000 per annum.

What is her breakeven point?

Solution

To break even we want just enough contribution to cover the total fixed costs of £40,000.

We therefore want total contribution of £40,000.

Each unit of sales gives contribution of 50 – 30 = £20.

Therefore the breakeven point in units

$$= \frac{\text{Total fixed costs}}{\text{Contribution per unit}} = \frac{£40,000}{£20} = 2,000 \text{ units}$$

We can show that this calculation is correct as below.

	£
Total contribution (2,000 units × £20)	40,000
Total fixed costs	(40,000)
Profit/loss	NIL

6.1 Margin of safety

The margin of safety is the amount by which the anticipated (budgeted) sales can fall before the business makes a loss. It can be expressed in absolute units or relative percentage terms.

In units: Margin of safety = Budgeted sales units – Breakeven sales units

In %: Margin of safety =

$$\frac{\text{Budgeted sales units - Breakeven sales units}}{\text{Budgeted sales unit}} \times 100\%$$

For the 'Steadyarm' product above, if Rachel is expecting to achieve sales of 3,600 units:

Margin of safety (units) = 3,600 – 2,000 = 1,600 units

As a %: $\frac{1,600}{3,600} \times 100 = 44.4\%$

Actual sales can fall by 44.4% of budgeted level before the Steadyarm will start to make a loss.

Margin of safety can also be expressed in sales revenue terms.

Activity 13

Camilla Ng

Camilla makes a single product, the Wocket. During 20X5 she plans to make and sell 3,000 Wockets and has estimated the following:

	Cost per unit
	£
Material	3
Labour	5
Variable overhead	2
	—
Total variable cost per unit	10
	—

Total fixed costs are budgeted to be £12,000

Estimated selling price £15

Required

(a) Calculate the contribution per unit earned by each Wocket.

(b) Calculate Camilla's budgeted profit.

(c) Calculate Camilla's breakeven point and margin of safety.

Solution

(a) **Contribution per unit**

= Selling price per unit – Variable cost per unit

= £__________

(b) **Budgeted Profit**

= Total contribution – Fixed costs

= £__________

(c) **Breakeven point**

= Total fixed costs / Contribution per unit

= ______________units

Margin of safety

= (budgeted sales – breakeven point)/budgeted sales × 100%

= ______________%

6.2 Achieving a target profit

A similar approach can be used to find the sales volume at which a particular profit is made.

Sales volume to achieve a particular profit

$$= \frac{\text{Total fixed costs} + \text{required profit}}{\text{Contribution/unit}}$$

Example

Achieving a target profit

Information as with Rachel above but we now want to know how many units must be sold to make a profit of £100,000.

To achieve a profit of £100,000, we require sufficient contribution firstly to cover the fixed costs (£40,000) and secondly, having covered fixed costs, we require sufficient contribution to give a profit of £100,000. Therefore our required contribution is £140,000.

Sales volume to achieve a profit of £100,000

$$= \frac{\text{Total fixed costs} + \text{required profit}}{\text{Contribution/unit}}$$

$$= \frac{£40{,}000 + £100{,}000}{£20}$$

= 7,000 units

We can show that this is the case with a summarised income statement.

	£
Revenue (7,000 × £50)	350,000
Variable cost (7,000 × £30)	(210,000)
Total fixed costs	(40,000)
Profit	100,000

6.3 C/S ratio

The contribution to sales (C/S) ratio can also be used to calculate a breakeven point but in terms of sales (£).

The £ amount of sales to breakeven is calculated using:

$$\frac{\text{Total fixed costs}}{\text{C/S ratio}}$$

The C/S ratio is calculated by dividing contribution by sales value (either per unit in each part of the formula, or in total in both parts of the formula).

For example, if contribution per unit is £20 and the sales price per unit is £50 then the C/S ratio is 0.4 or 40%.

Activity 14

A company budgets to sell 500 units but has calculated that it will breakeven at 400 units. The margin of safety is:

20%

25%

Activity 15

A company budgets to sell 16,000 units of a product at a selling price of £25. Variable costs are £15 per unit and fixed costs are £75,000 in total.

The contribution per unit is £ ☐

The breakeven point in units is ☐

The margin of safety in units is ☐

The margin of safety as a percentage (to 2 decimal places) is ☐

The contribution to sales (C/S) ratio (to 2 decimal places) is ☐

The break even sales are £ ☐

Activity 16

A company budgets to sell 1,000 units of a product at a selling price of £2. Variable costs are £0.50 per unit and fixed costs are £900 in total.

The contribution per unit is £ [ ]

The breakeven point in units is [ ]

The margin of safety in units is [ ]

The margin of safety as a percentage (to 2 decimal places) is [ ]

The contribution to sales (C/S) ratio (to 2 decimal places) is [ ]

The break even sales are £ [ ]

7 Limiting factor analysis

7.1 Marginal costing and decision-making

In the section on overheads we compared total absorption costing (TAC) with marginal costing (MC), where only directly attributable variable overheads are absorbed into cost units. The key reason for using MC is to assist in decision making. If a decision has to be made it is sensible only to take into account those costs which will actually be affected by the decision. Since most overheads are fixed the decision to make one extra unit of production will not affect that cost, so it should be ignored. Only the marginal cost of making one extra unit should be considered in decision making and therefore should be added to the cost unit.

This approach to costing has two key uses:

- It affects inventory valuation (inventory valued under an MC approach is of lower value than that under TAC since fixed overheads have not been absorbed).
- It enables us to make decisions when there is a scarcity of resources, which is when the shortage of one resource means that that resource limits the entire capacity of the operation: this is the limiting factor.

7.2 Single limiting factor

A company may have two products, each requiring materials and labour. There may be a limit as to the amount of labour or materials that is available for the coming month. How can the company make the most possible profit subject to such a constraint?

Since fixed costs are independent of production they are irrelevant (they will have to be paid however many units of each product are manufactured). The above problem therefore requires us to maximise contribution taking into account the limiting factor.

Example

Barbecue Limited manufactures two products for which the following details are available.

	Product X		*Product Y*
Selling price	£38		£38
Direct materials 8 units @ £1	£8	4 units @ £1	£4
Labour 4 hours @ £2	£8	6 hours @ £2	£12
Variable overhead 4 machine hours @ £3	£12	3 machine hours @ £3	£9
Fixed overheads	£5		£7

Maximum demand for X is 2,500 units.

Maximum demand for Y is 2,000 units.

Required

Calculate the optimum production plan for Barbecue in each of the following two situations:

(a) Labour in the next period is limited to *16,000* hours, with no limit on machine hours.

(b) Machine hours in the next period are limited to *12,000* hours, with no limit on labour hours.

Solution

We would like to produce Xs and Ys up to the point where maximum demand is reached. (There is no point producing beyond this, because customers do not want any more.) So ideally we would like to produce 2,500 X and 2,000 Y. To do this we would require the following resources.

	Labour hours	*Machine hours*
2,500 X	10,000	10,000
2,000 Y	12,000	6,000
	22,000	16,000

If labour is limited to 16,000 hours we will not have enough labour hours to achieve this. Similarly, if machine hours are limited to 12,000 our production will be restricted.

To tackle this problem we begin by calculating the contribution earned per unit of each product.

Contribution for each unit of X = £ (38 – 8 – 8 – 12) = £10 per unit
Contribution for each unit of Y = £ (38 – 4 – 12 – 9) = £13 per unit

(a) Labour is limited so we calculate the contribution earned per labour hour for each product.

X = £10/4 = £2.50 per labour hour

Y = £13/6 = £2.17 per labour hour

You get more contribution per labour hour for × than for Y so make as many Xs as possible.

Available hours = 16,000 2,500 Xs require 10,000 hrs

The remaining hours are all used to make as many Ys as possible.

Remaining Ys will take six hours each to make so produce 6,000/6 = 1,000 Ys.

Contribution = (2,500 × £10) + (1,000 × £13) = £38,000

(b) In this case, machine hours are the scarce resource so we calculate contribution per machine hour.

X = £10/4 = £2.50 per machine hour

Y = £13/3 = £4.33 per machine hour

Now it is better to make Ys. Making 2,000 Ys requires 2,000 × 3 = 6,000 machine hours. That leaves us a further 6,000 machine hours for making Xs.

6,000 remaining hours for X means making 6,000/4 = 1,500 Xs

Contribution = (1,500 × £10) + (2,000 × £13) = £41,000

Note that in the examination, if you are told the maximum demand for a product it is a big hint that this method should be used.

Activity 17

Roger

Roger makes three products – X Y and Z. He would like to make 500 of each product in the next year.

	X	Y	Z
Selling price	90	80	75
Materials (£3 per kg)	15	18	12
Labour	15	12	24
Variable overheads	8	6	10
Fixed overheads	4	4	4

Required

(a) Calculate the contribution earned by each product.

(b) If material supplies are limited to 7,000 kg calculate the production plan which will optimise Roger's profit for the year.

(a) Contribution per unit

Selling price per unit – Variable cost per unit

	X	Y	Z
	£	£	£
Selling price	90	80	75
Materials			
Labour			
Variable overhead	38		
Contribution	52	44	29
	1	2	3

(b)

Contribution	52	44	29
Per limiting factor	15/3 = 5kg	18/3 = 6	12/3 = 4
Contribution per kg	10.40	7.33	7.25
Rank	1	2	3

Make X first using

Make Y next using   2500 X 500

4500 kg left   3000 Y 500

Available   7,000 kg

375

Optimal production plan is Y

7.3 Absorption costing versus marginal costing in decision-making

We need to understand how absorption costing and marginal costing can be used in tasks which measure performance and which consider ways of enhancing value.

Absorption costing may be relevant for measuring the performance of a business and it may also be appropriate to use in enhancing value. For example, a product may be re-engineered in order to reduce production costs and it would be perfectly appropriate to consider the full absorption cost of the redesigned product.

Lifecycle costing (see later chapters) needs to consider both fixed and variable costs. However, it may be inappropriate to use absorption costing in certain circumstances. For example, if the business is considering contracting out the manufacture of a product, selling surplus capacity or some other limiting factor decision, then the marginal cost is the appropriate method as fixed costs will not change as a result of the decision.

However, it must be understood that certain fixed costs may change and the incremental cost in these circumstances may include both variable and fixed elements.

8 Summary

This chapter has revised several fundamental cost accounting topics from your earlier studies, in particular the treatment of overheads including:

- allocation/apportionment/absorption;
- service departments;
- over-/under-absorption;
- activity based costing approach;
- breakeven analysis;
- limiting factor analysis.

Answers to chapter activities

Activity 1

C Factory rental could be apportioned on the basis of the floor area occupied by the various cost centres.

Activity 2

A Traditionally, overheads have been absorbed as a rate per labour hour.

Activity 3

Lorus Limited

(a) *Memorandum re overheads*

MEMORANDUM

To: Managing Director

Copy: Production heads – sawing, assembly, finishing, materials handling (MH), maintenance

From: Management Accountant

Date: X-X-XX

Subject: Statement to show allotment of overhead

	Sawing	*Assembly*	*Finishing*	*MH*	*Maintenance*
	£	£	£	£	£
Overhead	75,000	50,000	20,000	9,000	20,000
Apportion maintenance department overhead	6,000	8,000	4,000	2,000	(20,000)
Apportion MH Overhead	5,500	2,200	3,300	(11,000)	–
Total allotted	86,500	60,200	27,300	–	–

Note: Service department overhead has been apportioned to production departments on the basis of percentage estimates of relative benefit, as specified.

(b) 4,000 cupboards were produced with the following costs incurred:

	Sawing	*Assembly*	*Finishing*	*Total*	*Unit cost*
	£	£	£	£	£
Materials	120,000	80,000	20,000	220,000	55.00
Wages	50,000	25,000	40,000	115,000	28.75
Overheads	86,500	60,200	27,300	174,000	43.50
	256,500	165,200	87,300	509,000	127.25

The unit cost of a cupboard is £127.25.

Activity 4

Overhead recovery rates for each cost centre:

Machining $\frac{£36,000}{4,000 \text{ machine hours}}$ = £9.00 per machine hour

Fabrication $\frac{£41,600}{5,200 \text{ machine hours}}$ = £8.00 per machine hour

Outside contract work $\frac{£28,600}{1,950 \text{ labour hours}}$ = £14.67 per direct labour hr

Production cost of contract:

		£
Direct material		3,100
Direct labour:		
Machining	12 hours	
Fabrication	8 hours	
Outside work	6 hours	
	26 hours × £7.50	195
Overheads:		
Machining	12 hours × £9.00	108
Fabrication	8 hours × £8.00	64
Outside work	6 hours × £14.67	88
Production cost		3,555
Add 10% for admin, selling and distribution		356
		£3,911
Selling price/contract price (£3,911/75) × 100 =		£5,215

Check:

	£
Contract price/selling price	5,215
Cost	3,911
Profit	£1,304

Profit = 25% of selling price as required.

Activity 5

Overhead recovery rate:

Overheads		£
Building occupancy		9,100
Telephone, postage and stationery		4,700
Other overheads		11,200
Administrator's salary		14,500
		£39,500
Labour hours		9,400
Overhead rate per labour hour	£39,500/9,400 =	£4.20
Partners' labour charge-out rate	£30,000/1,880 =	£15.96 per hour
Qualified senior	£18,500/1,880 =	£9.84 per hour
Trainee (1)	£10,500/1,880 =	£5.59 per hour
Trainee (2)	£12,000/1,880 =	£6.38 per hour

White Rose Hotel estimated fees:

		£
Direct labour:		
Partners	5 hours × £15.96 =	79.80
Qualified senior	12 hours × £9.84 =	118.08
Trainee (1)	3 hours × £5.59 =	16.77
Trainee (2)	3 hours × £6.38 =	19.14
		233.79
Overheads:		
23 hours × £4.20		96.60
Total cost		330.39
Thus charge to client	(£330.39/70) × 100 =	£471.99

Activity 6

Task

(a) **Sandsend Engineers Ltd overhead recovered:**

		£
Machining	4,250 machine hours × £9.00	38,250
Fabrication	5,300 machine hours × £8.00	42,400
Outside work	1,975 labour hours × £14.67	28,973
		£109,623

(b)

Overhead control account

	£		£
Actual:		*Recovered in work-in-progress*	
Machining	37,800	Machining	32,250
Fabrication	42,000	Fabrication	42,400
Outside work	29,100	Outside work	28,973
Over-recovered – I.S (bal)	723		
	109,623		109,623

Activity 7

Products X and Y

	X	*Y*
	£	£
Material cost	1.50	4.00
Labour cost	7.00	3.50
	8.50	7.50
Overhead cost:		
Set-up		
$\frac{20,000}{40}$ = £500 per set-up		
$\frac{500 \times 30}{45,000}$	0.33	
$\frac{500 \times 10}{5,000}$		1.00
Purchasing		
$\frac{16,000}{80}$ = £200 per order		
$\frac{70 \times 200}{45,000}$	0.31	
$\frac{10 \times 200}{5,000}$		0.40
Labour supervision		
$\frac{23,750}{47,500}$ = £0.50 per labour hour	0.50	0.25
Total unit cost	£9.64	£9.15

Activity 8

A ABC gives the most accurate product costing.

Activity 9

(a) **Cost driver rates:**

Activity	*Cost pool* £	*Cost driver volume*	*Cost driver rate*
Process set up	260,000	200 set ups	£1,300 / set up
Material procurement	74,000	50 purchase orders	£1,480 per purchase order
Maintenance	64,000	12 maintenance plans	£5,333 per plan
Material handling	120,000	2,500 material movements	£48 per movement
Quality costs	80,000	200 inspections	£400 per inspection
Order processing	30,000	1,000 customers	£30 per customer

(b) Using the ABC method, the following overhead would be recovered for each 1,000 tonnes of output:

			£
17 set ups	×	£1,300	22,100
4 purchase orders	×	£1,480	5,920
1 maintenance plan	×	£5,333	5,333
210 material movements	×	£48	10,080
16 inspections	×	£400	6,400
80 customers	×	£30	2,400
			£52,233

Thus the overhead cost per tonne of product would be:

£52,233/1,000 = £52.23 per tonne

Activity 10 (June 2002)

(a) **Allocation of overheads**

		Mainframe £		Desktop £
Set up costs	10,000	Nil		
Rent and power – production	120,000 × 10/50	24,000	120,000 × 40/50	96,000
Rent – stores	50,000 × 400/800	25,000	50,000 × 400/800	25,000
Salaries – store issue staff	40,000 × 2,000/10,000	8,000	40,000 × 8,000/10,000	32,000
Total		67,000		153,000

(b) **Fixed overheads per unit**

Number of computers	5		5,000
Fixed overhead per computer	£67,000/5 £13,400	£153,000/5,000	£30.60

Activity 11

Absorption costing gives a higher inventory valuation than marginal costing since it includes fixed production costs which marginal costing does not.

Activity 12

Roger Morton

(a) **Total fixed overhead**

Fixed overhead per unit based on planned output

£4 per unit × 10,000 = £40,000

(b) **Contribution per unit**

Selling price per unit – Variable cost per unit

£75 – £46 = £29

(c) **Profit**

Contribution – Fixed costs

£29 × 2,000 – £40,000 = £18,000

Activity 13

(a) **Contribution per unit**

= Selling price per unit – Variable cost per unit

= £15 – £10 = £5

(b) **Budgeted Profit**

= Total contribution – Fixed costs

= £5 × 3,000 – £12,000 = £3,000

(c) **Breakeven point**

= Total fixed costs / Contribution per unit

= £12,000/£5 = 2,400 units

Margin of safety

= (budgeted sales – breakeven point)/budgeted sales × 100%

= (3,000 – 2,400)/3,000 × 100% = 20%

Activity 14

Budgeted sales – breakeven sales / Budgeted sales

= (500 – 400) / 500

= 20%

Activity 15

The contribution per unit is selling price – variable costs = £25 - £15 = £10

The breakeven point in units is fixed costs / contribution per unit = £75,000 / £10 = 7,500

The margin of safety in units is budgeted sales – breakeven sales = 16,000 – 7,500 = 8,500

The margin of safety as a percentage (to 2 decimal places) is 8,500 / 16,000 x 100% = 53.13%

The contribution to sales (C/S) ratio is £10 / £25 = 0.4

The breakeven sales volume is fixed costs / c/s ratio = £75,000 / 0.4 = £187,500

(Check this by taking breakeven units x selling price: 7,500 units x £25 = £187,500)

Activity 16

The contribution per unit is selling price – variable costs = £2 - £0.50 = £1.50

The breakeven point in units is fixed costs / contribution per unit = £900 / £1.50 = 600

The margin of safety in units is budgeted sales – breakeven sales = 1,000 – 900 = 100

The margin of safety as a percentage (to 2 decimal places) is 100 / 1,000 x 100% = 10.00%

The contribution to sales (C/S) ratio is £1.50 / £2.00 = 0.75

The breakeven sales volume is fixed costs / c/s ratio = £900 / 0.75 = £1,200

(Check this by taking breakeven units x selling price: 600 units x £2.00 = £1,200)

Activity 17

(a) **Contribution per unit**

Selling price per unit – Variable cost per unit

	X	*Y*	*Z*
	£	£	£
Selling price	90	80	75
Materials	(15)	(18)	(12)
Labour	(15)	(12)	(24)
Variable overhead	(8)	(6)	(4)
Contribution	52	44	29

(b)

Contribution	£52	£44	£29
Per limiting factor	£15 / £3 = 5kg	£18 / £3 = 6kg	£12 / £3 = 4kg
Contribution per kg	£10.40	£7.33	£7.25
Rank	1	2	3

Make 500 X first using 500 x 5 kg =	2,500 kg
Make 500 Y next using 500 x 6 kg =	3,000 kg
	5,500 kg
1,500 kg left	1,500 kg
Available	7,000 kg

Each Z requires 4kg; therefore (1,500kg / 4kg) 375 Z can be produced.

Optimal production plan is 500 X, 500 Y and 375 Z.

9 Test your knowledge

Workbook Activity 18

Luda Limited manufactures three products: P, Q and R. Each product is started in the machining area and completed in the finishing shop. The direct unit costs associated with each product forecast for the next trading period are as follows.

	P	*Q*	*R*
	£	£	£
Materials	18.50	15.00	22.50
Wages			
Machining area @ £5 per hour	10.00	5.00	10.00
Finishing shop @ £4 per hour	6.00	4.00	8.00
	34.50	24.00	40.50

There are machines in both departments and the machine hours required to complete one of each product are:

	P	*Q*	*R*
Machining area	4.0	1.5	3.0
Finishing shop	0.5	0.5	1.0
Budgeted output in units	6,000	8,000	2,000
Fixed overheads			
Machining area		£100,800	
Finishing shop		£94,500	

Required

(a) Calculate the overhead absorption rate for fixed overheads using:

(i) a labour hour rate for each department.

(ii) a machine hour rate for each department.

(b) Calculate the total cost of each product using:

(i) the labour hour rate.

(ii) the machine hour rate

as calculated in (a) above.

Luda Limited

(a) *Fixed overhead absorption rates*

			Machine area	Finishing shop
			£	£
	Fixed overhead			
			Hours	*Hours*
(i)	Labour hours	P		
		Q		
		R		
	Overhead absorption rate per labour hour			
(ii)	Machine hours	P		
		Q		
		R		
	Overhead absorption rate per machine hr			

(b) *Product costs*

	P	Q	R
	£	£	£
Materials			
Wages			
Prime cost			

(i) *Labour hour rate absorption*

	P	*Q*	*R*
	£	£	£
Prime costs as above			
Fixed overheads:			
Machine area			
Finishing shop			

(ii) *Machine hour rate absorption*

	P	Q	R
	£	£	£
Prime costs as above			
Fixed overheads:			
Machine area			
Finishing shop			

Workbook Activity 19

Blidworth Loam Ltd manufacture a single product 'Cricketloam' and supply this product to cricket clubs for grounds at professional level through to village greens.

Its cost specification includes the following budgeted details per tonne of product, together with budgeted data for the current year:

Direct labour hours	4.5
Labour rate per hour	£8.50
Direct material	1.1 tonnes per tonne of good output
Material cost	£25 per tonne
Variable production overheads (total)	£378,000
Fixed production overheads (total)	£250,000
Selling price per tonne	£132
Production volume	12,000 tonnes
Sales volume	11,500 tonnes

Task

Considering the above information, what is the budgeted marginal cost per tonne of product?

A £65.75

B £59.00

C £97.25

D £118.08

	£
Direct labour	
Direct material	
Variable overhead	
	–––––
Marginal cost = Total variable costs per tonne	
	–––––

Workbook Activity 20

Task

Using the information in Question 19, what is the contribution per tonne of product?

A £66.25

B £73.00

C £13.92

D £34.75

Workbook Activity 21

Task

Using the information in Question 19:

(a) Prepare a budgeted operating statement for the company in both marginal costing and full absorption costing format.

(b) Reconcile the difference in reported profit shown in your two statements produced in part (a).

(a) **Blidworth Loam Ltd**

Budgeted operating statement for the year

	Marginal costing format	*Absorption costing format*
Production (tonnes)	12000	12000
Sales (tonnes)	11500	11500
	£	£
Revenue	1518,000	1,518,000
Variable costs		
Direct labour	459000	459 000
Direct material	330000	330 000
Variable overhead	378000	378 000
Closing inventory for marginal costing	(48625)	
	1118375	
Contribution	399625	
Fixed costs	250 000	250 000
Closing inventory for absorption costing		(59042)
Operating profit	149625	160 042

(b) The difference in profit can be proved as:

Cost management

4

Introduction

In this chapter the focus is on long-term investment decisions – usually lasting more than one year. This could vary from the decision to build a new factory to whether or not to discontinue a product range.

There are many different investment appraisal techniques that could be used but the discounted cashflow method is presented here. This was covered in Costs and Revenues and therefore should be revision.

Lifecycle costing and the product lifecycle are also covered.

KNOWLEDGE

Explain the principles of discounted cash flow (3.2)

Describe and recognise when to use lifecycle costing and target costing (3.6)

SKILLS

Prepare estimates of capital investment projects using discounted cash flow techniques (2.9)

CONTENTS

1 Predicting future cash flows
2 The time value of money and discounting
3 Long-term investments in more detail
4 Lifecycle costing
5 Product lifecycle

1 Predicting future cash flows

The first stage in evaluating a proposed investment is to estimate the future cash flow implications. This will involve estimating future sales, costs, capital expenditure, disposal proceeds and so on.

As well as knowing what the future cash flows will be, we also need to know when they will occur. To simplify matters, we start the clock (time t = 0) when the initial investment happens.

To simplify things further, subsequent future cash flows are assumed to happen at year-ends, e.g. all of the sales and costs for the first year are assumed to be paid at the end of the first year – call this t = 1.

If we do this for all the future cash flows of the project, then we will typically end up with a table like the following:

	t = 0 £000	*Year 1* *(t = 1)* £000	*Year 2* *(t = 2)* £000	*Year 3* *(t = 3)* £000	*Year 4* *(t = 4)* £000	*Year 5* *(t = 5)* £000
Invest	(100)					
Sales		40	50	60	50	40
Variable costs		(10)	(12)	(15)	(13)	(11)
Net cash flow	(100)	30	38	45	37	29

Note that when estimating future cash flows we want to identify what difference the project will make – only future incremental cash flows are relevant, e.g. the factory rent may be unaffected by the proposed project and would not be included when assessing the investment.

2 The time value of money and discounting

2.1 The time value of money

A key concept in long-term decision-making is that of money having a time value.

Suppose you were offered £100 now or £100 in one year's time. Even though the sums are the same, most people would prefer the money now. The £100 in the future is effectively worth less to us than £100 now – the timing of the cash makes a difference.

The main reasons for this are as follows:

- **Investment opportunities**: the £100 received now could be deposited into a bank account and earn interest. It would therefore grow to become more than £100 in one year.
- **Inflation**: the £100 now will buy more goods than £100 in one year due to inflation.
- **Cost of capital**: the £100 received now could be used to reduce a loan or overdraft and save interest.
- **Risk**: the £100 now is more certain than the offer of money in the future.

What if the offer were changed to £100 now or £105 in one year? Many would still prefer the £100 now, even though it is the smaller amount!

To do calculations using the time value of money it needs to be expressed as an interest rate (often known as a cost of capital, a required return or a discount rate)

Suppose we felt that £100 now was worth the same to us as £110 offered in one year's time. We could say that our time value of money was estimated at 10% per annum.

While this would incorporate all four of the factors mentioned above (investment opportunities, inflation, costs of capital and risk), it is easiest to imagine that we have a bank account paying 10% interest per annum.

The £100 now could be invested for a year and would grow to £110.

Therefore £100 now is worth the same as £110 offered in one year. Alternatively we say that the £110 in one year has a present value of £100 now. This process of taking future cash flows and converting them into their equivalent present value now is called discounting.

To calculate the present value of any future cash flow we multiply the cash flow by a suitable discount factor (or present value factor):

Present value = future cash flow $\times$ discount factor

Discount factors are provided in assessments and simulations – you do not need to be able to calculate them.

For example, with a 10% discount rate, the discount factor for a cash flow at t = 1 is 0.909. Thus the offer of receiving £100 in one year's time is worth in today's terms

Present value = 100 $\times$ 0.909 = £90.90

2.2 Net Present Value (NPV)

The main implication of the time value of money is that we cannot simply add up and net off cash flows at different times – they are not comparable.

To get round this we do the following:

Step 1 Identify future, incremental cash flows.

Step 2 Discount the cash flows so they are in today's terms (present values).

Step 3 Now the present values can be added up and netted off to give a net present value or NPV.

Step 4 If the NPV is positive, then it means that the cash inflows are worth more than the outflows and the project should be accepted.

Using the previous example with a discount rate of 10%, this could be set out as follows:

	t = 0 £000	*Year 1 (t = 1)* £000	*Year 2 (t = 2)* £000	*Year 3 (t = 3)* £000	*Year 4 (t = 4)* £000	*Year 5 (t = 5)* £000
Net cash flow	(100)	30	38	45	37	29
Discount factor	1	0.909	0.826	0.751	0.683	0.621
Present value	(100)	27.3	31.4	33.8	25.3	18.0

Net Present Value = (100) + 27.3 + 31.4 + 33.8 + 25.3 + 18.0 = 35.8

This is positive, so the project should be undertaken.

An alternative layout could be as follows:

Time	*Cash flow* £000	*Discount factor @ 10%*	*Present value* £000
t = 0	(100)	1	(100)
t = 1	30	0.909	27.3
t = 2	38	0.826	31.4
t = 3	45	0.751	33.8
t = 4	37	0.638	25.3
t = 5	29	0.621	18.0
	Net Present Value		35.8

Activity 1

A machine costs £80,000 now. We expect cash receipts of £20,000 in one year's time, £50,000 in two years' time, £40,000 in three years' time and £10,000 in four years' time. The rate of interest applicable is 15%. Should we accept or reject the machine?

The relevant present value factors are:

	Year 1	*Year 2*	*Year 3*	*Year 4*
15%	0.870	0.756	0.658	0.572

Year		*Cashflow*	*DF@15%*	*PV*
		£		£
0	Cost			
1	Inflow			
2	Inflow			
3	Inflow			
4	Inflow			
			NPV =	________

Since the net present value is __________ we should __________ the machine.

Activity 2

Machine A costs £100,000, payable immediately. Machine B costs £120,000, half payable immediately and half payable in one year's time. The cash receipts expected are as follows.

	A	*B*
	£	£
at the end of 1 year	20,000	–
at the end of 2 years	60,000	60,000
at the end of 3 years	40,000	60,000
at the end of 4 years	30,000	80,000
at the end of 5 years	20,000	–

With interest at 5%, which machine should be selected?

The relevant present value factors are:

	Year 1	*Year 2*	*Year 3*	*Year 4*	*Year 5*
5%	0.952	0.907	0.864	0.823	0.784

Machine A				**Machine B**		
Year	*Cashflow*	*DF@5%*	*PV*	*Cashflow*	*DF@5%*	*PV*
	£		£	£		£
0						
1						
2						
3						
4						
5						
			________			________
NPV =			________	NPV =		________

Since machine ________ has the higher NPV, our decision should be to select machine ________.

Activity 3

Highscore Ltd manufacture cricket bats. They are considering investing £30,000 in a new delivery vehicle which will generate savings compared with sub-contracting out the delivery service. The vehicle will have a life of six years, with zero scrap value.

The accounting technician and the transport manager have prepared the following estimates relating to the savings.

The cash flows from the project are:

		£
Year	1	9,000
	2	11,000
	3	10,000
	4	10,500
	5	10,200
	6	10,100

The business cost of capital is 15%.

Required

Prepare an appraisal of the project using the discounted cash flow (NPV method) technique.

The relevant present value factors are:

	Year 1	*Year 2*	*Year 3*	*Year 4*	*Year 5*	*Year 6*
15%	0.870	0.756	0.658	0.572	0.497	0.432

Highscore Ltd

Discounted cash flow – Net Present Value method – appraisal

Year	*Cash flow*	*15% discount factor*	*NPV*
0			
1			
2			
3			
4			
5			
6			
		NPV	

Activity 4

Whitby Engineering Factors are considering an investment in a new machine tool with an estimated useful life of five years.

The investment will require capital expenditure of £50,000 and the accounting technician has prepared the following estimates of cash flow over the five-year period:

		£
Year	1	18,000
	2	20,000
	3	21,000
	4	22,000
	5	18,000

The firm's cost of capital is considered to be 12% and it uses this rate to appraise any future projects.

Required

- Prepare an appraisal of the project using the discounted cash flow (NPV method) technique.
- State with reasons whether you would accept or reject the project.

The relevant present value factors are:

	Year 1	*Year 2*	*Year 3*	*Year 4*	*Year 5*
12%	0.893	0.797	0.712	0.636	0.567

Discounted cash flow (NPV method)

Year	*Cash flow*	*12% discount factor*	*NPV*
0			
1			
2			
3			
4			
5			
		NPV	

As the NPV is positive, the project is achieving a rate of return in excess of 12% – the business' cost of capital.

The business should therefore _____________ the project.

Activity 5

Four projects have been assessed using NPV. Which project should be chosen for investment?

A £12,500

B £33,450

C (£44,777)

D (£13,456)

2.3 Merits and demerits of discounted cash flows

Merits

(a) Cash flows are less subjective than profits.

(b) Profit measures rely on such things as depreciation and other policies which are to a certain extent subjective. Cash, being tangible, suffers from no 'definition' problems and hence leads perhaps to a more objective measure of performance.

Demerits

(a) We are forced to make impractical assumptions or be faced with over-complicated calculations.

In the examples given so far we have assumed flows at yearly intervals, ignored taxation, ignored inflation – to mention just three simplifying assumptions.

(b) Discounted cash flow as a concept is more difficult for a layman to grasp.

It would clearly be beneficial for the person on whose behalf we are performing the calculation to have a grasp of the basic concept underlying the technique.

2.4 Annuity factors

In the event of a cash flow occurring each year in a calculation it is time consuming to apply each individual years discount factor to each cash flow.

Annuity factors are cumulative discount factors. The net present value of a cash flow which occurs each year can be calculated in one, quick way.

For example, using the individual discount factors:

Time	*Cash flow* £000	*Discount factor @ 10%*	*Present value* £000
t = 1	30	0.909	27.27
t = 2	30	0.826	24.78
t = 3	30	0.751	22.53
Net Present Value			74.58

However, given the annuity factor of 2.486 (0.909 + 0.826 + 0.751) this can be calculated much more quickly:

30 x 2.486 = 74.58 (as before)

If you were to need the annuity factors in the assessment, the assessor would provide them.

2.5 Net present cost

Net present cost is very similar to net present value, except that only costs feature in the calculation. That is, revenues or savings generated are not included perhaps because they are too uncertain, or perhaps because they are the same under various options.

In any event, the calculation required will be performed in the same way as any other NPV calculation except that the answers would be negative and then common sense dictates that if you have to choose from a range of negative / cost alternatives, you would pick the smallest one.

This does not mean that the project should be rejected necessarily, since the savings or revenues were consciously left out of the decision for the earlier stated reasons.

This method could be used when a company is making a purchasing decision between two machines. They might both raise revenues or make equivalent savings, but their investment and maintenance costs may be very different. Because the savings are the same they are omitted, and just the costs are discounted. Then the smallest negative NPV machine would be chosen.

2.6 Net terminal cost

Net terminal cost is very similar to net present cost except that instead of converting costs to their present value at time 0, they are compared at some time in the future.

In order to do this compounding must be used. This is the opposite of discounting. The formula for compounding is:

$$(1 + r)^n$$

The easiest way to calculate a terminal value is to work out the present value and then use the compounding formula. For example, if a company has worked out that the proposed purchase of a machine and its maintenance costs has an NPV of £12,345 when discounted at 10%, then its net terminal cost after, say, 5 years would be:

£12,345 × $(1+ 0.1)^n$ where $^n = 5$

= £19,882

Activity 6

A company is considering whether to buy a machine for £20,000 today with maintenance costs of £1,000 per year for 3 years. It will be sold at the end of the third year for £3,000. The company uses a discount rate of 10%.

(a) What is the net present cost?

(b) What is the net terminal cost?

Discount factors are:

Year	*1*	*2*	*3*
	0.909	0.826	0.751

Activity 7

The terminal cost for two projects has been calculated. For Project A it was (£12,000) and for Project B it was (£15,000). Which project should be accepted?

3 Long-term investments in more detail

Definition

Capital investment project

The key characteristic of a capital investment project is the tying up of capital for a number of years, in order to earn profits or returns over the period. Pulling out of the project earlier than originally intended will normally cause the return on investment to be considerably lower and may even cause a loss.

This differentiates this type of investment from the type more commonly undertaken by individuals, such as the purchasing of shares or depositing money at a building society, where the capital can often be recovered with a reasonable return at any time.

3.1 What will the capital be invested in?

The most common investment you will encounter will be in **tangible fixed assets**, such as a new machine, factory or premises from which to operate a new service business.

Other less tangible forms of investment include **research and development**, **patent rights or goodwill** obtained on the purchase of an existing business.

3.2 What form will the returns take?

The purchase of a new fixed asset will often be with the intention of starting a new line of business – say the manufacturing of a new product, or the provision of a new or extended service. The returns will be the **net income** generated by the new business.

Alternatively, the investment may be to benefit the existing operations, such that **revenues are increased** (where existing products/services are improved technologically or in quality) or **costs are reduced** (where production processes are updated or personnel reorganised). The returns will be measured as the **increase in net income or net reduction in costs** resulting from the investment.

3.3 Authorisation for a capital project

For projects involving a significant amount of capital investment, **authorisation** for its go-ahead will usually be given by the main board, or a sub-committee formed from the board for this purpose. Smaller projects (such as the replacement of an existing machine) may be within the authorisation limits of the manager of the area of business involved.

The decision will be based upon a **project proposal** using methods such as discounted cash flow.

3.4 Importance of non-financial factors

Although these appraisal methods will usually give a basis for a **recommendation as to whether or not the project should be accepted,** they will only be able to take account of monetary costs and benefits. **Qualitative factors** will also need to be considered when reaching a final decision – such as possible effects on staff morale (for example, if the project involves increased automation or considerable overtime), the environment, customer satisfaction and the business's status/reputation.

4 Lifecycle costing

Lifecycle costing is the maintenance of cost records for assets over their entire life, so that decisions concerning the acquisition, use or disposal of the assets can be made in a way that achieves the optimum asset usage at the lowest possible cost to the entity.

For example, when buying a machine, a business might be offered either a poor quality machine for £20,000 or a high quality machine for £50,000. If the poor quality machine is expected to continually break down and need to be repaired all the time, while the high quality machine is expected never to break down, then life cycle costing might argue that the high quality machine should be bought, despite it being more expensive, since its total cost of ownership over its entire life will be less than the poor quality alternative.

Activity 8

A company is going to renew a machine and is undecided between two options.

Machine A costs £50,000 immediately while machine B costs £80,000. Both machines will last 4 years. They will generate net savings after maintenance costs of:

Year 1	£20,000	£30,000
Year 2	£20,000	£20,000
Year 3	£20,000	£20,000
Year 4	£10,000	£20,000

At the end of their lives they will be disposed of generating an inflow of £10,000 for machine A and £30,000 for machine B.

Required

Calculate the Net Present Values of the two proposals when the interest rate is 10%.

The relevant present value factors are:

	Year 1	*Year 2*	*Year 3*	*Year 4*
10%	0.909	0.826	0.751	0.683

Y0						
Y1						
Y2						
Y3						
Y4						
		NPV	£		NPV	£

Therefore machine ____________ is the better option.

5 Product lifecycle

5.1 Revenue forecasts

When forecasting revenue figures, consideration should be given to the position of the product within its lifecycle. Most products have a limited life and there are generally thought to be five stages of the product lifecycle – development, launch, growth, maturity and decline, each of which will have different characteristics.

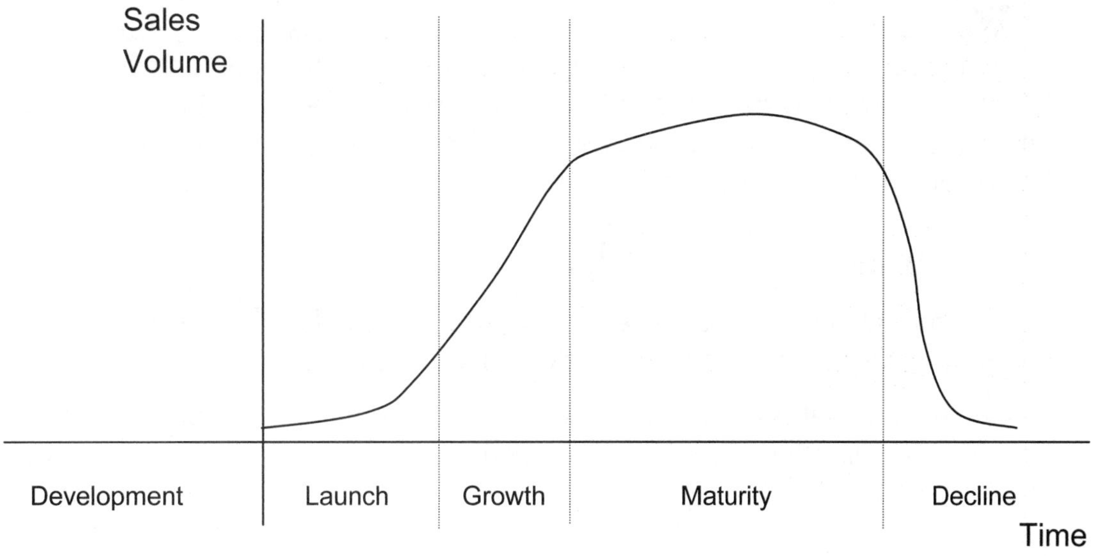

5.2 Development stage

During this time of the product's life there is likely to be a large amount of cost incurred on research and development but no revenue will be generated yet.

5.3 Launch stage

In the early stages of the product's life, immediately after its launch, sales levels are likely to be quite low. However, some eagerly awaited products, for example the PlayStation 3 games console, have had incredibly high sales levels in the launch stage.

Advertising costs will be very high, as will production costs building up inventory ready for the launch.

5.4 Growth stage

If the product is successfully launched then the product is likely to show fairly large increases in revenue indicated by a steep upward trend. However, such large revenue increases are unlikely to continue indefinitely.

As revenues increase, production will increase in order to match demand. Mechanisation may be preferred over labour intensive processes in order to speed up production. Economies of scale may be achieved through discounts received on bulk purchases of materials.

5.5 Maturity stage

During this stage the demand for the product is likely to start to slow or at least become more constant. The trend line in this stage will not show such a steep curve. It is probable that Heinz Baked Beans are at this stage.

Advertising costs are low and economies of scale have been achieved. There will probably be a switch from traditionally variable costs to fixed costs, for materials and labour, as production levels are now stable. Profits are probably maximised in this stage.

5.6 Decline stage

Most products will eventually reach the end of their life and revenues will begin to decline, with the trend line now also declining.

Costs will also fall as production stops and the remaining inventory is sold off. Profits will reduce considerably possibly to a loss.

5.7 Time series analysis and product lifecycle

Due to the changes in sales demand throughout the lifecycle of a product, care should be taken when using time series analysis to estimate the trend of future revenues. If the time series figures are based upon the growth stage then the trend line in this stage is unlikely to continue but will be likely to become less steep.

Activity 9

The stage in the product lifecycle with the highest units of sales is:

Introduction	☐
Growth	☐
Maturity	☐
Decline	☐

6 Summary

In this chapter we have considered the mechanics, the advantages and the disadvantages of the Discounted Cash Flow (DCF) or Net Present Value (NPV) technique.

The Net Present Value is an appraisal technique that takes the time value of money into account. As a general rule, if a project has a positive NPV, then it should be accepted, whereas a project with a negative NPV should be rejected.

Lifecycle costing and how it can be used to aid cost management has been considered.

This chapter has also considered the product lifecycle and how costs will change throughout the life of a product.

Answers to chapter activities

Activity 1

Year		*Cash flows*	*DF @ 15%*	*Present value*
		£		£
0	Cost	(80,000)	1	(80,000)
1	Inflows	20,000	0.870	17,400
2		50,000	0.756	37,800
3		40,000	0.658	26,320
4		10,000	0.572	5,720
			NPV =	7,240

Since the net present value is positive (i.e. a cash surplus) we should accept the machine.

Activity 2

Machine A

Year	*Cash flows*	*DF @ 5%*	*Present value*
	£		£
0	(100,000)	1	(100,000)
1	20,000	0.952	19,040
2	60,000	0.907	54,420
3	40,000	0.864	34,560
4	30,000	0.823	24,690
5	20,000	0.784	15,680
		NPV =	48,390

Machine B

Year	*Cash flows*	*DF @ 5%*	*Present value*
	£		£
0	(60,000)	1	(60,000)
1	(60,000)	0.952	(57,120)
2	60,000	0.907	54,420
3	60,000	0.864	51,840
4	80,000	0.823	65,840
		NPV =	54,980

Since machine B has the higher NPV, our decision should be to select machine B.

Activity 3

Highscore Ltd

Discounted cash flow – Net Present Value method – appraisal

Year	*Cash flow*	*15% discount factor*	*NPV*
0	(30,000)	1.00	(30,000)
1	9,000	0.870	7,830
2	11,000	0.756	8,316
3	10,000	0.658	6,580
4	10,500	0.572	6,006
5	10,200	0.497	5,069
6	10,100	0.432	4,363
		NPV	£8,164

Activity 4

Whitby Engineering Factors

Discounted cash flow (NPV method)

Year	*Cash flow*	*12% discount factor*	*NPV*
0	(50,000)	1.00	(50,000)
1	18,000	0.893	16,074
2	20,000	0.797	15,940
3	21,000	0.712	14,952
4	22,000	0.636	13,992
5	18,000	0.567	10,206
		NPV	£21,164

As the NPV is positive, the project is achieving a rate of return in excess of 12% – the business' cost of capital.

The business should therefore accept the project.

Activity 5

Project B has the highest NPV and should be selected.

Activity 6

(a) The net present cost is: £20,233.

Year	*Cost*	*DF@10%*	*PV*
0	(20,000)	1	(20,000)
1	(1,000)	0.909	(909)
2	(1,000)	0.826	(826)
3	2,000	0.751	1,502
		NPC =	(20,233)

(b) The net terminal cost is:

(20,233) × $1{\cdot}1^n$ where ^{n} is 3

= (£26,930)

Activity 7

Project A is the least cost and should be selected.

Activity 8

0	(£50,000)	1	(50,000)	(£80,000)	1	(80,000)
1	£20,000	0.909	18,180	£30,000	0.909	27,270
2	£20,000	0.826	16,520	£20,00	0.826	16,520
3	£20,000	0.751	15,020	£20,000	0.751	15,020
4	£20,000	0.683	13,660	£50,000	0.683	34,150
		NPV	£13,380		NPV	£12,960

Therefore machine A is the better option.

Activity 9

The maturity stage has the highest revenue level. (The growth stage has the highest revenue growth.)

7 Test your knowledge

Workbook Activity 10

A transport company is considering purchasing an automatic vehicle-cleansing machine. At present, all vehicles are cleaned by hand.

The machine will cost £80,000 to purchase and install in year 0 and it will have a useful life of four years with no residual value.

The company uses a discount rate of 10% to appraise all capital projects.

The cash savings from the machine will be:

Year	£
0	–
1	29,600
2	29,200
3	28,780
4	28,339

Task

As assistant management accountant, you are asked to carry out an appraisal of the proposal to purchase the machine and prepare a report to the general manager of the company. Your report should contain the following information:

(1) the net present value of the cash flows from the project

(2) recommend as to whether or not the proposal should be accepted.

In your calculations, you should assume that all cash flows occur at the end of the year.

Note: The present value of £1 at a discount rate of 10% is as follows:

Number of years from the present	£
1	0.909
2	0.826
3	0.751
4	0.683

Transport company

REPORT

To:

From:

Date:

Subject: Report on proposal to purchase vehicle cleansing machine

Appendix: appraisal calculations

Year	*Total cash flow* £	*Discount factor*	*Present value* £
0			
1			
2			
3			
4			
Net present value			

Workbook Activity 11

Data

RBG plc is a large quoted company using a 25% rate of interest for appraising capital projects. One of its divisional directors has put forward plans to make a new product, the AI. This will involve buying a machine specifically for that task. The machine will cost £600,000 and have a life of 5 years. However, because of the nature of the product, the machine will have no residual value at any time.

The annual cash flow will be as follows:

	£
Turnover per annum	380,000
Material	(90,000)
Labour	(30,000)
Overheads	(20,000)
Annual cash inflow	£240,000

Task

You are asked to write a report to the divisional accountant:

(a) appraising the divisional director's proposal using the net present value method of evaluating discounted cash flows and interpreting the result

For the calculation of the net present value, it can be assumed that cash flows occur at the end of each year. The present value of £1 at a discount rate of 25% is as follows:

End of year	£	*End of year*	£
1	0.800	4	0.410
2	0.640	5	0.328
3	0.512	6	0.262

REPORT

To:

From:

Date:

Subject:

Recommendation

Appendix 1 Investment appraisal (£)

End of year	*Cash flow £*	*Discount factor*	*Discounted cash flow*
0			
1			
2			
3			
4			
5			
		NPV =	

Time series, sampling and index numbers 5

Introduction

We use the time series techniques to forecast future trends.

You may also be asked to use the results of the linear regression technique to produce a trend for a series of data.

You should be able not only to use the time series techniques to forecast future trends and seasonal variations but also understand the weaknesses of time series analysis and the problems of using historical data to predict the future.

Sampling and index numbers are also important topics and are covered in this chapter.

KNOWLEDGE

Explain the use and purpose of indexing, sampling and time series (3.4)

SKILLS

Monitor and analyse on a regular basis current and forecast trends in prices and market conditions (2.2)

Compare trends with previous data and identify potential implications (2.3)

Consult relevant staff in the organisation about the analysis of trends and variances (2.4)

CONTENTS

1 Time series analysis
2 Isolating the trend
3 Moving averages
4 Linear regression
5 Finding the seasonal variations
6 Forecasting with time series analysis
7 Collecting information
8 Index numbers

1 Time series analysis

1.1 Introduction

The process of forecasting will inevitably involve some analysis of historic data (revenues, costs, share prices, etc) in order that future values may be predicted.

The data may concern the economy as a whole, the particular industry with which the organisation is involved (or wants to be) or the organisation itself.

Definitions

A **time series** is a set of values for some variable (e.g. monthly production) which varies with time. The set of observations will be taken at specific times, usually at regular intervals. Examples of figures which can be plotted as a time series are:

- monthly rainfall in London;
- daily closing price of a share on the Stock Exchange;
- monthly revenues in a department store.

Time series analysis takes historic data and breaks it down into component parts that are easier to extrapolate (predict future values of). In particular, it will isolate the underlying trend.

1.2 Plotting the graph of a time series

The basic pattern of a time series can be identified by plotting the recent points of the values on a graph, such as below.

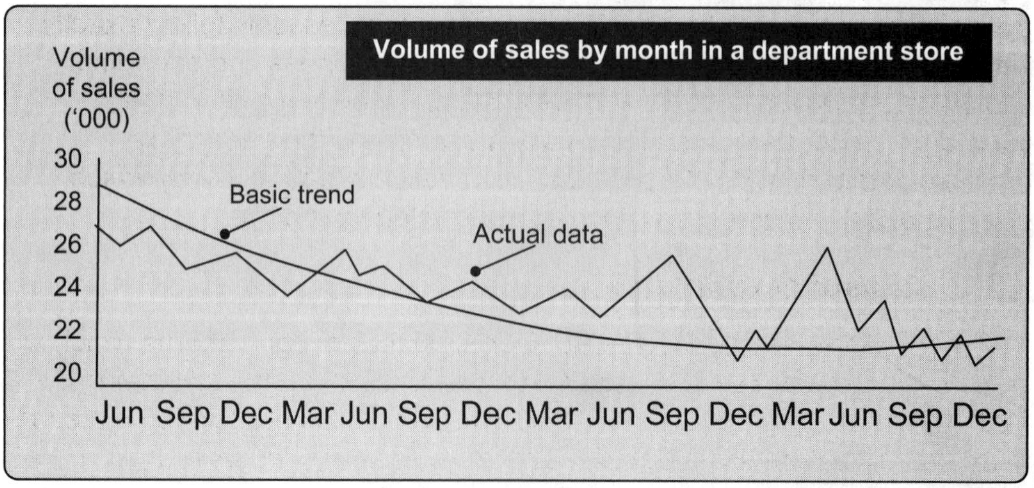

In such a graph time is always plotted on the horizontal x axis. Each point is joined by a straight line hence the typically 'jagged' appearance. Don't try to draw a smooth curve which will pass through all the points on a time series graph. You will find it practically impossible and, in any case, it is incorrect to do so. The only reason for joining the points at all is to give a clearer picture of the pattern, which would be more difficult to interpret from a series of dots.

On the graph above you will see that, having completed the time series graph, we have sketched in a 'basic trend' line. But what does it tell us? We need to look in more detail at what factors are at play in a time series.

1.3 Characteristic time series components

Analysis of time series has revealed certain characteristic movements or variations, the components of the time series. Analysis of these components is essential for forecasting purposes.

The four main types of component are as follows:

- basic trend (long-term);
- cyclical variations (not so long-term);
- seasonal variations (short-term);
- random variations (short-term).

1.4 Basic trend

The basic trend refers to the general direction in which the graph of a time series goes over a long interval of time once the short-term variations have been smoothed out. This movement can be represented on the graph by a basic trend curve or line.

1.5 Cyclical variations

Cyclical variations refer to long term swings around the basic trend. These cycles may or may not be periodic; they do not necessarily follow exactly similar patterns after equal intervals of time. In business and economic situations movements are said to be cyclical if they recur after time intervals of more than one year. A good example is the trade cycle, representing intervals of boom, decline, recession, and recovery which has, historically, followed an approximate seven year cycle.

1.6 Seasonal variations

Seasonal variations are the identical, or almost identical, patterns which a time series follows during corresponding intervals of successive periods. Such movements are due to recurring events such as the sudden increase in department store sales before Christmas. Although, in general, seasonal movements refer to a period of one year, this is not always the case and periods of hours, days, weeks, months, etc may also be considered depending on the type of data available.

1.7 Random variations

Random variations are the sporadic motions of time series due to chance events such as floods, strikes, elections, etc.

By their very nature they are unpredictable and therefore cannot play a large part in any forecasting, but it is possible to isolate the random variations by calculating all other types of variation and removing them from the time series data. It is important to extract any significant random variations from the data before using them for forecasting.

Random variations will not feature in your examination.

2 Isolating the trend

As we shall now see, there are three ways of isolating the trend:

- drawing a scattergraph;
- using moving averages;
- using linear regression.

2.1 Scattergraph – sketching a basic trend line

A basic trend line was drawn in on the time series graph shown earlier in this chapter. Indeed one way of isolating the trend is simply to draw it in freehand on the graph. This is called a 'scattergraph'.

This is actually a very helpful method. Once a time series has been prepared as a graph, it is usually a fairly simple matter to sketch in a basic trend line which manages to echo the overall long-term trend of the time series. There are some advantages to doing it this way:

- It is quick and easy.
- It allows one to interpolate a value easily. If you have monthly data for, say, Months 1, 3, 5, 7, 9 and 11 only, plotting those values and sketching a trend line will allow you to see what the likely value for months 2, 4, 6, 8 and 10 might have been. On the graph below you will see that we have interpolated the values of £125,000 for Month 6 of 20X4, and 175,000 for Month 12 of 20X4.
- It is possible to extrapolate a figure past the end of the data available (see the dotted line on the graph below). It is always worth bearing in mind, however, that data cannot be extrapolated very far ahead.

Common sense suggests, for instance, that the trend line in the graph below is unlikely to continue in a horizontal line for very long - it is bound either to rise or fall. So the extrapolation of 175,000 for Month 7 in 20X5 is not unreasonable, but it would not be helpful to extrapolate the line and make the same prediction for, say, Month 1 of 20X6.

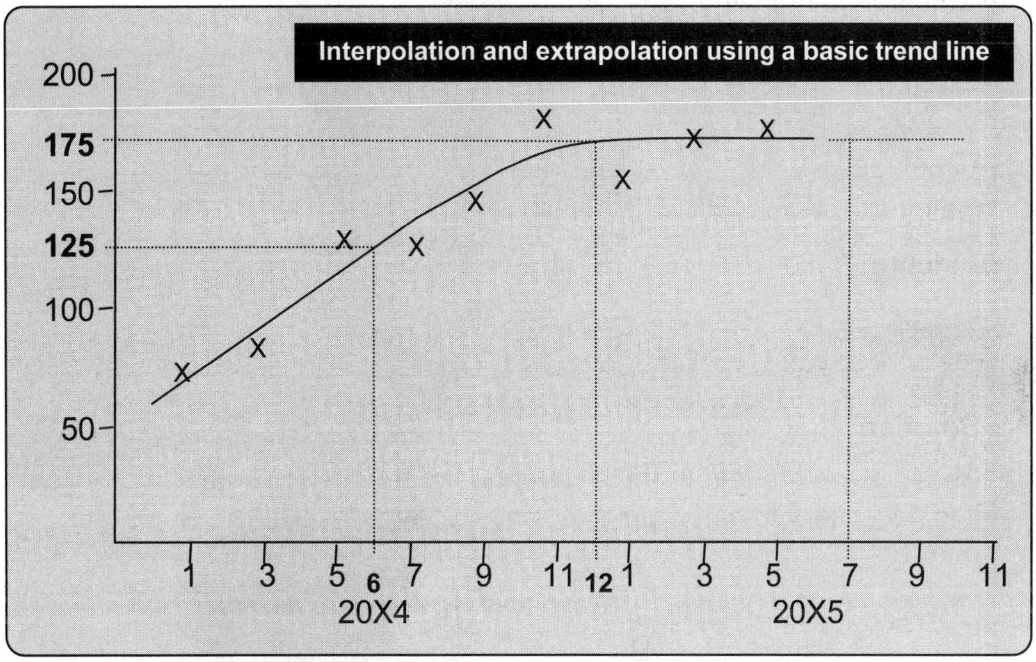

Two other common methods for isolating the trend are as follows:

- using moving averages
- using regression analysis.

We shall consider these in more detail.

3 Moving averages

3.1 Introduction

By using moving averages, the effect of any seasonal variation in a time series can be eliminated to show the basic trend. This elimination process will only work if the moving average is calculated over the correct number of values (being the number of values in one complete cycle). For instance, if a seasonal variation present in a time series is repeated every fourth period, then moving averages with a cycle of four should be used.

This will become clearer as you follow through this simple example.

Example

The following time series shows a set of revenue figures for eight quarters which are clearly increasing. At first sight, however, this increase appears to be quite erratic. We can however produce this trend by the use of moving averages.

Year	*Quarter*	*Revenues*
		£000
20X4	1	3
	2	5
	3	5
	4	5
20X5	1	7
	2	9
	3	9
	4	9

Solution

Because we are told that the revenue figures are for quarters of a year, it is necessary to calculate a moving average for all the sets of four quarters.

Year	*Quarter*	*Revenues*	*4-quarter moving average*
		£000	£000
20X4	1	3	
	2	5	
			4½ (W1)
	3	5	
			5½
	4	5	
			6½
20X5	1	7	
			7½
	2	9	
			8½
	3	9	
	4	9	

Workings

The moving average for the first four quarters is calculated as

$$\frac{3+5+5+5}{4} = 4½$$

Each moving average value is calculated and then placed in the centre of the numbers that were used in the calculation. For example, the first 4-value moving average is calculated as the average of the first four numbers, and then placed mid-way between the 2nd and 3rd quarter values of 2004

The moving average of four values captures the steadily increasing basic trend.

It will usually be fairly obvious which is the appropriate order in an examination question due to the way in which the data are presented, e.g. in 'quarters' (order 4) or days of the working week (order 5).

Be sure that you have understood the positioning of the moving averages in the above table. Each average has been written exactly opposite the middle of the figures from which it has been calculated. This results in the moving averages for even numbers of values (four in this case) being suspended halfway between two of the original figures.

Where you have a moving average for an even number of values, it is necessary to realign the moving averages so that they fall opposite the original values by calculating a centred moving average for every two moving average values.

Year	*Quarter*	*Original time series*	*Moving average (4 values)*	*Centred moving average order 4*
20X4	1	3		
	2	5		
			4½	
	3	5		5 (W)
			5½	
	4	5		6
			6½	
20X5	1	7		7
			7½	
	2	9		8
			8½	
	3	9		
	4	9		

As you can see by the centring process, the centred moving average is the basic trend.

(W) (4½ + 5½) ÷ 2 = 5

Example

The following data represents the revenues for TS Limited for the eight quarters shown.

	Quarter			
	1	2	3	4
Year 1	74	100	94	127
Year *2*	84	106	120	141

Calculate the trend using moving averages.

Solution

Year	*Qtr*	*Value*	*4-quarter moving total*	*4-quarter average*	*Trend*
1	1	74			
	2	100			
			395	99	
	3	94			100
			405	101	
	4	127			102
			411	103	
2	1	84			106
			437	109	
	2	106			111
			451	113	
	3	120			
	4	141			

3.2 Disadvantages of moving averages

- Values at the beginning and end of the series are lost – therefore the moving averages do not cover the complete period.
- The moving averages may generate cycles or other variations that were not present in the original data.
- The averages are strongly affected by extreme values. To overcome this a 'weighted' moving average is sometimes used giving the largest weights to central items and small weights to extreme values.

Activity 1

Using the table below, calculate the moving average of the following sales figures to:

(a) order 3;

(b) order 4.

Month	*Value* £
1	10
2	12
3	14
4	17
5	21
6	19
7	17
8	17

Solution

Month	*Value* £000	*Moving average order 3*	*Moving average order 4*
1	10		
2	12		
3	14		
4	17		
5	21		
6	19		
7	17		
8	17		

Activity 2

Ski Fun Ltd

Ski Fun Ltd owns a number of chalets in Switzerland that it lets out for holidays. Given below is data showing the number of people who stayed in the chalets each quarter.

	Quarter 1	*Quarter 2*	*Quarter 3*	*Quarter 4*
20X1			92	195
20X2	433	324	95	202
20X3	486	347	98	218
20X4	499	360	104	236

Calculate the trend of the number of visitors. Use a four-period moving average and round to the nearest whole number where necessary.

Ski Fun Ltd

Quarter		*Numbers*	*Four-period moving total Step 1*	*Four-period moving average Step 2*	*Trend Step 3*
20X1 –	3	92			
	4	195			
20X2 –	1	433			
	2	324			
	3	95			
	4	202			
20X3 –	1	486			
	2	347			
	3	98			
	4	218			

20X4 –	1	499			
	2	360			
	3	104			
	4	236			

Activity 3 (June 2004)

Sam Thomas is concerned about the rise in prices of direct materials used to make desks and has asked you to investigate.

The prices per kg of direct materials charged by suppliers for the period January 2004 to May 2004 are as follows.

	£
January	5.05
February	5.02
March	5.08
April	5.11
May	5.20

Task

(a) Calculate the moving average of monthly direct material prices over a period of three months.

(b) Write a memo to Sam Thomas to:

(i) explain what the trend in direct material prices, based on the moving average series, shows

(ii) suggest ONE possible use of the trend in setting the standard cost of direct materials for 2004

(iii) give TWO more pieces of information needed to set the standard cost of direct materials for 2004.

Task

(a) Average prices in the period January to March were:

Average prices in the period February to April were:

Average prices in the period March to May were:

(b)

MEMO

To:

From:

Date:

Subject: Trend in material prices

Use of trend in setting standards

Other information

Two other pieces of information are as follows:

(i)

(ii)

Activity 4 (June 2000)

Data

Garden Care is a division of Alton Products plc. The sales director of Garden Care, Hazel Brown, has noticed a distinct trend and pattern of seasonal variations for one of Garden Care's products since the product was introduced in the third quarter of 1997. She provides you with the following sales volumes for the product.

UNITS SOLD BY QUARTER

Year	*Quarter 1*	*Quarter 2*	*Quarter 3*	*Quarter 4*
1997			142	142
1998	150	150	142	158
1999	150	166	142	174
2000	150	182*		

*Estimate

Task

Hazel Brown asks you to:

(a) Calculate the *Centred Four-Point Moving Average Trend* figures.

(b) Calculate the seasonal variations on the assumption that the seasonal variations are additive.

(c) Use your results in (a) and (b) to forecast the sales volume for quarter 2 of year 2000.

(a) Trend and seasonal variations

Year	*Quarter*	*Actual*	*4 quarter total*	*4 quarter average*	*Centred trend*	*Seasonal variation*
1997	3	142				
	4	142				
1998	1	150				
	2	150				
	3	142				
	4	158				
1999	1	150				
	2	166				
	3	142				
	4	174				
2000	1	150				
	2	182				

(b) Analysis of seasonal variations

	Quarter 1	*Quarter 2*	*Quarter 3*	*Quarter 4*	*Residual*
1998					
1999					
Total					
Average					
Adjustment for residual					
Seasonal variations					0

(c) **Forecast demand – quarter 2**

Trend (160 + 2 + 2)	
Seasonal variation	
	____
Forecast	
Actual (estimate)	
Residual	
	____

The forecast demand for quarter 2 of 2000 is ___________units.

4 Linear regression

4.1 Introduction

The third way of isolating a trend is to use a mathematical technique called 'linear regression'. Only a broad understanding of linear regression is required in the context of producing a trend for a time series.

Regression analysis is a technique for estimating the line of best fit, given a series of data. It is essentially a statistical technique, and the description that follows is only a working guide for applying the technique.

Regression analysis is based on the concept of 'drawing the line that minimises the sum of the squares of the deviations of the line from the observed data' (so it is sometimes referred to as the least squares method). The regression line of *y* on x is used when an estimate of *y* (the **dependent** variable) is required for a given value of x (the **independent** variable).

4.2 Equation of the regression line

The general equation for the regression line is given as:

$$y = a + bx$$

Where:

x is the independent variable

y is the dependent variable

a is the fixed element

b is the variable element

You do not have to understand how this equation is calculated, but you do need to be able to use it.

In particular, you must understand that the independent variable (x) in some way causes the dependent variable (y) to have the value given by the equation.

Thus, if we were calculating the value of umbrellas sold for given amounts of monthly rainfall, the rainfall would be the independent variable (x) and the sales value would be the dependent variable (y) (rainfall causes umbrella sales and not vice versa).

Example

X Ltd is forecasting its sales for the four quarters of 20X5. It has carried out a linear regression exercise on its past revenue data and established the following:

a = 20

b = 0.7

The equation of the regression line is therefore:

y = 20 + 0.7x

Where x is number of the quarter and y is revenue in £000s.

Calculate the revenue for each of the quarters in 20X5.

Solution

		£000
Quarter 1	y = 20 + (0.7 × 1) =	20.7
Quarter 2	y = 20 + (0.7 × 2) =	21.4
Quarter 3	y = 20 + (0.7 × 3) =	22.1
Quarter 4	y = 20 + (0.7 × 4) =	22.8

Activity 5

Regression line

A regression line has been calculated as y = 192 + 2.40x, where x is the output and y is the total cost. You are required to:

(a) Fill in the blanks:

In the formula y = a + bx, y represents total cost (the ____________ variable), x represents the units of activity (the ____________ variable), 192 represents the ____________ cost element (£), 2.40 represents the ____________ cost per unit (£).

(Choose from: Variable, Fixed, Dependent, Independent)

The formula is estimating a linear relationship between activity level and total cost.

(b) Use it to predict the total cost for (i) 500 units and (ii) 1,500 units.

(i) x = 500

y =

= £ ____________

(ii) x = 1,500

y =

= £ ____________

Activity 6 (December 2003)

Data

Telford plc has a subsidiary, Ironbridge Ltd. This was formed on 1 January 1999. Ironbridge makes a single product, the Delta. The directors of Ironbridge are considering using time series to improve revenue forecasting.

The company has collected quarterly revenue data for its first 19 quarters of trading. Quarter 1 was the first three months of 1999; quarter 2 the second three months of 1999; quarter 5 the first three months of 2000; and quarter 19 the three months ended 30 September 2003.

Two models have been suggested.

Model A

This uses the linear regression formula of y = a + bx to describe the trend. The term y represents the forecast trend (or seasonally adjusted) revenue, a is a constant and x represents the quarter number being forecast. Applying the 19 quarters' data resulted in the development of the following formula:

$$y = £200{,}000 + £58{,}000x$$

For quarter 19, the three months ended 30 September 2003, x would be 19. The effect of this formula is for the forecast trend to increase by a constant £58,000 per quarter.

Model B

The formula for model B is $y = a + z(1 + g)^X$. In this model, a is a constant, x is the quarter number being forecast and g is a constant growth percentage. Applying the 19 quarters' data produced the following formula:

$$y = £1{,}000{,}000 + £60{,}000(1.1)^X$$

Barry Jones explained how the formula for model B worked. The first term, the £1,000,000, is a constant. However, the value of the second term, £60,000(1.1)X, increases quarterly by 10% over the previous quarter's figure.

To demonstrate this, Barry explained that the value of the second term for quarter 16 was £275,698, and so the value for quarter 17 would be 10% more, £303,268. Similarly, the value of the second term for quarter 18 would be 10% more than the value for quarter 17, a total of £333,595.

Barry gives you the actual seasonally adjusted data for the first three quarters of 2003.

Seasonally adjusted actual data	*Quarter 17*	*Quarter 18*	*Quarter 19*
Three months ended	31 March 2003	30 June 2003	30 September 2003
	£1,300,000	£1,350,000	£1,390,000

Task

(a) Calculate the forecast revenue for quarters 17, 18 and 19 using both models.

(b) Identify the model that gives the better estimate of the seasonal adjusted actual data. Give ONE reason for your answer.

(c) Write a memo to Barry Jones. In your memo, you should:

(i) use the model that gives the better estimate to forecast the seasonally adjusted revenue for quarter 20, the three months ending 31 December 2003;

(ii) identify TWO limitations to using that model as a forecasting technique.

(a) **Model A: a + bx =y**

Quarter 17:		
Quarter 18:		
Quarter 19:		

Model B: $a + z(1 + g)^x = y$

Quarter 17:		
Quarter 18:		
Quarter 19:		

(b) **Model A**

Y	*Actual*	*Difference*
	£1,300,000	
	£1,350,000	
	£1,390,000	

(b) **Model B**

Y	*Actual*	*Difference*
	£1,300,000	
	£1,350,000	
	£1,390,000	

The better fit is model __________as the difference between the actual results and the forecast results are smaller than with model _________.

(c)

MEMO

To:

From:

Date:

Subject:

(i) The model that gives the better estimate:

(ii) The limitations of using model B are as follows:

4.3 The assumptions of regression analysis

Regression analysis is based on sample data and if we selected a different sample it is probable that a different regression line would be constructed. For this reason, regression analysis is most suited to conditions where there is a relatively stable relationship between cost and activity level.

Assumptions we are making:

- The relationship is a linear one.
- The data used is representative of future trends.

5 Finding the seasonal variations

5.1 Introduction

Having isolated the trend we need to consider how to deal with the seasonal variations. We will look at two models – the additive model and the multiplicative model.

The additive model is the simplest model and is satisfactory when the variations around the trend are within a constant band width. If, as is more usual, the variations around the trend increase as the trend itself rises, it is better to use the multiplicative model.

5.2 The additive model – finding the seasonal variations

The additive model we will use expresses variations in absolute terms, with above and below average figures being shown as positives or negatives.

The four components of a time series (T = trend; S = seasonal variation; C = cyclical variation; R = random variation) are expressed as absolute values which are simply added together to produce the actual figures:

Actual data (time series) = T + S + C + R

For unsophisticated analyses over a relatively short period of time cyclical variations (C) and random variations (R) are ignored. Random variations are ignored because they are unpredictable and would not normally exhibit any repetitive pattern, whereas cyclical variations (long-term oscillations) are ignored because their effect is negligible over short periods of time. The model therefore simplifies to:

Actual data = T + S

The seasonal variation is therefore the difference between the computed trend figure and the original time series figure. Thus:

S = Actual – T

Example

The seasonal variations can be extracted by subtracting each trend value (using the moving averages method) from its corresponding time series value.

Solution

Quarter	*Original time series*	*Underlying trend*	*Seasonal variation (S)*
	(a)	(b)	(a) – (b)
3	94	100	(6)
4	127	102	25
1	84	106	(22)
2	106	111	(5)

6 Forecasting with time series analysis

6.1 Introduction

Earlier we noted that the analysis of a time series into its component parts would make extrapolation easier for forecasting future values for planning purposes.

In general, for short-term forecasts, only the trend and seasonal variations will be used; the cyclical variations will only have a significant effect over quite a long period of time and the random variations are, by their *very* nature, unpredictable.

Thus the approach to forecasting will be to:

- extrapolate the trend to the appropriate future time; and
- adjust the extrapolated trend value by the appropriate seasonal variation.

6.2 Extrapolating the trend

There is no unique method for extrapolation of the basic trend, as it will very much depend upon its particular shape (if, indeed, it has a discernible shape).

In practice, computers will be of great help in producing various possible equations for the trend, which can be rapidly tested against the data available to determine which fits best.

If the moving averages method has been used, a certain amount of judgement will be necessary. Possible approaches include the following:

- Plot the trend values on a graph and extrapolate by eye. (In fact, an initial sketch graph can be useful anyway to get a visual impression of the trend, before using one of the following methods to predict it.)
- Look at the increments between each trend value for any approximate pattern (e.g. roughly equal, which makes the trend approximately linear or steadily increasing) and continue this pattern to the future time required.
- If the increments appear to vary randomly, an average increment for the period may be calculated and used in the forecast.
- If the pattern of the trend appears to change significantly over the period, you may restrict your prediction technique to later data values only, as being more representative of future values.

Example

We will now use the time series analysis from paragraph 5.2 to forecast the sales value for quarter 4 of year 3, given that the time series figures are the quarterly revenues in £000.

Solution

The trend values obtained by moving averages have been plotted on a graph (unless specifically required, it is unlikely that you would have time to do this in an examination).

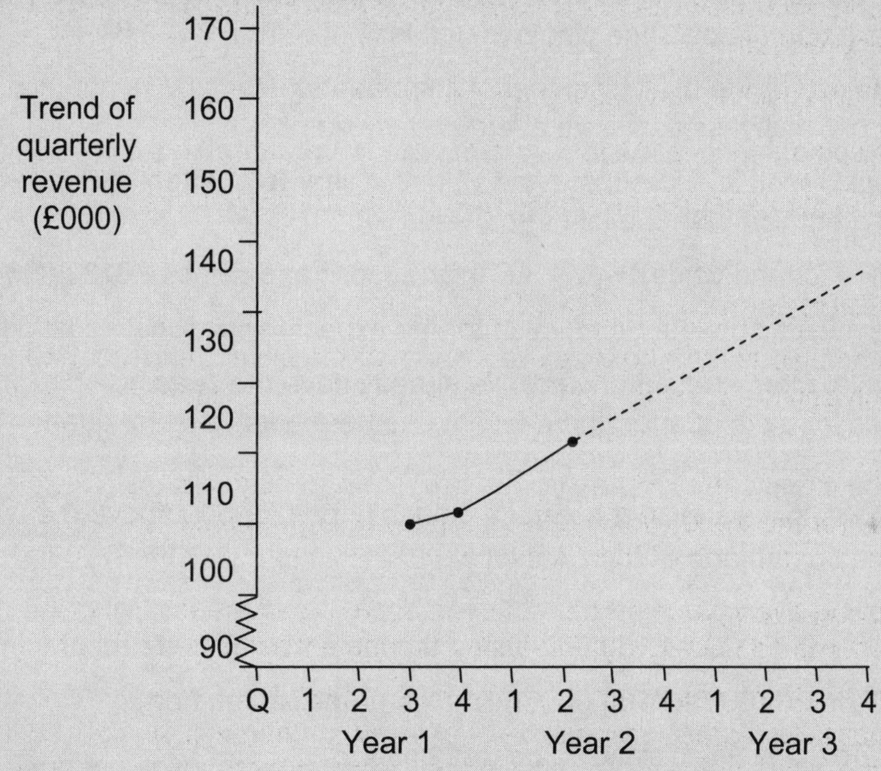

The graph shows an upward sloping trend, very approximately linear, but which becomes increasingly steep.

If we were to use the graphical approach to extrapolate, one approach would be to extend the line using the later, steeper gradient (although it should be noted that the earlier part of the curve shows that this may, in fact, revert to a shallower gradient). This approach may be over-optimistic. Perhaps it would be more prudent to assume that the earlier gradient will continue. The dashed line on the above graph shows a compromise between the two and produces a forecast for *Q4* of Year *3* of approximately *135,* indicating a trend value for revenue of *£135,000.*

Now consider the increments (the differences between each successive pair of trend values). Note that you do not need to work these out exactly; they will just be used to detect any pattern or change.

From previous quarter to		*Trend*	*Approximate Increment*
Year	*Quarter*		
1	3	100	–
	4	102	2
2	1	106	4
	2	111	5

There is no clear pattern, so some average increment may be used. The average increment over the whole period is (111 – 100)/3 $\cong$ 3.67

(Note that we divide by the number of increments or 'gaps' (3), not the number of trend values; we are averaging the 'gaps'.)

This would result in a forecast trend value for year 3, quarter 4 (which is six increments on from the last trend value) of:

111 (the last trend value) + (6 × 3.67) = 133, or trend sales of £133,000.

Now we must adjust the trend value for the expected seasonal variation.

This is a lot more straightforward! We already have the seasonal variations for each quarter, the relevant one here being that for quarter 4: +25

This means that we expect quarter 4 values to be £25,000 above the trend value. Thus, seasonally-adjusted predictions for quarter 4, year 3 would be:

£133,000 + £25,000 = £158,000 (using the incremental method); or

£135,000 + £25,000 = £160,000 (using the graphical method)

depending upon which trend value was used.

In an examination, you should only make one prediction, justifying the approach used. There will rarely be one 'correct' way, so do not spend too long deciding how you are going to do it.

Activity 7

Your organisation (AAT CA D94)

Your organisation is about to commence work on the preparation of the forthcoming year's annual budget.

As assistant management accountant, you have been asked to assist budget-holders and to respond to any queries which they may raise in the course of submitting their budget proposals.

Your organisation's revenue analyst had made some progress in preparing the revenue forecasts for year 5 when she unexpectedly needed to take leave for personal reasons.

She has left you the following memo.

MEMORANDUM

To: Assistant Management Accountant

From: Revenue Analyst

Date: 12 December 20X4

Subject: Revenue forecasts for year 5

In preparing the sales volume forecasts for year 5, I have got as far as establishing the following trend figures and average seasonal variations.

	Quarter 1 units	*Quarter 2 units*	*Quarter 3 units*	*Quarter 4 units*
Year 3 – trend figures	3,270	3,313	3,358	3,407
Year 4 – trend figures	3,452	3,496	3,541	3,587
Average seasonal variation	(50)	22	60	(32)

As a basis for extrapolating the trend line, I forecast that the trend will continue to increase in year 5 at the same average amount per quarter as during year 4.

Sorry to leave you with this unfinished job, but it should be possible to prepare an outline forecast for year 5 with this data.

Required

Prepare a forecast of sales volumes for each of the four quarters of year 5, based on the data contained in the analyst's memo.

Your organisation

Sales volume forecasts

Year	*Quarter*	*Trend*	*Increase in trend*	
		(units)	*(units)*	
3	4	3,407		
4	1	3,452		
	2	3,496		
	3	3,541		
	4	3,587		
			——	
				Average = units
			——	

Sales volume forecast for year 5

	Quarter 1	*Quarter 2*	*Quarter 3*	*Quarter 4*
	units	*units*	*units*	*units*
Trend (W1)	3,632			
Seasonal adjustment	–50			
	——	——	——	——
Forecast	3,582			
	——	——	——	——

(W1) Q 1 trend = Year 4 Q 4 trend + average quarterly trend

= 3,587 + 45

= 3,632

6.3 Seasonal variations and the multiplicative model

In some examinations you may be given the trend figures and seasonal variations but, instead of the seasonal variations being given in absolute figures as in the additive model that we have used so far, the seasonal variations may be given as percentage figures. This is the case if the multiplicative model is used for the time series analysis.

In order to find the forecast figures in this case, simply multiply the trend figure by the seasonal variation percentage and either add it to the trend or deduct it from the trend.

Example

Given below are the estimated trend figures for a company's revenue for the next four quarters:

20X3	*Trend*
	£
Quarter 1	560,000
Quarter 2	580,000
Quarter 3	605,000
Quarter 4	632,000

The seasonal variations using the multiplicative model have been calculated as:

Quarter 1	+ 15%
Quarter 2	+ 10%
Quarter 3	– 5%
Quarter 4	– 20%

Calculate the forecast revenue figures for each of the next four quarters.

Solution

Quarter 1	£560,000 + (560,000 × 0.15) =	£644,000
Quarter 2	£580,000 + (580,000 × 0.10) =	£638,000
Quarter 3	£605,000 – (605,000 × 0.05) =	£574,750
Quarter 4	£632,000 – (632,000 × 0.20) =	£505,600

6.4 Problems with forecasting

There are a number of problems with using time series analysis in order to estimate or forecast future results.

- The main problem is the inherent weakness of extrapolation. In order to estimate the trend for the future the trend line is extended on the graph and the figures read off. However, although the time series has moved in that particular manner in the past, it does not necessarily mean that it will continue to do so in the future.
- The seasonal adjustments used to find the forecast for the future are again based upon historic figures that may well be out of date. There is no guarantee that the seasonal variations will remain the same in the future. If the time series has a large residual or random variation element, then this will make any forecasts even less reliable.

7 Collecting information

7.1 Introduction

As we have seen, the purpose of the management information system and the management accountant is to provide useful information to the management of the business. In order to do this the management accountant will have to collect the information in the first place. However, before collecting information, it will be necessary to determine what the population is that we are interested in.

Definition

The population is simply all of the items of information that the collector is interested in. For example, if the management accountant wanted to know the proportion of defective units produced by a machine in a day then the population would be all of the units of product produced by the machine in the day.

7.2 Census or sampling approach

If information is required about a particular topic then there are two main approaches to obtaining the information, the census approach or the sampling approach.

The question here is whether we examine every item in the population, the census approach, or take a sample of the population. In business contexts it is rare to use the census approach so some form of sampling technique will be used. When sampling is used only a small number of items in the population are examined or tested.

Care must be taken when selecting a sample as the reliability of the results will be dependent upon how unbiased the sample is.

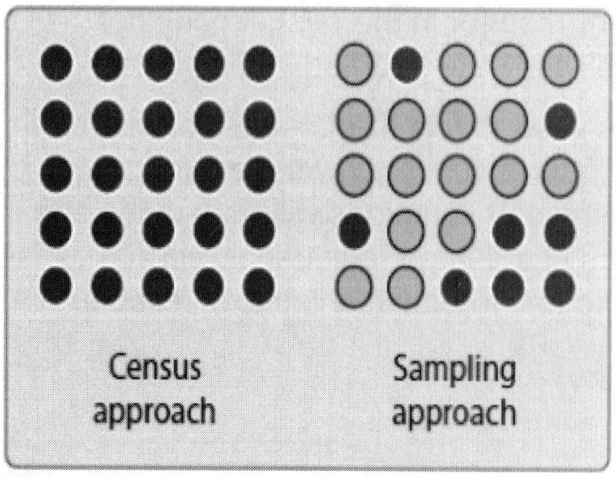

The census approach examines every item in the population

7.3 Random sampling

Random sampling is the best method of producing a totally unbiased sample; each item in the population has an equal chance of being included in the sample. In order for random sampling to be used each item in the population must be known and must have a consecutive number assigned to it. The sample is then chosen by random numbers taken from random number tables or a random number generator (your scientific calculator).

It is rare in practice for all items of the population to be known and for pure random sampling to be used. Therefore there are a number of other quasi-random methods of sampling that could be used:

- systematic sampling;
- stratified sampling;
- multi-stage sampling.

7.4 Systematic sampling

Systematic sampling is a simpler method of random sampling where again all of the items in the population must be known and each item must have a consecutive number assigned to it. Under systematic sampling the first item in the sample is chosen using a random number. Thereafter, every nth item in the population is taken to make up the sample. For example, the 14th item followed by every 50th item would produce a sample of 20 items from a population of 1,000 items.

7.5 Stratified sampling

Stratified sampling can be used if the population falls into distinct layers or groups. The population is split into these groups and the sample is then chosen from each group in proportion to the size of the group compared to the total population.

7.6 Multi-stage sampling

Again this is a method that can be used if the population naturally fall into fairly large groups or areas. Initially a number of groups or areas are selected randomly. The next stage is to take each group that has been selected and to split them into smaller groups from which again a sample is chosen randomly. This can be done any number of times until the final sample has been chosen.

7.7 Non-random sampling methods

In some instances it may not be cost effective to carry out random sampling techniques and therefore some form of non-random sampling is used. These methods will not produce such accurate results as the random sampling methods but the information collected can still be useful. Typical non-random sampling methods that can be used are:

- quota sampling;
- cluster sampling.

7.8 Quota sampling

This is particularly useful when market research is being carried out. Quota sampling can be used when there are a number of different groups in the population, for example men under 30, women over 30, etc. The number of sample members required from each group is determined and these samples are taken on a non-random basis from the group until the required number has been reached.

7.9 Cluster sampling

Cluster sampling is where one or more areas of the population are determined to be representative of the population as a whole and therefore the sample is taken from that group alone. For example, if a business was carrying out market research into the buying habits of supermarket shoppers countrywide then it may be decided that customers shopping at three different supermarkets in Birmingham are representative of nationwide supermarket shoppers and the sample can then be taken from shoppers at these three supermarkets only.

Activity 8

The method of sampling that assumes that specific groups of the population will be representative of the population as a whole and selected items are taken from specified groups rather than the entire population is:

A Random sampling

B Quota sampling

C Cluster sampling

D Stratified sampling

Activity 9

A method of sampling whereby each item in the population has an equal chance of being included in the sample is called:

A Random sampling

B Systematic sampling

C Stratified sampling

D Quota sampling

8 Index numbers

8.1 Introduction

We have seen that the trend of revenue or costs can be estimated using time series analysis. However, this method is quite complex and time-consuming. There are other methods of indicating the trend of figures for income or costs and one of these is to use index numbers.

8.2 Use of index numbers

A time series of figures for costs or income can be easily converted into an index. This is done firstly by choosing a base year and allocating to this year's figure an index of 100. Each subsequent period's figure is then converted into a relevant index number using the formula:

$$\text{Index} = \frac{\text{Current year figure}}{\text{Base year figure}} \times 100$$

Example

The materials costs for a business for the last six months were:

	£
March	427,000
April	442,000
May	460,000
June	433,000
July	447,000
August	470,000

If the index for March is 100, what are the index numbers of the costs for each of the subsequent months and what do these index numbers tell us?

Solution

Month		*Index*
March	Base year	100.0
April	$\frac{442,000}{427,000} \times 100$	103.5
May	$\frac{460,000}{427,000} \times 100$	107.7
June	$\frac{433,000}{427,000} \times 100$	101.4
July	$\frac{447,000}{427,000} \times 100$	104.7
August	$\frac{470,000}{427,000} \times 100$	110.1

The index shows that the materials costs are generally rising although there is a fall back in June which has been made up for by the highest level yet in August.

8.3 Indices to measure inflation

Published indices that can be useful to the management accountant are the Consumer Price Index (CPI) and the Retail Price Index (RPI). These indices published on a monthly basis by the Government and are used as measures of general price changes and inflation.

If we have a series of cost or revenue figures measured over a fairly long time period then they could have been distorted by price changes over the period and may not necessarily show the correct position.

We can use the RPI to adjust all of the figures in the time series into current day prices by using the formula:

$$\text{Current price adjusted figure} = \text{Actual revenue} \times \frac{\text{RPI in current year}}{\text{RPI in year of sales}}$$

Example

Suppose that a company has recorded annual revenue over the last six years as follows:

	£
20X0	735,000
20X1	764,000
20X2	791,000
20X3	811,000
20X4	833,000
20X5	856,000

The average RPI for each of those years was as follows:

	RPI
20X0	144.3
20X1	149.8
20X2	153.0
20X3	157.2
20X4	161.9
20X5	170.0

Show the revenue for the last six years in terms of current year (20X5) prices and explain what this shows.

Solution

	Actual revenue	*RPI adjustment*	*Price adjusted revenue*
	£		£
20X0	735,000	× 170.0/144.3	865,900
20X1	764,000	× 170.0/149.8	867,000
20X2	791,000	× 170.0/153.0	878,900
20X3	811,000	× 170.0/157.2	877,000
20X4	833,000	× 170.0/161.9	874,700
20X5	856,000		856,000

The original, unadjusted figures indicated a fairly substantial increase in revenue over the period, but once the revenues are adjusted to current prices, a different picture appears. In fact the revenue increased very gradually until 20X2 and has been in decline for the last three years.

When comparing costs or revenue over time the accountant should consider the effects of either general inflation by using the RPI or more specific price changes that affect the cost or revenue by using a price index specifically related to that cost or revenue.

Activity 10

Price indices

A product which cost £12.50 in 20X0, cost £13.65 in 20X1. Calculate the simple price index for 20X1 based on 20X0.

Simple price index $= \frac{P_1}{P_0} \times 100$

= £____________

This means that the price has increased by ____________% of its base year price of £12.50.

Activity 11

If a machine costs £2,000 on 1 January 20X2 and the relevant cost index has risen from 125.0 to 133.4 from January to April 20X2, how much would the machine be expected to cost in April 20X2?

Activity 12

Restating revenue figures

Given below are the revenue figures of an organisation and the Retail Price Index for a number of years.

	Revenues £000	*Retail Price Index*
20X1	500	131
20X2	510	139
20X3	540	149
20X4	580	154
20X5	650	164

Restate the revenue figures for each year on the following bases:

(a) deflating each year's revenue in order to take out the effect of inflation;

(b) restating each year's figures in terms of *20X5* prices.

Comment on your findings.

Restating Revenue Figures

(a) Deflation of figures

20X1 £500,000 × $\frac{131}{131}$ = £500,000

20X2 £510,000 × _____ =

20X3 £540,000 × _____ =

20X4 £580,000 × _____ =

20X5 £650,000 x _____ =

(b) Inflation to current year prices

20X1 £500,000 × =

20X2 £510,000 × =

20X3 £540,000 × =

20X4 £580,000 × =

20X5 £650,000 × =

Comment

8.4 Contracts

Indices can be used as a method of securing contracts to reduce the risk of rising prices. Particularly in the building industry, some building contracts may span several years. For example the building of the Olympic village for the 2012 Olympic Games in London has taken several years. The price of the contract will probably have been agreed up front. If there is inflation then the final receipt will be worth less than when the contract price was agreed years earlier. It is for this reason that often inflation is built into the contract, whereby the final price paid will be increased by an agreed inflation level.

9 Summary

Forecasts of future events are normally based on historical information. Information may be available from a wide variety of sources both internal and external to the business.

Time series analysis helps with the isolation of trends, although these still may not be easy to extrapolate into the future. Remember that you are using historic data which will not reflect future economic and environmental changes.

Also, you must be able to calculate the seasonal variations and be able to de-seasonalise data if required.

In this chapter we also looked briefly at sampling techniques and you should be aware of the definitions of the main sampling methods. Finally, we studied index numbers.

Answers to chapter activities

Activity 1

Month	*Value* £000	*Moving average order 3*	*Moving average order 4*
1	10		
2	12	12.0	
			13.25
3	14	14.3	
			16.00
4	17	17.3	
			17.75
5	21	19.0	
			18.50
6	19	19.0	
			18.50
7	17	17.6	
8	17		

Activity 2

Ski Fun Ltd

Quarter		*Numbers*	*Four-period moving total Step 1*	*Four-period moving average Step 2*	*Trend Step 3*
20X1 –	3	92			
	4	195			
			1,044	261	
20X2 –	1	433			262
			1,047	262	
	2	324			263
			1,054	264	
	3	95			271
			1,107	277	
	4	202			280
			1,130	283	

20X3 –	1	486			283
			1,133	283	
	2	347			285
			1,149	287	
	3	98			289
			1,162	291	
	4	218			293
			1,175	294	
20X4 –	1	499			295
			1,181	295	
	2	360			298
			1,199	300	
	3	104			
	4	236			

Activity 3 (June 2004)

Task

(a) Average prices in the period January to March were:

$$\frac{5.05 + 5.02 + 5.08}{3} = \frac{15.15}{3} = £5.05$$

Average prices in the period February to April were:

$$\frac{5.02 + 5.08 + 5.11}{3} = \frac{15.21}{3} = £5.07$$

Average prices in the period March to May were:

$$\frac{5.08 + 5.11 + 5.20}{3} = \frac{15.39}{3} = £5.13$$

(b)

MEMO

To: Sam Thomas

From: Accounting Technician

Date: June 2004

Subject: Material prices

Trend in material prices

The trend shows an upward movement in prices over the period. By smoothing the individual prices, the trend is more apparent than in the original data where the upward and downward monthly prices show a less clear picture.

Use of trend in setting standards

The trend can be extrapolated to indicate what future prices are likely to be in the remainder of 2004. This may cause the organisation to alter the standard for material prices if the expected prices are going to diverge significantly from the current standard.

Other information

Two other pieces of information are as follows:

(i) The amount of materials used to make a desk. This may be unchanged but it is possible that the desk could be re-engineered to simplify its construction, possibly using less material.

(ii) The overall demand for desks – if demand were to increase significantly, the greater demand for desks would generate an increased demand for materials. The company may be able to buy these materials cheaper by obtaining quantity discounts.

Activity 4 (June 2000)

(a) **Trend and seasonal variations**

Year	*Quarter*	*Actual*	*4 quarter total*	*4 quarter average*	*Centred trend*	*Seasonal variation*
1997	3	142				
	4	142				
			584	146		
1998	1	150			146	4
			584	146		
	2	150			148	2
			600	150		
	3	142			150	– 8
			600	150		
	4	158			152	6
			616	154		
1999	1	150			154	– 4
			616	154		
	2	166			156	10
			632	158		
	3	142			158	– 16
			632	158		
	4	174			160	14
			648	162		
2000	1	150				
	2	182				

(b) **Analysis of seasonal variations**

	Quarter 1	*Quarter 2*	*Quarter 3*	*Quarter 4*	*Residual*
1998	4	2	– 8	6	
1999	– 4	10	– 16	14	
Total	0	12	– 24	20	
Average	0	6	– 12	10	4
Adjustment for residual	– 1	– 1	– 1	– 1	– 4
Seasonal variations	– 1	5	– 13	9	0

(c) **Forecast demand – quarter 2**

Trend (160 + 2 + 2)	164
Seasonal variation	5
Forecast	169
Actual (estimate)	182
Residual	13

The forecast demand for quarter 2 of 2000 is 169 units.

Activity 5

Regression line

(a) In the formula y represents total cost (the dependent variable), x represents the units of activity (the independent variable), 192 represents the fixed cost element (£), 2.40 represents the variable cost per unit (£).

The formula is estimating a linear relationship between activity level and total cost.

(b) (i) x = 500

y = 192 + 2.40 (500)

= £1,392

(ii) x = 1,500

y = 192 + 2.40 (1,500)

= £3,792

Activity 6

(a) **Model A: a + bx =y**

Quarter 17:	£200,000 + (£58,000 × 17)	£1,186,000
Quarter 18:	£200,000 + (£58,000 × 18)	£1,244,000
Quarter 19:	£200,000 + (£58,000 × 19)	£1,302,000

Model B: a + z(1 + g)^x = y

Quarter 17:	£1,000,000 + £303,268	£1,303,268
Quarter 18:	£1,000,000 + £333,595	£1,333,595
Quarter 19:	£1,000,000 + £366,955 (W)	£1,366,955

Working

£333,595 × 1.1 = £366,955

(b) **Model A**

Y	*Actual*	*Difference*
£1,186,000 –	£1,300,000 =	– £114,000
£1,244,000 –	£1,350,000 =	– £106,000
£1,302,000 –	£1,390,000 =	– £88,000

(b) **Model B**

Y	*Actual*	*Difference*
£1,303,268 –	£1,300,000	£3,268
£1,333,595 –	£1,350,000	– £16,405
£1,366,955 –	£1,390,000	– £23,045

The better fit is model B as the difference between the actual results and the forecast results are smaller than with model A.

(c)

MEMO

To: Barry Jones

From: Accounting

Date: 4 December 2003

Subject: Forecasting

(i) Model B provides the more accurate forecast. It assumes a constant percentage rate of growth which is more in line with the results analysed.

For period 19, the second term of the equation was £366,955, and so for period 20 the second term will be £366,955 × 1.1 = 403,650. This gives a total forecast of £1,403,650.

(ii) The limitations of using model B are as follows.

It assumes that time is the only variable. This may not be the case and in the longer term such things as income, tastes and interest rates may be important.

It is unlikely that a constant rate of growth will be sustained over even a fairly short period of time. Seasonal variations will upset this trend as will some of the other factors referred to above, particularly interest rates.

The sample of 19 is very small and the figures should be kept under review until a stable pattern emerges.

Activity 7

Your organisation

(a) (i) Seasonal variations are regular patterns of fluctuations which occur over the year. For example, the seasonal variation for quarter 1 is minus 50 units. This indicates that the sales volume for quarter 1 is on average 50 units below the general trend in sales. Similarly, the sales volume for quarter 2 is generally 22 units above the general trend.

(ii) A trend line is the underlying direction in which a time series of data is moving. The trend is determined by removing the effect of seasonal variations, usually by using the technique of moving averages.

In the data provided, the monthly sales volume appears to be increasing by an average of 45 units in each quarter, after eliminating the seasonal variations. This is the underlying trend in the data, which the analyst suggests should be used to project the sales data into the future. This is known as extrapolating the trend (i.e. continuing its general direction as a basis for the sales forecast).

(b) **Sales volume forecasts**

Working: calculating the average quarterly increase in the trend

Year	*Quarter*	*Trend*	*Increase in trend*	
		(units)	*(units)*	
3	4	3,407		
4	1	3,452	45	
	2	3,496	44	
	3	3,541	45	
	4	3,587	46	
			——	
			180	Average = 180/4 = 45 units
			——	

Sales volume forecast for year 5

	Quarter 1	*Quarter 2*	*Quarter 3*	*Quarter 4*
	units	*units*	*units*	*units*
Trend	3,632	3,677	3,722	3,767
Seasonal adjustment	–50	+22	+60	–32
	–––––	–––––	–––––	–––––
Forecast	3,582	3,699	3,782	3,735
	–––––	–––––	–––––	–––––

Quarter 1 trend = Year 4 Quarter 4 trend + average quarterly trend

= 3,587 + 45

= 3,632

Activity 8

C Cluster sampling makes the assumption that specific groups of the population will be representative of the population as a whole and selects items from specified groups rather than the entire population.

Activity 9

A Random sampling is a method of sampling whereby each item in the population has an equal chance of being included in the sample.

Activity 10

Price indices

$$\text{Simple price index} = \frac{P_1}{P_0} \times 100$$

$$= \frac{13.65}{£12.50} \times 100$$

$$= 1.092 \times 100$$

$$= 109.2$$

This means that the price has increased by 9.2% of its base year price of £12.50.

Activity 11

$$£2,000 \times \frac{133.4}{125.0} = £2,134.40$$

Activity 12

Restating Revenue Figures

(a) Deflation of figures

$$20X1\ £500,000 \times \frac{131}{131} = £500,000$$

$$20X2\ £510,000 \times \frac{131}{139} = £480,647$$

$$20X3\ £540,000 \times \frac{131}{149} = £474,765$$

$$20X4\ £580,000 \times \frac{131}{154} = £493,377$$

$$20X1\ £500,000 \times \frac{131}{131} = £500,000$$

$$20X5\ £650,000 \times \frac{131}{164} = £519,207$$

(b) Inflation to current year prices

20X1 £500,000 × $\frac{164}{131}$ = £625,954

20X2 £510,000 × $\frac{164}{139}$ = £601,727

20X3 £540,000 × $\frac{164}{149}$ = £594,362

20X4 £580,000 × $\frac{164}{154}$ = £617,662

20X5 £650,000 × $\frac{164}{164}$ = £650,000

Comment

The revenue figures alone show increases year after year. However, once inflation is taken into account the result is different.

Both sets of figures, once deflated by one method or the other, show that in real terms revenues decreased in *20X2* and *20X3* and increased again in *20X4* and *20X5.* By *20X5,* even in real terms, revenues were higher than in *20X1.*

Activity 13

Task

(a) Average prices in the period January to March were:

$$\frac{5.05 + 5.02 + 5.08}{3} = \frac{15.15}{3} = £5.05$$

Average prices in the period February to April were:

$$\frac{5.02 + 5.08 + 5.11}{3} = \frac{15.21}{3} = £5.07$$

Average prices in the period March to May were:

$$\frac{5.08 + 5.11 + 5.20}{3} = \frac{15.39}{3} = £5.13$$

(b)

MEMO

To: Sam Thomas

From: Accounting Technician

Date: June 2004

Subject: Material prices

Trend in material prices

The trend shows an upward movement in prices over the period. By smoothing the individual prices, the trend is more apparent than in the original data where the upward and downward monthly prices show a less clear picture.

Use of trend in setting standards

The trend can be extrapolated to indicate what future prices are likely to be in the remainder of 2004. This may cause the organisation to alter the standard for material prices if the expected prices are going to diverge significantly from the current standard.

Other information

Two other pieces of information are as follows:

(i) The amount of materials used to make a desk. This may be unchanged but it is possible that the desk could be re-engineered to simplify its construction, possibly using less material.

(ii) The overall demand for desks – if demand were to increase significantly, the greater demand for desks would generate an increased demand for materials. The company may be able to buy these materials cheaper by obtaining quantity discounts.

10 Test your knowledge

Workbook Activity 14

Star Fuel (AAT Specimen paper) – amended

A software package outputs the following information:

Regression line y = £2,000,000 + £40,000 x Seasonal variation

Quarter	*A*	*B*	*C*	*D*
Amount	+£350,000	+£250,000	–£400,000	–£200,000
Percentage	+15%	+10%	–15%	–10%

Quarter A refers to the first quarter of annual data, B to the second quarter, C to the third and D to the fourth. The pattern then repeats itself. In terms of the specific data you input, seasonal variation A refers to Quarter 17, B to Quarter 18, C to Quarter 19 and D to Quarter 20.

Actual results

Quarter	*17*	*18*	*19*	*20*
Revenues	£3,079,500	£3,002,400	£2,346,500	£2,490,200

Task 1

Making use of the formula for the regression line, complete the table below by calculating the forecast revenues for quarters 17 to 20 using:

(a) the absolute seasonal variations;

(b) the percentage seasonal variations.

Solution

Quarter	*Season*	*Trend (W1)*	*Absolute variance*	*(a) Forecast (absolute)*	*Percentage variance*	*(b) Forecast (percentage)*
17	A	2680000	350000	3030 000	115	3082000
18	B	2720 000	250 000	2970 000	110	2992000
19	C	2760000	-400 000	2360 000	85	2346000
20	D	280000	-200000	2600 000	-90	252000

(W1) Trend for quarter 17

Trend (y) = 2000 000 + (40 000 x 17)

680 000

= 2,680,000

Task 2

(a) From your answers to Task 1, complete the table below to determine which method of calculating seasonal variations gives the best estimate of actual revenue.

(b) Having identified the preferred method, use that method to complete the table forecasting the revenue for quarters 21 to 24.

Solution

(a)

Quarter		*Actual*	*Forecast (absolute)*	*Error forecast*	*Forecast (percentage)*	*Error forecast*
17		3,079,500	3030 000	− 49500	3082000	2500
18		3,002,400	2970 000	−32400	2992000	−10400
19		2,346,500	2360 000	+ 13500	2346000	−500
20		2,490,200	2600 000	109800	2520000	+29800

The percentage seasonal variation always results in a lower error than the absolute variance; therefore the percentage seasonal variation appears to be the more accurate method. (Choose from: percentage, absolute.)

(b)

Quarter	*Season*	*Trend (W1)*	*Seasonal variation* %	*Forecast*
21	A	2,840,000	115	3,266,000
22	B	2 880 000	110	3 168 000
23	C	2920 000	85	2482 000
24	D	2 960 000	90	2664 000

(W1) y = 2000 000 + (40000 X 21)

840 000

Workbook Activity 15

Eastoft Feeds and Fertilisers Ltd use a number of standard raw materials for its product range. Product F4's main raw material is 'EF1'. The average price per tonne for this material, which is subject to seasonal change, for each quarter during 2001 was as below. The material is in short supply.

2001	*Q1*	*Q2*	*Q3*	*Q4*
Average price per tonne	£40	£44	£64	£76
Seasonal variation	–£4	–£8	+£4	+£8

Task

(a) Determine the seasonally adjusted price per tonne for raw material 'EF1' for each of the four quarters of 2001.

(b) If a similar pattern of price movements were to continue, determine the likely purchase price per tonne for each of the four quarters of 2002.

(a) **2001**

	Q1	*Q2*	*Q3*	*Q4*
Actual price per tonne	40	44	64	76
Seasonal variation	-4	-8	+4	+8
Trend	44	52	60	68

(b) **2002**

Trend +8	76	84	92	100
Seasonal variation	-4	-8	+4	+8
Forecast price per tonne	72	76	96	108

Workbook Activity 16

Eastoft Feeds and Fertilisers use a system of standard costing as a basis for their monthly management reporting.

Standards are revised on a quarterly basis to account for changes in price based on an index for specific categories of cost. The following information relates to current standards.

Category of cost	*Standard*
Direct labour rate per hour	£7.00
Raw material cost per tonne	£55.00
Fixed overhead recovery rate per hour	£12.50

The current price index for these categories and the index for each quarter were:

	Current	*Q1*	*Q2*	*Q3*	*Q4*
Direct labour	105.00	108.15	108.15	108.15	108.15
Raw material	110.00	112.75	113.87	114.45	114.45
Fixed overhead	108.00	109.08	109.62	110.17	110.50

Task

Revise the standards for each quarter on the basis of the changes highlighted in the index for each category of cost shown above.

Revision of standards based on changes in the index

Category of cost	*Current standard*	*Revised standards*			
		Q1	Q2	Q3	Q4
Direct labour hour rate	105	7.21	7.21	7.21	7.21
Raw material cost/tonne	110	56.38	56.94	57.23	57.23
Fixed overhead recovery rate per hour	108	12.63	12.68	12.75	12.79

Standard costing and variance analysis

6

Introduction

In this chapter, we examine how standards costs are set for the various inputs that go into production. This is called 'standard costing'. We then examine how and why the actual results may vary from the standard.

Examinations for Financial Performance will tend to concentrate on the calculation of variances for materials, labour and fixed overheads and the intelligent interpretation of these variances. Note that variances for revenue and variable overheads are not examined in Financial Performance.

KNOWLEDGE

Describe the use of standard units of inputs and outputs (2.2)

Explain the use of variance analysis in labour, materials and overhead costing (2.4)

SKILLS

Correctly identify variances and prepare relevant reports for management (1.7)

Analyse routine cost reports and compare with budget and standard costs to accurately identify any differences and the implications of these (1.6)

CONTENTS

1 Standard costing
2 Methods of developing standards
3 Setting standards
4 Standard cost card – absorption costing
5 Types of standard
6 Advantages and disadvantages of standard costing
7 Cost variances
8 Variance analysis – absorption costing
9 Raw material variances
10 Labour variances
11 Fixed overheads
12 Comparison of budgeted and actual results – operating statements
13 Variance analysis – marginal costing
14 Materials variances with inventory
15 Using variances backwards
16 Journal entries

1 Standard costing

1.1 Introduction

Standard costing provides us with a system that provides more immediate and detailed information to management as to why actual performance differs from expected performance.

Standard costing systems are widely used because they provide cost data which can be used for many different purposes, including the following:

(a) To assist in budget setting and evaluating performance.

(b) To act as a control device by highlighting those activities that do not conform to plan and thus alerting managers to those situations which may be 'out of control' and hence in need of corrective action.

(c) To provide a prediction of future costs to be used in decision-making.

(d) To simplify the task of tracing costs to products for inventory valuation.

(e) To provide a challenging target that individuals are motivated to achieve.

An effective standard costing system relies on standard cost reports, with variances clearly identified, to be presented in an intelligible form to management as part of the overall cost reporting cycle.

Definitions

A **standard cost** is a predetermined cost which is calculated from management's standards of efficient operation and the relevant necessary expenditure. It may be used as a basis for fixing selling prices, for valuing inventory and work in progress, and to provide control over actual costs through the process of variance analysis.

Standard costing is the preparation and use of standard costs, their comparison with actual costs, and the analysis of variances to their causes.

2 Methods of developing standards

2.1 The nature of standards

Whenever identical operations are performed or identical products are manufactured time and time again, it should be possible to decide in advance not only what they are likely to cost but also what they ought to cost. In other words, it is possible to set a standard cost for each operation or product unit, taking account of:

(a) technical standards for the quantities of material to be used and the working time required;

(b) cost standards for the material prices and hourly rates that should be paid.

2.2 Standards from past records

Past data can be used to predict future costs if operating conditions are fairly constant between past and future time periods. This method may not be appropriate for newly introduced operations.

The main disadvantage with this method is that past data may contain inefficiencies which would then be built into the standards.

2.3 Engineering standards

This involves engineers developing standards for materials, direct labour and variable overheads by studying the product and the production process, possibly with the help of time and motion studies. This method is particularly useful when managers are evaluating new products.

The main disadvantage is that engineering standards may be too tight as they may not allow for the behaviour of the workers.

3 Setting standards

3.1 Standard material usage

In setting material usage standards, the first stage is to define what quantity of material input is theoretically required to achieve one unit of measured output.

In most manufacturing operations the quantity or volume of product emerging will be less than the quantity of materials introduced. This type of waste is normal to most operations and the usage figure would be increased by an allowance for this normal waste.

3.2 Standard time allowed

The standard or allowed time for an operation is a realistic estimate of the amount of productive time required to perform that operation based on work study methods. It is normally expressed in standard hours.

Various allowances may be added to the theoretical operating time, to take account of operator fatigue and personal needs, and periodic activities such as machine setting, clearing up, regrinding tools and on-line quality inspection. An allowance may also be made for spoilt work, or for rectification of defects appearing in the course of processing.

3.3 Basic approach to price standards

When setting cost standards, there are two basic approaches:

(a) **To use the prices or rates which are current at the time the standards are set.** This has the advantage that each standard is a clearly known fact. On the other hand, if prices are likely to change then the standards based on these prices will have limited value for planning purposes.

The standards would have to be revised in detail from time to time to ensure that they are up to date. If this is not done, then any differences between standard and actual costs are likely to be largely due to invalid standards.

(b) **To use a forecast of average prices or rates over the period for which the standard is to be used.**

This can postpone the need for revision, but has the disadvantages that the standard may never correspond with observed fact (so there will be a price variance on all transactions) and the forecast may be subject to significant error.

3.4 Material price standards

In setting material price standards, a particular item of material may be purchased from several suppliers at slightly different prices; which price shall be adopted as standard? There are three possible approaches:

(a) **To identify the major supplier and to use their price as the standard**

This is particularly appropriate where there is no intention of buying large quantities from the alternative suppliers, but merely to use them as a means of ensuring continuity of supply should there be any delay or failure by the principal supplier.

(b) **To use the lowest quoted price as the standard**

This method can be used if it is desirable to put pressure on the buyer to obtain price reductions from other suppliers.

(c) **To forecast the proportion of supplies to be bought from each supplier and to calculate a weighted average price as the costing standard**

This is the most satisfactory method for control purposes if the required forecast can be made with reasonable accuracy.

Another question in relation to material price standards is whether to include the cost of carriage inwards and other costs such as non-returnable packing and transit insurance.

The objective always will be to price incoming goods at their total delivered cost, so these costs should be included in the standards.

3.5 Standard labour rates

When setting standard labour rates, one can either use basic pay rates only, or incorporate overtime premiums as well. The nature of the overtime work and the approach to cost control adopted by management will decide this issue.

(a) If a normal level of overtime work can be identified and is accepted as necessary, or if overtime is planned for the company's convenience, then the relative overtime premium payments will normally be included in the standard labour rate.

(b) If it is a management objective to reduce or eliminate overtime working, the standard rate may be restricted to basic pay.

4 Standard cost card – absorption costing

A standard cost card is built up using the technical specification for one unit.

A simple standard cost card is as follows:

Standard cost card – absorption costing

For one unit of output:	£
Direct material: 1.5 sq m @ £28 per sq m	42.00
Direct labour: 4 hours @ £5.25 per hour	21.00
Fixed overheads: 4 hours @ £7 per hour	28.00
Total standard cost	91.00

You can see that:

(a) Standard direct material cost

= Standard quantity of material × standard material price.

(b) Standard direct labour cost

= Standard direct labour hours × standard labour rate.

(c) Fixed overheads are absorbed using the direct labour hour overhead absorption rate.

(Note that variable overheads are not in the syllabus.)

5 Types of standard

5.1 Introduction

The way in which control is exercised and the interpretation and use of variances from standards will depend on which type of standard is used.

5.2 Ideal standards

In some cases standards are established on the assumption that machines and employees will work with optimal efficiency at all times, and that there will be no stoppages and no losses of material or services. Such standards would represent an ideal state of affairs and therefore the objectives they set are never achieved.

Managers who are responsible for the costs can hardly approve of targets which they can never reach and which, therefore, result in large adverse variances from the standards. This is demotivating for managers (and their staff), particularly if there is an element of performance-related pay in their remuneration. Managers and staff have often been found to 'give up' when faced with these standards.

5.3 Attainable (expected) standards

In other cases the standards set will be those which are reasonably attainable, consideration being given to the state of efficiency which can be achieved from the existing facilities. There is no question of assuming, as for ideal standard costs, that production resources will be used at maximum efficiency.

A positive effort is still made to achieve a high level of efficiency, but there is no question of going beyond what is attainable.

Management and staff are usually most motivated using this method.

5.4 Basic standards

A basic standard is one which, having been fixed, is not generally revised with changing conditions, but remains in force for a long period of time. It may be set originally having regard to either ideal or expected conditions. Under circumstances of rapid technological change or of significant price changes, basic standards are of limited value in relation to the achievement of the benefits outlined above since they will be out of date.

There may be variations on these methods, but the aim should be to select the standard cost which is likely to be the most realistic for the business concerned. It should be remembered that standards are the yardstick against which efficiency is measured and therefore, if they are unrealistic then any variances calculated will be of little meaning.

Activity 1

The setting of ideal standards should be motivational to employees.

True	
False	

6 Advantages and disadvantages of standard costing

6.1 Advantages

The advantages of standard costing fall into two broad categories: planning and control.

Planning

Predetermined standards make the preparation of forecasts and budgets much easier. If the standards are to be used for these operational decisions then they must obviously be as accurate as possible. This again means that standards should be revised on a frequent basis.

Control

Control is primarily exercised through the comparison of standard and actual results, and the isolation of variances. This is done by breaking down the simple variance identified in a budgetary control system into components based upon an expected outcome. This will highlight areas of apparent efficiency and inefficiency, and as necessary investigations as to the causes of the variance can be made. If these investigations discover the causes of the variances, then corrective action can be taken to improve efficiency in the future or alter the standards if necessary.

In addition to the above, there are subsidiary advantages such as:

(a) if the standards are perceived to be attainable, then they will serve to motivate the employees concerned;

(b) a standard costing bookkeeping system can be set up that will fulfil all requirements, for both internal and external reporting;

(c) recording of stock issues is simplified, as it is done at the standard price.

6.2 Disadvantages

A standard costing system is costly to set up and maintain, and standards must be revised on a regular basis to maintain effectiveness. It is for this reason that standard costing is most effective for well-established and repetitive processes, so that the revisions of standards are kept to a minimum.

7 Cost variances

7.1 Introduction

Definition

A cost variance is the difference between the standard cost of a product and its actual cost.

Cost variances are usually calculated for each element of cost separately, e.g. material, labour and fixed overheads.

We have seen how management will develop standard costs in advance of the period under review. During the course of that period actual costs will then be compared with standard costs, and any differences isolated for investigation as to their causes. This will then enable any corrective action to be taken as soon as possible.

If we consider top level management within the firm, perhaps the board of directors, then they will want to see a clear and succinct summary of the results for a given period. In particular they will wish to see a reconciliation between budgeted profit and actual profit that highlights the factors causing the difference.

7.2 Diagrammatic view of cost variances

Consider the cost of materials for producing 1,000 units of product X.

The standard cost of one unit is calculated as 2 kg of material at £2 per kg = £4 per unit.

To produce 1,000 units in period 1, the process actually uses 2,200 kg which cost £2.30 per kg.

The actual and standard costs for materials can be calculated as follows:

Standard cost of 1,000 units = 2,000 kg × £2 £4,000

Actual cost of 1,000 units = 2,200 kg × £2.30 £5,060

Total cost variance £1,060 (adverse)

This can be shown in a diagram as follows:

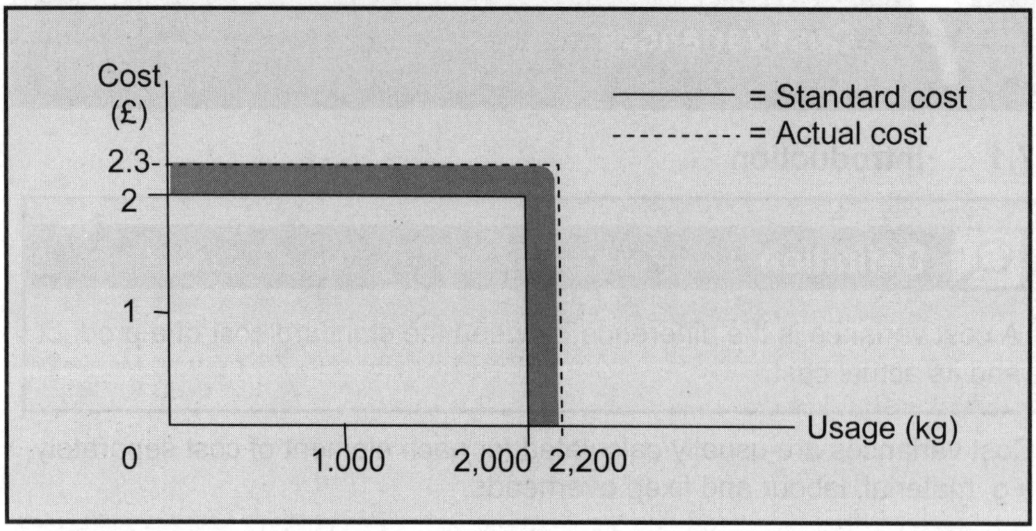

The shaded area shows the excess of the total actual cost over the total standard cost.

We need to analyse this into two parts:

(a) the price variance, i.e. the amount of the excess cost caused by actually paying £2.30 rather than standard £2.00 per unit;

(b) the usage variance, i.e. the amount of the excess cost caused by actually using 2,200 kg rather than the standard 2,000 kg.

This is shown in the diagram by dividing the shaded area of total excess cost into two parts as shown below:

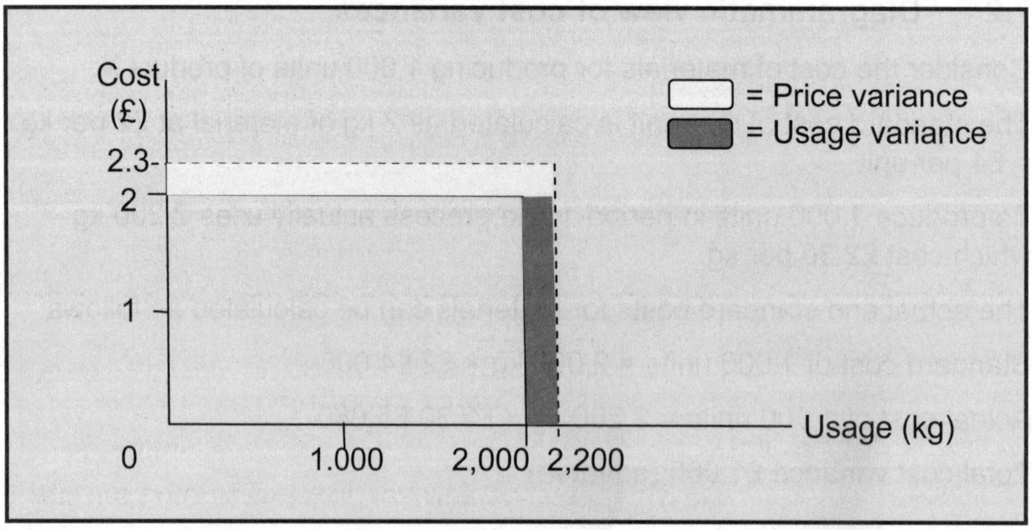

(a) The price variance is calculated as:

Quantity actually purchased × Actual price

Compared to:

Quantity actually purchased × Standard price

2,200 kg × £2.30 = £5,060

Compared to:

2,200 kg × £2.00 = £4,400

This is an adverse variance of £660 as we actually paid more than we should have paid.

(b) The usage variance is calculated as:

Quantity actually purchased × Standard price

Compared to:

Quantity that should have been used × Standard price

2,200 kg × £2.00 = £4,400

Compared to:

1,000 units x 2 kg × £2.00 = £4,000

This is an adverse variance of £400 as we actually used more than we should have used.

The two variances give the total variance as follows:

	£
Price variance	660 (adverse)
Usage variance	400 (adverse)
Total material variance	£1,060 (adverse)

7.3 A commonsense approach

The important thing to realise is that variances are quite easy if you understand what you are calculating.

All you are calculating is the difference between what something **should have cost** and what it **actually did cost**.

We shall see this time and time again as we work through the variances.

8 Variance analysis – absorption costing

8.1 Illustration

The following illustration will be used to show the computation of all necessary cost variances.

Katzman Ltd produces soap in bulk.

The standard cost per drum of soap is made up as follows:

Raw materials	100 kg costing £2 per kg
Labour	12 hours costing £3 per hour

Fixed production costs per month are budgeted at £90,000. For April 20X8, budgeted production was 7,500 drums.

The actual costs incurred in the month were:

Raw materials (900,000 kg purchased)	£1,755,000
Labour (110,000 hours paid)	£341,000
	£2,096,000
Fixed production costs	£86,000
	£2,182,000

During April 7,800 drums of soap were actually produced. There were no raw materials stocks at the start or end of the period.

8.2 Standard cost card

When standards have been set for individual operations or items of material, they can be combined to give the standard costs for products, components or other units of output.

The standard cost card for a drum of soap would appear as below:

	£
Raw materials (100 kg × £2)	200
Labour (12 hours × £3)	36
Fixed production overheads (12 hours × £1) (see working below)	12
Standard cost per drum	248

Working

The only figure requiring explanation here is the hourly fixed production overhead rate.

Based on our budgeted output, we planned to produce 7,500 drums, each taking 12 hours. Thus, budgeted hours are (7,500 × 12) = 90,000.

This gives us a standard fixed overhead absorption rate per hour of

$$\frac{£90,000}{90,000} = £1/\text{hour}$$

Notice here that we have assumed two things:

- we are operating a total absorption costing system, so that all production costs are absorbed into units produced; and
- the basis for absorbing fixed overheads is labour hours.

8.3 A simplistic comparison

Let us now compare the standard total costs with the actual total costs incurred.

	Standard cost	*Actual cost*	*Variance*	
Output (drums)	7,500	7,800	300	F
	£	£	£	
Direct materials	1,500,000 (W1)	1,755,000	255,000	A
Labour	270,000 (W2)	341,000	71,000	A
Fixed production overheads	90,000	86,000	4,000	F
	1,860,000	2,182,000	322,000	A

(A = Adverse, F = Favourable)

Workings

(W1) Total direct materials at standard= 7,500 drums × (100 kg × £2) = £1,500,000

(W2) Total labour cost at standard = 7,500 drums × (12 hours × £3) = £270,000

The standard and actual costs are not directly comparable. The budgeted activity level was 7,500 drums, but 7,800 were actually produced. It is not surprising therefore that total actual costs exceed the budget.

It would be much more useful to management to compare the actual costs of producing 7,800 drums with the standard costs of producing that same quantity.

8.4 A better comparison

A better comparison as suggested above is to compare the standard and actual costs of the actual quantity produced. This is done by what is known as 'flexing the budget'.

	Standard cost of budgeted output	*Standard cost of actual output*	*Actual cost of actual output*	*Variance*	
Output (drums)	7,500	7,800	7,800	–	
	£	£	£	£	
Direct materials	1,500,000	1,560,000 (W1)	1,755,000	195,000	A
Labour	270,000	280,800 (W2)	341,000	60,200	A
Fixed production overheads	90,000	90,000 (W3)	86,000	4,000	F
	1,860,000	1,930,800	2,182,000	251,200	A

Workings

(W1) 7,800 drums × 100 kg × £2 = 1,560,000

(W2) 7,800 drums × 12 hours × £3 = 280,800

(W3) Remember that the definition of a fixed cost is a cost that does not change as the output changes.

The above table shows the revised variances caused by comparing the standard and actual costs for the actual output of 7,800 drums.

Note: The preparation of variances may be beginning to seem a little arbitrary; we appear to be able to compare different things and produce a different version of what the variances are - surely there must be a right way of doing it? The important point to remember is that you are producing the most useful information for management. There is no right or unique way of doing this. The most useful way to produce the variances is to 'flex the budget' and that is how variances are always produced.

9 Raw material variances

9.1 Introduction

Let us now begin our detailed analysis of the difference between standard and actual cost, by looking at raw materials.

9.2 Total material cost variance

(a) To produce 7,800 drums we should have used (7,800 × 100 kg) = 780,000 kg. The material should have cost £2 per kg.

	£
Therefore, 7,800 drums should have cost 780,000 kg × £2 =	1,560,000
(b) To produce 7,800 drums we actually used 900,000 kg. This actually cost	1,755,000
Total cost variance (adverse)	195,000

The budgeted level of 7,500 drums is irrelevant here, since we must compute the standard cost for **actual** production.

We shall now analyse this total variance into a price and usage variance.

9.3 Materials price variance

We actually purchased 900,000 kg.

The price variance is simply the difference between what 900,000 kg should have cost and what they did actually cost.

	£
At actual price per kg, they did cost	1,755,000
Actual quantity x Standard Price 900,000 kg x £2	1,800,000
Price variance (favourable)	45,000

Therefore, there is a favourable price variance of £45,000.

This means that the actual price per kg purchased must have been less than standard. We can compute the actual price as follows:

$$\frac{\text{Actual cost}}{\text{Quantity purchased}} = \frac{£1{,}755{,}000}{900{,}000} = £1.95\,/\,\text{kg}$$

Thus, for every kg we purchased, we actually paid £0.05 less than the standard price. Clearly, since this is a cost saving, it gives rise to a favourable variance.

9.4 Materials usage variance

We actually produced 7,800 drums.

	£
Actual quantity x Standard price	
900,000 kg x £2	= 1,800,000
Standard quantity x Standard price	= 1,560,000
7,800 units x 100 kg x £2	
Usage variance (adverse)	240,000

Remember, this over-usage is valued at the standard price per kg.

Clearly, the variance is adverse, since the additional usage above standard incurs extra cost.

Reconciliation

We can summarise the above computations as follows:

£

	Calculations		£	
Step 1	Actual quantity purchased at actual cost	900,000 kg	1,755,000	Price variance £45,000 F
Step 2	Actual quantity purchased at standard cost	900,000 kg × £2	1,800,000	Usage variance £240,000 A
Step 3	Standard quantity that should have been used at standard cost	780,000 kg × £2	1,560,000	Total variance £195,000 A

This tabulation is the method that we will use to compute the variances.

Thus, what we have really done is the following:

Actual quantity × Actual price	Price variance
Actual quantity × Standard price	
Standard quantity for actual production × Standard price	Usage variance

Activity 2

The standard direct material usage per unit of product K is 0.4 tonnes. The standard price of the material is £30/tonne.

During April, 500 units of K were produced using 223 tonnes of material costing £6,913. Calculate the direct material usage variance.

Standard usage of 500 units of K:

Actual usage		
Excess usage		tonnes

Valued at standard price of £30/tonne:

Direct material usage variance is:

£______________

9.5 The style of examination question – materials

A typical example is shown below for materials.

Example

Materials Ltd makes boxes and the budget and actual results for June 2008 were as follows.

		Budget		*Actual*
Production (units)		1,000		1,200
Direct materials	500 kgs	£5,000	530 kgs	£5,700

Calculate the following variances:

-Variance	£	A/F
Direct Material Price	400	A
Direct Material Usage	700	F

Workings

Standard price of materials per kilogram £5,000/500kg = £10 / kg

Standard usage for one unit = 500kg/1,000 = 0.5 kg

Standard usage for actual production = 0.5 × 1,200 = 600kg

(a) Direct materials price variance

530 kg did cost	£5,700
530 kg should have cost 530 × £10	£5,300
Price variance	400 (A)

(b) Direct materials usage variance

1,200 units did use 530 kg	
which should have cost at standard price 530 × £10	£5,300
1,200 units should have used 600 kg	
which should have cost at standard price 600 × £10	£6,000
Usage variance	£700 (F)

Tutorial note

You are not asked to reconcile the total materials variance, but you could do this as follows.

Total material budget cost of 1,200 units from data in question =

(£5,000/1,000 units) × 1,200 units =	£6,000
Total actual cost from data in question	£5,700
Total variance	£300 (F)
Variances per answer	
Price	£400 (A)
Usage	£700 (F)
	£300 (F)

9.6 Interpretation of the variances

The variances computed in 9.4 above act as error signals to management. They in no way explain why we have used more material than the standard allowed, or why we have succeeded in purchasing material more cheaply than the standard price.

If management decided that these exceptional performances (compared to budget) demanded explanation, then investigation would have to be carried out as to their causes. This would enable responsibility for the variance to be identified, and management could then take any corrective action considered necessary.

Some possible causes of the variances in 9.4 above are listed below.

Price variance

Purchase of a cheaper substitute than the material per the standard cost and specification. Such an action may be a deliberate policy of the buying department (and therefore controllable), or may result from uncontrollable external factors such as market shortages.

- Bulk buying leading to discounts that the standard had not envisaged.
- Market factors leading to a lower price than anticipated (this would apply for example where raw materials depend upon random factors such as the weather affecting harvests).
- Using different suppliers from normal.
- The standard may have been set at a 'mid-year' price, anticipating future price rises. Thus we would expect favourable variances initially.

Usage variance

- Sub-standard raw materials. Notice the possibility here of interdependence between the variances. If the favourable price variance is due to buying a cheaper substitute, this may well cause operating inefficiencies leading to an adverse usage variance. Thus, in allocating responsibility for the variances, after investigation we may hold the purchasing manager responsible for the usage variance!
- Mechanical breakdown leading to spoilage of raw materials.
- The standard itself could be too tight (is it an ideal standard that is unattainable in practice?).

- Measurement errors. For example, if there are raw materials closing stocks that have not been recorded, this would overstate actual usage for the current period, but underestimate usage in the next period. Widely fluctuating variances from period to period may be indicative of such errors.
- Operating inefficiencies.

Activity 3

Total material variance

The standard direct material cost of product A is £5. During August 600 units of product A were made (standard usage of material is 1 kg per unit) and the actual direct material cost was £3,200. Calculate the direct material total cost variance for the period.

Solution

Variance	£	F/A
Direct material total cost		

Activity 4

Materials price and usage variance

A raw material, used in the manufacture of product F has a standard price of £1.30 per litre. During May, 2,300 litres were bought and used at a cost of £3,128. The 600 units made should have used 4 litres per unit. Calculate the direct material price and usage variance for May.

Variance	£	F/A
Direct material price		
Direct material usage		

10 Labour variances

10.1 Total labour cost variance

Referring back to the original example, you will see that the standard for labour per drum of soap is 12 hours at £3 per hour.

The actual results were:

Hours paid	110,000	costing £341,000
Actual production	7,800 drums	

Total labour cost variance

To produce 7,800 drums we should have taken (7,800 × 12 hours) = 93,600 hours

	£
This did cost	341,000
This should have cost, at the standard rate, (93,600 × £3)	280,800
Total cost variance (adverse)	60,200

Note that, just as for materials variances:

- the variance is adverse because the actual labour cost exceeds the standard cost for actual production;
- the budgeted production level of 7,500 drums is again irrelevant;
- again, we would obtain more useful management information if we could analyse the total cost variance further into the rate of pay and efficiency variances.

10.2 Labour rate variance

We actually paid for 110,000 hours.

	£
This did cost	341,000
At standard rate per hour, this should have cost (110,000 × £3)	330,000
Rate variance (adverse)	11,000

This means that the actual rate of pay per hour must have been more than the standard.

The actual rate is $\frac{\text{Actual cost}}{\text{Hours paid}} = \frac{£341{,}000}{110{,}000} = £3.10/\text{hour}$

Thus, for every hour paid for, we have actually paid £0.10 more than the standard price, and so the labour rate of pay variance is adverse.

10.3 Labour efficiency variance

We actually produced 7,800 drums.

		£
This did take 110,000 hrs which should have cost £3/hr	=	330,000
At standard efficiency, this should have taken (7,800 × 12)		
93,600 hrs which should have cost £3/hr	=	280,800
Efficiency variance		49,200

This variance is adverse, because we have taken more hours, and therefore incurred more cost, to produce 7,800 drums than the standard allowed.

Reconciliation

We can summarise the above computations as follows:

			£	£
Step 1	Actual hours paid at actual rate (actual cost)	110,000 hrs	341,000	11,000 A Rate of pay variance
Step 2	Actual hours paid at standard rate	110,000 hrs × £3	330,000	
Step 3	Standard hours that should have been paid at standard rate (standard cost)	93,600 hrs × £3	280,800	49,200 A Efficiency variance

Again, we can show the above in 'shorthand' as:

Actual hours paid	×	Actual rate	Rate variance
Actual hours paid	×	Standard rate	
Standard hours for actual production	×	Standard rate	Efficiency variance

Activity 5

The standard direct labour cost of product H is £7. During January 450 units of product H were made and the actual direct labour cost was £3,450. Calculate the direct labour total cost variance of the period.

	£
Standard direct labour cost of 450 units:	
Actual direct labour cost	
Direct labour total cost variance	

10.4 Examination style questions – labour

Example

Labour Ltd makes boxes and the budget and actual results for June 2008 were as follows.

		Budget		*Actual*
Production (units)		1,000		1,200
Direct labour	300 hrs	£4,500	340 hrs	£5,440

Calculate the following

(a) Direct labour rate variance

(b) Direct labour efficiency variance

Solution

Variance	£	A/F
Direct labour rate	340	A
Direct labour efficiency	300	F

Standard labour rate per hour

£4,500/300hr = £15 per hr

Standard labour hours for one unit = 300/1,000 = 0.3 hrs

Standard labour hours for actual production = 0.3 × 1,200 = 360 hrs

(a) Direct labour rate variance

340 hrs did cost	£5,440
340 hrs should have cost 340 × £15 =	£5,100
Labour rate variance	£340 (A)

(b) Direct labour efficiency variance

1,200 units did use 340 hrs	
which should have cost at standard price 340 × £15	£5,100
1,200 units should have used 360 hrs	
which should have cost at standard rate 360 × £15	£5,400
Labour efficiency variance	£300 (F)

Tutorial note

You are not asked to reconcile the total materials variance, but you could do this as follows.

Total labour budget cost of 1,200 units from data in question

= (£4,500/1,000 units) × 1,200 units =	£5,400
Total actual cost from data in question	£5,440
Total variance	£40 (A)

Variances per answer

Labour rate	£340 (A)
Labour efficiency	£300 (F)
	£40 A

10.5 Idle time

The labour force can be paid for a greater number of hours than they actually work. This may be due to a late delivery of raw materials preventing production and causing the workers to stand idle. If this is the case, then this idle time affects the labour efficiency variance and needs to be separated from it.

Actual hours paid × actual labour rate

Rate variance

Actual hours paid × standard labour rate

Idle time variance

Actual hours worked × standard labour rate

Efficiency variance

Standard labour hours × standard labour rate

For example, if the labour force were paid a standard rate of £10 per hour and in January they were paid for 6500 hours, but only worked 6000 hours. During the month 620 units were made that take 10 hours each.

Calculate the idle time and efficiency variances.

6,500 × £10 = £65,000

Idle time = £5,000 A

6,000 × £10 = £60,000

Efficiency = £2,000 F

620 × 10 × £10 = £62,000

All idle time variances are adverse.

10.6 Interpretation of labour variances

Some possible causes of labour variances may be:

Rate of pay variances

(i) Failure to include overtime premiums in the standard, or failure to allow for pay increases during the period.

(ii) Rush orders necessitating costly overtime working.

(iii) Using different grades of labour compared to that budgeted for, which could of course lead to an adverse or favourable variance.

Idle time variances

(i) Shortage of work

(ii) Machine breakdown

(iii) Shortage of material

Efficiency variances

(i) Good quality raw materials could lead to favourable labour efficiency, or of course sub-standard materials could cause inefficiencies. Time could be lost in setting up machines after breakdowns, or rectifying poor quality output.

(ii) Random fluctuations such as high morale due to the local football team's winning streak.

(iii) Although this last example is somewhat flippant, it does illustrate an important point. We are dealing here with labour – a human asset. As such its efficiency will depend greatly upon behavioural factors.

The plan itself could be wrong! Remember that to compute the variance we compare standard labour time with actual labour time. If the standard represents an ideal time, then adverse variances are inevitable. Alternatively, if the standard is outdated due to technical innovations or revised working practices, then again we would expect to see variances.

Activity 6

The following data relates to product C:

Actual production of C (units)	700
Standard wage rate/hour	£4
Standard time allowance per unit of C (hours)	1.50
Actual hours worked	1,000
Actual hours paid	1,050
Actual wage cost	£4,200

Calculate (a) the direct labour rate variance, (b) the idle time variance and (c) the efficiency variance from the above data.

(a) Actual hours paid did cost

Actual hours paid should cost

______

Rate variance

______

(b) Idle time:

Hours paid =

Hours worked =

Idle time variance = ______

(c) Standard hours produced:

Actual hours worked =

Efficiency variance ______

Activity 7

Compute labour variances for the following examples:

(a) Standard — 2 hours per unit at £3 per hour
Hours paid and worked — 5,000 hours, cost £14,000
Units produced — 2,800 units

Variances	£	A/F
Direct labour rate		
Direct labour efficiency		

(b) Standard — 3 hours per unit, £12 per unit
Original budget — 20,000 units
Production — 18,000 units
Hours worked — 48,000 hours
Hours paid — 50,000 hours, cost £210,000

Variances	£	A/F
Direct labour rate		
Idle time		
Direct labour efficiency		

11 Fixed overheads

11.1 Introduction

Remember that, in order to set a fixed overhead absorption rate per hour, we had to make an estimate of activity level in hours, as well as of the fixed cost itself.

The relevant information from the example is:

Budgeted fixed production costs	=	£90,000
Standard hours per drum	=	12 hours
Budgeted production	=	7,500 drums

The actual results were:

Labour	=	110,000 hours paid
Fixed production costs	=	£86,000
Production	=	7,800 drums

From these estimates we obtained the standard fixed overhead absorption rate per hour:

$$\frac{\text{Budgeted cost}}{\text{Budgeted hours}} = \frac{£90{,}000}{(7{,}500 \times 12)} = £1/\text{hour}$$

This means that, as units are produced, we will absorb £12 (12 hours at the standard of £1) per unit. Thus, there may be a variance due to the over or under absorption of fixed overheads.

For example, if actual fixed costs were exactly as per budget of £90,000, but we actually produced 8,000 units, then we would absorb 8,000 × 12 hours × £1 = £96,000.

Thus we would have over-absorbed £6,000, due to the increased production compared to budget. Finished goods will therefore be valued at £6,000 more than actual cost, and so a favourable variance would be needed to reduce this standard cost back to actual cost. This variance is called the volume variance, and only arises because we have chosen to absorb fixed overheads into production.

11.2 Fixed overheads – total cost variance

	£
The actual cost was	86,000
In producing 7,800 drums we have absorbed (7,800 × £12)	93,600
Total cost variance (favourable)	7,600

11.3 Fixed overhead expenditure variance

Since fixed costs do not vary with the level of production, the expenditure variance is simply a comparison of budgeted and actual fixed costs.

	£
Actual total cost	86,000
Budgeted cost	90,000
Expenditure variance (favourable)	4,000

Thus we have actually incurred, regardless of activity level, £4,000 less fixed costs than budgeted. The variance is therefore favourable.

11.4 Fixed overhead volume variance

We actually produced 7,800 drums.

	£
Budgeted absorption (7,500 × £12)	90,000
Actual absorption (7,800 × £12)	93,600
Volume variance (favourable)	3,600

Remember that the variance is favourable because we have over absorbed fixed overheads. We thus require a favourable variance to compensate for this over-absorption.

We have produced 300 units more than budget, thus over-absorbing fixed overheads by 300 × the standard rate of £12 per unit i.e. £3,600 favourable volume variance.

11.5 Sub-division of the volume variance

The volume variance as computed above can be subdivided further to explain why the level of activity was different from budget. In other words, how did we manage to produce 300 units more than the budget of 7,500?

- Capacity variance

  This compares actual hours worked with the budgeted hours, and is favourable where actual hours exceed budgeted hours since squeezing more hours out of our factory enables us to make extra units.

- Efficiency variance

  This compares standard hours that should have been worked with actual hours worked, and so is the usual measure of efficiency seen already for both labour and variable overheads.

These sub-variances can be calculated as shown below:

Capacity variance

	Hours	£
Budgeted hours at the standard rate	90,000	90,000
Actual hours worked at the standard rate	110,000	110,000
Capacity variance (favourable)	20,000	20,000

Efficiency variance

	Hours	£
Actual hours worked at the standard rate	110,000	110,000
Standard hours that should have been worked at the standard rate	93,600	93,600
Efficiency variance (adverse)	16,400	16,400

Reconciliation

	Hours	£
Budgeted hours at actual total cost	90,000	86,000
Expenditure variance (favourable)	–	4,000
Budgeted hours at standard cost	90,000	90,000
Capacity variance (favourable)	20,000	20,000
Actual hours at standard cost	110,000	110,000
Efficiency variance (adverse)	16,400	16,400
Standard hours at standard cost	93,600	93,600

Thus, if we absorb fixed overheads on the basis of labour hours it enables us to split the volume variance further into capacity and efficiency elements. The total cost variance must remain the same. The 'variance tree' below may help as a convenient way of remembering this.

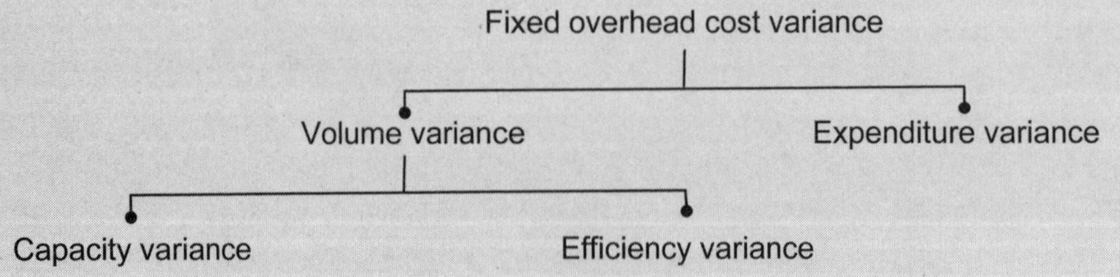

11.6 Examination style questions – fixed overheads

Example

Fixed Ltd makes boxes and the budget and actual results for June 2008 were as follows

	Budget		*Actual*
Production (units)	1,000		1,200
Fixed overheads	£2,000		£2,500

Calculate the following

(a) Budgeted overhead absorption rate per unit

(b) Fixed overheads absorbed into actual production

(c) Fixed overhead expenditure variance

(d) Fixed overhead volume variance

Solution

(a) Budgeted overhead absorption rate per unit

£2,000/1,000 = £2 per unit

(b) Fixed overheads absorbed into actual production

Units actually produced = 1,200 units

Overheads absorbed into actual production = 1,200 × £2 = £2,400

(c) Fixed overhead expenditure variance

£2,000 – £2,500 = £500 (A)

(d) Fixed overhead volume variance

Actual overhead absorbed =	£2,400
Budgeted overhead =	£2,000
Variance	£400 (F)

Tutorial note

You are not asked to reconcile the fixed overhead variance, but you could do this as follows.

Overhead absorbed	2,400
Actual overhead	2,500
Total variance	£100 (A)
Variances per answer	
Expenditure variance	£500 (A)
Volume variance	£400 (F)
	£100 (A)

11.7 Usefulness of fixed overhead variances

We must be clear throughout the above analysis that we are dealing with a fixed cost. Refer back to the earlier sections on materials and labour, and you will see that there are no volume variances for these items. The volume variance arises for fixed overheads purely because of our desire to absorb fixed costs into production, and the consequent setting up of an arbitrary absorption basis such as labour hours.

Conflict

Thus we are really seeing a conflict between the use of standard costing for control purposes, and the use of standards for product costing. We may for example base our selling price on cost plus a fixed mark-up, in which case a production cost inclusive of fixed costs may be desired. However, for control purposes the only variance of any real significance is the expenditure variance. Since we are dealing with a fixed cost, then the cost will not change simply because we are operating at something other than budgeted output level.

Thus the volume variance is really uncontrollable, and arises due to our failure to operate at the budgeted activity level.

A partial solution

One solution to this criticism is to sub-divide the volume variance into capacity and efficiency. The capacity variance compares actual hours worked with budgeted hours that should have been worked. When actual hours exceed budgeted hours, the capacity variance is favourable, because we are making better use of our facilities than expected. In other words, we have obtained more productive hours worth of output for the same fixed cost.

If the capacity variance is of some use in terms of explaining utilisation of facilities, then how can we use the efficiency variance? The answer is that the fixed overhead efficiency variance is very different from the efficiency variances computed for labour. Efficient use of the latter can reduce actual cost, but fixed overhead cost cannot be affected by efficiency in the short-run. Further, there is little to be gained in terms of information to management since they are already aware of inefficiencies through the variable cost reports.

Activity 8

PD

PD has the following data concerning its fixed production overheads:

Budget cost	£50,000
Budget production	10,000 units
Budget labour hours	20,000
Actual cost	£47,500
Actual production	8,450 units
Actual labour hours	16,600

Calculate the fixed overhead total variance assuming an absorption system based upon labour hours.

PD

Absorption rate = £____________ per std hour

Actual output in standard hours = ______________ standard hours

	£
Overhead cost	
Overhead absorbed	
Variance	

11.8 Exam style questions

Example

The accountant of Back Ltd has calculated the fixed overhead capacity variance as £8,000 adverse for the month of July 2008.

Fixed overhead incurred in the month was £90,000. Budgeted production for the month was 85,000 boxes Actual production was 80,000 boxes. The overhead recovery rate was £1 per box

Calculate

(a) Budgeted overheads

(b) Fixed overhead expenditure variance

(c) Fixed overhead volume variance

(d) Fixed overhead efficiency variance

Solution

(**Tutorial note** – most of the question is normal variance analysis. It is in part (d) (step 4 below) that you have to use details of the capacity variance given in the question to work back to the efficiency variance asked for).

(a) Budgeted overhead was £85,000. Budgeted production was 85,000 boxes and the recovery rate was set as £1.

(b) **Calculate the expenditure variance**

	£
Actual overhead	90,000
Budgeted overhead	85,000
	5,000 (A)

(c) **Calculate the volume variance**

	£
Budgeted overhead	85,000
Actual overhead absorbed (80,000 × £1)	80,000
	5,000 (A)

(The business fell short of budgeted absorption by £5,000)

(d) **Calculate the overhead efficiency variance**

Volume variance = capacity + efficiency variance

	£
Volume variance =	5,000 (A)
Capacity variance = (per question)	8,000 (A)
Efficiency variance	3,000 (F)

(The volume variance shows that the business did not produce as much as budget and under-absorbed £5,000 of overhead. The capacity variance shows that £8,000 was under-absorbed due to insufficient hours being worked. This means that £3,000 was recovered by the workforce producing more goods in the time worked).

Activity 9

From the information below calculate (a) the fixed overhead variance and (b) all the sub-variances, using absorption costing.

TP has the following data concerning its fixed production overheads:

Budget fixed overhead	£44,000
Budget production	8,000 units
Budget labour hours	16,000
Actual fixed overhead	£47,500
Actual production	8,450 units
Actual labour hours	16,600

Fixed overhead recovery rate =

Standard hours per unit =

(a) **Fixed overhead total variance**

(b) **Sub-variances**

(i) Fixed overhead expenditure variance:

(ii) Fixed overhead volume variance:

The volume variance can be analysed into a capacity and efficiency variance.

(iii) Fixed overhead capacity variance:

(iv) Fixed overhead efficiency variance:

Activity 10

Malik Brothers run a taxi and courier service both locally and a specific service to Manchester Airport for holiday makers and business personnel.

On the Manchester Airport run the 'round trip' is benchmarked as 5 standard hours. In the quarter ended 31 March 2002, 182 standard trips are planned. (Overheads are recovered based on standard trips.)

The fixed costs incurred by the business, including the drivers' salary, are budgeted to be £11,500 for the period.

The actual fixed costs for the period were £12,400 and 175 standard trips were made. The actual hours worked were 940.

Task

Calculate:

(a) The standard hours in the budget.

(b) The fixed overhead recovery rate per standard hour.

(c) The fixed overhead recovered in the quarter ended 31 March 2002.

(d) The fixed overhead total variance.

(e) The fixed overhead expenditure variance.

(f) The fixed overhead volume variance.

(g) The fixed overhead capacity variance.

(h) The fixed overhead efficiency variance.

(a) **Standard hours in the budget**

(b) **Fixed overhead recovery rate per standard hour**

£ per standard hour

(c) **Fixed overhead recovered**

(d) Fixed overhead total variance

(e) Fixed overhead expenditure variance

(f) Fixed overhead volume variance

(g) Fixed overhead capacity variance

(h) Fixed overhead efficiency variance

12 Comparison of budgeted and actual results – operating statements

The Operating Statement with absorption costing is a statement that reconciles:

- the total standard cost of actual output (production), with
- the total actual cost of actual output (production).

Note that the 'total standard cost of actual production' is not the same as the original budgeted cost (£1,860,000 in the example per paragraph 8.4) or even the flexed budgeted cost (£1,930,800 in that example).

It is the standard cost per unit × the actual output of the period, i.e.

£248 × 7,800 units = £1,934,400

The reason for this difference is that the total standard cost of actual output includes the fixed overhead absorption rate for all units produced (£12 × 7,800 = £93,600) whereas the original and flexed budget only includes the fixed overhead budget figure of £90,000.

		£	£	£
Total standard cost of actual output (7,800 × £248)				1,934,400
Cost variances		*Adverse*	*Favourable*	
Materials	price		45,000	
	usage	240,000		
Labour	rate of pay	11,000		
	efficiency	49,200		
Fixed overheads	expenditure		4,000	
	capacity		20,000	
	efficiency	16,400		
Net variances (adverse, therefore increase costs)		316,600	69,000	247,600
Actual cost				2,182,000

13 Variance analysis – marginal costing

13.1 Standard cost card

So far in this chapter we have dealt exclusively with the calculations for absorption costing. We shall now look at the calculations for marginal costing.

There is only one very important difference between the two. As we have seen, with absorption costing we absorb the fixed overheads into the units produced at a standard absorption rate based on labour hours.

With marginal costing, we don't attempt to absorb the fixed overheads into the units produced.

The standard cost card will look as follows.

Standard cost card – marginal costing

	£
Raw material: 100 g × £2	200.00
Labour: 12 hours @ £3 per hour	36.00
Total standard cost	236.00

You can see that the standard costs for direct material and labour are calculated exactly as before:

(a) Standard direct material cost = Standard quantity of material × standard material price.

(b) Standard direct labour cost = Standard direct labour hours × standard labour rate.

The only difference is that there is no standard amount for fixed overheads absorbed into the units.

13.2 Variance analysis – marginal costing

Having mastered the sometimes tricky calculations in this chapter so far, you will be delighted to know that the calculations of the material and labour variances are exactly the same as before (and so we don't calculate them again here). Even better, if you struggled a little with the fixed overhead variances, the calculation of the fixed overhead variance in marginal costing is very easy.

13.3 The fixed overhead variance

Taking the same example as before, the fixed overhead variance is simply the expenditure variance (the difference between the budgeted fixed cost and the actual fixed cost incurred). There is no volume or other variance because we are not attempting to absorb the fixed overheads into the units – hence no volume variance can arise.

Actual fixed cost	£86,000
Budgeted fixed cost	£90,000
Fixed cost variance	£4,000

13.4 Comparison of budgeted and actual results – marginal costing

Having computed all of the variances, we can now reconcile the budgeted and actual cost. Remember that we are dealing here with marginal costing.

		£	£	£
Budgeted cost (7,800 × £236)				1,840,800
Cost variances		*Adverse*	*Favourable*	
Materials	price		45,000	
	usage	240,000		
Labour	rate of pay	11,000		
	efficiency	49,200		
		300,200	45,000	255,200
				2,096,000
Add budgeted fixed overhead				90,000
Fixed overheads variance	expenditure		4,000	(4,000)
Actual cost				2,182,000

Activity 11

The following budgetary control report has been provided for Drug Limited:

	Budget		*Actual*	
Production		14,700		13,500
Direct material	4,140 kgs	£20,520	3,750 kgs	£20,000
Direct labour	920 hrs	£4,238	890 hrs	£3,971
Fixed overheads		£10,250		£9,600
Total cost		£35,008		£33,571

The following variances have been calculated:

Direct materials	1,413 A
Direct materials	258 F
Direct labour rate	129 F
Direct labour efficiency	208 A
Fixed overhead expenditure	650 F
Fixed overhead volume	837 A

Produce an operating statement under absorption costing.

Budgeted/standard cost for actual production			32150
Variances	**F**	**A**	
Direct materials price	500	1413	
Direct materials usage	258		
Direct labour rate	129		
Direct labour efficiency		208	
Fixed overhead expenditure	650		
Fixed overhead volume		837	
Total variance	1037	2458	1421
Actual cost of actual production			33571

Produce an operating statement under ~~marginal~~ costing.

Budgeted/standard variable cost for ~~actual~~ production			22737
Budgeted fixed costs			10250
Variances	**F**	**A**	
Direct materials price	258		
Direct materials usage		1413	
Direct labour rate	129		
Direct labour efficiency		208	
Fixed overhead expenditure	650		
Total variance	1037	1621	584
Actual cost of actual production			33571

14 Materials variances with inventory

14.1 Introduction

So far we have only considered an example where all the materials purchased were used so that there is no inventory at the end of the period.

We need to consider cases where all the materials purchased are not used and inventory therefore remains at the end of the period.

14.2 Materials price variance calculated on purchases

The most important thing to understand is that the materials price variance is calculated on the total of all the materials purchased in the period, whether they are used or not.

This means that any inventory carried to the next period is carried at its standard cost.

Note that the materials usage variance is based on the quantity of materials used as before.

Example

X Ltd purchases 4,000 kg of material at a cost of £8,400. It uses 3,300 kg to produce 600 of product A. Product A's standard cost card for material is as follows:

	Standard cost per unit
	£
Material – 5 kg at £2 per kg	10.00

Calculate:

(a) the price variance;

(b) the usage variance;

(c) the value of closing inventory in the cost records.

Solution

(a) **Price variance**

This is calculated on all the materials purchased whether they are used in production or not.

			£	
Actual cost of 4,000 kg		=	8,400	
Actual quantity purchased x Standard price	= 4,000 × £2	=	8,000	
			——	
Price variance (adverse)			400	(A)
			——	

(b) **Usage variance**

			£	
Actual quantity used x Standard price	= 3,300 kg × £2	=	6,600	
Standard cost of producing 600 units	= 600 × 5kg ×£2	=	6,000	
			——	
Usage variance (adverse)			600	(A)
			——	

(c) **Closing inventory**

Closing inventory will be valued at standard cost

Purchased	4,000 kg
Used	3,300 kg
Closing inventory	700 kg

Value per cost accounts = 700 × £2 = £1,400.

Activity 12

Y Ltd

Y Ltd produces a product B which has the following standard cost for materials.

	Standard cost per unit
	£
Material – 5 kg at £3 per kg	15.00

Y Ltd produces 100 units of B in a period. It purchased 750 kg of material at a cost of £2,500 and uses 600 kg for production.

Calculate:

(a) the price variance;

(b) the value of closing inventory of material in the cost records;

(c) the usage variance.

(a)

	£
Actual cost of materials purchased	
Standard cost of materials purchased	

(b) Closing inventory (kg) = Purchase quantity – quantity used

= ___________

Valued at standard cost, this gives a closing inventory valuation of £ _________.

(c)

	£
Actual materials used at standard price	
Standard cost of producing 100 B	

15 Using variances backwards

15.1 Introduction

So far, variance calculations have started with standard and actual costs given in the question and you have been required to calculate the variances.

The examiner may also set questions where the question will, for example, give the standard and the variance and ask you to calculate the actual.

Example

A Ltd purchases 1,000 kg of material at a cost of £550.

The adverse price variance is £50. What was the standard cost of 1 kg of material?

Solution

	£
Actual cost of 1,000 kg	550
Adverse variance	(50) (A)
Therefore, standard cost of 1,000 kg	500
Therefore, standard cost of 1 kg	0.50

Example

Alternatively, you could be given data on the standard cost and variance and be asked to calculate the actual cost paid.

For example, B Ltd purchases 200 litres of oil which should have cost £1 per litre at standard. The adverse price variance is £0.10 per litre. Calculate the actual cost of the 200 litres purchased.

Solution

	£
200 litres should have cost 200 × £1	200
Price variance = 200 × £0.10	20 (A)
Therefore, 200 litres did cost	£220

Example

An added complication could involve a change in inventory, for example.

C Ltd produces 600 widgets in March.

The standard cost card for a widget shows the following:

	Standard cost per unit
	£
Material – 3 kg at £2 per kg	6.00

There was no materials usage variance.

There was no opening inventory but closing inventory of material was 200 kg.

There was a £200 adverse price variance.

Calculate the actual amount paid for materials purchased in March.

Solution

	Kg
Standard amount of material used (600 × 3 kg)	1,800
No usage variance, therefore actual amount used	1,800
Closing inventory	200
Total purchased	2,000

	£
Standard cost of purchases 2,000 × £2	4,000
Price variance	200 (A)
Actual cost	4,200

16 Journal entries

16.1 Introduction

A ledger account is usually kept for each variance. As a general rule, all variances are recorded at the point at which they arise.

16.2 General rules

You will find the following general rules helpful when recording variances in the ledger accounts:

(a) The materials price variance is recorded in the materials inventory account.

(b) The labour rate variance is recorded in the wages control account.

(c) The material usage and labour efficiency variances are recorded in the work in progress account.

(d) The fixed production overhead expenditure variance is recorded in the production overhead control account while the volume, capacity or efficiency variances are recorded in work in progress.

At the end of a period the variance accounts are totalled and transferred to the profit and loss account. **Adverse** variances are **debited** and **favourable** variances are **credited** to the profit and loss account.

Example

A management accountant has calculated the following variances for the month of March:

	£
Materials price	4,500 A
Materials usage	200 F
Labour rate	1,050 F
Labour efficiency	1,200 A
Fixed overhead expenditure	2,100 A
Fixed overhead efficiency	400 A

Required

Record the variances in the ledger accounts.

Solution

Dr	Material price variance account	4,500
Cr	Raw material stores control account	4,500
Dr	Work in progress account	200
Cr	Material usage variance account	200
Dr	Wages control account	1,050
Cr	Labour rate variance account	1,050
Dr	Labour efficiency variance account	1,200
Cr	Work in progress account	1,200
Dr	Fixed overhead expenditure variance account	2,100
Cr	Production overhead control account	2,100
Dr	Fixed overhead efficiency variance account	400
Cr	Work in progress account	400

Activity 13

An adverse labour efficiency variance has arisen at J plc. The management accountant will record it in the ledger accounts as:

A Dr Labour efficiency variance: Cr Wages control account

B Dr Labour efficiency variance; Cr Work in progress account

C Dr Wages control account; Cr Labour efficiency variance

D Dr Work in progress account; Cr Labour efficiency variance

Activity 14 (June 2002) (Amended)

Data

You are employed as a financial analyst at Drampton plc, a computer retailer. One of your duties is to prepare a standard costing reconciliation statement for the finance director.

The company sells two types of computer, desktop computers for individual use and mainframe computers for large organisations. Desktop computers are sold by advertising in newspapers. Customers telephone Drampton to place an order and the telephone call is answered by trained operators. Drampton pays the cost of the telephone call. The total standard cost of one telephone call is shown below.

STANDARD COST OF ONE CALL

Expense	*Quantity*	*Cost*	*Cost per call*
Telephone cost	1 unit	£0.07 per unit	£0.07
Operators' wages	6 minutes	£3.50 per hour	£0.35
Fixed overheads[1]	6 minutes	£6.50 per hour	£0.65
Standard cost of one telephone call			£1.07

[1] Fixed overheads are based on budgeted operator hours.

Drampton's finance director gives you the following information for the three months ended 31 May 2002.

• Budgeted number of calls		900,000 calls
• Actual number of calls		1,000,000 calls
• Actual expenses	*Quantity*	*Cost*
• Telephone cost	1,200,000 units	£79,200
• Operators' wages	114,000 hours	£478,800
• Fixed overheads		£540,000
Actual cost of actual operations		£1,098,400

Task

(a) Calculate the following information:

(a)	(i)	Actual cost of a telephone unit:		
			=	0.066
	(ii)	Actual hourly wage rate of operators:		
			=	4.20
	(iii)	Standard number of operator hours for 1,000,000 calls:		
			=	100 000
	(iv)	Budgeted cost of fixed overheads:		
			=	585 000
	(v)	Budgeted number of operator hours:		
			=	90 000
	(vi)	Standard cost of actual operations:		
			=	1070 000

(b) Using the data given and your answers to part (a), calculate the following variances:

(b)	(i)	Price variance for telephone calls:		
			=	4800 (f)
	(ii)	Usage variance for telephone calls:		
			=	14000 (A)
	(iii)	Labour rate variance:		
			=	79800 (a)
	(iv)	Labour efficiency variance:		
			=	49000 (a)
	(v)	Fixed overhead expenditure variance:		
			=	45000 ?
	(vi)	Fixed overhead volume variance:		
			=	650 000 (f)
	(vii)	Fixed overhead capacity variance:		
			=	
	(viii)	Fixed overhead efficiency variance		
			=	91000

(c) Prepare a statement for the three months ended 31 May 2002 reconciling the standard cost of actual operations to the actual cost of actual operations.

(c)	**Standard costing reconciliation statement – 3 months ended 31 May 2002**		
		£	£
	Standard cost of actual operations		
	Price variance, telephone calls		
	Usage variance, telephone calls		
	Labour rate variance		
	Labour efficiency variance		
	Fixed overhead expenditure variance		
	Fixed overhead capacity variance		
	Fixed overhead efficiency variance		
		———	———
	Actual cost of actual operations		
			———

17 Summary

In this chapter we have looked at the various ways of establishing standard costs within a standard cost reporting system. We have also examined the causes of variances and outlined techniques which may be used to decide whether to investigate them.

We have revised the computation and interpretations of variances; in particular, fixed overhead variances which are a little more taxing.

Remember that the fixed overhead expenditure variance simply compares the budgeted cost with the actual cost. The volume variance compares the budgeted activity level with the standard activity level and can be split further into a capacity and efficiency variance.

Answers to chapter activities

Activity 1

False. It is impossible to be 100% certain, since different managers will react in different ways, but generally ideal standards will demotivate since adverse variances will continually be reported.

Activity 2

Standard usage of 500 units of K:

500 × 0.4 tonnes	200 tonnes
Actual usage	223 tonnes
Excess usage	23 tonnes

Valued at standard price of £30/tonne:

Direct material usage variance is:

23 tonnes × £30/tonne = £690 Adverse

i.e.: (Standard usage – actual usage) × standard price = (200 – 223) × £30 = £690 Adverse.

Activity 3

Total material variance

	£
Actual direct material cost	3,200
Standard direct material cost of 600 units i.e. standard cost of actual production £5 × 600	3,000
Direct material total cost variance – Adverse	200

Activity 4

Materials price variance

	£
Actual cost of 2,300 litres	3,128
Standard cost of 2,300 litres:	
2,300 litres × £1.30/litre	2,990
Direct material price variance – Adverse	138

Materials usage variance	
Actual usage 2,300 × £1.30	2,990
Standard usage 600 × 4 × £1.30	3,120
Materials usage variance – Favourable	130

Activity 5

	£
Actual direct labour cost	3,450
Standard direct labour cost of 450 units:	
£7 × 450	3,150
Direct labour total cost variance – Adverse	300

Activity 6

(a) Actual hours paid did cost £4,200

Actual hours paid should cost

1,050 × £4 = £4,200

Rate variance NIL

(b) Idle time:

Hours paid = 1,050 × 4 = 4,200

Hours worked 1,000 × 4 = 4,000

200 adverse

(c) Standard hours produced:

700 units × 1.50 standard hours = 1,050 standard hours

Actual hours worked = 1,000, thus efficiency variance

1,000 x £4 = £4,000

1,050 x £4 = £4,200

= £200 favourable – the hours worked were less than those allowed.

Activity 7

(a)

	Hours	£
Actual hours paid at actual rate per hour	5,000	14,000
Actual hours paid at standard rate per hour 5,000 x £3	5,000	15,000
Direct labour rate variance	–	1,000 F
Actual hours worked at standard rate per hour	5,000	15,000
Standard hours for production achieved at standard rate per hour 2,800 x 2 hrs x £3	5,600	16,800
Direct labour efficiency variance	600	1,800 F

(b)

	Hours	£
Actual hours paid at actual rate per hour	50,000	210,000
Actual hours paid at standard rate per hour 50,000 x £4 per hour	50,000	200,000
Direct labour rate variance	–	10,000 A

		£
Actual hours paid at standard rate per hour		200,000
Actual hours worked at standard rate per hour 48,000 x £4		192,000
Idle time variance		8,000 A

	Hours	£
Actual hours worked at standard rate per hour	48,000	192,000
Standard hours for production achieved at standard rate per hour 18,000 x 3 hrs x £4	54,000	216,000
Direct labour efficiency variance	6,000	24,000 F

Activity 8

PD

$$\text{Absorption rate} = \frac{\text{Budgeted cost}}{\text{Budgeted hours}} = \frac{£50,000}{20,000} = £2.50/\text{std hour}$$

$$\text{Actual output in standard hours} = 8,450 \times \frac{20,000}{10,000} = 16,900 \text{ std hrs}$$

Actual overheads	£47,500
Amount absorbed = 16,900 × £2.50 =	£42,250
Variance – under-recovery	£5,250 A

Activity 9

Fixed overhead recovery rate $\frac{\text{Budget overhead}}{\text{Budget hours}} = \frac{£44,000}{16,000} = £2.75/\text{hr}$

Standard hours per unit = $\frac{16,000}{8,000}$ = 2 hrs per unit

(a) **Fixed overhead variance**

Fixed overhead recovered in production achieved

= 8,450 × 2 = 16,900 hours

	£
Fixed overhead recovered = 16,900 × £2.75/hr =	46,475
Actual fixed overhead incurred =	47,500
Variance (under-recovered)	1,025 (A)

(b) **Sub-variances**

(i) Fixed overhead expenditure variance:

	£
Actual cost	47,500
Budgeted overhead	44,000
	£3,500 A

£3,500 adverse, represents an overspend

(ii) Fixed overhead volume variance:

Budget overhead	44,000
Actual production 16,900 x £2.75	46,475
Over-recovery	£2,475 F

The volume variance can be analysed into a capacity and efficiency variance.

(iii) Fixed overhead capacity variance:

Budgeted overhead	44,000
Actual hours worked 16,600 x £2.75	45,650
	£1,650 F

Activity 10

(a) **Standard hours in the budget**

182 trips × 5 standard hours

= 910 standard hours

(b) **Fixed overhead recovery rate per standard hour**

£11,500/910 = £12.637 per standard hour

(c) **Fixed overhead recovered**

175 × 5 standard hours

= 875 standard hours × £12.637

= £11,058

(d) **Fixed overhead total variance**

	£
Actual fixed cost	12,400
Fixed overhead recovered	11,058
	1,342 Adverse

(e) **Fixed overhead expenditure variance**

	£
Actual fixed costs	12,400
Budgeted fixed costs	11,500
	£900 Adverse

(f) **Fixed overhead volume variance**

	£
Budgeted hours × FORR	
910 x £12.637	11,500
Standard hours x FORR	
875 × £12.637	11,057
	£443 Adverse

(g) **Fixed overhead capacity variance**

	£
Budgeted hours × FORR	
910 x £12.637	11,500
Actual hours x FORR	
940 × £12.637	11,878
	£ 378 Favourable

(h) **Fixed overhead efficiency variance**

	£
Actual hours × FORR	
940 x £12.637	11,878
Standard hours x FORR	
875 × £12.637	11,057
	£ 821 Adverse

Activity 11

Budgeted/standard cost for actual production (W1)			32,150
Variances	**F**	**A**	
Direct materials price		1,413	
Direct materials usage	258		
Direct labour rate	129		
Direct labour efficiency		208	
Fixed overhead expenditure	650		
Fixed overhead volume		837	
Total variance	1,037	2,458	1,421
Actual cost of actual production			33,571

(W1) £35,008 x 13,500 / 14,700 = £32,150

Budgeted/standard variable cost for actual production (W2)			22,737
Budgeted fixed costs			10,250
Variances	**F**	**A**	
Direct materials price		1,413	
Direct materials usage	258		
Direct labour rate	129		
Direct labour efficiency		208	
Fixed overhead expenditure	650		
Total variance	1,037	1,621	584
Actual cost of actual production			33,571

(W2) £20,520 + £4,238 = £24,758 x 13,500 / 14,700 = £22,737

Activity 12

Y Ltd

(a)

	£
Actual cost of materials purchased =	2,500
Standard cost of materials purchased = 750 × £3 =	2,250
	250 (A)

(b) Closing inventory (kg) = Purchase – quantity used
= 750 – 600
= 150 kg

Valued at standard cost, this gives a closing inventory valuation of 150 × 3 = £450

(c)

	£
Actual materials used at standard price 600 kg x £3	1,800
Standard cost of producing 100 B 100 x 5 kg x £3	1,500
	300 (A)

Activity 13

B Dr Labour efficiency variance, Cr. WIP

Activity 14 (June 2002)

(a) (i) Actual cost of a telephone unit:

£79,200/1,200,000 units	=	£0.066

(ii) Actual hourly wage rate of operators:

£478,800/114,000 hours	=	£4.20

(iii) Standard number of operator hours for 1,000,000 calls:

1,000,000 × 6/60	=	100,000

(iv) Budgeted cost of fixed overheads:

900,000 × £0.65	=	£585,000

(v) Budgeted number of operator hours:

900,000 × 6/60	=	90,000

(vi) Standard cost of actual operations:

1,000,000 × £1.07	=	£1,070,000

(b) (i) Price variance for telephone calls:

1,200,000 x £0.066	=	
1,200,000 x £0.070		£4,800 (F)

(ii) Usage variance for telephone calls:

1,200,000 x £0.070	=	
1,000,000 x £0.070		£14,000 (A)

(iii) Labour rate variance:

114,000 x £4.20	=	
114,000 x £3.50		£79,800 (A)

(iv) Labour efficiency variance:

114,000 x £3.50	=	
100,000 x £3.50		£49,000 (A)

(v) Fixed overhead expenditure variance:

£540,400 – £585,000	=	£44,600 (F)

(vi) Fixed overhead volume variance:

90,000 x £6.50	=	
100,000 x £6.50		£65,000 (F)

(vii) Fixed overhead capacity variance:

90,000 x £6.50	=	
114,000 x £6.50		£156,000 (F)

(viii) Fixed overhead efficiency variance

114,000 x £6.50	=	£91,000 (A)
100,000 x £6.50		

(c) Standard costing reconciliation statement – 3 months ended 31 May 2002

	£	£
Standard cost of actual operations		1,070,000
Price variance, telephone calls	4,800 (F)	
Usage variance, telephone calls	(14,000) (A)	
Labour rate variance	(79,800) (A)	
Labour efficiency variance	(49,000) (A)	
Fixed overhead expenditure variance	44,600 (F)	
Fixed overhead capacity variance	156,000 (F)	
Fixed overhead efficiency variance	(91,000) (A)	28,400 (A)
Actual cost of actual operations		1,098,400

18 Test your knowledge

Workbook Activity 15

A company used 2,000 hours of labour paying £10 per hour. During this time the company made 2,050 units whilst the budget had been for 2,500 units. The standard number of hours allowed was one hour per unit, and the budgeted rate per hour was £9.80.

Complete the following table.

			£
Budgeted/Standard cost of labour for actual production			
Variances	**F**	**A**	
Direct labour rate			
Direct labour efficiency			
Total variance			
Actual cost of labour for actual production			

Workbook Activity 16

A company has budgeted fixed overheads of £40,000 and budgeted output is 20,000 units.

Actual output was 19,000 units and actual overheads were £39,000.

Complete the following table.

			£
Budgeted/Standard fixed cost for actual production			
Variances	**F**	**A**	
Fixed overhead expenditure			
Fixed overhead volume			
Total variance			
Actual fixed cost for actual production			

Workbook Activity 17

A company used 24,000 hours of labour paying £8 per hour. During this time it managed to make 400 units whilst the budget had been for only 190 units. The standard number of hours allowed was 50 per unit, and the budgeted rate per hour was £7.90.

Complete the following table.

			£
Budgeted/Standard cost of labour for actual production			
Variances	**F**	**A**	
Direct labour rate			
Direct labour efficiency			
Total variance			
Actual cost of labour for actual production			

Workbook Activity 18

A company bought 112,000 kilograms of material paying £4 per kilogram. It managed to make 2,100 units whilst the budget had been for 1,900 units. The standard quantity of material allowed for in the budget was 56 kilograms per unit, and the budgeted price per kilogram was £4.50.

Complete the following table.

			£
Budgeted/Standard cost of materials for actual production			
Variances	**F**	**A**	
Direct materials price			
Direct materials usage			
Total variance			
Actual cost of materials for actual production			

Workbook Activity 19

A company has budgeted fixed overheads of £1,250,000 and budgeted output is 25,000 units.

Actual output was 24,100 units and actual overheads were £1,245,000.

Complete the following table.

			£
Budgeted/Standard fixed cost for actual production			
Variances	**F**	**A**	
Fixed overhead expenditure			
Fixed overhead volume			
Total variance			
Actual fixed cost for actual production			

Workbook Activity 20

A company bought 2,000 kilograms of material paying £5 per kilogram. It managed to make 400 units whilst the budget had been for 420 units. The standard quantity of material allowed for in the budget was 6 kilograms per unit, and the budgeted price per kilogram was £5.50.

Complete the following table.

			£
Budgeted/Standard cost of materials for actual production			
Variances	**F**	**A**	
Direct materials price			
Direct materials usage			
Total variance			
Actual cost of materials for actual production			

Workbook Activity 21 (December 2002) (Amended)

Data

You are a newly appointed trainee accounting technician with Primary Chemicals plc. One of your responsibilities is to prepare and monitor standard costing variances for the distillation department. The distillation department prepares barrels of a refined chemical using a continuous process.

Fixed overheads are charged to production on the basis of machine hours. This is because the machine hours required determines the speed of production.

The budgeted and actual results of the distillation department for the week ended 30 November 2002 are shown below.

Distillation Department – Operating results
week ended 30 November 2002

Production		*Budget* 2,500 barrels		*Actual* 2,400 barrels
		Standard cost		*Actual cost*
Material	12,500 litres	£106,250	11,520 litres	£99,072
Labour	10,000 labour hrs	£60,000	10,080 labour hrs	£61,488
Fixed overheads	20,000 machine hrs	£200,000	18,960 machine hrs	£185,808
Total cost		£366,250		£346,368

Task

(a) Calculate the following information:

(a)	(i)	Standard price of material per litre	
	(ii)	Actual price of material per litre	
	(iii)	Standard litres of material per barrel	
	(iv)	Standard labour rate per hour	
	(v)	Standard labour hours per barrel	
	(vi)	Standard machine hours per barrel	
	(vii)	Fixed overheads per budgeted machine hour	
	(viii)	Standard absorption cost per barrel	

(b) Using the data provided in the operating results and your answers to part (a), calculate the following variances:

(b)	(i)	Material price variance	
	(ii)	Material usage variance	
	(iii)	Labour rate variance	
	(iv)	Labour efficiency variance	
	(v)	Fixed overhead expenditure variance	
	(vi)	Fixed overhead volume variance	

	(vii)	Fixed overhead capacity variance	
			______
			______
	(viii)	Fixed overhead efficiency variance	
			______
			______

(c) Prepare a statement reconciling the standard absorption cost of actual operations to the actual absorption cost of actual operations.

(c)	Reconciliation statement week ended 30 November 2002		
	Standard cost of actual production		
	Material price variance		
	Material usage variance		
	Labour rate variance		
	Labour efficiency variance		
	Fixed overhead expenditure variance		
	Fixed overhead capacity variance		
	Fixed overhead efficiency variance		
		______	______
	Actual cost of actual production		
			______

Workbook Activity 22 (December 2003) (Amended)

Data

You are an accounting technician employed by Garforth Cookridge and Co, a firm of accountants and registered auditors. A new client is Econair Ltd. Econair is a small airline that operates two routes from its home airport.

One of your tasks is to prepare standard costing variances for Econair. To help you, the airline provides you with the following information for the 28 days ended 30 November 2003 for the route between the home airport and Alpha City.

Budgeted and actual operating results 28 days ended 30 November 2003

		Budget		*Actual*
Operating data				
Number of flights		168		160
Number of flying hours		672		768
Expenses	*Quantity*	£	*Quantity*	£
Fuel	33,600 gallons	50,400	38,400 gallons	61,440
Pilots' remuneration	1,344 pilot hours	67,200	1,536 pilot hours	79,872
Aircraft fixed overheads	672 flying hours	75,600	768 flying hours	76,200
Cost of operations		193,200		217,512

Other information

- Pilot hours are the same as labour hours for a manufacturer.
- Flying hours are the same as machine hours for a manufacturer.
- The number of flights is the same as production volume for a manufacturer. Fuel and pilots' remuneration are treated as variable costs. Fixed overheads are charged to operations on the basis of flying hours.

Task

(a) Use the budgeted data to calculate the following information:

(a)	(i)	Standard price of fuel per gallon:	
	(ii)	Standard fuel usage for 160 flights:	
	(iii)	Standard hourly rate for pilots:	

	(iv)	Standard pilot hours per flight:	
	(v)	Standard pilot hours for 160 flights:	
	(vi)	Standard fixed overhead cost per budgeted flying hour:	
	(vii)	Standard flying hours per flight:	
	(viii)	Standard flying hours for 160 flights:	
	(ix)	Standard fixed overhead absorbed by the 160 flights:	
	(x)	Standard cost of actual operations:	

(b) Using the data given and your answers to part (a),calculate the following variances:

(b)	(i)	Fuel price variance:	
	(ii)	Fuel usage variance:	
	(iii)	Rate variance for pilots:	
	(iv)	Efficiency variance for pilots:	
	(v)	Fixed overhead expenditure variance:	
	(vi)	Fixed overhead volume variance:	
	(vii)	Fixed overhead capacity variance:	
	(viii)	Fixed overhead efficiency variance:	

(c) Prepare a statement for the 28 days ended 30 November 2003 reconciling the standard cost of actual operations to the actual cost of actual operations.

Standard Costing Reconciliation Statement – 28 days ended 30 November 2003

	£	£
Standard cost of actual operations		
Fuel price variance		
Fuel usage variance		
Rate variance for pilots		
Efficiency variance for pilots		
Fixed overhead expenditure variance		
Fixed overhead capacity variance		
Fixed overhead efficiency variance		
	———	
		———
Actual cost of operations		
		———

Data

The Chief Executive of Econair, Lisa Margoli, is given a copy of the standard costing reconciliation statement you prepared. Lisa tells you she is concerned about the fixed overhead variances and gives you the following information.

- **Flight and passenger data:** During the 28 days to 30 November 2003, the actual number of flights to Alpha City was 8 less than budgeted. Although the budget assumed 70 passengers per flight, the actual number of passengers per flight was 80.
- **Current policy for apportioning and charging fixed overheads:** The second route operated by Econair is from the home airport to another country, Betaland. Econair's current practice is to apportion budgeted and actual fixed overheads between the two routes based on the number of aircraft. The apportioned fixed overheads are then charged to operations using flying hours.

- **Budgeted operating data for the 28 days to 30 November 2003**

Route	*Alpha City*	*Betaland*	*Total*
Number of aircraft	2	4	6
Number of flights per 28 days	168	448	616
Number of flying hours per 28 days	672	2,240	2,912
Insurance value of each aircraft	£10m	£20m	
Total aircraft insurance value per route	£20m	£80m	£100m

- **Analysis of total budgeted fixed overhead expenses for both routes for the 28 days to 30 November 2003**

Aircraft maintenance	£116,480
Insurance	£98,020
Luggage handling and in-flight facilities *	£12,300
Budgeted fixed overheads	£226,800

* Luggage handling and in-flight facilities only apply to the route to Betaland.

Budgeted fixed overhead per aircraft (£226,800/6 aircraft)	£37,800
Budgeted fixed overheads apportioned to Alpha City route (£37,800 × 2 aircraft)	£75,600

Task

Write a memo to Lisa Margoli. In your memo you should:

(a) identify a more appropriate method than flying hours for charging standard fixed overheads;

(b) briefly explain why your chosen method for charging standard fixed overheads would give different fixed overhead capacity and efficiency variances to those calculated in Task 23.1;

(c) use the analysis of budgeted fixed overhead expenses and the operating data to reallocate the budgeted fixed overheads apportioned to the Alpha City route.

Task

MEMO

To:

From:

Date:

Subject:

Thank you for raising your concerns with me about the fixed overheads for the Alpha City route.

(a)

(b)

(c)

Fixed overhead	*Driver*	*Apportionment*	*Total*
Aircraft maintenance	Flying hours		
Insurance	Insurance value		

Workbook Activity 23 (June 2004) (Amended)

Data

Brown Ltd manufactures and sells office furniture. The company operates an integrated standard cost system in which:

- purchases of materials are recorded at standard cost;
- finished goods are recorded at standard cost;
- direct materials and direct labour costs are both variable costs;
- fixed production overheads are absorbed using direct labour hours.

You are an accounting technician at Brown Ltd. You report to Sam Thomas, the Finance Director.

The company's most popular product is an executive desk. Its standard cost is as follows:

Product: Executive desk

Inputs	*Quantity*	*Unit price*	*Total cost*
		£	£
Direct materials	30 kgs	5.00	150.00
Direct labour	5 hours	6.00	30.00
Fixed production overheads	5 hours	4.00	20.00
Standard cost			200.00

Actual and budgeted data for the manufacture of executive desks for May 2004 are shown below:

- 27,500 kg of direct materials were purchased for £143,000.
- Issues from stores to production totalled 27,500 kg.
- The actual output for the month was 900 desks.
- The budgeted output for the month was 1,000 desks.
- 4,200 direct labour hours were worked at a cost of £26,040.
- Actual fixed production overheads were £23,000.

Task

(a) Calculate the following information for May:

(a)	(i)	Actual price of materials per kg	=	
	(ii)	Standard usage of materials for actual production	=	
	(iii)	Actual labour rate per hour	=	
	(iv)	Standard labour time for actual production	=	
	(v)	Budgeted production overheads	=	

(b) Calculate the following variances for the production of executive desks for May:

(b)	(i)	The material price variance		
	(ii)	The material usage variance		
	(iii)	The labour rate variance		

	(iv)	The labour efficiency variance		
	(v)	The fixed overhead expenditure variance		
	(vi)	The fixed overhead volume variance		
	(vii)	The fixed overhead capacity variance		
	(viii)	The fixed overhead efficiency variance		

(c) Prepare an operating statement for May which reconciles the standard absorption cost of total actual production with the actual absorption cost of total actual production.

Operating statement for May 2004

	£	£	£
Standard absorption cost of actual production			
	Favourable	*Adverse*	
Material price variance			
Material usage variance			
Labour rate variance			
Labour efficiency variance			
Fixed overhead capacity variance			
Fixed overhead efficiency variance			
			———
Actual absorption cost of actual production			
			———

(d) Write a memo for Sam Thomas to present to the Board of Directors. Your memo should comment on the usefulness, or otherwise, of the statement you have prepared in your answer to (c) above.

(d) **MEMO**

To:

From:

Date:

Subject:

Investigating and reporting variances

7

Introduction

In this chapter we shall start by revising the variances we calculated in the previous chapter. We shall then concentrate on the ways in which management uses these variances. This will include investigating the causes of the variances, seeking ways to control the variances and ways in which the variances can be reported.

KNOWLEDGE

Explain the use of variance analysis in labour, materials and overhead costing (2.4)

SKILLS

Compare results over time using methods that allow for changing price levels (2.1)

Prepare reports in the most appropriate format and present them to management within the required timescale (3.1)

Prepare exception reports to identify matters which require further investigation (3.2)

Make specific recommendations to management in a clear and appropriate form (3.3)

CONTENTS

1 Reconciliations
2 Measuring the significance of variances
3 Investigation of variances
4 Responsibility accounting and the interdependence of variances

1 Reconciliations

1.1 Introduction

We have seen that standard costs are developed in advance of the period under review. During the course of that period, actual costs are compared with standard costs. Any variances are isolated for investigation as to their cause, enabling corrective action to be taken as soon as possible.

Management will wish to see a clear and succinct summary of the results for the period and in particular will want any unusual or unexpected items to be brought to their attention (exception reporting). In general, this will take the form of a reconciliation between budgeted and actual profits which highlights the variances between them. To be useful as a management tool, the reconciliation should be part of an overall report to management.

Example

You have already covered in the previous chapter the calculation of basic cost variances.

The following budgeted and actual data for TJB Limited for 20X9 will be used to revise the principles and computations, and lead on to reporting these variances.

TJB Limited – Budgeted profit for the year ending 31 December 20X9

Produce and sell 10,000 units

		Produce and sell 10,000 units	
		£	£
Budgeted revenue units	10,000		100,000
Production cost	£/unit		
Direct materials – 10,000 tons @ £1 per ton (1 ton per unit)	1.00	10,000	
Direct labour – 20,000 hours @ 50p per hour (2 hours per unit)	1.00	10,000	
Fixed production overhead – 20,000 hours @ 75p per hour	1.50	15,000	
Total budgeted production cost	3.50		35,000
Budgeted profit for the period			65,000

During the year to 31 December 20X9, the following actual results were obtained.

TJB Limited – Actual profit for the year ending 31 December 20X9

Production and sales 8,000 units

	£	£
Revenue		96,000
Production cost		
Direct materials – 7,750 tons purchased and used (£1.0968 per ton)	8,500	
Direct labour – 16,500 hours paid (£0.4545 per hour)	7,500	
Fixed production overhead incurred	15,500	
Total actual production cost		31,500
Total profit		64,500

The purpose of a cost analysis is to reconcile the budgeted costs of £35,000 to the actual costs of £31,500.

Such a reconciliation is a budgetary control statement or budgetary control report.

Solution

Cost variances

	Flexed budget cost of producing 8,000 units	*Actual cost of producing 8,000 units*	*Difference (variance)*	
	£	£	£	
Direct materials	8,000	8,500	500	A
Direct labour	8,000	7,500	500	F
Fixed production overhead	12,000	15,500	3,500	A
Total	28,000	31,500	3,500	A

All these total variances can be analysed into at least two further types of variance:

(a) a price variance;

(b) a usage or utilisation variance, which in some cases can be broken down further.

Total direct material cost variance

		£	
(a)	The actual amount of material used at the actual price	8,500	
(b)	The standard amount of material that should have been used for the actual production at the standard price – 8,000 tons × £1	8,000	
	Total variance	500	A

To analyse this further we need first to get the actual amount of material used at the standard price: the direct materials price variance.

Direct materials price variance

	Tons	£	
Actual materials purchased, at actual price	7,750	8,500	
Actual materials purchased, at standard price per ton (£1)	7,750	7,750	
Materials price variance	–	750	A

We next need to compare this with the standard materials that should have been used for that level of production: the direct materials usage variance.

Direct materials usage variance

	Tons	£	
Actual materials used at standard price	7,750	7,750	
Standard materials allowed for production achieved at standard price	8,000	8,000	
Materials usage variance (@ £1 per ton)	250	250	F

Total direct material cost variance = £750 A + £250 F
= £500 A

Total direct labour cost variance

		£	
(a)	The actual hours paid at the actual rate per hour	7,500	
(b)	The standard time allowed to produce the output, priced at the standard rate per hour (16,000 × £0.50)	8,000	
	Total variance	500	F

The total variance can be analysed into rate and efficiency variances as with materials.

Labour rate variance

	Hours	£	
Actual hours paid at actual rate per hour	16,500	7,500	
Actual hours paid at standard rate per hour (50p/hour)	16,500	8,250	
Direct labour rate variance	–	750	F

Total labour efficiency variance

	Hours	£	
Actual hours paid at standard rate per hour	16,500	8,250	
Standard hours allowed for production achieved at standard rate per hour (50p)	16,000	8,000	
Direct labour usage variance		250	A

Total direct labour cost variance = £750 F + £250 A
= £500 F

Total fixed overhead cost variance

	£	
Actual fixed overhead cost	15,500	
Standard cost absorbed into actual production (8,000 × £1.50 per unit)	12,000	
Total fixed overhead cost variance	3,500	A

This is then analysed into price (expenditure) and volume variances. The volume variance is then sub-analysed into usage (efficiency) and capacity variances.

Fixed overhead expenditure variance

	£	
Actual fixed overhead cost	15,500	
Budgeted fixed overhead cost	15,000	
Fixed overhead expenditure variance	500	A

Fixed overhead volume variance

This is the under-absorption (at standard rates) due to the lower actual production level than that budgeted.

	Units	£	
Budgeted production x standard rate of £1.50	10,000	15,000	
Actual production x standard rate of £1.50	8,000	12,000	
Fixed overhead volume variance (in units)	2,000		
Valued at standard absorption rate		3,000	A

The variance is adverse because we have under-absorbed fixed overhead by 2,000 units' worth. We thus require an extra charge to the cost account to compensate for this under-absorption.

The £3,000 adverse volume variance can be analysed further.

Fixed overhead capacity variance

	Hours		
Budgeted hours x standard rate of £0.75	20,000	15,000	
Actual hours worked x standard rate of £0.75	16,500	12,375	
Capacity variance	3,500	= £2,625	A

Fixed overhead efficiency variance

	Hours		
Actual hours worked x standard rate of £0.75	16,500	12,375	
Standard hours allowed for actual production achieved x standard rate of £0.75	16,000	12,000	
Efficiency variance @ £0.75 per hour	500	= £375	A

The two variances add up to the volume variance (£375 + £2,625 = £3,000 adverse), and shows that the principal reason for our under-production was a failure to devote sufficient hours to production (3,500 hours short).

Having computed all the variances, we can now reconcile budgeted costs with actual costs.

		Adverse	*Favourable*	
		£	£	£
Total budgeted cost				28,000
Cost variances				
Materials	Price	750		
	Usage		250	
Labour	Rate		750	
	Efficiency	250		
Fixed overheads	Expenditure	500		
	Usage	375		
	Capacity	2,625		
Total/net cost variances		4,500	1,000	3,500
Total actual cost				31,500

Activity 1

(a) The budget for product A for a period is as follows:

Production	2,000 units
Revenue	2,000 units: £15 per unit
Direct material cost	6,000 kg of XYZ: £2 per kg
Direct labour cost	4,000 hours: £2 per hour

Actual results for the period were:

Production	2,500 units
Revenue	2,250 units: £15 per unit
Direct materials	5,000 kg purchased and consumed at a total cost of £12,000
Direct labour	6,000 hours at a total cost of £9,000

There were no opening inventories. It is company policy to value inventory at standard cost.

(i) Prepare a statement of actual profit for the period.

(ii) Calculate the following:

- Material price variance
- Material usage variance
- Labour rate variance
- Labour efficiency variance

(i) **Actual profit for the period**

	£	£
Revenue (2,250 units × £15)		
Production cost (2,500 units)		
Direct materials		
Direct labour		
	_______	
Less: Closing inventory		
(250 units at £10 per unit) (W1)		
	_______	
Cost of sales		
		_______
Actual profit		
		_______

(ii)

	£
Material price variance	
Material usage variance	
Labour rate variance	
Labour efficiency variance	

1.2 Marginal costing

The previous example of TJB Limited was based upon total absorption costing as the fixed production overhead was absorbed into the standard cost of the product. Under marginal costing the fixed overhead is charged to the income statement as a period cost and is not absorbed into the cost of the product.

For the purpose of variances this means that the only fixed overhead variance that exists is the fixed overhead price or expenditure variance. There is no volume variance.

1.3 Materials price variance and price changes

In some examination tasks you may be given information about specific price indices that have affected the materials prices during the period. In these circumstances it is then possible to split the materials price variance into that element that relates to the price increase and any other cause of the variance.

Example

The standard material cost for a business' single product is 4 kg at a price of £12.00 per kg. The standard price was set when the index for this material price stood at 120. During August, 10,000 units of the product were made using 42,000 kgs at a total cost of £525,000. The August price index for this material is 122.

What is the total materials price variance, the element relating to the price increase and the element relating to other causes?

Solution

Total materials price variance

		£
Actual cost		525,000
Standard cost of actual materials	42,000 × £12.00	504,000
		21,000 Adverse

This adverse variance of £21,000 can then be split into the element relating to the price increase and the element relating to other factors:

Variance relating to other factors

		£
Actual cost		525,000
Revised price for actual materials	42,000 × (£12.00 × 122/120)	512,400
		12,600 Adverse

This part of the variance is controllable and should be investigated.

Variance relating to price increase

		£
Revised price for actual materials	42,000 × (£12.00 × 122/120)	512,400
Standard cost of actual materials	42,000 × £12.00	504,000
		8,400 Adverse

This part of the variance is uncontrollable by the company since it cannot dictate inflation levels.

Variances can be broken down like this for many reasons, not just because of price changes. Any decision that has been taken and needs to be isolated should be calculated in this way.

Activity 2

A company produces and sells a single product.

One product should use 2.5 kg of materials. The quantity index was set when the index was 100.

The material has a standard cost of £5 per kg (set when the price index was 100).

During July, the standard material price per kg was revised due to the price index rising to 105. Its standard material usage was also revised as the quantity index had risen to 110.

Actual results were:

Production: 1,000 units

Direct materials: 2,550 kg purchased and used at a cost of £12,000

The controllable material price variance is £ ______

The uncontrollable material price variance is £ ______

The controllable material usage variance is £ ______

The uncontrollable material usage variance is £ ______

(Answers should be to 2 decimal places.)

2 Measuring the significance of variances

2.1 Introduction

As we have seen, the key tool for management control within a standard costing system is some form of variance analysis report or budgetary control statement. The aim is to prepare a report to management on a routine basis in which variances are clearly identified and can be acted upon as appropriate.

In exercising control, it is generally impracticable to review every variance in detail at each accounting period and attention will usually be concentrated on those variances which have the greatest impact on the achievement of the budget plan.

2.2 Identifying significant variances

One method of identifying significant variances is to express each variance as a percentage of the related budget allowance or standard value. Those showing the highest percentage deviation would then be given the most urgent attention.

This method, however, could result in lack of attention to variances which, although representing a small percentage of the standard value, nevertheless involve significant sums of money. Both percentages and absolute values should be looked at in deciding where the priorities for control actually lie.

In practice, management will review the variance report presented to them and decide which variances should be investigated on the basis of whether the costs of investigation are outweighed by the benefits (called a cost-benefit analysis).

Management will often request a more detailed analysis and explanation of specific variances to be produced as the decision as to whether or not a variance merits investigation may need more information than is provided in the original variance report.

2.3 Fluctuating variances – looking at trends

The variances of a particular period may not be representative of a general trend. Items like stationery costs can fluctuate widely from month to month, dependent on the amount of stationery that has been invoiced.

Sometimes, the accountant will make estimated adjustments to either the budget or the actual figures in an attempt to give a better picture of the underlying trend but this is not a completely satisfactory way of dealing with the matter.

The simplest way of getting the month's figures into context is to show also the accumulated cost for the year to date. High cost and low cost periods will then be revealed but will balance out in the cumulative figures.

A development of the above idea is also to report each period the manager's latest forecast compared with the annual budget. It will then be possible to see whether variances from budget currently being reported are likely to continue to accumulate during the remainder of the year, or whether they will be offset by later opposite variances.

Although this technique of forecasting is dependent on managers' subjective assessments, it is a good way of ensuring that the correct control action gets taken on the current figures.

Example

You might like to spend a few minutes considering what the report below tells you about the business.

Income Statement – Seven periods cumulative to ... 20...

	Period 7			**Cumulative**			**Whole year**	
	Budget	*Actual*	*Variances for (A)*	*Budget*	*Actual*	*Variances for (A)*	*Budget*	*Latest forecast*
	£000	£000	£000	£000	£000	£000	£000	£000
Revenue	500	600	100	3,500	3,420	(80)	6,000	6,200
Direct cost of sales	280	322	(42)	1,960	1,951	9	3,500	3,850
Factory overhead	58	69	(11)	420	400	20	700	750
Administration and selling costs	122	123	(1)	840	800	40	1,320	1,147
Total costs	460	514	(54)	3,220	3,151	69	5,520	5,747
Operating profit	40	86	46	280	269	(11)	480	453
Profit: Revenue %	8	14.3	–	8	7.9	–	8	7.3

Solution

(a) Revenues, which had obviously been below budget for the first six periods of the year, are significantly in excess of budget for period 7 (reducing the cumulative shortfall to £80,000), and are now expected to exceed the budget for the year as a whole.

(b) Direct costs are naturally higher when revenues are higher. The percentage of direct costs to revenue is not consistent, however, as the following calculations show:

	Budget	*Actual*
Period 7	56.0%	53.7%
Cumulative to date	56.0%	57.0%
Forecast for whole year	58.3%	62.1%

For the seven periods as a whole, direct costs have been in excess of the budgeted percentage and even though the budget for the twelve months provides for an increase in that percentage the forecast actual increase is still higher. Period 7 in isolation shows an anomalous result, perhaps due to some peculiarity in sales mix.

(c) The variance on factory overhead, which is favourable over the seven periods as a whole, has become adverse in period 7 and is forecast as adverse for the year as a whole (though not at the rate experienced in period 7).Failure to budget adequately for inflationary increases is one possibility.

(d) Administration and selling costs have a cumulative favourable variance to date of £40,000 against a budget of £840,000, i.e. 4.8%. By the end of the year a favourable variance of £173,000 (13.1% on budget) is expected. It would appear that considerable economies are planned, and have already commenced. The fact that period 7 above shows a small adverse variance is not significant. Such results can emerge in administration costs, which can be influenced by random occurrences like a large purchase of stationery or a major visit overseas by the managing director.

2.4 Comparing against forecasts

Some large organisations in the UK have taken the idea of comparing against forecasts a step further. Many companies employ the following comparisons.

	Comparison	*Information*
1	Budget v actual	What progress have we made towards achieving objectives?
2	Budget v forecast	Will we continue to progress towards achievement of objectives?
3	Budget v revised forecast	Will suggested corrective actions lead us back to achievement of objectives?
4	Latest forecast v previous	Why are the forecasts different and are circumstances getting better or worse?
5	Actual v past forecast	Why were forecasts incorrect and can they be improved?

It may not be necessary to perform each of these control comparisons every month or quarter. The actual versus past forecast may only be necessary annually or less frequently.

It must be remembered that managers will need to be motivated to produce these forecasts and use them. They must be educated to recognise why and how they can use them to enable them to do a better job and not feel that they are just another means for higher level management to check on them and apply pressure.

Finally, this year's results are sometimes compared with those for the corresponding period last year. In some cases this may be helpful in establishing a trend, but it must never be forgotten that the budget is this year's plan, and it is against that plan that performance must be controlled.

3 Investigation of variances

3.1 Introduction

Variance analysis, if properly carried out, can be a useful cost-controlling and cost-saving tool. However, the traditional variance analysis seen so far is only a step towards the final goal of controlling and saving costs.

3.2 Generalised reasons for variances

The causes of variances can be classified under four headings:

- Planning errors
- Measurement errors
- Random factors
- Operational causes

Planning errors lead to the setting of inappropriate standards or budgets. This may be due to carelessness on the part of the standard setter (not taking account of known changes in the production process or expected price rises, for example) or due to unexpected external changes (a market shortage of a resource leading to increased price. These need to be isolated from hindsight information and a revision of the standard considered for future budgets.

Measurement errors include errors caused by inaccurate completion of timesheets or job cards, inaccurate measurement of quantities issued from stores, etc. The rectification of such errors or errors caused by random factors will probably not give rise to any cost savings (though this is a generalisation).

Random factors are by definition uncontrollable, although they need careful monitoring to ensure that they are not, in fact, one of the other types of variance.

3.3 Operational causes of variances

Examples of some specific reasons for individual variances are shown below.

Variance		*Possible causes*
Materials:	Price	Bulk discounts Different suppliers/ Different Materials Unexpected delivery costs Different buying procedures
	Usage	Different quality material Theft, obsolescence, deterioration Different quality of staff Different mix of material Different batch sizes and trim loss
Labour:	Rate	Different class of labour Excessive overtime Productivity bonuses National wage negotiations Union action
	Idle time	Shortage of material Breakdown of machinery
	Efficiency	Different levels of skill Different working conditions The learning effect Lack of supervision Works to rule Machine breakdowns Lack of material Lack of orders Strikes (if paid) Too long over coffee breaks
Overhead:	Expenditure	Change in nature of overhead Unforeseen price changes
	Volume	Excessive idle time Increase in workforce

It will nearly always be useful to consult staff working in operational departments to resolve any queries in the data as they will have 'local' knowledge of the day-to-day operations.

Example

An adverse materials usage variance of £50,000 arose in a month as follows:

Standard cost per kg	£10
Actual cost per kg	£12
Units produced	2,000
Standard quantity per unit	25 kg
Actual quantity used	55,000 kg

	£
Standard cost of actual usage (55,000 kg × £10)	550,000
Standard cost of standard usage (2,000 × 25 kg × £10)	500,000
Adverse usage variance	50,000

On further investigation, the following is ascertained.

1. The actual quantity used was based on estimated stock figures. A stocktake showed that 53,000 kg were in fact used.
2. 3,000 kg is the best estimate for what might politely be called the monthly 'shrinkage' but, in less polite circles, theft.
3. 2,000 kg of stock were damaged by children who broke into the stores through some of the shaky panelling.
4. The supervisor feels that existing machinery is outmoded and more efficient machinery could save 1,000 kg a month.

Additional considerations

1. A security guard would cost £9,000 a year to employ and would stop 20% of all theft. Resultant dissatisfaction amongst works staff might cost £20,000 per annum.
2. Given the easy access to stores, vandals might be expected to break in every other month; £10,000 would make the stores vandal-proof.
3. New machinery would cost £720,000.

Analyse the usage variance in the light of this information and comment on your results.

Solution

The original £50,000 usage variance could be analysed as follows:

		Adverse/(favourable) variance
		£
(a)	Bad measurement (53,000 – 55,000) × £10	20,000
(b)	Theft (3,000 × £10)	30,000
(c)	Damage (2,000 × £10)	20,000
(d)	Obsolete machinery (1,000 × £10)	10,000
(e)	Other operational factors (balance)	(30,000)
		50,000

In each case, the variances should be studied and compared with the cost of rectification.

(a) **Bad measurement** – Assuming no costly decisions were made, or are likely to be made in the future, such as over-stocking, the component is of no future consequence.

(b) **Theft** – Annual cost due to theft is 12 × £30,000 or £360,000; 20% of this saved would amount to £72,000 at a cost of £9,000 + £20,000, thus the security guard is worth employing.

(c) **Damage** – Annual cost due to vandalism is 6 × £20,000 or £120,000; this would presumably be avoided by spending £10,000 now; again worthwhile.

(d) **Obsolete machinery** – Annual cost of using old machines is 12 × £10,000 or £120,000; the cost of making this saving (the saving would increase as purchase prices increased or if production increased) is £720,000; the decision over this investment would require further consideration such as discounted cash flow analysis.

(e) **Other factors** – We now see a favourable usage variance once all known factors above have been accounted for. This may need further investigation, particularly if it affects the quality of goods produced.

Activity 3

An adverse materials price variance might mean that __________

quality material was bought than standard. The employees found it easier to work with this high quality material, so worked

__________efficiently than standard.

(Gap fill from: Better; Worse; More; Less)

Activity 4

If better quality material was bought than had been allowed for in the standard cost, which four of the following variances are most likely to result?

Favourable material price;	☐
Adverse material price	☐
Favourable material usage	☐
Adverse material usage	☐
Favourable labour efficiency	☐
Adverse labour efficiency	☐
Favourable labour rate	☐
Adverse labour rate	☐
Favourable variable overhead efficiency	☐
Adverse variable overhead efficiency	☐

3.4 Fixed overhead variances

These are worth a special note, due to the particular nature of the fixed overhead volume variance.

We have seen that the volume variance is a product of the TAC system, and represents the adjustment for over-/under-absorption of fixed costs due to actual production being higher or lower than budgeted. Unlike the other variances, it does not actually represent a cost saving or overspend.

If this is the case, is it worth spending any time on the investigation of fixed overhead volume variances? Does it really matter if overheads are under-/over-absorbed, since it will all be adjusted for in the end?

The problem with having an inappropriate absorption rate is that decisions may have been taken on a unit cost that is too high or too low – for example, in setting the price of a product. If this is too high, sales may have been unnecessarily lost; if it is too low, profit margins may have been significantly eroded.

To minimise such effects of over-/under-absorption, regular reviews should be conducted of expenditure and activity levels arising throughout the period. The absorption rate can then be adjusted if it is felt necessary to reflect more recent estimates of expenditure and activity levels.

3.5 The cost of variance analysis

The provision of any information involves the costs of collecting the basic data, processing it, and reporting the results. Variance analysis is no exception and, as with other forms of management information, the benefits to which it gives rise must be commensurate with the costs incurred.

(a) Variance analysis allows 'management by exception' and it is presumably for this purpose that a standard costing system has been introduced.

(b) When variances are known to exist, failure to make adequate investigations, even on a random basis, will weaken the control system and thus the motivation of managers.

(c) The amount of analysis required can sometimes be reduced by defining levels of significance below which detailed investigation is not required.

(d) The costs of clerical work can be over-estimated. In most working days there will be some spare capacity that can be utilised without extra cost.

What has to be considered, therefore, is the amount of detail that can be incorporated usefully in variance analysis. This will fall into two categories:

(a) **Including more detailed codings** in source documents indicating causes and responsibilities. Such coding is likely to involve people outside the accounts department, who may be unwilling to give time to the task. How useful the analysis will be, will depend on whether or not it is practicable to identify causes and responsibilities at the time the document is initiated.

(b) **Investigations and re-analysis of variances after the event**. This can involve the time of quite senior people, but the process of investigation may well be more useful from the point of view of the management of the business than any quantity of formal variance calculations.

4 Responsibility accounting and the interdependence of variances

4.1 Introduction

It is part of any system aimed at improving the performance of a business or any part of the business, that actions shall be traced to the person responsible. This may give the impression of 'laying the blame', but it is equally possible to award praise (and remunerate accordingly).

We have seen that responsibility accounting is a system which recognises various decision centres within a business and traces costs (and possibly revenues) to the individual managers who are primarily responsible for making decisions about the items in question.

Example

An opportunity arises for a buying department to obtain a consignment of a particular material at an exceptionally low price. The purchase is made; a favourable price variance is recorded and the buying department is duly praised.

Subsequently, when products are being manufactured using this type of material, significant adverse material usage variances and labour efficiency variances are recorded, and are initially regarded as the responsibility of the department where the work is done.

Is it fair to blame the adverse variances on the operational departments?

Solution

Investigations may reveal a number of relevant facts, for example:

- The 'cheap' material was of poor quality, and in consequence much of it was wasted in the process of machining. The resultant material usage and labour efficiency variances should presumably be regarded as the responsibility of the buying department, to offset the favourable price variance.

- Due to an employee leaving it had been necessary to use an operator who was not familiar with the job. At least part of the excess usage of materials could be attributed to this cause; but whether it should be regarded as the responsibility of the operating department or of the personnel department (for failing to recruit a replacement) is still open to question. If the employee who left had been highly paid, his removal might cause a favourable wage rate variance in the period under review – an offset to the adverse efficiency variance.
- The tools used had been badly worn, thus causing excessive time on the job. It would be necessary to consider whether this condition was attributable to the operating department (failing to sharpen tools or to requisition replacements) or to the tools store-keeper or to the buying department (for failing to buy on time or for buying poor quality items again).

The important points to bear in mind are as follows:

- Different types of variance can be inter-linked by a common cause.
- In many cases, the responsibility for variances cannot be identified merely by reference to the cost centre where the variance has been reported. Responsibility may be shared by several managers or may lie completely outside the cost centre in which the variance has arisen.
- In some instances, after questioning the managers as to the cause of a variance an independent assessment needs to take place. For example, the production manager may say that the quality of raw materials, the old machinery or the unskilled staff may have caused the adverse material usage variance, when the material price variance was also adverse. However, it could be that the buyer bought an inferior material but still paid more than the standard. An independent assessment of the material quality might need to take place.

Activity 6

WH Limited (AAT CA D94)

WH Limited uses a standard costing system which produces monthly control statements to manufacture product M, a perishable, high quality raw material which is carefully weighed by direct employees. Some wastage and quality control rejects occur at this stage. The employees then compress the material to change its shape and create product M.

All direct employees are paid a basic hourly rate appropriate to their individual skill level and a bonus scheme is in operation. Bonuses are paid according to the daily rate of output achieved by each individual.

A standard allowance for all of the above operational factors is included in the standard cost of product M. Standard cost data for one unit of product M is as follows:

		Standard cost *£ per unit*
Direct material X:	4.5 kg × £4.90 per kg	22.05
Direct labour:	10.3 hours × £3.50 per hour	36.05
Standard direct cost		58.10

The production manager has approached you for further explanations concerning the standard costing control system. He is particularly interested in understanding how the standard price is set per kg of material used.

Task

Write a memo to the production manager, explaining the following:

(a) what information would be needed to determine the standard price per kg of material X;

(b) the possible sources from which this information might be obtained.

Further data:

During November, the following costs were incurred producing 400 units of product M:

		Actual costs
		£
Direct material X:	2,100 kg @ £4.60 per kg	9,660
Direct labour:	4,000 hrs@ £4.00 per hr	16,000
Actual direct cost		25,660

Task

(a) Calculate the following direct cost variances for product M for November:

(i) direct material price;

(ii) direct material usage;

(iii) direct labour rate;

(iv) direct labour utilisation or efficiency;

(b) Present the variances in a statement which reconciles the total standard direct cost of production with the actual direct cost for product M in November.

Further data

The production manager receives a copy of the standard costing control statement for product M every month. However, he has recently confessed to you that he does not really have a clear understanding of the meaning of the variances.

He has also been baffled by the following statement made by the finance director at a recent meeting of senior managers: 'Assigning responsibility for variances can be complicated if the variances are interdependent, for example if an adverse variance in one part of the organisation is caused by a favourable variance elsewhere.'

Task

As assistant accountant for WH Limited, you are asked to write a memo to the production manager which explains the following:

(a) the meaning of each of the direct cost variances calculated for product M;

(b) two possible causes of each of the variances which you have calculated for product M for November;

(c) two examples of interdependence which may be present in the variances which you have calculated for product M for November. Explain clearly why the variances may be interdependent, so that the manager can better understand the meaning of the finance director's statement.

WH Limited

MEMORANDUM

To: Production Manager
From: Assistant Accountant
Date: 12 December 20X4
Subject: Determining the standard price per kg of material X

As requested I detail below the information which would be needed to determine the standard price of material X and possible sources of the information.

(a) *The information which is needed*	(b) *Possible sources*
•	
•	
•	
•	
•	
•	

((a) (i) Direct material price variance =

(ii) Direct material usage variance =

(iii) Direct labour rate variance =

(iv) Direct labour efficiency variance =

(b) Reconciliation of standard direct cost of production with actual direct cost for November:

	£	£
Standard direct cost of production		
Direct cost variances:		
Direct material – price		
– usage		
Direct labour – rate		
– efficiency		
		———
Actual direct cost of production		
		———

Note: A = adverse variance; F = favourable variance

Task

(a) – (c)

WH Limited

MEMORANDUM

To:

From:

Date:

Subject:

As requested I detail below explanations of the direct cost variances and possible suggestions as to their cause in November.

(a) *The meaning of the variances*

Direct material price variance

Direct material usage variance

Direct labour rate variance

Direct labour efficiency variance

(b) *Possible causes of the variances*

Favourable direct material price variance

Adverse direct material usage variance

Adverse direct labour rate variance

Favourable direct labour efficiency variance

(c) Two examples of interdependence, where one variance can be related to others, could include the following.

Activity 7

Revamp Furniture Limited

Revamp Furniture Limited manufacture a lounge chair by subjecting plasticised metal to a moulding process, thereby producing the chair in one piece.

(a) From the information provided below, you are required to analyse the cost variances and prepare a reconciliation of budgeted with actual cost incorporating the result of your analysis.

Standard/budget data

Unit variable costs:	
Direct material	6 lb at 50p per lb
Direct labour	2 hours at 160p per hour
Budgeted fixed overhead for the year (240 working days)	£30,000
Budgeted production/sales for the year	60,000 chairs
Actual data for period 1	
Number of working days	20
Production/sales	5,200 chairs

Direct material received and used:

Delivery No 1	12,000 lb	Cost	£5,880
Delivery No 2	14,000 lb	Cost	£6,790
Delivery No 3	6,000 lb	Cost	£3,060
Direct labour hours worked	10,080	Cost	£17,540
Fixed overhead			£2,550

(b) 'Cost variances are often found, upon investigation of causes, to be interdependent.'

Briefly explain this statement using as illustrations:

(i) material price and usage variances;

(ii) labour rate and efficiency variances;

taken from your answer to (a) above and comment briefly on any possible interdependence between material cost variances and labour cost variances.

Revamp Furniture Limited

(a) Reconciliation for Period 1 (see workings)

	£	£	£
Flexed budgeted cost (W1)			
Cost variances			
Materials (W2)			
Price			
Usage			
Rate of pay			
Efficiency			
Fixed overhead (W4)			
Expenditure			
Efficiency			
Capacity			
	______	______	
	______	______	______
Actual cost (W5)			
			______

(b) (i)

(ii)

Workings

1 *Standard cost per unit*

	£
Materials	
Labour	
Fixed overhead	
	——
	——
Flexed budgeted cost	

2 *Materials*

(i) *Price variance*

	£

(ii) *Usage variance*

	£

3 *Labour*

(i) *Rate of pay*

	£

(iii) *Efficiency*

	£

4 *Fixed overhead*

(i) *Expenditure variance*

	£

(ii) *Efficiency variance*

	£

(iii) *Capacity variance*

	£
	———
	———

5 *Actual cost statement*

	£
Materials	
Labour	
Fixed overhead	
	———
	———

6 Summary

In this chapter we have examined ways of measuring the significance of variances and the way in which management might introduce controls based on the variance reports provided to them. The investigation of variances is a part of this process and it is important that you understand the causes of variances and their typical remedies.

We then considered briefly responsibility accounting and the possible interaction of variances. This is a very important area in the context of management appraisal. As we have seen, purchasing of cheap materials may cause a knock-on effect into the working of those materials thereby giving the impression that the workforce (and by implication the managers of the workforce) are inefficient. This will not be the case as the problems are caused by poor purchasing of materials rather than inefficient labour.

Answers to chapter activities

Activity 1

(a) (i) *Actual profit for the period*

	£	£
Revenue (2,250 units × £15)		33,750
Production cost (2,500 units)		
Direct materials	12,000	
Direct labour	9,000	
	21,000	
Less: Closing inventory (250 units at £10 per unit) (W1)	2,500	
Cost of sales		18,500
Actual profit		15,250

Working

	£
Standard cost data per unit	
Direct materials ($\frac{6,000 \text{ kg}}{2,000 \text{ units}}$ @ £2/kg)	6.00
Direct labour ($\frac{4,000 \text{ hours}}{2,000 \text{ units}}$ @ £2/hour)	4.00
	10.00

(ii) *Material price variance*

	£
Actual usage (5,000 kg) at actual cost	12,000
Actual usage (5,000 kg) at standard cost (£2/kg)	10,000
	2,000 (A)

	£
Actual usage (5,000 kg) at standard cost (£2/kg)	10,000
Standard usage for actual production (7,500 kg) at standard cost (£2/kg)	15,000
	5,000 (F)

Labour rate variance	£
Actual hours (6,000 hours at actual rate (£1.50/hour)	9,000
Actual hours (6,000 hours) at standard rate (£2/hour)	12,000
	3,000 (F)

Labour efficiency variance	£
Actual hours (6,000 hours) at standard rate (£2/hour)	12,000
Standard hours for actual production (5,000 hours) at standard rate (£2/hour)	10,000
Labour efficiency variance	2,000 (A)

Activity 2

Revised price = £5 x 105 / 100 = £5.25

Revised quantity = 2.5 kg x 110 / 100 = 2.75 kg

AQ × AP

2,550 kg × £? = £12,000

AQ × RP

2,550 × £5.25 = £13,387.50

Controllable price variance = £1,387.50 F

AQ × RP

2,550 × £5.25 = £13,387.50

AQ x SP

2,550 x £5 = £12,750

Uncontrollable price variance = £637.50 A

AQ × SP

2,550 x £5 = £12,750

RQ × SP

1,000 × 2.75 kg × £5 = £13,750

Controllable usage variance = £1,000.00 F

RQ × SP

1,000 × 2.75 kg × £5 = £13,750

SQ x SP

1,000 x 2.5 kg x £5 = £12,500

Uncontrollable usage variance = £1,250.00 A

Activity 3

An adverse material price variance might mean that better quality material was bought than standard. The employees found it easier to work with this high quality material, so worked more efficiently than standard.

Activity 4

Adverse material price; favourable material usage; favourable labour efficiency; favourable variable overhead efficiency.

Activity 5

Actual cost	£2,000	
		Operating = £235 A
Exchange rate adjusted cost 1,000 × (1.50 × 2/1.70)	£1,765	
		Planning = £265 A
Original standard cost 1,000 kg × £1.50	£1,500	
Total variance		£500 A

Activity 6

WH Limited

Task 1

WH Limited

MEMORANDUM

To: Production Manager

From: Assistant Accountant

Date: 12 December 20X4

Subject: Determining the standard price per kg of material X

As requested I detail below the information which would be needed to determine the standard price of material X and possible sources of the information.

(a) *The information which is needed*	(b) *Possible sources*
• Type and quality of material	Technical specification
• Quantity and timing of purchases, for determining any bulk discounts	Production and purchasing schedules
• Past trend in prices	Historical records in company Supplier records Government statistics Trade association statistics Movements in price indexes
• Future trend in prices	Discussions/negotiations with suppliers Trade association forecasts Financial press forecasts Government forecasts of key indexes

• Carriage costs to be added	Historical records in company Supplier records
• Type of standard to be set, e.g. average for year, or increasing with inflation	Company policy on standard setting

Task 2

(a) (i) Direct material price variance

2,100 x £4.60

2,100 x £4.90

= £630 favourable

(ii) Direct material usage variance

2,100 x £4.90

400 x 4.5 x £4.90

= £1,470 adverse

(iii) Direct labour rate variance

4,000 x £4.00

4,000 x £3.50

= £2,000 adverse

(iv) Direct labour efficiency variance

4,000 x £3.50

400 x 10.3 x £3.50

= £420 favourable

(b) Reconciliation of standard direct cost of production with actual direct cost for November:

		£	£
Standard direct cost of production (400 × £58.10)			23,240
Direct cost variances:			
Direct material	– price	630 (F)	
	– usage	(1,470) (A)	
			(840) (A)
Direct labour	– rate	(2,000) (A)	
	– efficiency	420 (F)	
			(1,580) (A)
Actual direct cost of production			25,660

Note that adverse variances are added to the standard cost to give the actual cost.

Note: A = adverse variance; F = favourable variance

Task 3

(a) – (c)

WH Limited

MEMORANDUM

To: Production Manager
From: Assistant Accountant
Date: 12 December 20X4
Subject: Direct cost variances for November

As requested I detail below explanations of the direct cost variances and possible suggestions as to their cause in November. Page 1 of 3

(a) *The meaning of the variances*

Direct material price variance

This variance shows the saving or overspending which resulted from paying a lower or higher price than standard for the direct material used in the period. The favourable variance indicates that a lower than standard price was paid.

Direct material usage variance

This variance shows the saving or overspending, at standard prices, which resulted from using less or more material than standard to manufacture the production for the period. The adverse variance indicates that more material was used than standard.

Direct labour rate variance

This variance shows the saving or overspending which resulted from paying a lower or higher hourly rate than standard for the hours worked in the period. The adverse variance indicates that a higher than standard hourly rate was paid.

Direct labour efficiency variance

This variance shows the saving or overspending, at standard rates, which resulted from working less or more hours than standard to manufacture the production for the period. The favourable variance indicates that fewer hours were worked than standard.

(b) *Possible causes of the variances*

Favourable direct material price variance

Bulk discounts were received which were not allowed for in the standard. The standard price of material was set too high. A lower quality material was purchased, at a lower price than standard. Effective negotiations by the buyer secured a price lower than the standard.

Adverse direct material usage variance

Material wastage was higher than allowed in the standard. The standard usage was set too low. There was a higher than standard level of rejects. Theft of material.

Adverse direct labour rate variance

High levels of overtime were paid for compared with the standard allowance. The standard wage rate was set too low.

A higher grade of labour was used.

Bonus payments were higher than standard.

Favourable direct labour efficiency variance

Employees were working faster than standard. More skilled employees were used.

There were savings through the learning effect.

The standard labour time was set too high.

The material was easy to process, leading to savings against the standard time.

(c) Two examples of interdependence, where one variance can be related to others, could include the following.

The savings made on material price (favourable material price variance) may indicate that poor quality material was purchased, leading to high wastage, rejects and an adverse usage variance.

Bulk discounts may have resulted in the saving on material price. However, the consequent excessive stocks may have led to deterioration and write-offs, hence the adverse usage variance.

Direct workers may have been of a higher grade than standard, resulting in higher hourly rates and the adverse rate variance. However, the higher skill level may have led to time savings and the favourable efficiency variance.

Higher than standard bonus payments may have caused the adverse labour rate variance, but the bonuses may have resulted from faster working and hence the favourable efficiency variance.

Faster working resulted in the favourable efficiency variance, but less care may have been taken over weighing and handling the material, hence the adverse material usage variance.

Activity 7

Revamp Furniture Limited

(a) Reconciliation for Period 1 (see workings)

	£	£	£
Flexed budgeted cost (W1)			34,840
Cost variances			
Materials (W2)			
Price	270		
Usage		400	
Labour (W3)			
Rate of pay		1,412	
Efficiency	512		
Fixed overhead (W4)			
Expenditure		50	
Efficiency	80		
Capacity	20		
	882	1,862	980
Actual cost (W5)			35,820

(b) (i) Although standard costing has, as one of its purposes, the allocation of responsibility for cost variances, it is often found in practice that the analysis of variances is merely the beginning of a further task of investigation before ultimate responsibility can be fairly assigned.

On the operating statement submitted for part (a) of this question there is disclosed a favourable material price variance and an adverse usage variance. Theoretically this should indicate that the buyer is operating efficiently and the production manager inefficiently. This need not necessarily be true, however. The buyer could have taken advantage of a special offer of material at less than standard price, not appreciating that the material was slightly below standard quality. It is very likely that the inferior material would give rise to production problems of machining, handling and possibly others which could well result in excess usage; hence the adverse usage variance.

(ii) As regards labour, the payment of higher than standard rates (suggested by the adverse rate of pay variance in the operating statement) may well have had the effect of providing greater motivation, and hence speedier work, which is reflected in the favourable efficiency variance.

There may well be interdependence between the material and labour cost variances; for instance, the speedier work suggested by the favourable labour efficiency variance may have been accomplished by disregarding material usage standards.

From the foregoing it will be seen that not only is there possible interdependence between the variances of each element of cost, but also cross-interdependence between the elements of cost.

Workings

1 *Standard cost per unit*

	£
Materials (6 × 50p)	3.00
Labour (2 × £1.60)	3.20
Fixed overhead $\frac{£30,000}{120,000}$ = 25p per hour × 2 hours	0.50
	6.70

Flexed budgeted cost 5,200 × £6.70 £34,840

(Fixed overhead is budgeted to be absorbed over (60,000 × 2 hours) = 120,000 hours

2 *Materials*

(i) *Price variance*

	£
Actual cost of 32,000 lb (5,880 + 6,790 + 3,060)	15,730
Standard cost	16,000
	270 (F)

(ii) *Usage variance*

	£
Actual usage	16,000
Expected usage (5,200 x 6) x £50p	16,400
	£400 (A)

3 *Labour*

(i) *Rate of pay*

	£
Actual cost of 10,080 hours	17,540
Standard cost (10,080 × £1.60)	16,128
	1,412 (A)

(ii) *Efficiency*

	£
Standard cost (10,080 × £1.60)	16,128
Standard time allowed x £1.60 10,400 x £1.60	16,640
	512 (F)

4 *Fixed overhead*

(i) *Expenditure variance*

	£
Actual cost	2,550
Budgeted cost (30,000 x 20/240)	2,500
	50 (A)

(ii) *Capacity variance*

	£
Budgeted 20/240 × 120,000 x 25p	2,500
Actual hours worked 10,080 x 25p	2,520
	20 (F)

(iii) *Efficiency variance*

	£
Actual hours worked 10,080 x 25p	2,520
Standard hours 10,400 x 25p	2,600
	80 (F)

(The absorption rate is calculated by dividing the budgeted cost by the budgeted number of hours to be worked: £30,000/ (60,000 × 2 hours) = 25p.)

5 *Actual cost statement*

	£
Materials (5,880 + 6,790 + 3,060)	15,730
Labour	17,540
Fixed overhead	2,550
	35,820

7 Test your knowledge

Workbook Activity 8 (December 2001) (Amended)

Data

You are employed as a trainee Accounting Technician with Gransden, Yelling and Co, a firm of accountants and registered auditors. One of your clients is CD Products Ltd.

CD Products uses expensive equipment to make compact discs for customers in other companies. It has two manufacturing departments: the CD pressing department and the finishing department. The CD pressing department uses one machine to write digital data from a master disc to blank discs. The finishing department then prints information on the front of the discs, packages them and sends the completed discs to the customers.

CD Products uses standard costs to help prepare quotations for customers but does not yet use them for reporting purposes. Details of the standard costs used in the pressing department are shown below.

STANDARD COST PER MACHINE HOUR – CD PRESSING DEPARTMENT	
Blank compact discs: 800 × £0.20 each	£160.00
Labour: 8 labour hours × £7.00	£56.00
Fixed overheads	£200.00
	———
Standard cost of pressing 800 compact discs per machine hour	£416.00
	———

CD Products has prepared the following financial and operating information for the week ended 30 November 2001.

CD Pressing Department information:

- Budgeted labour hours — 880 hours
- Actual number of compact discs manufactured — 96,000 CDs
- Actual cost of blank compact discs issued to production — £20,790
- Actual price paid for each blank compact disc — £0.21
- Actual labour hours worked — 980 hours
- Actual cost of labour — £7,252

Factory information:

- Budgeted total factory fixed costs — £33,000
- Actual total factory fixed costs — £34,500
- Budgeted total factory labour hours — 1,320 hours
- Both budgeted and actual fixed overheads are apportioned between the pressing and finishing departments on the basis of budgeted labour hours.

The Chief Executive of CD Products is Jamil Baharundin. He tells you that the weekly financial and operating information does not help him manage the business. You suggest a standard costing statement might be more helpful. Jamil asks you to prepare a standard costing statement for the CD Pressing Department, using the information for the week ended 30 November 2001.

Task

(a) Calculate the following information for the CD Pressing Department for the week ended 30 November 2001:

(a)	(i)	Standard number of compact discs produced per labour hour:		
			=	
	(ii)	Budgeted machine hours of the department:		
			=	
	(iii)	Budgeted departmental fixed overheads:		
			=	
	(iv)	Actual fixed overheads:		
			=	

	(v)	Standard fixed overhead rate per labour hour:		
			=	
	(vi)	Standard labour hours produced:		
			=	
	(vii)	Actual number of blank CDs issued to production:		
			=	
	(viii)	Actual cost of actual production including fixed overheads:		
		Labour		
		Material		
		Fixed overhead		
	(ix)	Standard cost of actual production:		
			=	

(b) Calculate the following variances for the CD Pressing Department:

(b)	(i)	Material price variance:		
			=	
	(ii)	Material usage variance:		
			=	
	(iii)	Labour rate variance:		
			=	
	(iv)	Labour efficiency variance:		
			=	
	(v)	Fixed overhead expenditure variance:		
			=	

	(vi)	Fixed overhead volume variance:		
			=	
	(vii)	Fixed overhead capacity variance:		
			=	
	(viii)	Fixed overhead efficiency variance		
			=	

(c) Prepare a statement for the CD Pressing Department reconciling the standard absorption cost of actual production to the actual absorption cost of actual production.

(c)	**Standard costing reconciliation statement – week ended 30 November 2001**		
			£
	Standard cost of actual production		
			———
	Summary of variances:		
	Material price		
	Material usage		
	Labour rate		
	Labour efficiency		
	Fixed overhead expenditure		
	Fixed overhead volume		
			———
			———
	Actual cost of production		
			———

Data

In a letter to you, Jamil tells you that your standard costing statement helped explain why CD Products' profits have recently been falling. He plans to use similar statements in the future but, before doing so, he raises the following issues:

- He is not certain if all variances should be investigated. As an example, he explains that for every 100 fault-free compact discs produced in the week ended 30 November 2001, two had to be scrapped. As the unit cost of a blank CD is so small, he feels it is not worth investigating the other reasons for the material usage variance.

- The standard costs for quotation purposes assumed customers would want their discs to be both pressed and finished. The demand for disc pressing is so high that it exceeds the capacity of the CD Pressing Department but most customers then take the pressed compact discs elsewhere for finishing.
- The CD Pressing Department requires a dust-free, air-conditioned environment using an expensive machine but the Finishing Department does not use any expensive resources.

An analysis of the budgeted factory fixed overheads showing their usage by department was included in the letter and is reproduced below.

	CD Pressing	*Finishing*	*Total*
Rent, rates and insurance	£8,600	£1,300	£9,900
Air conditioning, heat, light and power	£9,600	£900	£10,500
Depreciation and maintenance	£12,600		£12,600
	£30,800	£2,200	£33,000

Task

Write a letter to Jamil Baharundin. In your letter you should:

(a) Identify FOUR issues to consider before deciding to investigate a variance.

(b) Sub-divide the material usage variance into that part due to discs being scrapped and that part due to other reasons.

(c) *Briefly* explain, with reasons, why there might be excess demand for the CD Pressing Department but much less demand for the Finishing Department.

Task

LETTER

Gransden, Yelling and Co
Accountants and Registered Auditors

5 December 2001

Jamil Baharundin
CD Products Ltd
Anytown

Dear Mr Baharundin

Thank you for your letter and observations regarding the introduction of the new reporting format based on the standing costing technique.

I list my response to your questions below:

(a) **Issues to consider before investigating a variance**

(b) **Sub-division of the material usage variance**

(c) **Demand for pressing and finishing**

Yours sincerely
AAT Student

Workbook Activity 9 (December 2000) (Amended)

Data

You are employed as a management accountant in the head office of Travel Holdings plc. Travel Holdings owns a number of transport businesses. One of them is Travel Ferries Ltd. Travel Ferries operates ferries which carry passengers and vehicles across a large river. Each year, standard costs are used to develop the budget for Travel Ferries Ltd. The latest budgeted and actual operating results are shown below.

Travel Ferries Ltd

Budgeted and actual operating results for the year to 30 November 2000

Operating data:	*Budget*		*Actual*	
Number of ferry crossings		6,480		5,760
Operating hours of ferries		7,776		7,488
		£		£
Cost data:				
Fuel	1,244,160 litres	497,664	1,232,800 litres	567,088
Labour	93,312 hours	466,560	89,856 hours	471,744
Fixed overheads		466,560		472,440
		————		————
Cost of operations		1,430,784		1,511,272

Other accounting information:

- Fuel and labour are variable costs.
- Fixed overheads are absorbed on the basis of budgeted operating hours.

One of your duties is to prepare costing information and a standard costing reconciliation statement for the Chief Executive of Travel Holdings.

Task

(a) Calculate the following information:

	(i)	Standard price of fuel per litre:		
			=	
	(ii)	Standard litres of fuel for 5,760 ferry crossings:		
			=	
	(iii)	Standard labour rate per hour:		
			=	
	(iv)	Standard labour hours for 5,760 ferry crossings:		
			=	
	(v)	Standard fixed overhead per budgeted operating hour:		
			=	
	(vi)	Standard operating hours for 5,760 crossings:		
			=	
	(vii)	Standard fixed overhead cost absorbed by the actual 5,760 ferry crossings:		
			=	

(b) Using the data provided in the operating results and your answers to part (a), calculate the following variances:

	(i)	Material price variance:		
			=	
	(ii)	Material usage variance:		
			=	
	(iii)	Labour rate variance:		
			=	
	(iv)	Labour efficiency variance:		
			=	
	(v)	Fixed overhead expenditure variance:		
	(vi)	Fixed overhead volume variance:		
			=	

	(vii)	Fixed overhead capacity variance:		
			=	
	(viii)	Fixed overhead capacity variance:		
			=	

(c) Prepare a statement reconciling the actual cost of operations to the standard cost of operations for the year to 30 November 2000.

Travel Ferries Ltd – Reconciliation statement for the year ended 30 November 2000

F = Favourable

A = Adverse

	£
Standard cost of actual operations	
	–––––––
Summary of variances:	
Material price	
Material usage	
Labour rate	
Labour efficiency	
Fixed overhead expenditure	
Fixed overhead volume	
	–––––––
Actual cost	
	–––––––

Task

Write a memo to the Chief Executive. Your memo should:

(a) Sub-divide the material price variance into:

  (i) that part arising from the standard price being different from the actual market price of fuel, and

  (ii) that part due to other reasons.

(b) Identify ONE variance which is not controllable and give ONE reason why the variance is not controllable.

(c) Identify TWO variances which are controllable and which should be investigated. For each variance, give ONE reason why it is controllable.

MEMO

To:

From:

Date:

Subject:

I refer to the concern you have expressed recently regarding the adverse variances in the report on Travel Ferries' operations for the year ended 30 November.

In reply to your comments, I wish to make the following observations concerning:

- further analysis of the material price variance.
- identification of uncontrollable variances.
- controllable variances and their investigation.

(a)

(b)

(c)

Workbook Activity 10 (June 2000) (Amended)

Data

NGJ Ltd is a furniture manufacturer. It makes 3 products: the Basic, the Grand and the Super. You are the management accountant reporting to the product line manager for the Basic. Reproduced below is NGJ's unit standard material and labour cost data and budgeted production for the year to 31 May 2000 together with details of the budgeted and actual factory fixed overheads for the year.

Unit standard material and labour cost data by product for the year to 31 May 2000

Product	*Basic*	*Grand*	*Super*
Material at £12 per metre	6 metres	8 metres	10 metres
Labour at £5.00 per hour	6 hours	1 hour	1 hour
Budgeted production	10,000 units	70,000 units	70,000 units

Total budgeted and actual factory fixed overheads for the year to 31 May 2000

	Budgeted	*Actual*
	£	£
Rent and rates	100,000	100,000
Depreciation	200,000	200,000
Light, heat and power	60,000	70,000
Indirect labour	240,000	260,000
Total factory fixed overheads	600,000	630,000

Apportionment policy:

As all products are made in the same factory, budgeted and actual total factory fixed overheads are apportioned to each product on the basis of budgeted total labour hours per product.

During the year 11,500 *Basics* were made. The actual amount of material used, labour hours worked and costs incurred were as follows:

Actual material and labour cost of producing 11,500 Basics for the year to 31 May 2000		
	Units	*Total cost*
Material	69,230 metres	£872,298
Labour	70,150 hours	£343,735

Task

(a) Calculate the following information:

(i) Budgeted labour hours of production for NGJ Ltd:

	Labour hours	*Budgeted hours per unit*	*Budgeted production*	*Budgeted hours*
	Basic			
	Grand			
	Super			
				———
	Total budgeted labour hours			
				———

(ii)	Standard factory fixed overhead rate per labour hour:	
(iii)	*Basic* budgeted factory fixed overhead:	
	Basic actual factory fixed overhead:	
(iv)	Actual material cost per metre:	
	Actual labour hourly rate:	
(v)	Standard absorption cost of actual *Basic* production:	
	Material	
	Labour	
	Factory fixed overheads	
		———
		———

(vi)	Actual absorption cost of actual *Basic* production:	
	Material	
	Labour	
	Factory fixed overheads	

(b) Calculate the following variances for *Basic* production:

(i)	Material price variance		
		=	
(ii)	Material usage variance:		
		=	
(iii)	Labour rate variance:		
		=	
(iv)	Labour efficiency variance:		
		=	
(v)	Fixed overhead expenditure variance:		
		=	
(vi)	Fixed overhead volume variance:		
		=	
(vii)	Fixed overhead capacity variance:		
		=	
(viii)	Fixed overhead efficiency variance:		
		=	

(c) Prepare a statement reconciling the actual absorption cost of actual *Basic* production with the standard absorption cost of actual *Basic* production.

Standard costing reconciliation statement – year ended 31 May 2000

		£
Standard cost of actual production		
Summary of variances:		
Material price		
Material usage		
Labour rate		
Labour efficiency		
Fixed overhead expenditure		
Fixed overhead volume		
	———	
		———
Actual cost of production		
		———
F = Favourable		
(A) = Adverse		

Data

The product line manager for the *Basic is* of the opinion that the standard costs and variances do not fairly reflect the effort put in by staff. The manager made the following points:

- Because of a shortage of materials for the *Basic,* the purchasing manager had entered into a contract for the year with a single supplier in order to guarantee supplies.
- The actual price paid for the material per metre was 10% less than the market price throughout the year.
- The *Basic is* a hand-made product made in a small, separate part of the factory and uses none of the expensive machines shared by the *Grand* and the *Super.*
- *Grand* and *Super* production uses the same highly mechanised manufacturing facilities and only one of those products can be made at any one time. A change in production from one product to another involves halting production in order to set up the necessary tools and production line.

In response to a request from the *Basic* product line manager, a colleague has re-analysed the budgeted and actual factory fixed overheads by function. The revised analysis is reproduced below.

Functional analysis of factory fixed overheads for the year ended 31 May 2000

	Budget	*Actual*
	£	£
Setting up of tools and production lines	202,000	228,000
Depreciation attributable to production	170,000	170,000
Stores	60,000	59,000
Maintenance	40,000	48,000
Light, heat and power directly attributable to production	48,000	45,000
Rent and rates directly attributable to production	80,000	80,000
Total factory fixed overheads	600,000	630,000

Task

Write a memo to the *Basic* product line manager. Your memo should:

(a) Identify the market price of the material used in the *Basic.*

(b) Sub-divide the material price variance into that part due to the contracted price being different from the market price and that due to other reasons.

(c) Identify ONE benefit to NGJ Ltd, which is not reflected in the variances, arising from the purchasing manager's decision to enter into a contract for the supply of materials.

(d) *Briefly* explain what is meant by activity-based costing.

(e) Refer to the task data, where appropriate, to *briefly* discuss whether or not activity-based costing would have reduced the budgeted and actual fixed overheads of *Basic* production.

MEMO

To:

From:

Date:

Subject:

Further to your comments on the variances relating to Basic production, I wish to make the following observations.

(a)

(b)

(c)

(d)

(e)

Workbook Activity 11 (December 1999)

You are the assistant management accountant at the Bare Foot Hotel complex on the tropical island of St Nicolas. The hotel complex is a luxury development. All meals and entertainment are included in the price of the holidays and guests only have to pay for drinks.

The Bare Foot complex aims to create a relaxing atmosphere. Because of this, meals are available throughout the day and guests can eat as many times as they wish.

The draft performance report for the hotel for the seven days ended 27 November 1999 is reproduced below.

Bare Foot Hotel Complex

Draft performance report for seven days ended 27 November 1999

Guests	*Notes*		*Budget* [540]		*Actual* [648]
		$	$	$	$
Variable costs					
Meal costs	1		34,020		49,896
Catering staff costs	2, 3		3,780		5,280
Total variable costs			37,800		55,176
Fixed overhead costs					
Salaries of other staff		5,840		6,000	
Local taxes		4,500		4,200	
Light, heat and power		2,500		2,600	
Depreciation of buildings and equipment		5,000		4,000	
Entertainment		20,500		21,000	
Total fixed overheads			38,340		37,800
Total cost of providing for guests			76,140		92,976

Notes

1 Budgeted cost of meals: number of guests × 3 meals per day × 7 days × $3 per meal.

2 Budgeted cost of catering staff: each member of the catering staff is to prepare and serve 12 meals per hour. Cost = (number of guests × 3 meals per day × 7 days ÷ 12 meals per hour) × $4 per hour.

3 Actual hours worked by catering staff = 1,200 hours.

Other notes

The amount of food per meal has been kept under strict portion control. Since preparing the draft performance report, however, it has been discovered that guests have eaten, on average, four meals per day.

You report to Alice Groves, the general manager of the hotel, who feels that the format of the draft performance report could be improved to provide her with more meaningful management information. She suggests that the budgeted and actual data given in the existing draft performance report is rearranged in the form of a standard costing report.

Task

(a) Use the budget data, the actual data and the notes to the performance report to calculate the following for the seven days ended 27 November 1999:

(a)	Budget and actual data		
(i)	Actual number of meals:		
		=	
(ii)	Standard number of meals:		
		=	
(iii)	Actual hourly rate for catering staff:		
		=	
(iv)	Standard hours allowed to serve three meals:		
		=	
(v)	Standard overhead per guest:		
		=	
(vi)	Standard cost of providing for 648 guests:		
		=	
	Catering staff	=	
	Fixed overheads:		
			______
		=	
			______

(b) Use the data given earlier and your answers to part (a) to calculate the following variances for the seven days ended 27 November 1999:

(i)	Material price variance:		
		=	
(ii)	Material usage variance:		
		=	
(iii)	Labour rate variance:		
		=	
(iv)	Labour efficiency variance:		
		=	
(v)	Fixed overhead expenditure variance:		
		=	
(vi)	Fixed overhead volume variance:		
		=	

(c) Prepare a statement reconciling the standard cost for the actual number of guests to the actual cost for the actual number of guests for the seven days ended 27 November 1999.

		$
	Standard cost of providing for guests	
	Summary of variances:	
	Material price variance	
	Material usage variance	
	Labour rate variance	
	Labour efficiency variance	
	Fixed overhead expenditure variance	
	Fixed overhead volume variance	
		———
		———
	Actual cost of providing for guests	
		———

Data

On receiving your reconciliation statement, Alice Groves asks the following questions:

- How much of the labour efficiency variance is due to guests taking, on average, four meals per day rather than the three provided for in the budget and how much is due to other reasons?
- Would it be feasible to sub-divide the fixed overhead volume variance into a capacity and efficiency variance?

Task

Write a memo to Alice Groves. Your memo should:

(a) Divide the labour efficiency variance into that part due to guests taking more meals than planned and that part due to other efficiency reasons.

(b) Explain the meaning of the fixed overhead capacity and efficiency variances.

(c) *Briefly* discuss whether or not it is feasible to calculate the fixed overhead capacity and efficiency variances for the Bare Foot Hotel Complex.

MEMO

To:

From:

Date:

Subject

(a)

(b)

(c)

Workbook Activity 12 (June 1999) (Amended)

Data

You are the management accountant at Brighter Chemicals Ltd. Brighter Chemicals makes a single product, Zed, which is sold in 5-litre tins.

One of your responsibilities is to prepare a report each month for the management team comparing the actual cost of Zed production with its standard cost of production. This involves taking data from a computer printout, preparing standard cost variances and reconciling the standard cost of actual production to the actual cost of actual production. After the data is analysed, you attend a management meeting where the performance of the company is discussed. The printout for May 1999 is reproduced below.

Brighter chemicals Ltd – Production report for May 1999						
Number of tins of Zed	*Budgeted production 1,750*				*Actual production 1,700*	
Inputs	*Units of input*	*Standard cost per unit of input*	*Standard cost per tin of Zed*	*Standard cost of budgeted production*	*Actual cost per unit of input*	*Actual cost of actual production*
Material	5 litres	£40.00	£200.00	£350,000	£40.20	£338,283
Labour	10 hrs	£6.00	£60.00	£105,000	£5.90	£110,330
Fixed overheads	10 hrs	£24.00	£240.00	£420,000		£410,000
			£500,000	£875,000		£858,613

Task

In preparation for the management meeting:

(a) Calculate the:

(i)	Actual litres used:		
(ii)	Actual hours worked:		
(iii)	Standard litres for 1,700 tins of Zed:		
(iv)	Standard labour hours for 1,700 tins of Zed:		
(v)	Standard hours of fixed overheads charged to budgeted production:		
(vi)	Standard hours of fixed overheads charged to actual production:		

(b) Calculate the following variances:

(b)(i)	Material price variance:		
		=	
(ii)	Material usage variance:		
		=	
(iii)	Labour rate variance:		
		=	
(iv)	Labour efficiency variance:		
		=	
(v)	Fixed overhead expenditure variance:		
		=	
(vi)	Fixed overhead volume variance:		
		=	
(vii)	Fixed overhead capacity variance:		
		=	
(viii)	Fixed overhead efficiency variance:		
		=	

(c) Prepare a report reconciling the standard cost of *actual* production to the actual cost of *actual* production.

	£
Standard cost of actual production	
	———
Summary of variances:	
Material price	
Material usage	
Labour rate	
Labour efficiency	
Fixed overhead expenditure	
Fixed overhead volume	
	———
	———
Actual cost of production	
	———

Data

On receiving your report, the production director makes the following comments:

- The material used in Zed production is purchased in drums. A notice on each drum states that the minimum content per drum is 50 litres.
- Finished production of Zed is automatically poured into tins by a machine which also measures the contents. An error of 0.5% either way in the accuracy of measurement is acceptable.
- The reported material price variance does not truly reflect the efficiency of the purchasing department. An index of raw material prices stood at 124.00 when the standard price was set but stood at 125.86 in May.
- It seems unnecessary to investigate favourable variances. Favourable variances improve profitability and should be encouraged. Only adverse variances should be investigated.

Task

Write a *short* memo to the production director. Your memo should:

(a) Sub-divide the material price variance calculated into that part caused by the change in the standard cost as measured by the material price index and that part caused by the efficiency or inefficiency of the purchasing department.

(b) Give THREE separate reasons why Zed production might result in a favourable material usage variance.

MEMO

To:

From:

Date:

Subject:

I refer to your observations regarding the material variances shown on my recent standard costing reconciliation statement.

If the standard price of material had been revised to incorporate the index then the price would have been:

(a) It is possible, using this additional information, to sub-divide the price variance to that element due to the price increase highlighted in the index and that attributed to the efficiency of the purchasing department:

Revised standard price		Revised standard price	
Original standard price		Actual price	
Difference		Difference	
Actual quantity (litres)		Actual quantity (litres)	
Price variance due to revised price		Price variance due to purchasing	

(b) There can be a number of factors which influence the reporting of a favourable usage variance; these include:

Performance indicators

8

Introduction

Cost variances, covered earlier, give one type of performance indicator – how individual operational managers perform against pre-set budget and standard cost targets. Here we continue this theme, but look at measures for productivity, efficiency etc; ratios that assist in assessment of resource utilisation; and overall profitability measures that may be applied to operating divisions and the business as a whole. We also look at the particular performance evaluation aspects of service industries, in particular the measurement of quality of service. The objective will always be to highlight activities, processes, products and business units that need some attention in order to enhance their value to the business.

KNOWLEDGE

Identify appropriate performance indicators: efficiency, effectiveness, productivity; balanced scorecard, benchmarking; unit costs; control ratios (efficiency, capacity and activity), scenario planning ('what if' analysis) (3.3)

Describe the contribution of functional specialists in an organisation to cost reduction and value enhancement (1.2)

Identify the relevant performance and quality measures to use to monitor financial performance (3.1)

Identify the correct ratios to monitor financial performance (3.5)

Describe and recognise when life cycle costing and target costing should be used (3.6)

CONTENTS

1 Types of performance indicator
2 Ratio analysis
3 Profitability
4 Liquidity
5 Gearing
6 Manufacturing industries
7 Service departments
8 Service sectors
9 Total quality management (TQM)
10 The balanced scorecard
11 Cost reduction and value enhancement

SKILLS

Calculate ratios, performance indicators and measures of value added (2.5)

Prepare relevant performance indicators (2.6)

Interpret the results of relevant performance indicators, identify potential improvements and estimate the value of such improvements (2.7)

Identify ways to reduce costs and enhance values, consulting specialists as necessary (2.8)

Prepare reports in the most appropriate format and present them to management within the required timescales (3.1)

Prepare exception reports to identify matters which require further investigation (3.2)

Make specific recommendations to management in a clear and appropriate form (3.3)

1 Types of performance indicator

1.1 Introduction

Performance indicators may be categorised as quantitative or qualitative.

1.2 Quantitative performance indicators

Quantitative measures are expressed in numerical terms which include the following:

(a) variances;

(b) profit, sales, costs, etc;

(c) ratios and percentages;

(d) indices.

1.3 Qualitative performance indicators

Qualitative indicators are far more subjective and cannot be expressed as an objective, numerical measure. Examples relevant to business and managerial performance would include the following:

(a) level of customer satisfaction: expressed as a subjective level 'very satisfied' … to …'not at all satisfied';

(b) staff performance grades: 'excellent', 'average', 'poor', etc;

(c) company performance: 'steady', 'volatile results', 'disappointing', etc.

1.4 Efficiency and effectiveness

Performance indicators can be used to measure the efficiency and effectiveness of organisations.

Definition

Efficiency can be defined as the relationship between inputs and outputs achieved. The fewer the inputs used by an organisation to achieve any given output, the more efficient is that organisation. In commercial organisations, efficiency is usually measured in terms of profitability, often in relation to assets employed.

Effectiveness is the degree to which an objective or target is met.

2 Ratio analysis

2.1 Introduction

Ratio analysis is one of the main tools utilised in appraising the performance of a company, the main advantage being that the magnitude of the individual figures is eliminated allowing the appraiser to concentrate on relative movements.

Ratio analysis is generally utilised in two ways as follows:

(a) comparison of performance year to year;

(b) comparison with other companies.

The techniques covered here occur in many branches of accountancy and it is important that you can calculate and interpret appropriate ratios.

2.2 Types of ratios

The main types of ratio used are:

(a) profitability ratios;

(b) liquidity ratios;

(c) gearing ratios;

(d) investment ratios.

Of these, profitability and liquidity ratios are of the greatest significance to the management accountant.

Example

In order to illustrate the most common ratios, let's look at some calculations based on the summarised accounts of Knotty plc. The information from Knotty plc's financial statements will be used in the following sections.

Income statement for the year ended 31 July 20X9

	Notes	*20X9*		*20X8*	
		£000	£000	£000	£000
Revenue			37,589		30,209
Cost of sales			(28,380)		(22,808)
Gross profit			9,209		7,401
Distribution costs		(3,755)		(3,098)	
Administrative expenses		(2,291)		(2,030)	
			(6,046)		(5,128)
			3,163		2,273
Other operating income			108		0,279
Operating profit			3,271		2,552
Interest receivable			7		28
			3,278		2,580
Finance costs			(442)		(471)
Profit on ordinary activities before taxation			2,836		2,109
Tax on profit on ordinary activities			(1,038)		(650)
Profit on ordinary activities after taxation			1,798		1,459
Preference dividend			(6)		(6)
			1,792		1,453
Ordinary dividends			(606)		(441)
Profit for the year			1,186		1,012

Statement of financial position as at 31 July 20X9

	Notes	*20X9*		*20X8*	
		£000	£000	£000	£000
Non-current assets					
Tangible assets			8,687		5,669
Investments			15		15
			8,702		5,684
Current assets					
Inventories		8,486		6,519	
Receivables	1	8,836		6,261	
Cash and cash equivalents		479		250	
		17,801		13,030	
Payables: amounts falling due within one year					
Bank loans and overdrafts		(929)		(511)	
Other amounts falling due within one year		(9,178)		(6,645)	
		(10,107)		(7,156)	
Net current assets			7,694		5,874
Total assets less current liabilities			16,396		11,558
Payables: amounts falling due after more than one year					
Debentures			(2,840)		(2,853)
Net assets			13,556		8,705
Equity					
Called up share capital					
Ordinary shares of 20p each	2		2,003		1,762
4.2% cumulative preference shares of £1 each			150		150
			2,153		1,912
Share premium account			123		123
Other reserves			2,576		–
Retained earnings			8,704		6,670
			13,556		8,705

Notes

1 Receivables at 31 July 20X9 include trade receivables of £8,233,000 (20X8 £5,735,000).

2 The number of ordinary shares in issue at 31 July 20X9 was 10,014,514 (20X8: 8,808,214).

3 Profitability

3.1 Return on capital employed (ROCE)

Return on capital employed (ROCE) expresses profit as a percentage of the assets in use (the capital employed in the business) and can be further subdivided into profit margin and asset turnover (use of assets):

Profit margin × Asset turnover = Return on capital employed (ROCE)

$$\frac{\text{Profit}}{\text{Turnover}} \times \frac{\text{Turnover}}{\text{Assets}} = \frac{\text{Profit}}{\text{Assets}}$$

The equation helps to demonstrate how management can influence the rate of return on capital employed:

(a) By increasing profit margins:

- (i) increase sales prices;
- (ii) reduce costs.

(b) By increasing asset turnover (use of assets):

- (i) increase revenues;
- (ii) reduce assets (capital employed).

3.2 Year-end or average capital employed

Ideally, the profits for the year ended 31 July 20X9 should be related to the assets in use throughout the year (the average capital employed). In practice, the ratio is usually computed using the assets at the year-end (the year-end capital employed). Using year-end figures of capital employed can distort trends and inter-company comparison; if new investment has been undertaken near to the year-end and financed (for example) by the issue of new shares, the capital employed will have risen by the total finance raised, whereas the profits will only have a month or two of the new investment's contribution.

A range of different acceptable measures of the assets in use is available; the matter of principle should be that the profit figure which is related to the capital employed should include all types of return on those assets.

Solution

For Knotty plc, a suitable calculation would be as follows.

	20X9	*20X8*
	£000	£000
Equity	13,556	8,705
Add: Debentures	2,840	2,853
Year-end capital employed	16,396	11,558

	20X9	*20X8*
	£000	£000
Operating profit	3,271	2,552
Interest receivable	7	28
Profit before finance costs and tax	3,278	2,580

So the return on capital employed is calculated as:

$$\frac{\text{Profit before finance costs and tax}}{\text{Equity and long-term debt}} \times 100\%$$

20X9 $\frac{3,278}{16,396} \times 100 = 20.0\%$

20X8 $\frac{2,580}{11,558} \times 100 = 22.3\%$

The capital employed figure includes the long-term debt, the debentures. Therefore, the profit used must be that available to these providers of capital, the profit before finance costs.

The rate of return on year-end capital employed has fallen in 20X9 compared with 20X8 and might indicate less effective management. To comment further, we need to sub-analyse the ratio into profit margin and asset turnover.

We also need to understand that the way in which business managers are assessed can have a great influence on the decisions that they make. The use of ratios such as ROCE can lead to a lack of goal congruence where managers improve the performance of certain ratios but this may not be in the best interests of the organisation as a whole.

For example, a manager may not be prepared to invest in new machinery if the increase in the net asset position will reduce the ROCE, even though the investment may reduce other costs, leading to zero defects or an increase in customer satisfaction.

3.3 Profit margin

If the profitability ratios are to interlock perfectly, the profit margin will be calculated expressing the same profit before interest payable and tax as a percentage of revenue:

$$\frac{\text{Profit before finance costs and tax}}{\text{Revenue}} \times 100\%$$

A small problem with the approach in this example is that the profit includes interest receivable which is not represented in revenue; however, as the amount is small, this can be ignored.

In order that the profit can be related more fairly to revenue, profit margin is sometimes calculated using operating profit.

Solution

For Knotty plc: 20X9 $\frac{3,271}{37,589} \times 100 = 8.7\%$

20X8 $\frac{2,552}{30,209} \times 100 = 8.4\%$

Operating profit margins have improved slightly over the last year, possibly due to better cost control.

Sectors which have traditionally generated relatively high margins include publishing, electronics manufacturing, distillers and brewers, whereas food retailing and motor vehicle distribution are examples of low margin businesses.

Low margins within a sector may arise from a policy designed to increase market share by cutting selling prices, or may be due to high development costs associated with new products, both of which may be positive factors for the future. However, low margins are often associated with inefficiency and poor quality management.

Conversely, high margins relative to competitors, or improving margins, are usually taken as indicators of efficiency and good management. High margins achieved by dominating a particular market may, however, attract competitors into that market and imply lower margins in the longer term.

3.4 Costs as a % of revenue

The calculation of any type of cost as a % of revenue is simply performed using the formula:

$$\frac{\text{Cost}}{\text{Revenue}} \times 100\%$$

Solution

For the distribution costs in our example:

$$\text{Distribution cost as a \% of revenue} = \frac{\text{Distribution cost}}{\text{Revenue}} \times 100\%$$

20X9 $\frac{3,755}{37,589} \times 100\% = 9.99\%$ 20X8 $\frac{3,098}{30,209} \times 100\% = 10.26\%$

3.5 Asset turnover

Another aspect of efficient management is to 'make the assets work'. This may involve disposing of those 'underperforming' assets which cannot be made to generate revenue, as well as developing and marketing the company's products or services.

Solution

Once again, the simplest method of computing the ratio is to relate revenue to the same figure of year-end capital employed used in calculating return on capital employed:

$$\text{Asset turnover} = \frac{\text{Revenue}}{\text{Capital employed}}$$

20X9 $\frac{37,589}{16,396} = 2.3$ times 20X8 $\frac{38,209}{11,558} = 2.6$ times

However, as with profit margins, certain assets represented by capital employed have no turnover implications. One method of avoiding this illogicality is to exclude long and short-term investments from capital employed. For companies with substantial investments this will make a considerable difference.

Asset turnover will tend to be lower in capital-intensive manufacturing industries, which carry substantial tangible non-current assets, inventories and trade receivables, than in service industries where the principal resource is people rather than plant and machinery, and where inventories are low.

There are often trade-offs between asset turnover and profit margins in different sectors. For example, food retailers have relatively low profit margins compared to electronic equipment manufacturers, but asset turnover is higher. Typical numbers might be:

	Profit *margin* %	×	Asset *turnover*	=	*ROCE* %
Food retailer	3.7	×	6.7	=	24.8
Electronic equipment manufacturer	10.3	×	2.3	=	23.7

3.6 Gross profit margin

The profit margin given above used a profit figure that included non-productive overheads and sundry items of income. The gross profit margin looks at the profitability of the pure trading activities of the business:

$$\frac{\text{Gross profit}}{\text{Revenue}} \times 100\%$$

Solution

For Knotty plc: 20X9 $\frac{9,209}{37,589} \times 100 = 24.5\%$

20X8 $\frac{7,401}{30,209} \times 100 = 24.5\%$

The company has maintained its gross profit margin; thus the slight rise in net profit margin must be due to overhead costs being better controlled.

Activity 1

WH Limited (AAT D94)

WH Limited is a member of a trade association which operates an inter-company comparison scheme. The scheme is designed to help its member companies to monitor their own performance against that of other companies in the same industry.

At the end of each year, the member companies submit detailed annual accounts to the scheme organisers. The results are processed and a number of accounting ratios are published and circulated to members. The ratios indicate the average results for all member companies.

Your manager has given you the following extract, which shows the average profitability and asset turnover ratios for the latest year. For comparison purposes, WH Limited's accounts analyst has added the ratios for your company.

	Results for year 4	
	Trade association average	*WH Limited*
Return on capital employed	20.5%	18.4%
Net (operating) profit margin	5.4%	6.8%
Asset turnover	3.8 times	2.7 times
Gross margin	14.2%	12.9%

Required

As assistant accountant for WH Limited, your manager has asked you to prepare a report for the senior management committee. The report should cover the following points:

(a) an explanation of what each ratio is designed to show;

(b) an interpretation of WH Limited's profitability and asset turnover compared with the trade association average;

(c) comments on any limitations of these ratios and of comparisons made on this basis.

Activity 1

WH Limited

REPORT

To:

From:

Date:

Subject:

We have received the Trade Association results for year 4 and this report looks in detail at the profitability and asset turnover ratios.

(a) **What each ratio is designed to show**

(i) *Return on capital employed (ROCE)*

(ii) *Net operating profit margin*

(iii) Asset *turnover*

(iv) Gross *margin*

(b) **WH Limited's profitability and asset turnover**

(c) **Limitations of the ratios and of inter-company comparisons**

4 Liquidity

4.1 Current ratio and quick ratio

When analysing a company's balance sheet without access to management information, it is customary to calculate two ratios as indicators of the company's ability to pay its way:

$$\text{Current ratio} = \frac{\text{Current assets}}{\text{Current liabilities}}$$

$$\text{Quick ratio (or acid test ratio)} = \frac{\text{Current assets less inventories}}{\text{Current liabilities}}$$

Solution

For Knotty plc:

		20X9	*20X8*
(a)	Current ratio	$\frac{17,801}{10,107} = 1.76$	$\frac{13,030}{7,156} = 1.82$
(a)	Quick ratio	$\frac{9,315}{10,107} = 0.92$	$\frac{6,511}{7,156} = 0.91$

4.2 Cash and funds flow analysis

Although current and quick ratios are used to measure liquidity, they are limited insofar as they concentrate on only one area of the statement of financial position. If the company needs adequate cash to meet its obligations, there are sources other than the sale of inventories and the collection of amounts owed by receivables.

Analysis of cash flows is a more comprehensive method of assessing liquidity, although significant variations in the liquidity ratios may indicate important changes.

4.3 Other working capital ratios

A more detailed analysis of the movement in the elements of working capital can be made with the help of the following ratios.

4.4 Inventory holding period (inventory days)

Inventory holding periods can be compared if they relate costs of sales as a measure of activity to inventories which are usually included at cost:

$$\frac{\text{Inventories}}{\text{Cost of sales}} \times 365 \text{ days}$$

Solution

20X9 $\frac{8,486}{28,380} \times 365 = 109$ days

20X8 $\frac{6,519}{22,808} \times 365 = 104$ days

There has been a slight increase in the holding period, indicating inventory is taking longer to sell. A review of inventories may be necessary to determine whether levels of obsolete or damaged inventories are increasing. There may be a deliberate policy to increase inventories.

4.5 Trade receivables collection period (trade receivable days)

This calculation is always made using revenue since trade receivables includes the profit element:

$$\frac{\text{Trade receivables}}{\text{Revenue}} \times 365 \text{ days}$$

Solution

20X9 $\frac{8,233}{37,589} \times 365 = 80$ days

20X8 $\frac{5,735}{30,209} \times 365 = 69$ days

The company is taking approximately 11 days longer, on average, to collect its debts.

As the year-end figures may be unrepresentative (due perhaps to seasonality of revenues), an average receivables figure for the year might be used if this were available.

4.6 Trade payables payment period (trade payable days)

A similar calculation can be made to determine the trade payables payment (settlement) period:

$$\frac{\text{Trade payables}}{\text{Purchases or cost of sales}} \times 365 \text{ days}$$

Purchases should normally be used for this ratio but if it is not available from the information then cost of sales can be used as a substitute.

Activity 2

Two liquidity ratios are:

- Inventory turnover ☐
- Receivables days ☐
- Return on capital employed ☐
- Gearing ☐

Activity 3

Homely Limited

Data

Stately Hotels plc is considering making an offer to buy a small privately owned chain of hotels, Homely Limited. In order to carry out an initial appraisal, you have been provided with an abbreviated set of their accounts for 20X4.

Homely Limited – Income statement for the year ended 31 December 20X4 (extract)

	£000
Revenue	820
Operating costs	754
Operating profit	66
Finance costs	4
Profit before tax	62
Taxation	18
Profit after tax	44
Dividends	22
Profit for the year	22

Homely Limited – Statement of financial position as at 31 December 20X4 (extract)

	£000
Non-current assets at carrying amount	230
Net current assets	70
Total assets less current liabilities	300
Long-term loans	50
Equity	250
Number of employees (full-time equivalents)	20
Number of rooms, each available for 365 nights	18
Number of room nights achieved in 20X4	5,900

Stately Hotels plc uses a number of key accounting ratios to monitor the performance of the group of hotels and of individual hotels in the chain. An extract from the target ratios for 20X4 is as follows:

Stately Hotels plc – target ratios for 20X4 (extract)

(i)	Return on capital employed, based on profit before finance costs and tax	26%
(ii)	Operating profit percentage	13%
(iii)	Asset turnover	2 times
(iv)	Working capital period = $\frac{\text{Working capital}}{\text{Operating costs}} \times 365$	20 days
(v)	Percentage room occupancy = $\frac{\text{Number of room nights let}}{\text{Number of room nights available}} \times 100\%$	85%
(vi)	Revenue per employee (full-time equivalent)	£30,000

Required

(a) Calculate the six target ratios above based on Homely Limited's accounts and present them in a table which enables easy comparison with Stately Hotels' target ratios for 20X4.

(b) Prepare a memorandum for the management accountant of Stately Hotels plc, giving your initial assessment of Homely Limited based on a comparison of these ratios with Stately Hotels' target ratios. Your memorandum should provide the following information for each of the six ratios.

   (i) Comments on the performance of Homely Limited and suggestions about the management action which might be necessary to correct any apparent adverse performance.

   (ii) A discussion of any limitations in the use of the ratio for this performance comparison.

Activity 3

Homely Limited

(a) *Target ratios*

Return on capital employed =

Operating profit percentage =

Asset turnover =

Working capital period =

Percentage room occupancy =

Revenue per employee =

Key ratios for 20X4

	Stately Hotels plc target	*Homely Limited actual*
Return on capital employed	26%	
Operating profit percentage	13%	
Asset turnover	2.0 times	
Working capital period	20 days	
Percentage room occupancy	85%	
Revenue per employee	£30,000	

WH Limited

MEMORANDUM

To:

From:

Date:

Subject:

I have carried out an initial assessment of Homely Limited, based on an extract from their accounts for 20X4. I have calculated their key accounting ratios and compared them with our company's target ratios and my conclusions and recommendations are as follows.

Return on capital employed (ROCE)

Operating profit percentage

Asset turnover

Working capital period

Percentage room occupancy

Revenue per employee

Example

Work through the following example to ensure that you understand how to calculate and interpret basic ratios.

The outline statements of financial position of the Nantred Trading Co Limited were as shown below.

Statement of financial position as at 30 September

	20X9		*20X8*	
	£	£	£	£
Non-current assets (at carrying amount)				
Premises	98,000		40,000	
Plant and equipment	162,000		65,000	
		260,000		105,000
Current assets				
Inventories	95,300		31,200	
Trade receivables	30,700		19,700	
Cash and cash equivalents	26,500		15,600	
	152,500		66,500	
Current liabilities				
Trade payables	55,800		23,900	
Corporation tax	13,100		11,400	
Proposed dividends	17,000		17,000	
	85,900		52,300	
Working capital		66,600		14,200
Net assets employed		326,600		119,200
Financed by				
Ordinary share capital	200,000		100,000	
Reserves	26,600		19,200	
Equity		226,600		119,200
7% debentures		100,000		–
		326,600		119,200

The only other information available is that:

- revenue for the years ended 30 September 20X8 and 20X9 was £202,900 and £490,700 respectively;
- profit before tax and finance costs (operating profit) for the years to 30 September 20X8 and 20X9 was £21,500 and £44,500 respectively.

(a) Calculate, for each of the two years, two suitable ratios to highlight the liquidity and two suitable ratios to highlight the profitability of the company.

(b) Comment on the situation revealed by the figures you have calculated in your answer to (a) above.

Solution

(a)

		20X9	20X8
(i)	$\frac{\text{Current assets}}{\text{Current liabilities}}$	$\frac{152,500}{85,900} = 1.78:1$	$\frac{66,500}{52,300} = 1.27:1$
(ii)	$\frac{\text{Current assets} - \text{Inventories}}{\text{Current liabilities}}$	$\frac{57,200}{85,900} = 0.67:1$	$\frac{35,300}{52,300} = 0.67:1$
(iii)	$\frac{\text{Profit before tax and finance costs}}{\text{Capital (net assets) employed}}$	$\frac{44,500}{326,600} \times 100 = 13.6\%$	$\frac{21,500}{119,200} \times 100 = 18.0\%$
(iv)	$\frac{\text{Profit before tax and finance costs}}{\text{Revenue}}$	$\frac{44,500}{490,700} \times 100 = 9.1\%$	$\frac{21,500}{202,900} \times 100 = 10.6\%$

(b) The situation revealed by the ratios calculated in (a) above may be summarised as follows.

Liquidity ratios (i) and (ii)

The current ratio indicates a substantial surplus of current assets over current liabilities and this has improved over the year. The liquid assets (receivables and cash) to current liabilities ratio shows no change and based on past experience does not signify any liquidity difficulties.

Profitability ratios (iii) and (iv)

The overall return on capital employed has decreased by a substantial amount. This may be because full benefit has not yet been received from the additional investment of £100,000 from the debentures issued during the year. The level of net profit per £ of revenue has also decreased and this may be due to the same reasons. Fortunately the overall return is high enough to mean that the 7% paid to the debenture holders is still easily achieved and the surplus return will improve returns to the ordinary shareholders, compensating them for the risk they have undertaken in introducing gearing (the debentures) into the organisation.

4.7 Comparing entities using performance indicators

Comparing an entity with a similar one may come up as a very practical task in an examination. The likely situation is where you have two firms in competition with each other, and one of them sets itself a performance indicator as a target to help it achieve a competitive advantage. The other firm must try to match or better that target.

4.8 What if? analysis

'What if? analysis' or 'scenario planning' is a technique used to test the effect on a set of figures of altering one of the variables that produced those figures. Flexible budgeting is a form of what if? analysis – what if we produce 20,000 units rather than 15,000, say?

With 'what if? analysis' or 'scenario planning' we need to understand that elements of the income statement and statement of financial position are linked. For example, a 10% increase in sales volume will lead to a 10% increase in variable costs as more units are produced but no increase in fixed costs, assuming that capacity exists. A 10% increase in sales price, however, will not lead to any changes in costs. The increase in costs will change the profit and, if no dividends are paid, this will increase the net assets of the business. The change in revenue will therefore affect several ratios.

Example

Theta division makes only one product, the Devon. In the year to 30 June 20X9, its results were as follows:

	£
Revenue	500,000
Receivables at 30 June 20X9	105,000
Cash at 30 June 20X9	20,000

The main competitor in the Devon market is Gamma Co, which sells Devons at a 15% higher price than Theta. It has been estimated that Theta could also charge a higher price without reducing sales volume. Gamma's results for the same period as Theta are as follows:

	£
Revenues	700,000
Receivables	72,500
Cash	10,000

What would be the effect on the cash balance of Theta achieving Gamma's success?

Solution

The requirement in this example can be read as – what if Theta raised its prices and implemented credit controls to achieve Gamma's levels of revenue and receivables?

	Theta	*Gamma*
Receivable days	$\frac{£105{,}000}{£500{,}000} \times 365 = 77$	$\frac{£72{,}500}{£700{,}000} \times 365 = 38$

Theta's revised figures

	£	£
Existing cash		20,000
Revenue increase (£500,000 × 0.15)		75,000
Change in receivables: Revised receivables		
$(£500{,}000 \times 1.15) \times \frac{38}{365}$	59,863	
Existing receivables	105,000	
		45,137
Revised cash balance		140,137

Therefore Theta division would increase its cash balance by £120,137 by raising its prices.

Example

Break even analysis and the make or buy decision

X Ltd is considering the outsourcing of the production of P to a third party who would supply ready-made P's for £35 per unit. P currently has a production cost of:

	£
Material	20
Labour	15
Variable overhead	5
Fixed overhead	8

The expected production level or purchasing requirement for next year is 1,000 units. P's sell for £50 per unit.

If X does decide to outsource production the total fixed overhead is expected to increase by £2,000, and the capital employed will decrease from £40,000 to £30,000 due to the sale of some obsolete machinery.

Required

(a) Calculate the contribution per unit of P when it is made by X and when it is purchased.

(b) Calculate the total profit when P is made by X and when it is purchased.

(c) Calculate the net profit margin and the return on capital employed under both options.

(d) Calculate the breakeven point and margin of safety under both options.

(e) Explain whether production should be outsourced.

Solution

(a)		*Make*	*Buy*
		£	£
Selling price		50	50
Material		20	35
Labour		15	–
Variable overhead		5	–
Contribution		10	15

(b)		*Make*	*Buy*
		£	£
Contribution per unit		10	15
Units		1,000	1,000
Total contribution		10,000	15,000
Fixed overheads		8,000	10,000
Profit		2,000	5,000

(c)		*Make*	*Buy*
		£	£
Profit margin		$\frac{2,000}{50,000} \times 100\%$	$\frac{5,000}{50,000} \times 100\%$
		= 4%	= 10%
Return on capital employed		$\frac{2,000}{40,000} \times 100\%$	$\frac{5,000}{30,000} \times 100\%$
		= 5%	= 16.67%

(d)		*Make*	*Buy*
		£	£
BEP (units)		$\frac{8,000}{10}$	$\frac{10,000}{15}$
		= 800	= 667
Margin of safety		1,000 – 800	1,000 – 667
		= 200 units	= 333 units

(e) Production should be outsourced. Even though fixed costs will rise, the contribution per unit and total profit is higher when outsourced.

The profit margin and the return on capital employed are improved by outsourcing.

When outsourced, the breakeven point is lower which is good, and the margin of safety is greater which will make managers more comfortable.

Example

Limiting factors

Y makes two products – L and M. The selling price and cost per unit based on an expected production of 1,000 units each are:

	L	£	*M*	£
Selling price		20		30
Material	2 kg × £4	8	2.5 kg × £4	10
Labour	1 hr × £5	5	2 hrs × £5	10
Variable overhead	1 hr × £3	3	2 hrs × £3	6
Fixed overhead		2		2
Profit per unit		2		2

Material may be limited to 3,500 kg in the next period.

Required

(a) Calculate the total profit margin if material supplies are unlimited.

(b) Calculate the optimal production plan if material is limited.

(c) Calculate the profit margin if material is now limited.

Solution

(a)	£	£
Selling price	20	30
Material	(8)	(10)
Labour	(5)	(10)
Variable overhead	(3)	(6)
Contribution per unit	4	4
X units	1,000	1,000
Total contribution	4,000	4,000

	£
Total contribution	8,000
Fixed overheads (1,000 × £2 + 1,000 × £2)	(4,000)
Profit	4,000
Profit margin	$\frac{4,000}{50,000} \times 100\% = 8\%$

(b)	*L*	*M*
Contribution per unit	4	4
Per limiting factor	2 kg	2.5 kg
	£2	£1.60
Rank	1	2
	1,000 units × 2 kg	600 units × 2.5 kg
	= 2,000 kg	1,500 kg
Optimal production plan	1,000 units	600 units

(c)	*L*	*M*	*Total*
	£	£	£
Contribution per unit	4	4	
× units	1,000	600	
Total contribution	4,000	2,400	6,400
Fixed costs			4,000
Profit			2,400
Profit margin (Revenues = 1,000 × £20 + 600 × £30)			$\frac{2,400}{38,000} \times 100\%$ = 6.32%

Example

Closure of a business segment versus mechanisation

M Ltd has made losses for the past two years and the management has now decided that in order to cut costs and return to profit they must either transfer production overseas where the labour costs are lower and rents are cheaper, or mechanise their factory which would also lower the labour cost but require huge investment.

Current total costs and sales price at a production level of 10,000 units are:

		£
Sales		30 per unit
Materials		100,000
Labour		75,000
Variable overhead		50,000
Fixed overhead		100,000

If production is transferred overseas, labour costs and variable overhead would fall by 40% and rent of £50,000 (a fixed cost) would fall by 50%.

If the factory is mechanised the new machinery would cost £200,000, depreciation (a fixed cost) would be 25% per annum, and the labour cost would fall by 80%.

Required

(a) Should the company stay as they are, transfer overseas or mechanise?

(b) Calculate the break-even point in the three scenarios.

Solution

(a)	*Current*		*Overseas*		*Mechanise*
	£		£		£
Revenues	300,000		300,000		300,000
Materials	(100,000)		(100,000)		(100,000)
Labour	(75,000)	60%	(44,400)	20%	(15,000)
Variable overhead	(50,000)	60%	(30,000)	20%	(10,000)
Contribution	75,000		125,600		175,000
Fixed overhead	(100,000)	Less rent	(75,000)	Plus dep'n	(150,000)
Profit/(loss)	(25,000)		50,600		25,000

Therefore M Ltd should transfer production overseas in order to improve their profit.

(b)	£	£	£
Contribution	75,000	125,600	175,000
Per unit	7.50	12.56	17.50
Fixed costs	100,000	75,000	150,000
BEP (units)	$\frac{100,000}{7.50}$ = 13,333	$\frac{75,000}{12.56}$ = 5,971	$\frac{150,000}{17.50}$ = 8,571

Activity 4

Diamond Limited (AAT specimen paper)

Diamond Limited is a retail jeweller operating 30 branches in similar localities. Common accounting policies operate throughout all branches, including a policy of using straight-line depreciation for non-current assets.

All branches use rented premises. These are accounted for under 'other costs' in the operating statement. Non-current assets are predominantly fixtures and fittings.

Each branch is individually responsible for ordering inventory, the authorising of payments to trade payables and the control of trade receivables. Cash management, however, is managed by Diamond's head office with any cash received by a branch being paid into a head office bank account twice daily.

You are employed in the head office of Diamond Limited as a financial analyst monitoring the performance of all 30 branches. This involves calculating performance indicators for each branch and comparing each branch's performance with company standards. Financial data relating to Branch 24 is reproduced below.

Diamond Limited – Branch 24 – Year ended 31 December 20X9

Operating statement			*Operating net assets at year end*		
	£000	£000		£000	£000
Revenue		720.0	Non-current assets		
Opening inventory	80.0		Cost		225.0
Purchases	340.0		Accumulated depreciation		(90.0)
Closing inventory	(60.0)				
	———				———
		360.0	Carrying amount		135.0
		———			
Gross profit		360.0	*Working capital*		
Wages and salaries	220.6		Inventories	60.0	
Depreciation	45.0		Receivables	96.0	
Other costs	36.8		Payables	(51.0)	
	———			———	
					105.0
					———
		302.4	Net assets		240.0
		———			———
Operating profit		57.6			
		———			

Task 1

Prepare a statement showing the following performance indicators for Branch 24:

(a) the return on capital employed;

(b) the gross profit margin as a percentage;

(c) the asset turnover;

(d) the revenue (or net profit) margin as a percentage;

(e) the average age of receivables in months;

(f) the average age of payables in months;

(g) the average age of the closing inventory in months.

Data

The financial director of Diamond Limited is Charles Walden. He is concerned that Branch 24 is not performing as well as the other branches. All other branches are able to meet or exceed most of the performance standards laid down by the company.

Charles is particularly concerned the branches should achieve the standards for return on capital employed and for asset turnover. He also feels that managers should try to achieve the standards laid down for working capital management.

The relevant standards are:

Return on capital employed	40%
Asset turnover	4 times per annum
Average age of receivables	0.5 months
Average age of payables	3 months
Average age of closing inventory	1 month

Charles Walden has recently attended a course on financial modelling and scenario planning. Charles explains that scenario planning shows the likely performance of a business under different assumed circumstances. It requires an understanding of the relationship between the different elements within the financial statements and how these change as the circumstances being modelled change. As an example, he tells you that if the volume of branch revenue was to increase then the cost of sales would also increase but that all other expenses would remain the same as they are fixed costs.

He believes scenario planning would be particularly helpful to the manager of Branch 24, Angela Newton. Charles had previously discussed the performance of the branch with Angela and emphasised the importance of improving the asset turnover and maintaining control of working capital. However, Angela raised the following objections:

- Turning over assets is not important; making profit should be the main objective.
- Branch 24 has been in existence for two years less than all the other branches.

Task 2

Charles Walden asks you to write a memo to Angela Newton. Your memo should:

(a) show the return on capital employed that Branch 24 would have achieved had it been able to achieve the company's asset turnover during the year to 31 December 20X9 while maintaining prices and the existing capital employed;

(b) show the return on capital employed and the asset turnover for the year if Branch 24 had been able to achieve the company's standards for the average age of receivables, the average age of payables and the average age of finished inventory while maintaining its existing sales volume;

(c) using the data in task 1 and your solution to task 2 (a), address the issues raised by Angela Newton.

Activity 4

Diamond Limited

Task 1

Diamond Ltd
Performance report – Branch 24
Year ended 31 December 20X9

(a)	Return on capital employed	
(b)	Gross profit margin	
(c)	Asset turnover	
(d)	Revenue margin	
(e)	Average age of receivables	
(f)	Average age of payables	
(g)	Average age of inventory	

Task 2

Workings

(a)		£
	Revised revenue	
	Cost of sales = 50%	
		———
	Gross profit	
	Fixed costs	
		———
	Operating profit	
		———
	Revised return on capital employed	
(b)	*Revised working capital*	£
	Revised receivables	
	Revised inventory	
	Revised payables	
		———
	Revised working capital	
	Add non-current assets	
		———
	Revised capital employed	
		———
	Return on capital employed	
	Asset turnover	

MEMORANDUM

To:

From:

Date:

Subject:

5 Gearing

5.1 Calculating gearing

There are many ways to calculate the levels of debt versus equity in a company. Two such ways are:

$$\frac{\text{Debt}}{\text{Equity}} \quad \text{or} \quad \frac{\text{Debt}}{\text{Debt} + \text{Equity}}$$

The debt figure should include all sources of debt including long-term loans and short-term overdrafts.

If a company has a high gearing level then it is potentially more risky than a low geared company. This is because when interest rates rise the interest paid on the debt may rise and will place a strain on the profits generated by the company.

However, certain industries are more accepting than others of high gearing, so any gearing level calculated must be compared against similar companies in order to ascertain whether the company is at risk or not.

Solution

For Knotty plc:

		20X9	*20X8*
(a)	$\frac{\text{Debt}}{\text{Equity}}$	$\frac{2,840 + 929}{13,556} = 0.28$	$\frac{2,853 + 511}{8,705} = 0.39$
(b)	$\frac{\text{Debt}}{\text{Debt} + \text{Equity}}$	$\frac{2,840 + 929}{3,769 + 13,556} = 0.22$	$\frac{2,853 + 511}{3,364 + 8,705} = 0.28$

(Note: Technically preference shares are often deemed to be debt finance. However the examiner has never gone into this level of detail so they have been included as equity to keep this example simple.)

6 Manufacturing industries

6.1 Introduction

The performance of a manufacturing business and its constituent activities will commonly be measured in quantitative terms, mainly monetary. However, we shall also consider relevant non-monetary and qualitative factors that can be useful.

6.2 Productivity and effectiveness

Productivity is a measure of the efficiency of resource usage and expresses the rate of output in relation to resource used, often in non-financial terms.

Examples include the following:

(a) units produced per labour or machine hour;

(b) productive hours to total hours paid;

(c) actual output to full capacity output;

(d) number of operations undertaken per day;

(e) number of passengers transported per month;

(f) number of vehicles manufactured per week.

Productivity is closely linked with both efficiency and resource utilisation (which is considered later).

Effectiveness is about meeting the business objectives or targets. Effectiveness measures include:

(a) percentage of production free from defects;

(b) delivery time to customer

(c) number of trains running on time;

(d) percentage of students passing their exams first time.

6.3 Labour activity, capacity and efficiency ratios

Three control ratios are often used to measure productivity, as follows:

Activity ratio: $\frac{\text{Standard hours for actual production}}{\text{Budgeted hours}}$

Capacity ratio: $\frac{\text{Actual hours worked}}{\text{Budgeted hours}}$

Efficiency ratio: $\frac{\text{Standard hours for actual production}}{\text{Actual hours worked}}$

Example

	Budget	*Actual*
Output (units)	10,000	9,000
Hours worked	200	190

Calculate:

(a) the activity ratio;

(b) the capacity ratio;

(c) the efficiency ratio.

Solution

(a) Output per standard hour $= \frac{10,000}{200} = 50$ units

Actual output in standard hours $= \frac{9,000}{50} = 180$

Activity ratio: $\frac{180}{200} = 90\%$

In other words, the production level was only 90% of the budgeted level.

(b) Capacity ratio: $\frac{190}{200} = 95\%$

Only 95% of budgeted hours were actually worked and used to produce units.

(c) Efficiency ratio: $\frac{180}{190} = 94.74\%$

According to the budget, 50 units should have been produced in an hour and therefore in the 190 hours that were actually worked, 9,500 units should have been produced. Only 94.74% of that quantity (9,000) were actually produced.

Note that the three ratios are related to each other:

Efficiency ratio	×	Capacity ratio	=	Activity ratio
94.74%	×	95%	=	90%

6.4 Value added

Definition

Value added is the pool of wealth created, out of which a business provides for:

- payment of wages, salaries and other employee benefits;
- reward for providers of capital, in the form of interest and dividends;
- payment of government taxation;
- maintenance and expansion of assets.

It is also defined as:

- the value of revenue less the cost of bought in materials and services.

Example

Value added statement

Horn Ltd

	£m
Revenue	1.35
Bought in materials and services	0.55
Value added	0.80
Applied as:	
To pay employee wages and other benefits	0.28
Providers of capital dividends	0.13
Government taxation	0.04
Maintenance and expansion of assets	
Depreciation	0.15
Profit	0.20

Number of employees = 20

- Value added per '£' of employee costs

$$\frac{£0.80}{£0.28} = 2.86$$

- Value added per employee

  $$\frac{£0.80}{20} = £0.04m \text{ or } £40{,}000$$

- Value added per '£' of employee costs and depreciation

  $$\frac{£0.80}{£0.43m} = 1.86$$

or, in a highly mechanised process, related to use of machinery:

- production per machine hour;
- production per machine.

Activity 5

Task

(a) From the following information, draft the value added statement for the years 20X2 and 20X3.

Sandsend Engineering Ltd

Extract from Income statements for the years ended 31 December 20X2 and 20X3

	20X2	*20X3*
	£m	£m
Revenue	6.1	6.5
*Costs	4.2	4.5
Operating profit	1.9	2.0
Finance costs	0.6	0.6
	1.3	1.4
Taxation	0.3	0.3
	1.0	1.1
Dividends	0.2	0.2
Profit for the year	0.8	0.9

*Costs comprise:

	£m	£m
Wages and salaries	1.8	1.9
Depreciation	0.4	0.5
Other bought in items	2.0	2.1

	20X2	20X3
Revenue	£m	£m
	6.1	6.5
Less bought in materials and services	2.0	2.1
	—	—
Value added	4.1	4.4
	—	—
Applied as follows:		
To pay employees wages, salaries and other benefits	1.8	1.9
To pay providers of capital		
Finance costs	.6	.6
Dividends	.2	.2
To pay government taxation	.3	.3
To maintenance and expansion of assets		
Depreciation	.4	.5
Profit for the year	.8	.9
	—	—
Value added	4.1	4.4
	—	—

(b) Calculate for both years the value added per '£' of employee costs, and state why this measure is considered an indicator of labour productivity.

	20X2	20X3
Value added	£m	£m
	4.1	4.4
Employee costs	1.8	1.9
	—	—
Value added per '£' of employee costs	2.28	2.32
	—	—

Why value added is considered to be a measure of productivity:

Pg422

6.5 Unit costs

Unit costs are the actual average cost of production of each unit of product in the period. Management will attempt to drive down unit costs over time.

6.6 Resource utilisation

This is a measure of the extent to which resources were used in relation to maximum capacity. Examples of utilisation and related measures for different resources include the following:

Machines	–	utilisation (hours used : potential hours)
	–	down time (machine down hours : total hours)
Materials	–	wastage (normal/abnormal loss percentage)
	–	inventory turnover (linked to levels of slow-moving inventory)
Labour	–	utilisation (productive : total hours)
	–	absenteeism, lateness
	–	mix variances (where different grades are used)
	–	idle time (non-productive hours : total hours)
	–	labour turnover (leavers replaced : total employed)

6.7 Quality of service

For a manufacturing business, this can be categorised into quality of service to customers and quality of service from service departments. The latter is covered in the section on the service departments.

Quality of service to customers is essentially a subjective, qualitative measure, although some quantitative measures can be used in connection with it – for example, ratios such as customer returns to total sales and customer complaints per units sold. Speed of service can be measured in retail outlets or numbers waiting per checkout in a supermarket.

The main source of measure of customer satisfaction will generally be through some sort of questionnaire. This is all considered in more detail later in this chapter.

6.8 Other non-monetary measures

Quality is a particular area in which such indicators are required; two others that have recently been identified as important attributes of world-class manufacturing are innovation and flexibility.

6.9 Innovation

Innovation is concerned with the business's ability to beat their competitors in developing new products, improvements to existing ones or additional customer services.

Measurement of innovation must concentrate on its effectiveness as well as its existence – counting the number of new products developed is of little help without knowing the extent to which they have been accepted by the market. Possible measures include the following:

(a) research and development expenditure related to new revenues;

(b) viable new products to existing products;

(c) percentage of total profits relating to new products/ improvements.

6.10 Flexibility

Flexibility is concerned with the business's ability to respond to customers' needs, in terms of speed of delivery of existing products, speed of reaction to changes in demand patterns and ability to respond to particular customer requests or specifications.

In a manufacturing context, it is often the case that flexibility is connected with the amounts of products using common parts. If demand for one type of product falls, it is easier to switch stock and processing to another if there is a common base between them.

7 Service departments

7.1 Introduction

Many of the measures discussed above will be relevant in the assessment of the performance of service departments within a business. Unless an internal charge-out system operates (for example, the charging of user departments per hour of computer department time spent on their work), the emphasis will be on costs rather than profits.

7.2 Types of performance indicator

As well as the normal cost variances (with activity levels based on the departments' own cost unit, e.g. maintenance hours, meals served, data processing hours), other cost ratios will be appropriate, for example:

(a) meal cost per employee per period (canteen);

(b) running costs per van-mile (deliveries);

(c) cost per call-out (maintenance department).

Example

Consider a transport/distribution department. What type of cost performance indicators might be appropriate?

Solution

(a) **Standing costs** (ascertained as a rate per day), including:

- (i) Road tax
- (ii) Insurance
- (iii) Garage and administration costs
- (iv) Drivers' wages
- (v) Depreciation

(b) **Running costs** (ascertained as a rate per ton/mile), including:

- (i) Fuel and lubricants
- (ii) Tyres
- (iii) Repairs
- (iv) Maintenance

Standing costs will be incurred for vehicles owned whether or not they are in use and are in the nature of stepped fixed costs. Fixed because, for each vehicle, they do not vary in amount and 'stepped' because for each additional vehicle required, costs, on a graph, will rise by a further step and remain fixed for a further range of activity until another vehicle is required.

In addition to these, there will be depot administration and establishment costs to be absorbed. These should be ascertained in total and related to the activity of the depot. Statistical information such as mileage run, loaded and empty, and tonnages carried should also be collected so that a reasonable method of absorption may be derived.

The analysis of expenditure between fixed and variable costs (standing and running costs) gives potential for the use of marginal costing and the consequent improvements in management information.

With such information available, management will be better equipped to deal with:

(a) control over costs for each vehicle or group of similar vehicles;

(b) pricing;

(c) choice of most economic vehicle for specific tasks;

(d) acceptability of contracts;

(e) vehicle purchase and replacement decisions;

(f) many other day-to-day decisions.

8 Service sectors

8.1 Introduction

Service organisations include the following:

(a) **Professional services**, such as firms of accountants, architects, surveyors, solicitors, whose main assets will be their employees and who provide individual, personalised services to their customers.

(b) **Mass services**, such as transport, which are highly capital asset based and provide a standard range of services to a wide range of customers.

(c) **Public sector services**, such as health, education and local authorities.

8.2 Types of performance indicators

Service sector measures can be considered under very similar headings as those for manufacturing organisations, although there will be a different emphasis on their relative importance.

The main difference between the two types of organisation is the nature of their output.

Output from manufacturing businesses comprises tangible, clearly identifiable products, usually of a standard design and quality which can be rejected by a customer if not required or unsuitable, and produced in advance of demand and stored until needed.

Think about a service provided to you – can it be said to have any of these characteristics? This leads to a different approach needed for performance measurement where costs per product or units per hour are of little relevance or meaning. However, in earlier chapters, we have seen that cost units do not have to be in terms of products and that measures may be activity rather than product based.

So, using similar headings as before, particular areas to be considered about the performance indicators of service organisations are productivity, unit costs, resource utilisation, profitability and quality of service.

In examinations the tasks will ask for performance indicators which are tailored to the scenario set. Make sure that you read the scenario information carefully and actually calculate the indicators that are asked for.

8.3 Productivity

Productivity can be difficult to measure, because services rarely have a standard unit of output. For example, it would be meaningless to measure a conveyancing solicitor's productivity on the basis of 'property purchase completions per month', as each will have a different degree of complexity and value to the business. Similarly, it would be inappropriate to assess a bus line on the basis of 'journeys per day', as the contribution to the company's profits would depend upon the number of people carried at each stage of the journey and how many buses were operating on the line.

Meaningful measures of productivity or efficiency for a service depend upon a clearly defined measure of activity and resources.

So, for example, the measure of activity for the bus line might be 'passenger miles' and of the resource might be 'driver hours'.

Professional firms, such as accountants and solicitors, will generally use 'chargeable hours' as a measure of activity and employees' productivity will be judged by 'chargeable hours per employee'.

8.4 Unit costs

Again, the difficulty here is in defining an appropriate unit for the activity being measured. Once this has been established, appropriate costs need to be attributed to it. So the cost of a professional chargeable hour would mainly consist of employee costs (salaries, NICs, benefits, etc.) but will also include a recovery of general overheads.

The cost of a 'passenger mile' for a transport company will include driver costs, vehicle running costs and overheads.

8.5 Resource utilisation

Resource utilisation is the extent to which available resources are used for productive service. Examples of suitable measures for various types of service businesses are illustrated by the following ratios:

Professional	Chargeable hours : Total hours available
Transport	Passenger miles : Total train miles available
Hotel	Rooms occupied : Rooms available
Car hire	Car-days hired : Car-days available

8.6 Profitability

Clearly, for the service business overall, the usual measures can apply – ROCE, profit margins, etc. Unit profitability measures will again depend upon the clear definition of the cost unit or unit of activity. The profit can then be determined by comparison of the cost per unit (as discussed above) with the income generated (e.g. the charge-out rate for a professional chargeable hour or the average fare per mile on a bus/train route).

Activity 6

Transport company (AAT J94)

A transport company is reviewing the way in which it reports vehicle operating costs to the company management. In particular, it is interested in the use of performance ratios which will help to assess the efficiency and effectiveness of the use of its vehicles.

Information on the following items is available for each vehicle for the period as follows:

Costs

Variable costs	
Fuel	Tyres
Oil	Other parts
Hydraulic fluid	Repairs and maintenance
Fixed costs	
Road fund licence	Cleaning
Insurance	Depreciation
Drivers' wages	

Activity measures

Miles driven	Number of days available for use
Tonnes carried	Number of days vehicle actually used
Journeys made	

Required

You are asked to indicate six suitable performance ratios which could be used to monitor the effectiveness and efficiency of the usage of each vehicle.

Three of your ratios should relate to the efficient control of costs and three should relate to the effective usage of vehicles.

Activity 6

Transport company

Performance ratios

(i) **Costs**

(ii) **Usage**

8.7 Quality of service

This has arguably more significance in the service sector than in the manufacturing sector. Customers will make their buying decisions in the service sector on the basis of how well they expect the service to be provided.

The factors contributing to quality of service will vary according to the nature of the business. As an illustration, consider the service provided to trainee accountancy students by a private college. Possible factors that would influence a potential student in their choice of college and the ways in which these might be measured are as follows:

Factor	*Possible measures*
Technical expertise	Pass rates
Communication	Clarity of lectures, study material and administrative information
Access	Staff/student ratios Availability of tutorial help outside lecture hours Ease of finding department/member of staff required Location of college
Friendliness	Approachability of staff
Flexibility	Ability to tailor service to individual student's needs
Facilities	Availability and standard of canteen, library, phones, etc
Aesthetics	Appearance of college Staff presentation
Comfort	Roominess of classrooms Heating/air-conditioning Comfort of seats, size of desks

You can no doubt think of some more factors and different ways in which those given could be measured. For example, it is perhaps a little glib to use pass rates as a measure of the college's technical expertise, as these are also likely to be significantly influenced by the abilities and commitment of the students themselves.

8.8 Quantitative and qualitative performance indicators

Having identified what needs to be measured, how can this be achieved? Some are a matter of fact or record – like pass rates or the existence of facilities; most of the rest are qualitative judgement and would need to be measured by the use of questionnaires completed by students.

An overall measure of the quality of service provided by the college could be the trend in the number of students enrolling for courses, although again this can be affected by other factors, such as the location of the college and students, the policy of the students' employers and the size of the market for trainee accountants.

9 Total quality management (TQM)

Definition

Total quality management (TQM) can be defined as 'a continuous improvement in quality, efficiency and effectiveness'.

- It aims towards an environment of zero defects at a minimum cost – the principle of 'get it right first time'.
- It requires an awareness by all personnel of the quality requirements with supplying the customer with products of the agreed design specification.
- It aims towards the elimination of waste where waste is defined as anything other than the minimum essential amount of equipment, materials, space and workers' time.
- It must embrace all aspects of operations from pre-production to post-production stages in the business cycle.

Total quality management will, therefore, seek method changes which will help in achieving such objectives. Examples include the use of Just-in-time (JIT) production procedures whereby each component or product is produced or purchased only when needed by production or by a customer, rather than for inventory.

9.1 Quality circles

An important element of TQM is that every employee is involved and anyone with an idea about how to improve quality should be heard. This is done by forming groups of employees known as quality circles. These groups normally consist of about 10 employees of differing levels of seniority and with different skills who meet regularly to discuss quality problems and put forward ideas.

9.2 Indicators measuring quality and the cost of quality

Indicators to measure quality of service may include:

- The number of defects
- Units returned
- Warranty claims
- Customer complaints
- The cost of inspection
- Repairs
- Re-working

Traditionally failure rates, scrap and reworking were subsumed within the costs of production while other aspects of poor quality were accounted for in either production or marketing overheads. TQM does not accept the cost of poor quality as inevitable and requires that the cost of quality is highlighted in management reports. This enables alternative approaches (such as built-in quality at the design stage) to be developed.

Quality-related costs are the expenditure incurred in defect prevention and appraisal activities and the losses due to internal and external failure of a product or service through failure to meet agreed specifications.

9.3 Types of quality-related costs

Quality-related costs may be classified as follows:

(a) **Failure costs** are the costs required to evaluate, dispose of, and either correct or replace a defective or deficient product.

(i) Internal failure costs are costs discovered before the product is delivered to the customer. Examples include the following:

- Rework costs
- Net cost of scrap
- Disposal of defective products
- Downtime due to quality problems

(ii) External failure costs are costs discovered after the product is delivered to customers.

Examples include the following:

- Complaint investigation and processing
- Warranty claims
- Cost of lost sales
- Product recalls

(b) **Appraisal costs** are costs of monitoring and inspecting products in terms of specified standards before the products are released to the customer. Examples include the following:

- Measurement equipment
- Inspection and tests
- Product quality audits
- Process control monitoring
- Test equipment expense

(c) **Prevention costs** include investments in machinery, technology and education programs designed to reduce the number of defective products during production. Examples include the following:

- Customer surveys
- Research of customer needs
- Field trials
- Quality education and training programmes
- Supplier reviews
- Investment in improved production equipment
- Quality engineering
- Quality circles

Example

Carlton Limited makes and sells a single product.

The following information affects its costs and revenues.

1 5% of incoming material from suppliers is scrapped owing to poor receipt and storage organisation.

2 4% of material X input to the machine process is wasted owing to processing problems.

3 Inspection of storage of material X costs 10 pence per square metre purchased.

4 Inspection during the production cycle, calibration checks on inspection equipment and other checks cost £25,000 per period.

5 Production quantity is increased to allow for the downgrading of 12.5% of product units at the final inspection stage. Downgraded units are sold as 'second quality' units at a discount of 30% on the standard selling price.

6 Production quantity is increased to allow for returns from customers which are replaced free of charge. Returns are due to specification failure and account for 5% of units initially delivered to customers. Replacement units incur a delivery cost of £8 per unit. 80% of the returns from customers are rectified using 0.2 hours of machine running time per unit and are re-sold as 'third quality' products at a discount of 50% on the standard selling price. The remaining returned units are sold as scrap for £5 per unit.

7 Product liability and other claims by customers are estimated at 3% of sales revenue from standard product sales.

8 Machine idle time is 20% of gross machine hours used (i.e. running hours = 80% of gross hours).

9 Sundry costs of administration, selling and distribution total £60,000 per period.

10 Carlton Limited is aware of the problem of excess costs and currently spends £20,000 per period on training staff in efforts to prevent a number of such problems from occurring.

Give examples of internal and external failure costs, appraisal costs and prevention costs borne by Carlton Limited.

Solution

Internal failure costs. The machine processing losses, downgrading of products, and materials which are scrapped due to poor receipt and storage.

External failure costs. Product liability claims and the costs of making free replacements, including delivery costs.

Appraisal costs. Inspection during the production process, inspection of materials in storage and calibration checks.

Prevention costs. Training costs.

Whilst the general theory is that organisations should plan to have zero defects, we should be aware that there may be commercial reasons for allowing some defects, perhaps due to expensive quality assurance schemes. Ideally, a cost-benefit analysis should be performed.

Activity 7

An example of an external failure cost is:

A Customer survey

B Product recalls

C Inspection

D Rework

10 The balanced scorecard

10.1 Introduction

The balanced scorecard approach to performance indicators recognises that historically too much emphasis has been placed on financial ratios in assessing an entity's performance. A successful business will only succeed in the long-term if it keeps its customers happy as well as by making profits. The approach therefore combines financial measures with operational, organisational innovation and customer service measures. All of these perspectives must be managed by managers if the business is to prosper in the long-term.

The balanced scorecard becomes the manager's instrument panel for managing the complexity of the organisation within a dynamic external environment.

10.2 Four perspectives of the balanced scorecard

The table below is an example of a balanced scorecard performance management system which demonstrates the role of critical success factors (CSFs) and key performance indicators (KPIs) in this process.

The balanced scorecard

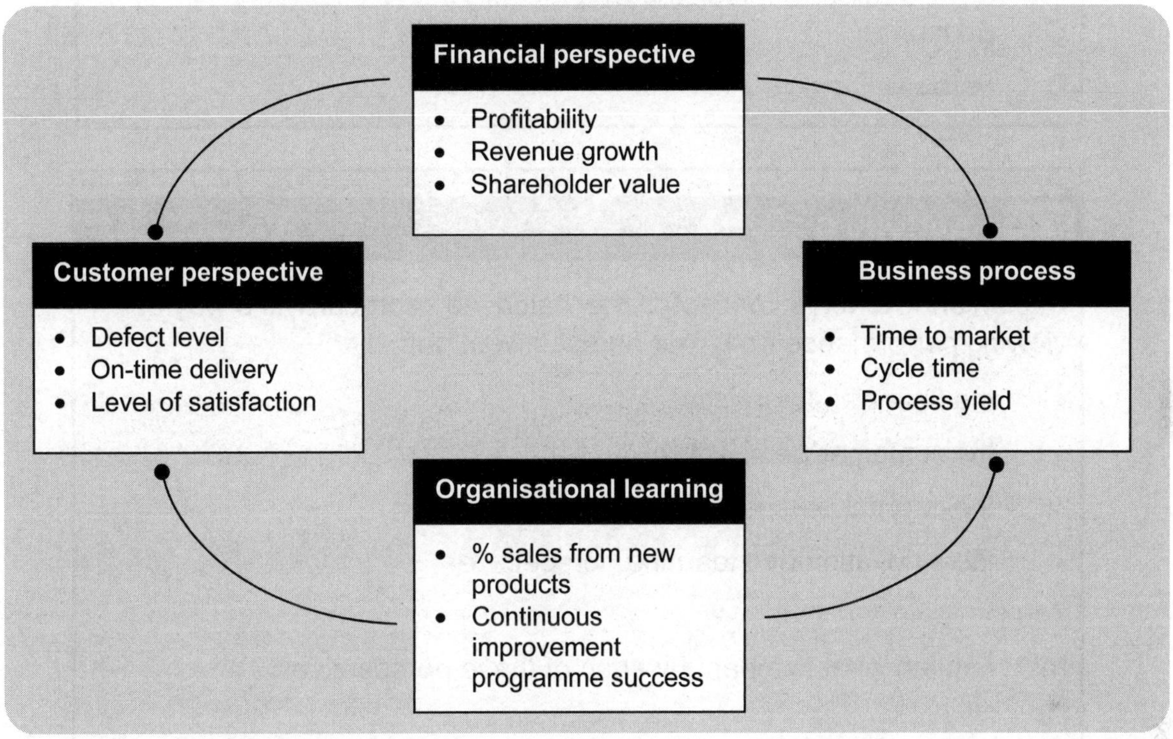

10.3 Key performance indicators

Typical key performance indicators for the balanced scorecard approach are illustrated below.

	Financial aspect	*Customer aspect*	*Business process aspect*	*Organisational learning aspect*
Strategic objective ▼	Shareholder satisfaction ▼	Customer satisfaction ▼	Manufacturing excellence ▼	New product innovation ▼
Critical success factor ▼	Grow shareholder wealth ▼	Achieve preferred supplier status ▼	State-of-the-art process plant ▼	Successful new product development ▼
Key performance indicators	ROCE	Number of new customers	Cycle times Unit cost % yield	% of revenue represented by new products

Activity 8

The four perspectives of the balanced scorecard include:

A Competitor

B Financial

C Economic

D Political

Activity 9

Kaplan and Norton's concept of the 'balanced scorecard' is a way of viewing performance from four perspectives, namely:

- the financial perspective;
- the customer perspective;
- the internal perspective;
- the innovation and learning perspective.

Task

(a) Explain what is meant by each of these perspectives.

The financial perspective

The customer perspective

The internal perspective

The innovation and learning perspective

(b) You work as an accounting technician in the business planning unit of a large company which has a number of subsidiaries. You use the balanced scorecard concept in appraising performance.

The following information relates to subsidiary A for the year ended 31 December 20X3.

	£m
Revenue	6.85
Cost of sales	5.71
Operating profit	1.14
Number of employees	75

Cost of sales includes training costs of £40,000 and quality assurance costs of £350,000. Assets employed by the subsidiary total £6.30m.

Analysis of revenue by products:

	£m
Existing products	4.85
New products	2.00

Analysis of revenue by customer:

	£m
Existing established customers	4.90
New customers	1.95

Identify a performance indicator for each of the four perspectives for subsidiary A for the year ended 31 December 20X3.

Financial perspective:

Customer perspective:

Internal perspective:

Innovation and learning perspective:

11 Cost reduction and value enhancement

11.1 Introduction

There are few organisations which would not benefit from real efforts to keep costs to a minimum. Businesses will make more money that way, assuming quality is not compromised.

Not-for-profit organisations will make their funds go further in providing necessary services, and will be better able to meet the requirements for 'good stewardship' normally imposed on them.

Definitions

Cost reduction is a process which leads to the achievement of real and permanent reductions in the unit costs of goods manufactured or services rendered without impairing their suitability for the use intended.

Cost control, on the other hand, aims simply to achieve the target costs originally accepted.

Note that cost reduction is aiming to reduce unit costs, i.e. the cost per item of output. It would be possible for a cost reduction programme to increase the total costs incurred, as long as the output volume rose even more, so that the unit cost was reduced.

11.2 Implementing a cost reduction programme

Once an organisation has adopted an objective of reducing costs, the following conditions need to apply if it is to be successful.

- A clear purpose – say, to reduce labour costs by 20%, or materials by 15%.
- A good reason – economic survival, say, or the ability in the future to compete with competitors with a lower cost base.
- Commitment and involvement by senior managers.
- Excellent and positive communication with workforce and, if possible, consultation.
- Gradual introduction.

11.3 Application of cost reduction techniques

Virtually all areas of businesses and not-for-profit organisations are open to the use of cost reduction techniques, including product design, production, purchasing, marketing, distribution, finance and personnel.

Two important cost reduction techniques are target costing and value engineering.

(a) **Target costing**

Target costing starts by subtracting a desired profit margin from the market price at which an item could be sold; this gives the target cost. It is then up to the designers to plan how the product can be manufactured for that cost. If the product is currently planned to cost more than the target cost, then the plan must be modified (which may mean that it is abandoned).

For example, if customers have indicated that they would pay £100 a new product, and the company that developed it usually makes a 20% profit margin on each product they sell, then the product would have to be manufactured for £80. If this was impossible, then the product would not make it as far as the production stage.

(b) **Value engineering**

Value engineering is a philosophy of designing products which meet customer needs at the lowest cost while assuring the required standard of quality and reliability. The idea is to understand what it is that customers want from your products, and save costs by eliminating items that add no value in customers' eyes. For example, a manufacturer of computer components may decide that its customers place no value on a paper instruction manual or on fancy packaging, and will decide to sell its products with no manual and in a plain cardboard box.

11.4 Value enhancement

The 'flip side' of cost reduction is value enhancement namely, getting the best value from the resources that are used in the organisation. Use of the performance indicators that we have seen in this chapter will provide useful comparative measures to assess value enhancement before and after an active 'value-for-money' programme.

It should be emphasised that cost reduction and value enhancement are not just the responsibility of the accounts department of a business. All the functional specialists (designers, marketing, engineering, quality control, etc) must pool their knowledge and work side-by-side to achieve the required objectives.

11.5 Benchmarking

One way of closely monitoring one's own business is to compare the results in your business with those of closely related businesses. **Benchmarking** is the establishment of targets and comparators, through whose use relative levels of performance (particularly areas of under-performance) can be identified. By the adoption of identified best practices it is hoped that performance can be improved.

One common example is internal benchmarking, where a company is split up into business divisions, all operating in more or less the same industry, and performance indicators are calculated and compared for each division. Perhaps it is then found that one division has receivables of four months revenue, while all the other divisions have receivables of less than two months revenue. The division with abnormally high receivables should be able to improve its liquidity by tightening up its credit control procedures.

Activity 10

Revenue less the cost of bought-in materials and services is called:

- Value added ☐
- Cost reduction ☐
- Value enhancement ☐

Activity 11

A pricing method whereby the starting point is the selling price followed by the deduction of a margin is called?

- Target costing ☐
- Loss leading ☐
- Competitor pricing ☐

Activity 12

Gransden Limited (AAT J96)

Gransden Limited makes and retails a variety of furniture products. One year ago, the directors realised that their traditional financial accounting system was not providing sufficient information for the managers. As a result, they established a management accounting department headed by William Jones. He quickly established standard costing throughout the organisation as well as introducing performance reports for each division in the company. Both techniques have been effective and, as a result, you were recently appointed as the Assistant Management Accountant to the company.

Some managers, however, are still having difficulty understanding the meaning of the standard costing reports prepared each month. One manager, Helen Dale, particularly feels that the report for May was misleading. Her department manufactures high quality wooden display cabinets. She wrote to William Jones about the report, and an extract from the letter is reproduced below.

'In May, my department produced 5,000 cabinets, 500 more than required in my budget. According to your own figures each cabinet requires five metres of wood at a standard price of £100 per metre, a total cost of £2,500,000. For some reason, you show the result of this as being an overall adverse material variance of £200,000, which you then break down into price and usage, despite my department only using 22,500 metres of wood in May.

Also, only yesterday, I read that the Retail Price Index stood at 168 compared with an index of 160 when the standards were agreed. This shows inflation at 3% and so the £200,000 overspend on standard cost is entirely due to price inflation, which is out of my control. Your standard costing information is not therefore particularly helpful to me as a manager.'

Required

William Jones plans to discuss with Helen the issues raised in her letter. Before doing so, however he has asked you to:

(a) (i) determine the material price and usage variances within the overall adverse variance;

(ii) check the accuracy of the index of inflation calculated by Helen Dale.

Increase in RPI

Current index

Index at beginning of period

Price inflation

(b) Identify three difficulties which might be experienced in interpreting the price variance, including the inflation element.

Difficulties in interpreting the price variance

(i)

(ii)

(iii)

Data

Another problem faced by William Jones has arisen from the splitting of the company into separate divisions. This restructuring had the full agreement of the Board of Directors, who viewed it as a way of giving responsibility to operating managers. Two functions, however, were deliberately retained at the centre: capital investment decisions and cash management.

Gransden's cash management system operates through a central accounting unit within the head office finance department. Divisions inform the unit when a payable is to be paid. The unit then makes the necessary arrangements for the payment to be made. Similarly, although the divisions retain overall responsibility for credit control, all remittances from receivables are handled directly by the central accounting unit. As a result of this, each division's capital employed is defined as non-current assets plus current assets (other than cash) less current liabilities.

Two divisions, the Northern Division and the Southern Division, are entirely retailing operations. Over the last year, anxieties have been expressed about the Southern Division not adequately contributing to overall company profitability. Details of their results for the year to 31 May 20X6 and the relevant management ratios for the Northern division are reproduced below.

Operating results for the year ending 31 May 20X6

	North		*South*	
	£000	£000	£000	£000
Revenue		135,000		191,000
Opening inventory	25,000		55,000	
Purchases	75,000		105,000	
Closing inventory	(20,000)		(40,000)	
Cost of sales		80,000		120,000
Gross *profit*		55,000		71,000
Wages and salaries	10,000		12,000	
Depreciation	10,000		16,000	
Other costs	9,688		8,620	
		29,688		36,620
Operating profit		25,312		34,380
Net assets				
Non-current assets		100,000		160,000
Depreciation		40,000		48,000
Net book value		60,000		112,000
Inventory		20,000		40,000
Receivables		16,875		46,750
Payables		(12,500)		(8,750)
Capital employed		84,375		190,000

Management ratios for the North Division

Return on capital employed	30.00%	Average age of receivables	1.5 months
Gross profit margin	40.75%	Average age of inventory	3 months
Revenue margin (operating profit/ revenue)	18.75%	Average age of payables	2 months
Asset turnover	1.6 times		

Required

You are informed by the Management Accountant that the Board plans to investigate ways of improving the efficiency of the Southern Division and a meeting has been called for this purpose in one week's time. William Jones has asked you to:

(c) Calculate the relevant management ratios for the Southern Division.

Return on capital employed

Gross profit margin

Revenue margin

Asset turnover

Average age of receivables

Average age of inventory

Average age of payables

(d) Estimate what the return on capital employed would have been for the Southern Division if:

(i) it has achieved the same asset turnover as the Northern Division;

(ii) it had the same average age of receivables, inventory and payables as the Northern Division.

Note: for the purpose of Task (d)(i) only, you should assume that the wages and salaries, the depreciation and the other costs are all fixed costs and that inventory, receivables and payables remain unaltered.

(i) Southern Division's return on capital employed with an asset turnover of 1.6 times:

	£
Revenues	
Gross profit @ 37%	
Less fixed costs	
Operating profit	
Capital employed	
Return on capital employed	

(ii) Southern Division's return on capital employed with Northern's working capital ratios:

	£
Non-current assets	
Inventories	
Receivables	
Payables	
Capital employed	
Operating profit	
Return on capital employed	

(e) Identify two limitations to your analysis in parts (c) and (d).

(i)

(ii)

12 Summary

As you have seen, there are numerous possible performance indicators and their relevance will depend upon the type of organisation and the aspect of performance being assessed.

The most important ratios for you to be able to compute (and interpret) are as follows:

Profitability:	Return on capital employed (ROCE) Gross and net profit margins
Liquidity:	Current ratio Quick (acid test) ratio Inventory turnover Receivables' collection period Payables' payment (settlement) period
Investor:	Gearing

Remember that a ratio on its own is not particularly useful information; it needs to be compared, internally or externally. This gives rise to problems of comparability, which you should be able to discuss.

Many of the ideas covered in earlier chapters will have relevance here (e.g. variance analysis and the use of indices).

Make sure you are quite clear about the necessary attributes of a cost unit (or unit of activity) in order for it to provide a useful basis for measurement. This is particularly important for service activities. Try to think of services you have had experience of yourself and how the various aspects may be measured.

There will rarely be a unique right or wrong answer, so do not be afraid to use your imagination!

Answers to chapter activities

Activity 1

WH Limited

REPORT

To: Senior Management Committee

From: Assistant Accountant

Date: 12 December 20X9

Subject: Profitability and asset turnover ratios

We have received the Trade Association results for year 4 and this report looks in detail at the profitability and asset turnover ratios.

(a) **What each ratio is designed to show**

(i) *Return on capital employed (ROCE)*

This ratio shows the percentage rate of profit which has been earned on the capital invested in the business (i.e. the return on the resources controlled by management). The expected return would vary depending on the type of business and it is usually calculated as follows:

$$\text{Return on capital employed} = \frac{\text{Profit before finance costs and tax}}{\text{Capital employed}} \times 100\%$$

Other profit figures can be used, as well as various definitions of capital employed.

(ii) *Net operating profit margin*

This ratio shows the operating profit as a percentage of revenue. The operating profit is calculated before finance costs and tax and it is the profit over which operational managers can exercise day to day control. It is the amount left out of revenue after all direct costs and overheads have been deducted.

$$\text{Net operating profit margin} = \frac{\text{Operating profit}}{\text{Revenue}} \times 100\%$$

(iii) *Asset turnover*

This ratio shows how effectively the assets of a business are being used to generate sales:

$$\text{Asset turnover} = \frac{\text{Revenue}}{\text{Capital employed}}$$

If the same figure for capital employed is used as in ROCE, then ratios (i) to (iii) can be related together as follows.

(i) ROCE = (ii) Net operating profit margin x (iii) Asset turnover

(iv) *Gross margin*

This ratio measures the profitability of revenue:

$$\text{Gross margin} = \frac{\text{Gross profit}}{\text{Revenue}} \times 100\%$$

The gross profit is calculated as the revenue less the cost of goods sold and this ratio therefore focuses on the company's manufacturing and trading activities.

(b) **WH Limited's profitability and asset turnover**

WH Limited's ROCE is lower than the trade association average, indicating either poor profitability (as measured by the net profit margin) or poor asset utilisation (as measured by the asset turnover) or both.

WH Limited's operating profit margin is higher than the trade association average, despite a lower than average gross profit margin. This suggests that overheads are lower relative to revenue in WH Limited.

WH Limited's asset turnover ratio is lower than the trade association average. This may mean that assets are not being used as effectively in our company and it is the cause of the lower than average ROCE.

WH Limited's gross profit margin is lower than the trade association average. This suggests either that WH's direct costs are higher than average, or that selling prices are lower.

(c) **Limitations of the ratios and of inter-company comparisons**

There are a number of limitations of which management should be aware before drawing any firm conclusions from a comparison of these ratios:

(i) The ratios are merely averages, based on year-end balance sheet data, which may not be representative.

(ii) One particular factor which could affect these ratios is if there has been any new investment towards the end of the financial year. This investment would increase the value of the assets or capital employed, but the profits from the investment would not yet have accumulated in the income statement. Generally, newer assets tend to depress the asset turnover and hence the ROCE in the short term. It is possible that this is the cause of our company's lower asset turnover and ROCE.

(iii) Although the trade association probably makes some attempt to standardise the data, different member companies may be using different accounting policies, for example in calculating depreciation and valuing inventory.

(iv) Our company's analyst may have used a different formula for calculating any of the ratios. For example, as noted above, there is a variety of ways of calculating capital employed. However, it is likely that the trade association would provide information on the basis of calculation of the ratios.

(v) The member companies will have some activities in common, hence their membership of the trade association. However, some may have a diversified range of activities, which will distort the ratios and make direct comparison difficult.

Activity 2

Two liquidity ratios are inventory turnover and receivable days.

Activity 3

Homely Limited

(a) *Target ratios*

Return on capital employed $= \frac{66}{300} \times 100\% = 22\%$

Operating profit percentage $= \frac{66}{820} \times 100\% = 8\%$

Asset turnover $= \frac{820}{300} = 2.7$ times

Working capital period $= \frac{70}{754} \times 365 = 34$ days

Percentage room occupancy $= \frac{5,900}{18 \times 365} \times 100\% = 90\%$

Revenue per employee $= \frac{820,000}{20} = £41,000$

Key ratios for 20X4

	Stately Hotels plc target	*Homely Limited actual*
Return on capital employed	26%	22%
Operating profit percentage	13%	8%
Asset turnover	2.0 times	2.7 times
Working capital period	20 days	34 days
Percentage room occupancy	85%	90%
Revenue per employee	£30,000	£41,000

WH Limited

MEMORANDUM

To: Management Accountant, Stately Hotels plc

From: Assistant to the Management Accountant

Date: 21 June X4

Subject: Initial assessment of the performance of Homely Limited

I have carried out an initial assessment of Homely Limited, based on an extract from their accounts for 20X4. I have calculated their key accounting ratios and compared them with our company's target ratios and my conclusions and recommendations are as follows.

Return on capital employed (ROCE)

At 22% the ROCE is below the target which we set for the hotels in our chain. Management action will be necessary to improve the return on capital employed, through improved profitability of operations, increased asset turnover, or both.

The main limitation in the use of this ratio is that the valuation of the capital employed can have a considerable effect on the apparent ROCE. For example, if the capital employed is undervalued, this will artificially inflate the ROCE.

Operating profit percentage

This is considerably below the target ratio set by Stately Hotels plc and it is the cause of the depressed ROCE. Management action will be necessary to improve this, either by increasing prices or by controlling operating costs relative to revenue. Since the former action may depress demand in Homely Limited's market, it is likely that management will need to focus on the control of operating costs.

A limitation in the use of this ratio is that Homely's operations may not be comparable to the average hotel in the Stately group. For example, they may not have conference facilities, which would affect the profile of their costs.

Asset turnover

At 2.7 times this is higher than the target ratio, indicating that, although Homely's operations are not as profitable, they generate more revenue per £ of capital employed. It may be that Homely has a different basis of operating, i.e. charging lower prices, and thus reducing the profitability of revenue, but in the process generating a higher revenue for the level of capital employed.

The main limitation of this ratio stems from the limitation of the ROCE, i.e. its accuracy relies on the correct valuation of capital employed.

Working capital period

This is 34 days of operating costs, almost double the level which we require in our target performance ratios. Working capital levels are probably unacceptably high and need to be reduced. This will require more attention to receivables control, reduction in inventory of, for example, consumable materials and foodstuffs, and an investigation into whether full use is being made of available credit facilities.

A limitation of this ratio is that it relies on the accurate valuation of working capital. For example, although inventories should not account for a high proportion of working capital in a hotel, their valuation can be very subjective.

Another major limitation is that the ratio is based on statement of financial position data, which depicts the working capital level on a single day. This may not be representative of the year as a whole and therefore incorrect conclusions may be drawn from the analysis.

Percentage room occupancy

Homely Limited is achieving a room occupancy rate which is above the level expected in our organisation's target ratios. This is a healthy sign which is encouraging.

Revenue per employee

Homely Limited's revenue per employee is also healthy. However, we must ensure that customer service and quality are not suffering as a result of operating with a lower level of staffing.

Overall, Homely Limited seems to have some strengths which would be worth exploiting. However, their control of operating costs and of working capital needs some attention.

Activity 4

Diamond Limited

Task 1

Diamond Ltd
Performance report – Branch 24
Year ended 31 December 20X9

(a)	Return on capital employed	57.6/240.0	24%
(b)	Gross profit margin	360.0/720.0	50%
(c)	Asset turnover	720.0/240.0	3 times
(d)	Revenue margin	57.6/720.0	8%
(e)	Average age of receivables	(96.0/720.0) × 12	1.6 months
(f)	Average age of payables	(51.0/340.0) × 12	1.8 months
(g)	Average age of inventory	(60.0/360.0) × 12	2.0 months

Task 2

Workings

(a)

		£
Revised revenue	£240,000 × 4	960,000
Cost of sales = 50%		480,000
Gross profit		480,000
Fixed costs		302,400
Operating profit		177,600
Revised return on capital employed	£177,600/£240,000	74%

(b)

Revised working capital		£
Revised receivables	(0.5 × £720,000)/12	30,000
Revised inventories	(1× £360,000)/12	30,000
Revised payables	(3 × £340,000)/12	(85,000)
Revised working capital		(25,000)
Add non-current assets		135,000
Revised capital employed		110,000
Return on capital employed	£57,600/£110,000	52%
Asset turnover	£720,000/£110,000	6.5 times

MEMORANDUM

To: Angela Newton

From: Financial analyst

Date: 5 January 20X0

Subject: Branch 24 performance indicators

Charles Walden has asked me to write to you concerning the performance indicators of Branch 24 and the extent of improvement possible if the branch was able to achieve the performance standards established by the company.

Had Branch 24 been able to achieve the same asset turnover as other branches, the return on capital employed would have been 74 per cent, comfortably in excess of the standard return on capital employed.

Likewise, had the branch controlled its working capital at standard levels, not only would the return on capital employed have been 52 per cent but it would also have achieved an asset turnover of 6.5 times.

You are quite correct to emphasise the need for profitability. If the asset turnover can be improved while maintaining the existing level of net assets, then turnover will increase. If the cost of this increased revenue is less than its value, then this will lead to both increased profits and an increase in the return on capital employed.

The suggestion that your performance might be less than other branches because your branch has been established for less time may be valid. From the financial data related to your branch, it would appear that Branch 24 was only opened two years ago. (The annual depreciation is £45,000 and the accumulated depreciation is £90,000.) If other branches have been established longer, then the accumulated depreciation will be greater, leading to a lower carrying amount and a lower capital employed. It is also possible that the older fixtures and fittings would have been purchased at a lower price, resulting in the annual depreciation charge also being less and hence increasing operating profit.

Activity 5

(a) **Value added statements**

	20X2	*20X3*
Revenue	£m	£m
	6.1	6.5
Less bought in materials and services	2.0	2.1
Value added	4.1	4.4
Applied as follows:		
To pay employees wages, salaries and other benefits	1.8	1.9
To pay providers of capital		
Finance costs	0.6	0.6
Dividends	0.2	0.2
To pay government taxation	0.3	0.3
To maintenance and expansion of assets		
Depreciation	0.4	0.5
Profit for the year	0.8	0.9
Value added	4.1	4.4

(b) **Value added per £ of employee costs**

	20X2	20X3
	£m	£m
Value added	4.1	4.4
Employee costs	1.8	1.9
Value added per '£' of employee costs	£2.28	£2.32

Bought in materials and services are consumed by value adding activities which are driven by labour and other resources to produce finished goods or services rendered. These outputs have a value in the form of revenue and when offset by the bought in items create a pool of wealth we know as value added.

Labour is a major resource which contributes to this wealth and therefore we can measure labour's productivity as:

$$\frac{\text{Value added}}{\text{Labour cost}}$$

If the productivity of labour increases then this ratio will increase.

In the case of the company above, the ratio has improved from £2.28 to £2.32 – showing an increase in labour productivity.

Activity 6

Transport company

Cost control performance ratios

Cost per mile
Cost per tonne carried
Cost per journey
Cost per tonne/mile

} each of these ratios could be calculated for fixed and variable costs separately

Fixed cost per available day
Fixed cost per working day

Usage performance ratios

Tonne/miles per period
Days available as a percentage of total working days
Days used as a percentage of available days
Tonnes carried per available day
Journeys made per available day
Tonnes/miles per journey

Activity 7

B External failure costs include the costs of product recalls.

Activity 8

B The balanced scorecard encompasses:

- the financial perspective;
- the customer perspective;
- the business perspective;
- the innovation and learning perspective.

Activity 9

(a) The four perspectives within the 'balanced scorecard' view of performance are:

- *The financial perspective*

  This is concerned with satisfying shareholders and measures used include the return on capital employed and the revenue margin.

- *The customer perspective*

  This attempts to measure how customers view the organisation and how they measure customer satisfaction. Examples include the speed of delivery and customer loyalty.

- *The internal perspective*

  This measures the quality of the organisation's output in terms of technical excellence and consumer needs. Examples include unit cost and total quality measurement.

- *The innovation and learning perspective*

  This emphasises the need for continual improvement of existing products and the ability to develop new products to meet customers' changing needs. In a 'for profit' organisation, this might be measured by the percentage of revenue attributable to new products.

(b) **Financial perspective:**

Shareholder satisfaction

Return on capital employed

$$\frac{\text{Operating profit}}{\text{Assets employed}} \times 100\%$$

$$\frac{1.14}{6.30} \times 100\% = 18.1\%$$

Customer perspective:

Customer satisfaction

% of revenue to established and existing customers

$$\frac{4.90}{6.85} \times 100\% = 71.5\%$$

Internal perspective:

Quality assurance costs as a % of total cost

$$\frac{0.35}{5.71} \times 100\% = 6.1\%$$

Innovation and learning perspective:

Revenue generated by new products as a % of total revenue

$$\frac{2.00}{6.85} \times 100\% = 29.2\%$$

Activity 10

Value added equals revenue less the cost of bought-in materials and services.

Activity 11

Target costing is the idea of identifying the cost at which a product must be made, and then choosing a design and production method that will meet that cost. This differs from the traditional idea of producing an item, seeing how much it has cost, and then adding a profit margin to set the selling price.

Activity 12

Gransden Limited

(a) (i) *Material price and usage variances*

	£		
Standard cost	2,500,000	Material price variance	
Total variance	200,000 (A)	(£120 – £100) × 22,500 metres =	£450,000 (A)
Actual cost	2,700,000	Material usage variance	
		Standard metres: £2,500,000/£100	25,000
Actual usage (metres)	22,500	Actual metres	22,500
Actual cost per metre	£120	Physical variance (metres)	2,500 (F)
		2,500 metres × £100 =	£250,000 (F)

(ii) *Increase in RPI*

Current index	168
Index at beginning of period	160
Price inflation (168/160 – 1) × 100	5%

(b) **Difficulties in interpreting the price variance**

(i) The original standard may not have been appropriate.

(ii) There might be a link between the adverse price variance and the favourable usage variance. This might occur if a superior, but more expensive, material has been used.

(iii) The Retail Price Index is a measure of the cost of living for the average household in the UK. It may not be an appropriate index for measuring price rises in manufacturing generally nor price rises for wood in particular.

(c) Return on capital employed $\frac{34,380}{190,000} \times 100$ = 18.09%

Gross profit margin $\frac{71,000}{191,000} \times 100$ = 37.17%

Revenue margin $\frac{34,380}{191,000} \times 100$ = 18.00%

Asset turnover $\frac{191,000}{190,000}$ = 1 time

Average age of receivables $\frac{47,750}{191,000} \times 12$ = 3 months

Average age of inventory $\frac{40,000}{120,000} \times 12$ = 4 months

Average age of payables $\frac{8,750}{105,000} \times 12$ = 1 month

(d) (i) Southern Division's return on capital employed with an asset turnover of 1.6 times:

	£
Revenue = £190,000 × 1.6	304,000
Gross profit @ 37%	112,480
Less fixed costs	36,620
Operating profit	75,860
Capital employed	£190,000
Return on capital employed	40%

(ii) Southern Division's return on capital employed with Northern's working capital ratios:

	£
Non-current assets	112,000
Inventories £120,000 × 3/12 =	30,000
Receivables £191,000 × 1.5/12 =	23,875
Payables £105,000 × 2/12 =	(17,500)
Capital employed	148,375
Operating profit	£34,380
Return on capital employed	23%

(e) (i) Both divisions appear to be charging straight-line depreciation at 10 per cent per annum. On that basis, the average age of Northern's non-current assets is four years old (£40,000/£10,000) while the comparable figure for the Southern Division is only three years (£48,000/£16,000). Because of this, Southern will have lower accumulated depreciation in relative terms and hence a higher capital employed.

(ii) Although the average age of payables and receivables result from past activity – buying and selling respectively – the average age of inventory has a different perspective. Although the cost of sales is backward looking in the same way as purchases and revenues, the inventory level at the year-end may not be a direct consequence of this activity. Inventory could be being built up in anticipation of higher sales levels next year.

(iii) Southern Division may be paying its payables more quickly to obtain cash discounts.

13 Test your understanding

Workbook Activity 13

What would the revenue need to have been for the asset turnover to be 5 times if the total assets are £50,000?

What would the operating profit need to have been for the ROCE to be 20% if the net assets are £400,000?

What would the gross profit need to have been if sales revenue was £1,000,000 and the gross profit margin was 20%?

What would the inventory value need to be if the current ratio was 2, current liabilities were £200,000, and receivables and cash totalled £120,000?

What would sales revenue need to be (to the nearest £) if receivable days were 80 days and receivables were £400,000?

What would be the 'value added' if sales revenue was £950,000, materials used were £400,000; labour employed was £150,000 and bought in services were £200,000?

What would payables need to be (to the nearest £) if sales were £1,200,000, cost of sales were £700,000 and the payables days were 30 days?

[ ]

During a period, the actual hours worked by employees totalled 1,630. Budgeted hours were 1,470 hours. The standard hours for the work totalled 1,502.

Calculate the:

Activity ratio = [ ] %

Efficiency ratio = [ ] %

Capacity ratio = [ ] %

(each to one decimal place).

Workbook Activity 14 (Amended)

Stonehill Quarries Ltd

You work as an accounting technician for Moran and Geoff, a firm of licensed accounting technicians.

One of your clients, Stonehill Quarries Ltd, has experienced an increase in revenue but a downturn in their overall financial performance in recent times. The company is owner managed by Ernie Heyes and a small management team.

The following is a summary of the Quarrying Trade Association's performance for the sector as a whole for the year 20X3.

Performance indicators

Return on capital employed	24%
Asset turnover	1.6
Net profit before finance costs and tax as a % of revenue	15%
Current ratio	1.5 : 1
Liquidity ratio (acid test)	1.03 : 1
Receivables collection period	60 days

Payables payment period	70 days
Finished goods inventory in days	38 days
Labour costs as % of revenue	18.1%
Operating costs as % of revenue	85.01%
Distribution costs as % of revenue	9.5%
Administrative costs as % of revenue	4.5%
Value added per '£' of employee costs	£1.95

An extract from the company's financial statements for the years 20X2 and 20X3 shows the following:

Income statements

	20X2	*20X3*
	£m	£m
Revenue	5.38	6.68
*Operating costs	4.43	5.82
	0.95	0.86
Finance costs	0.08	0.08
	0.87	0.78
Taxation	0.30	0.27
Profit after tax	0.57	0.51
Dividends	0.16	0.16
Profit for the year	0.41	0.35

*Operating costs comprise:

	£m	£m
Wages, salaries and other employee costs	0.98	1.25
Bought in materials and services	3.21	4.32
Depreciation	0.24	0.25
	4.43	5.82

Operating costs include the following:

	£m	£m
Distribution	0.49	0.61
Administration	0.22	0.27

Statements of financial position

		20X2	20X3
		£m	£m
Non-current assets		3.77	3.88
Current assets:			
Inventories	Raw materials	0.12	0.15
	Finished goods	0.43	0.45
Receivables		0.88	1.19
Cash and cash equivalents		0.04	0.05
		1.47	1.84
Less current liabilities:			
Trade payables		0.66	0.82
Taxation		0.30	0.27
Dividends		0.16	0.16
		1.12	1.25
Net current assets		0.35	0.59
Total assets less current liabilities		4.12	4.47
Less liabilities due after one year:			
Debentures		1.00	1.00
		3.12	3.47
Financed by:			
Equity		3.12	3.47

Task

(a) Calculate the ratios listed in the trade association statistics for Stonehill Quarries based on the accounts for the years 20X2 and 20X3.

Return on capital employed

20X2	*20X3*		
Asset turnover			
20X2	*20X3*		
Net profit before finance and tax as a % of revenue			
20X2	*20X3*		
Current ratio			
20X2	*20X3*		
Acid test			
20X2	*20X3*		
Receivables collection period			
20X2	*20X3*		
Payables payment period			
20X2	*20X3*		

Finished goods inventory in days			
20X2	*20X3*		
Labour cost % of revenue			
20X2	*20X3*		
Operating costs % of revenue			
20X2	*20X3*		
Distribution costs % of revenue			
20X2	*20X3*		
Admin costs % of revenue			
20X2	*20X3*		

Value added per '£' of employee costs			
	20X2	*20X3*	

Value added per '£' of employee costs			
20X2	*20X3*		

(b) Comment on the performance of Stonehill Quarries compared with the sector as a whole.

(b) **Return on capital employed**

Asset turnover

Profit margin

Current ratio and acid test

Receivables collection period

Payables payment period

Finished goods inventory in days

Labour costs % of revenue

Operating costs % of revenue

Distribution and admin costs to revenue

Value added per '£' of employee costs

Workbook Activity 15 (June 2001) (Amended)

Data

Smithex Ltd makes a single product, the Alpha, which is sold directly to domestic customers. Smithex is able to sell as many Alphas as it can produce.

Each Alpha contains a specialist part, the A10, which is in short supply. Smithex operates a just-in-time stock policy for the other material plus bought in services but not for the A10.

Smithex does not offer credit facilities to customers or hold any inventory of Alphas. The internal accounts of Smithex for the year to 31 May 2001 are shown below.

Operating statement for the year ended 31 May 2001

	Units	£	£
Revenue			6,480,000
Purchases A10	12,000	1,200,000	
Less returns	1,200	120,000	
Net purchases	10,800	1,080,000	
Add opening inventory	1,200	120,000	
Less closing inventory	(1,200)	(120,000)	
A10 issued to production	10,800	1,080,000	
Other material plus bought in services		108,000	
Production wages		1,296,000	
Variable cost of production and sales			2,484,000
Contribution			3,996,000
Production overhead		3,024,000	
Inspection cost of A10 goods received		69,600	
Cost of A10 returns		48,000	
Cost of remedial work		120,000	
Customer support for faulty products		194,400	
Administrative and distribution expenses		216,000	
Total fixed overheads			3,672,000
Net operating profit			324,000

Statement of financial position as at 31 May 2001

	£	£
Net non-current assets		1,600,000
Inventories	120,000	
Cash	80,000	
Payables	(180,000)	
Net current assets		20,000
Net assets		1,620,000
Financed by:		
Equity		800,000
Loans		820,000
		1,620,000

Other data

• Number of production employees	140
• Maximum production capacity per year	12,000
• Closing inventory only consists of units of A10	
• Payables only arise from purchases of A10	

You are employed by Smithex as its management accountant. One of your duties is to prepare management accounting information for Janet Noble, the Managing Director of Smithex.

Task

Janet Noble asks you to prepare the following performance indicators for Smithex:

(a)	**Revenue margin**		
(b)	**Return on capital employed**		
(c)	**Asset turnover**		

(d)	**Average age of inventory**			
(e)	**Average age of payables**		=	
(f)	**Added value per employee**			
	Revenue			
	Less: Material A10			
	Less: Other material and bought in services			
		———	———	
	Added value			
			———	
	Added value per employee		=	
(g)	**Wages per production employee**			
			=	
(h)	**Capacity ratio**			
			=	
(i)	**Contribution per Alpha**			
			———	

Data

At a board meeting to consider the performance indicators, the directors express concern about the high *cost of quality.* This is defined as the total of all costs incurred in preventing faults plus those costs involved in correcting faults once they have occurred. It is a single figure measuring all the explicit costs of quality – that is, those costs collected within the accounting system.

The directors have also asked the supplier of the A10 to implement a Total Quality Management (TQM) programme to avoid faulty units of A10 being purchased and to also operate a Just-in-Time (JIT) policy to eliminate the need for Smithex to carry inventory.

Janet Noble tells you that:

- All costs making up the cost of quality are caused by the faulty units of A10.
- The supplier would agree to the TQM and JIT proposals but:
  - the cost per A10 would increase by £10;
  - supplies of the A10 would be limited to the 12,000 currently provided but each A10 would be guaranteed fault-free;
  - supplies of the A10 would have to be paid for in the month received and no credit would be allowed.
- Smithex's cost of quality would be saved and inventory eliminated if the supplier implemented the TQM and JIT proposals.
- Smithex would want to keep its cash balance at £80,000.
- Any surplus cash arising from the proposals would be used to reduce the £820,000 of loans.

Janet Noble is interested in knowing what the results of Smithex would have been if the TQM and JIT proposals had been applied to the results for the year ended 31 May 2001.

Task

Janet Noble asks you to calculate the following:

(a) Cost of quality for Smithex Ltd.

Cost of remedial work		
Inspection costs of A10 goods received		
Cost of A10 returns		
Customer support for faulty products		
		________
Cost of quality		
		________

(b) Revised operating profit if the supplier's conditions were accepted.

Revised unit contribution		
Revised volume		
Revised total contribution		
Revised fixed costs:		
Existing		
Less: Saving in cost of quality		
	________	________
Revised profit		
		________

Workbook Activity 16 (December 2000) (Amended)

Data

Travel Bus Ltd is a company owned by Travel Holdings plc. It operates in the town of Camford. Camford is an old town with few parking facilities for motorists. Several years ago the Town Council built a car park on the edge of the town and awarded Travel Bus the contract to carry motorists and their passengers between the car park and the centre of the town.

Originally, the Council charged motorists £4.00 per day for the use of the car park but, to encourage motorists not to take their cars into the town centre, parking has been free since 1 December 1999.

The journey between the car park and the town centre is the only service operated by Travel Bus Ltd in Camford. A summary of the results for the first two years of operations, together with the net assets associated with the route and other operating data, is reproduced below.

Operating statement year ended 30 November

	1999	*2000*
	£	£
Revenue	432,000	633,600
Fuel	129,600	185,328
Wages	112,000	142,000
Other variable costs	86,720	84,512
Gross profit	103,680	221,760
Bus road tax and insurance	22,000	24,000
Depreciation of buses	12,000	12,000
Maintenance of buses	32,400	28,512
Fixed garaging costs	29,840	32,140
Administration	42,000	49,076
Net profit/(loss)	(34,560)	76,032

Extract from statement of financial position as at 30 November

	1999	*2000*
	£	£
Buses	240,000	240,000
Accumulated depreciation	168,000	180,000
Carrying amount	72,000	60,000
Net current assets	14,400	35,040
	86,400	95,040

Other operating data	*1999*	*2000*
Fare per passenger per journey	£0.80	£1.00
Miles per year	324,000	356,400
Miles per journey	18.0	18.0
Days per year	360	360
Wages per driver	£14,000	£14,200

Throughout the two years the drivers were paid a basic wage per week, no bonuses were paid and no overtime was incurred.

In two weeks there will be a meeting between officials of the Town Council and the Chief Executive of Travel Holdings to discuss the performance of Travel Bus for the year to 30 November 2000. The previous year's performance indicators were as follows:

Gross profit margin	24%
Net profit margin	–8%
Return on capital employed	–40%
Asset turnover	5 times
Number of passengers in the year	540,000
Total cost per mile	£1.44
Number of journeys per day	50
Maintenance cost per mile	£0.10
Passengers per day	1,500
Passengers per journey	30
Number of drivers	8

Task

In preparation for the meeting, you have been asked to calculate the following performance indicators for the year to 30 November 2000:

(a)	Gross profit margin:	
(b)	Net profit margin:	
(c)	Return on capital employed:	
(d)	Asset turnover:	
(e)	Number of passengers in the year:	
(f)	Total cost per mile:	
(g)	Number of journeys per day:	
(h)	Maintenance cost per mile:	
(i)	Passengers per day:	
(j)	Passengers per journey:	
(k)	Number of drivers:	

Data

On receiving your performance indicators, the Chief Executive of Travel Holdings raises the following issues with you:

- The drivers are claiming that the improved profitability of Travel Bus reflects their increased productivity.
- The managers believe that the change in performance is due to improved motivation arising from the introduction of performance related pay for managers during the year to 30 November 2000.
- The officials from the Town Council are concerned that Travel Bus is paying insufficient attention to satisfying passenger needs and safety.

The Chief Executive asks for your advice.

Task

Write a memo to the Chief Executive of Travel Holdings plc. Where relevant, you should make use of the data and answers to Task 32.1 to:

(a) *Briefly* discuss whether or not increased productivity always leads to increased profitability.

(b) Develop ONE possible measure of driver productivity and suggest whether or not the drivers' claim is valid.

(c) Suggest ONE reason, other than improved motivation, why the profitability of Travel Bus might have improved.

(d) Suggest:

   (i) ONE *existing* performance indicator which might measure the satisfaction of passenger needs; and

   (ii) ONE other possible performance indicator of passenger needs which cannot be measured from the existing performance data collected by Travel Bus.

(e) Suggest:

   (i) ONE *existing* performance indicator which might measure the safety aspect of Travel Bus's operations; and

   (ii) ONE other possible safety performance indicator which cannot be measured from the existing performance data collected by Travel Bus.

MEMO

To:

From:

Date:

Subject:

I refer to your observations relating to the performance of Travel Bus Ltd and detail my comments below.

(a) **Relationship between productivity and profitability**

(b) **Driver productivity**

(c) **Reasons for improved profitability**

(d) **Indicator of passenger satisfaction**

(e) **Possible safety indicators**

Workbook Activity 17 (June 2000) (Amended)

Data

LandAir and SeaAir are two small airlines operating flights to Waltonville. LandAir operates from an airport based at a town on the same island as Waltonville but SeaAir operates from an airport based on another island. In both cases, the flight to Waltonville is 150 air-miles. Each airline owns a single aircraft, an 80-seat commuter jet and both airlines operate flights for 360 days per year.

You are employed as the management accountant at SeaAir and report to Carol Jones, SeaAir's chief executive. Recently both airlines agreed to share each other's financial and operating data as a way of improving efficiency. The data for the year to 31 May 2000 for both airlines is reproduced below. The performance indicators for LandAir are reproduced further below.

Operating statement year ended 31 May 2000

	LandAir	*SeaAir*
	$000	$000
Revenue	51,840	29,700
Fuel and aircraft maintenance	29,160	14,580
Take-off and landing fees at Waltonville	4,320	2,160
Aircraft parking at Waltonville	720	2,880
Depreciation of aircraft	500	400
Salaries of flight crew	380	380
Home airport costs	15,464	8,112
Net profit	1,296	1,188

Extract from statement of financial position as at 31 May 2000

	LandAir	*SeaAir*
	$000	$000
Non-current assets		
Aircraft	10,000	10,000
Accumulated depreciation	2,500	4,000
Carrying amount	7,500	6,000
Net current assets	3,300	5,880
	10,800	11,880

Other operating data

Number of seats on aircraft	80	80
Return flights per day	12	6
Return fare	$200	$275
Air-miles per return flight	300	300

Performance indicators	*LandAir*
Return on capital employed	12.00%
Asset turnover per year	4.80
Revenue (or net profit) margin	2.50%
Actual number of return flights per year	4,320
Actual number of return passengers per year	259,200
Average seat occupancy[1]	75.00%
Actual number of passenger-miles[2]	77,760,000
Cost per passenger mile	$0.65

Notes:

1 Actual number of return passengers ÷ maximum possible number of return passengers from existing flights.

2 Actual number of passengers carried × number of miles flown.

Task

Carol Jones asks you to prepare the following performance indicators for SeaAir:

(a)	Return on capital employed:	
(b)	Asset turnover:	
(c)	Revenue (or net profit) margin:	
(d)	Actual number of return flights per year:	
(e)	Actual number of return passengers per year:	
(f)	Average seat occupancy:	
(g)	Actual number of passenger-miles:	
(h)	Cost per passenger mile:	

Data

Carol Jones is concerned that the overall performance of SeaAir is below that of LandAir, despite both airlines operating to the same destination and over a similar distance. She finds it all the more difficult to understand as LandAir has to compete with road and rail transport. Carol Jones has recently attended a seminar on maintaining competitive advantage and is eager to apply the concepts to SeaAir. She explains that there are two ways to gain a competitive advantage:

- by being the lowest cost business; or
- by having a unique aspect to the product or service allowing a higher price to be charged.

This involves managers attempting to eliminate costs which do not enhance value, that is, costs for which customers are not prepared to pay either in the form of a higher price or increased demand.

She makes the following proposals for next year, the year ending 31 May 2001:

- The number of return flights is increased to 9 per day.
- The estimated average seat occupancy will change to 55%.
- The price of a return fare will remain the same.

As a result of the proposals, there will be some changes in operating costs:

- Fuel and aircraft maintenance, and take-off and landing fees at Waltonville airport, will increase in proportion with the increase in flights.
- Aircraft parking at Waltonville will be halved.
- Aircraft depreciation will increase to $600,000 for the forthcoming year.
- Additional flight crew will cost an extra $58,000.
- There will be no other changes in costs.

Task

Carol Jones is interested in forecasting the performance of SeaAir for next year, the year to 31 May 2001. Write a memo to Carol Jones. In your memo you should:

(a) Calculate the forecast number of passengers next year for SeaAir.

(b) Calculate SeaAir's forecast net profit for next year.

(c) Show SeaAir's forecast return on capital employed for next year assuming no change in its net assets other than any additional depreciation.

(d) Identify ONE competitive advantage SeaAir has over LandAir.

(e) Identify ONE expense in SeaAir's operating statement which does not add value.

MEMO

To:

From:

Date:

Subject:

I outline below the forecast performance for SeaAir for the year to 31 May 2001.

(a)	Forecast number of passengers:	
(b)	Forecast net profit for the year to 31 May 2001:	
		$000
	Revenue:	
		–––––
	Fuel and aircraft maintenance	
	Take off and landing fees at Waltonville	
	Aircraft parking at Waltonville	
	Depreciation of aircraft	
	Salaries of flight crew	
	Home airport costs	
		–––––
	Net profit	
		–––––
(c)	Revised return on capital employed:	

(d)

(e)

Workbook Activity 18 (December 1999) (Amended)

Data

You are employed as a financial analyst with Denton Management Consultants and report to James Alexander, a local partner. Denton Management Consultants has recently been awarded the contract to implement accrual accounting in the St Nicolas Police Force and will shortly have to make a presentation to the Head of the Police Force. The presentation is concerned with showing how performance indicators are developed in 'for profit' organisations and how these can be adapted to help 'not for profit' organisations.

James Alexander has asked for your help in preparing a draft of the presentation that Denton Management Consultants will make to the Head of the Police Force. He suggests that a useful framework would be the balanced scorecard and examples of how this is used by private sector organisations.

The balanced scorecard views performance measurement in a 'for profit' organisation from four perspectives.

The financial perspective

This is concerned with satisfying shareholders and measures used include the return on capital employed and the revenue margin.

The customer perspective

This attempts to measure how customers view the organisation and how they measure customer satisfaction. Examples include the speed of delivery and customer loyalty.

The internal perspective

This measures the quality of the organisation's output in terms of technical excellence and consumer needs. Examples include unit cost and total quality measurement.

The innovation and learning perspective

This emphasises the need for continual improvement of existing products and the ability to develop new products to meet customers' changing needs. In a 'for profit' organisation, this might be measured by the percentage of revenue attributable to new products.

To help you demonstrate how performance indicators are developed in 'for profit' organisations, he gives you the following financial data relating to a manufacturing client of Denton Management Consultants.

Income statement
12 months ended 30 November 1999

	£000	£000
Revenue		240.0
Material	18.0	
Labour	26.0	
Production overheads	9.0	
Cost of production	53.0	
Opening finished inventory	12.0	
Closing finished inventory	(13.0)	
Cost of sales		52.0
Gross profit		188.0
Research & development	15.9	
Training	5.2	
Administration	118.9	
		140.0
Net profit		48.0

Extract from statement of financial position at 30 November 1999

	Opening balance £000	*Additions* £000	*Deletions* £000	*Closing balance* £000
Non-current assets				
Cost	200.0	40.0	10.0	230.0
Depreciation	80.0	8.0	8.0	80.0
Carrying amount				150.0
Net current assets				
Inventory of finished goods			13.0	
Receivables			40.0	
Cash			6.0	
Payables			(9.0)	
				50.0
Net assets				200.0

Task

James Alexander asks you to calculate the following performance indicators and, for each indicator, to identify ONE balanced scorecard perspective being measured:

(a)	Return on capital employed:		
		=	
	Scorecard:		
(b)	Revenue margin percentage		
		=	
	Scorecard:		
(c)	Asset turnover:		
		=	
	Scorecard:		
(d)	Research and development as percentage of production:		
		=	
	Scorecard:		

(e)	Training as percentage of labour costs:		
		=	
	Scorecard:		
(f)	Average age of finished inventory:		
		=	
	Scorecard:		

Data

On receiving your calculations, James Alexander tells you that he has recently received details of the current performance measures used by the St Nicolas Police Force. Four indicators are used:

- the percentage of cash expenditure to allocated funds for the year;
- the average police hours spent per crime investigated;
- the average police hours spent per crime solved;
- the clear-up rate (defined as number of crimes solved ÷ number of crimes investigated).

He also provides you with data for the current year used in developing the current indicators as follows:

- Funds allocated for the year: $3,000,000
- Cash expenditure during the year: $2,910,000
- Number of reported crimes in the last year: 8,000 crimes
- Number of crimes investigated in the year: 5,000 crimes
- Number of crimes solved in the year: 2,000 crimes
- Number of police hours spent on investigating and solving crimes: 40,000 hours
- Number of police hours spent on crime prevention: 500 hours

Task

James Alexander asks you to prepare short notes for him. Your notes should:

(a) Calculate the four indicators currently used by the St Nicolas Police Force.

(b) Identify ONE limitation in the calculation of the clear-up rate.

(c) Briefly suggest:

(i) ONE reason why the percentage of cash expenditure to allocated funds may be an inadequate measure of the financial perspective.

(ii) ONE reason why the clear-up rate might be an inadequate measure of the customer perspective other than because of the limitation identified in part (b).

(iii) ONE reason why the hours spent per crime investigated might be an inadequate measure of the internal perspective.

(iv) ONE measure which might focus on the innovation and learning perspective.

Notes on Performance Indicators for the St Nicolas Police Force

To:

Prepared by:

Date:

The following are my observations on the issues you raised on the performance indicators.

(a) **Calculation of the four indicators currently used by the St Nicolas Police Force**

- Percentage of cash expenditure to allocated funds for the year:

- Average police hours spent per crime investigated:

- Average police hours per crime solved:

- Clear-up rate:

(b) **Limitations to the clear-up rate**

(c) **Performance indicators and the balanced scorecard**

Workbook Activity 19 (June 1999) (Amended)

Data

You are employed by ALV Ltd as an accounting technician. Two companies owned by ALV Ltd are ALV (East) Ltd and ALV (West) Ltd. These two companies are located in the same town and make an identical electrical product which sells for £84.

Financial data relating to the two companies is reproduced below. In addition, performance indicators for ALV (East) Ltd are also enclosed. Both companies use the same straight-line depreciation policy and assume no residual value.

ALV (East) Ltd
Extract from statement of financial position as at 31 May 1999

	Cost	*Accumulated depreciation*	*Net book value*
	£000	£000	£000
Non-current assets			
Buildings	1,000	700	300
Plant & machinery	300	240	60
	1,300	940	360
Net current assets			
Inventory		45	
Receivables		30	
Cash		5	
Payables		(40)	40
			400

ALV (East) Ltd
Income statement – year to 31 May 1999

	£000
Revenue	840
Material and bought-in services	340
Production labour	180
Other production expenses	52
Depreciation – buildings	20
Dep'n – plant and machinery	30
Admin and other expenses	50
Operating profit	168

Other data

Number of employees	18	Units produced	10,000

Performance indicators for ALV (East) Ltd

Asset turnover	2.1 times	Production labour cost per unit	£18.00
Net profit margin	20.00%	Output per employee	556
Return on capital employed	42.00%	Added value per employee	£27,778
Wages per employee	£10,000	Profit per employee	£9,333

ALV (West) Ltd
Extract from statement of financial position as at 31 May 1999

	Cost £000	*Accumulated depreciation* £000	*Carrying amount* £000
Non-current assets			
Buildings	1,500	120	1,380
Plant & machinery	900	180	720
	2,400	300	2,100
Net current assets			
Inventory		20	
Receivables		30	
Cash		5	
Payables		(44)	Nil
			2,100

ALV (West) Ltd
Income statement – year to 31 May 1999

	£000
Revenue	2,520
Material and bought-in services	1,020
Production labour	260
Other production expenses	630
Depreciation – buildings	30
Dep'n – plant and machinery	90
Admin and other expenses	112
Operating profit	378

Other data

Number of employees	20	Units produced	30,000

ALV Ltd is considering closing one of the companies over the next two years. As a first step, the board of directors wish to hold a meeting to consider which is the more efficient and productive company.

Task

In preparation for the board meeting, calculate the following performance indicators for ALV (West) Ltd:

(a)	Asset turnover:		
(b)	Net profit margin:		
		=	
(c)	Return on capital employed:		
		=	
(d)	Wages per employee:		
		=	
(e)	Production labour cost per unit:		
		=	

(f)	Output per employee:		
		=	
(g)	Added value:		
	Added value per employee:		
		=	
(h)	Profit per employee:		
		=	

Data

Shortly after preparing the performance indicators for ALV (West) Ltd, the chief executive of ALV Ltd, Jill Morgan, issued a statement to a local newspaper. In that statement she said that the workforce at ALV (East) was far less productive than at the other company despite both companies making an identical product. She concluded that it was up to the workforce to improve productivity. In response, the employees stated that the normal way of measuring efficiency is profit and, therefore, ALV (East) was more efficient than ALV (West).

Jill Morgan asks you to prepare a report for the next board meeting to explain the issues involved so that all board members can be properly briefed.

Task

Write a report to Jill Morgan for distribution to the board of directors. Your report should:

(a) Explain what is meant by:

  (i) productivity;

  (ii) efficiency.

(b) Identify the best TWO performance indicators used by ALV to measure efficiency and use those indicators to identify which of the two companies is the more efficient.

(c) Identify the best TWO performance measures used by ALV to measure productivity and use those indicators to identify which of the two companies has the higher productivity.

(d) Use the NET NON-CURRENT ASSETS to derive a different measure of productivity for both companies.

(e) Use the data in Task 1 and your answer to Task 2 (d) to explain ONE reason why the productivity and efficiency measures might give different rankings.

REPORT ON THE EFFICIENCY AND PRODUCTIVITY OF ALV (EAST) AND ALV (WEST)

Prepared for:

Prepared by:

Date:

Introduction

The objective of this report is to define the terms 'productivity' and 'efficiency' and relate these concepts to the divisions within the company.

It then considers performance indicators for these concepts and compares divisional performance, finally deriving further measures of productivity relevant to both divisions.

(a) **The meaning of productivity and efficiency**

(b) **Two performance indicators to measure efficiency**

(c) **Two performance indicators to measure productivity**

(d) **An alternative measure of productivity**

(e) **One reason why productivity and efficiency measures give different rankings**

Workbook Activity 20 (June 2002) (Amended)

Data

Drampton plc is considering purchasing Hand Power Systems Ltd. Hand Power Systems makes a hand-held computer and has provided Drampton with its latest operating statement and statement of financial position. These are shown below together with details of the orders received during the year and information about the sales returns.

Hand Power Systems Ltd:
Operating statement for the year ended 31 May 2002

	Volume	£000	£000
Gross sales	21,000		6,300
Less sales returns	1,000		300
Revenue	20,000		6,000
Material		3,360	
Labour		960	
Production fixed overheads		480	
Cost of production	24,000	4,800	
Add opening finished inventory	1,000	300	
Less closing finished inventory	(5,000)	(1,350)	
Cost of sales	20,000		3,750
Gross profit			2,250
Research and development		768	
Training		576	
Customer support		240	
Marketing		200	
Administration		226	2,010
Net operating profit			240

Extract from statement of financial position as at 31 May 2002

	£000	£000
Non-current assets		
Machinery and equipment		
Cost		5,000
Accumulated depreciation		4,000
Carrying amount		1,000
Net current assets		
Inventory of finished goods	1,350	
Receivables	1,500	
Cash	(426)	
Payables	(424)	2,000
Net assets		3,000

Additional information

- Orders for 26,000 hand-held computers were received during the year ended 31 May 2002.
- Sales returns represent hand-held computers found to be faulty by customers. Customers had these replaced by fault-free computers.

Task

Prepare the following performance indicators for Drampton's finance director:

(a)	Gross profit margin:	
(b)	Net profit (or revenue) margin:	
(c)	Return on capital employed:	
(d)	Asset turnover:	
(e)	Average age of receivables:	
(f)	Research and development/Production:	
(g)	Training/Production:	
(h)	Customer support/Revenue	
(i)	Returns/Revenue	
(j)	Average delay in supplying customers:	

Data

The finance director believes that a balanced scorecard will help in the analysis of Hand Power Systems' performance and gives you the following information.

The balanced scorecard views performance measurement from four perspectives:

- the financial perspective: this is concerned with satisfying shareholders and measures used include the return on capital employed;
- the customer perspective: this attempts to measure how customers view the organisation and with measuring customer satisfaction. Examples include the speed of delivery and customer loyalty;
- the internal perspective: this measures the quality of the organisation's output in terms of technical excellence and consumer needs. Examples include unit cost and total quality measurement;
- the innovation and learning perspective: this emphasises the need for continual improvement of existing products and developing new products to meet customers' changing needs. In a 'for profit' organisation, this might be measured by the percentage of revenue attributable to new products.

Task

Name ONE balanced scorecard perspective being measured for each of the performance indicators.

(a) Gross profit margin:

(b) Net profit (or revenue) margin:

(c) Return on capital employed:

(d) Asset turnover:

(e) Average age of receivables:

(f) Research and development/Production:

(g) Training/Production:

(h) Customer support/Revenue:

(i) Returns/Revenue

(j) Average delay in supplying customers:

Data

The finance director gives you the following additional information relating to Hand Power Systems for the year to 31 May 2003.

Accounting policies

- Inventories: the closing inventory of finished goods is valued on a last-in, first-out basis and material prices have been falling throughout the year ended 31 May 2002.

  There are no raw material or work in progress inventories at any time.

- Depreciation: this is calculated on a straight-line basis assuming no residual value.

  The depreciation charge for the year was £1,000,000.

  Similar non-current assets in other companies have an average life of 10 years.

Other information

	Selling prices	*Material costs*	*Sales volume*
• Indices for this year and next year			
• Index year ended 31 May 2002	120	175	100
• Forecast index year ended 31 May 2003	100	140	130

- Total quality management will be introduced. As a result, there will no longer be any sales returns.
- The hand-held computers will be made to order and so there will be no closing inventories.
- As a result of this year's research and development, new machinery and equipment will be introduced from 1 June 2002. This will result in a 25% saving in the labour cost per hand-held computer.
- The new machinery and equipment will also result in savings of £160,000 in the production fixed overheads.

Task

Write a memo to the finance director. In your memo you should:

(a) briefly state and explain the effect of the following accounting policies on Hand Power Systems' profit for the year ended 31 May 2002:

  (i) inventory valuation

  (ii) depreciation

MEMO

To:

From:

Date:

Subject:

(a) **Accounting policies**

(i) **Inventory valuation:**

(ii) **Depreciation:**

(b) **Calculate the following forecast data for the year to 31 May 2003**

(i)	Selling price per computer:	
(ii)	Sales volume:	
(iii)	Sales revenue:	
(iv)	Unit material cost:	
(v)	Unit labour cost:	
(vi)	Production volume:	
	Sales volume	
	Less opening inventory	
	Production	

(vii)	Forecast cost of production:	
	Materials	
	Labour	
	Fixed overhead	
	Cost of production	
(viii)	Forecast cost of sales:	
	Cost of production	
	Add opening inventory	
	Cost of sales	
(ix)	Forecast gross profit	

Workbook Activity 21 (December 2002) (Amended)

Data

You are the Management Accountant of Care4, a registered charity. You report to Carol Jones, the Chief Executive. Care4 owns Highstone School, a residential school for children with special needs. One of your duties is to prepare performance indicators for Highstone School. The accounts for the year to 31 August 2002 are shown below.

Operating statement – year to 31 August 2002

	£	£
Fee income		1,760,000
Teacher salaries	600,000	
Nursing and support staff salaries	480,000	
Administrative expenses	120,000	
Power	128,000	
Housekeeping	160,000	
Depreciation	236,800	
Total expenses		1,724,800
Operating surplus		35,200

Statement of financial position extract at 31 August 2002

	Land	*Buildings and equipment*	*Total*
	£	£	£
Non-current assets			
Cost	4,502,800	11,840,000	16,342,800
Depreciation to date		9,708,800	9,708,800
Carrying amount	4,502,800	2,131,200	6,634,000
Net current assets			
Receivables	440,000		
Cash	62,000		
Payables	(96,000)		406,000
Net assets			7,040,000

Local authorities refer children with special needs to the school and pay the school fees. There is a standard contract that states the number of children per teacher and the number of nursing and support staff required. You are provided with the following additional information:

- The school fee per child for the year ended 31 August 2002 was £22,000.
- The contracts state there must be:
  - one teacher for every four children (The average salary per teacher is £30,000;)
  - one member of the nursing and support staff for every two children. (The average salary per member of the nursing and support staff is £12,000).
- The school can accommodate a maximum of 100 children.
- The buildings and equipment are depreciated by equal amounts each year and are assumed to have no residual value.
- Payables entirely relate to power and housekeeping.

Task

Prepare the following school performance indicators for Carol Jones:

(a)	Operating surplus/fee income	
(b)	Return on net assets	
(c)	Average age of receivables	
(d)	Average age of payables	
(e)	Number of children in school	
(f)	Occupancy rate of school	
(g)	Number of teachers	
(h)	Number of nursing and support staff	
(i)	Total cash-based expenses = total expenses – depreciation	
(j)	Number of months cash-based expenditure payable	

Data

On receiving your performance indicators, Carol Jones tells you she is worried about the financial viability of the school. Some payables are objecting to the late payment of their invoices and the cash balance is insufficient to pay expenses when due. She also tells you that the school wants to purchase new equipment costing £400,000 in September 2003.

Carol Jones feels that the productivity and efficiency of the school must be improved and sets the following targets for the year to 31 August 2003:

- Operating surplus as a percentage of fee income should double.
- Return on net assets should double.
- The school should generate sufficient cash to be able to:
  - pay for the new equipment; and
  - have a cash balance equivalent to one month's cash-based expenses.

She proposes the following action plan for the year to 31 August 2003.

Action plan – year to 31 August 2003

- The number of children will increase by 10%.
- The school fee per child will not change.
- The number of teachers and the number of nursing and support staff will increase according to the contract.
- There will be no change in the average salaries of either teachers or nursing and support staff.
- No other expenses will change.
- Receivables will only be allowed 1½ months to pay.
- The average age of payables will be 2 months.
- There will be no additional funding by Care4 nor will the school make any payments to Care4.

Task

Prepare the following forecast information for the year to 31 August 2003 using the assumptions of the action plan and before the purchase of the new equipment:

	Fee income		
	Teacher salaries		
	Nursing salaries		
	Administrative costs (no change)		
	Power (no change)		
	Housekeeping (no change)		
	Depreciation (no change)		
		————	————
			————
(b)	Receivables		
(c)	Payables		
(d)	Revised carrying amount of non-current assets:		
	Carrying amount as at 31 August 2002		
	Depreciation year to 31 August 2003		
			————
	Carrying amount as at 31 August 2003		
			————

(e)	Cash balance 31 August 2002			
	Add:	Operating surplus		
		Non-cash items (depreciation)		
		Change in receivables		
	Less:	Change in payables		
	Cash balance 31 August 2003			

Task

Write a memo to Carol Jones. In your memo you should:

(a) Calculate the following forecast information for the year ended 31 August 2003:

(i) operating surplus as a percentage of fee income;

(ii) return on net assets;

(iii) cash available after allowing for buying the new equipment;

(iv) number of months that cash-based expenses could be paid from the cash balance after allowing for buying the new equipment.

(b) State if the action plan achieves all of the proposed targets.

(c) Explain the difference between productivity and efficiency.

(d) Give ONE example of increased productivity as a result of implementing the action plan.

MEMO

To:

From:

Date:

Subject:

(a) If the action plan is achieved, the target results will be as follows:

(i) Operating surplus as a percentage of fee income

(ii) Return on net assets

(iii) Cash available after buying new equipment:

(iv) Number of months cash-based expenses can be paid from the cash balance:

Cash expenses

Number of months cash

(b)

(c)

(d)

Workbook Activity 22 (December 2003) (Amended)

You are employed as an accounting technician by Aspex Technologies Ltd. One of your duties is to prepare performance indicators and other information for Stuart Morgan, the Financial Director.

Aspex Technologies make a single product, the Zeta. In the year to 30 November 2003, the company has had problems with the quality of the material used to make Zetas and Stuart would like to know what the cost of quality has been for the year.

The cost of quality is defined as the total of all costs incurred in preventing faults plus those costs involved in correcting faults once they have occurred. It is a single figure measuring all the explicit costs of quality – that is, those costs collected within the accounting system.

Stuart provides you with the following financial statements and data.

Operating statement – year ended 30 November 2003

	Units	£000	£000
Revenue	360,000		14,400
Purchases	400,000	6,400	
Less returns	(40,000)	(640)	
Net purchases	360,000	5,760	
Add opening inventory	90,000	1,440	
Less closing inventory	(90,000)	(1,440)	
Material issued to production	360,000	5,760	
Production labour		3,600	
Variable cost of production and sales			9,360
Contribution			5,040
Heat, light and power		720	
Depreciation		1,000	
Inspection cost		80	
Production overhead		2,000	
Reworking of faulty production		40	
Customer support		200	
Marketing and administrative expenses		424	
Total fixed overheads			4,464
Operating profit			576

Statement of financial position as at 30 November 2003

	£000	£000
Non-current assets at cost		8,000
Cumulative depreciation		2,000
Carrying amount		6,000
Inventory	1,440	
Receivables	2,400	
Cash	960	
Payables	(1,200)	
Net current assets		3,600
		9,600
Financed by		
Debt		6,000
Equity		3,600
		9,600

- The number of production employees in the company is 180.
- Production labour is a variable expense.
- The demand for Zetas in the year to 30 November 2003 was 390,000 but not all could be produced and sold due to poor quality materials. Any orders not completed this year can be completed next year.
- The only reason for the reworking of faulty production and customer support expenses was the poor quality of the materials.
- Material and heat, light and power are the only bought-in expenses.
- Payables relate entirely to material purchases.
- There are no inventories of finished goods or work in progress.
- Depreciation is based on the straight-line method.

Task

Prepare the following information for Stuart Morgan:

(a)	Selling price per Zeta:		
(b)	Material cost per Zeta:		
(c)	Labour cost per Zeta:		
(d)	Contribution per Zeta:		
(e)	Contribution percentage:		
(f)	Net profit (or revenue) margin:		
(g)	Return on capital employed:		
(h)	Asset turnover:		
(i)	Average age of receivables in months:		
(j)	Average age of inventory in months:		
(k)	Average age of payables in months:		
(l)	Added value per employee		
	Revenue:		
	Material:		
	Heat, light and power:		
		———	
	Added value:		
		———	
	Added value per employee:		
(m)	Average delay in completing an order months		
	Order volume:		
	Sales volume:		
		———	
	Backlog:		
		———	
	Average delay:		
(n)	Cost of quality		
	Inspection:		
	Reworking:		
	Customer support:		

Data

Stuart Morgan tells you that the Directors of Aspex Technologies have agreed an action plan for the year to 30 November 2004. The plan involves:

- using market research to forecast likely sales volume and prices
- implementing total quality management and just-in-time stock control;
- greater working capital control.

Stuart provides you with the following

Market research

- Indices for this year and next year

	Selling price index	*Sales volume index*
Indices for year ended 30 November 2003	180	70
Forecast indices for year ending 30 November 2004	171	84

- The total fore
- cast sales volume for the year ending 30 November 2004 is made up of two elements:
  - a revised volume from applying the sales volume indices to the 360,000 Zetas sold in the year to 30 November 2003;
  - an additional volume from completing orders placed in the year to 30 November 2003 but not made in that year because of the poor quality materials.
- The forecast selling price applies to the total forecast sales volume using the selling price indices.

Total quality management and just-in-time inventory control

- The material supplier has agreed to take back the existing closing inventory and replace it with fault-free materials.
- The supplier has also agreed to guarantee all material will be fault-free next year and improve the speed and reliability of deliveries. In exchange, Aspex has agreed that the unit cost of material will remain the same as last year.
- Aspex will no longer keep inventories of material.
- The costs making up the cost of quality will be saved.

Working capital control and other matters

- The unit cost of production labour will remain the same and there will be no change in the remaining fixed overheads.
- The average age of receivables will be 2 months.
- Aspex has agreed that the average age of payables will be 1 month.
- The cash balance will remain the same. Any surplus cash will be used to pay off the existing loans.
- No non-current assets will be bought or sold during the year to 30 November 2004.

Task

Prepare the following estimates for the year to 30 November 2004 for Stuart Morgan:

(a)	Forecast demand:	
	Add backlog	
	Sales volume (units)	
(b)	Planned sales volume:	
	less available inventory of material	
	Purchases (units)	
(c)	Cost of purchases:	
(d)	Selling price per Zeta:	
(e)	Revenue:	
(f)	Total contribution. As the cost of material remains the same, the contribution is only affected by the selling price.	
	Reduction in selling price:	
	Revised unit contribution:	
	Total contribution:	

(g)	Fixed costs	
	Existing fixed costs:	
	less cost of quality	
(h)	Profit:	
(i)	Net assets	
	Net non-current assets last year:	
	less extra year's depreciation	
	Carrying amount	
	Receivables:	
	Cash (given)	
	Payables:	
	Net assets	
(j)	Revised NP (or revenue) margin:	
(k)	Revised return on capital employed:	

Workbook Activity 23 (June 2004)

Data

The actual and budgeted operating results for the sale and production of executive desks for the year to May 2004 are set out below.

	Actual	*Budget*
	£	£
Revenue	2,750,000	3,000,000
Cost of sales		
Opening finished goods inventory	200,000	200,000
Cost of production	2,329,600	2,400,000
Closing finished goods inventory	(240,000)	(200,000)
Cost of sales	2,289,600	2,400,000
Gross profit	460,400	600,000
Distribution and administration costs	345,000	360,000
Operating profit	115,400	240,000

Other data for the production and sale of executive desks for the year to May 2004 is as follows:

	Actual	*Budget*
Number of desks sold	11,000	12,000
Number of desks produced	11,200	12,000
Direct labour hours	58,200	60,000
Net assets employed	£1,075,400	£1,200,000

Task

(a) Calculate the following actual and budgeted performance indicators:

Note: All performance indicators – except (iv) – should be expressed as percentages.

	Actual	*Budget*
Gross profit margin		
Operating profit margin		
Return on capital employed		
Inventory turnover (in months)		
Labour capacity ratio		
Labour efficiency ratio		

(b) Write a memo to Sam Thomas. Your memo should include ONE course of action the company could take to improve EACH performance indicator.

MEMO

To:

From:

Date:

Subject:

(i) **Gross profit margin**

(ii) **Operating profit margin**

(iii) **Return on capital employed**

(iv) **Inventory turnover**

(v) **Labour capacity ratio**

(vi) **Labour efficiency ratio**

Data

Sam Thomas has been on a course on product management. He was particularly interested in the concept of value engineering or value analysis. This was explained to be a process which involves different specialists to evaluate a product's design. The objective of the process is to identify how a product may be redesigned to improve its value.

Task

Write a brief memo to Sam Thomas. Your memo should describe how value engineering or value analysis may be used to reduce the production cost of an item such as an executive desk.

MEMO

To:

From:

Date:

Subject:

WORKBOOK ACTIVITIES ANSWERS

ANSWERS

Workbook activity answers

2 Collection of cost information

Workbook Activity 7

Product 'EF3'

Quarter ended	*Volume tonnes*	*Fixed cost*	*Variable cost*	*Total cost*
		£	£	£
March	15,000	25,000	525,000	550,000
June	12,000	25,000	420,000	445,000
September	16,000	25,000	560,000	585,000
December	14,000	25,000	490,000	515,000

3 Accounting for overheads

Activity 18

Luda Limited

(a) *Fixed overhead absorption rates*

			Machine area	*Finishing shop*
			£	£
	Fixed overhead		100,800	94,500
			Hours	*Hours*
(i)	Labour hours	P 6,000 units × 2, 1.5	12,000	9,000
		Q 8,000 units × 1, 1	8,000	8,000
		R 2,000 units × 2, 2	4,000	4,000
			24,000	24,000
	Overhead absorption rate per labour hour		£4.20	£4.50

(ii)	Machine hours	P 6,000 × 4, 0.5	24,000	3,000
		Q 8,000 × 1.5, 0.5	12,000	4,000
		R 2,000 × 3, 1	6,000	9,000
			42,000	9,000
	Overhead absorption rate per machine hr		£2.40	£10.50

(b) *Product costs*

	P	*Q*	*R*
	£	£	£
Materials	18.50	15.00	22.50
Wages	16.00	9.00	18.00
Prime cost	34.50	24.00	40.50

(i) *Labour hour rate absorption*

	P	*Q*	*R*
	£	£	£
Prime costs as above	34.50	24.00	40.50
Fixed overheads:			
Machine area £4.20 × 2, 1, 2	8.40	4.20	8.40
Finishing shop £4.50 × 1.5, 1, 2	6.75	4.50	9.00
	49.65	32.70	57.90

(ii) *Machine hour rate absorption*

	P	*Q*	*R*
	£	£	£
Prime costs as above	34.50	24.00	40.50
Fixed overheads:			
Machine area £2.40 × 4, 1.5, 3	9.60	3.60	7.20
Finishing shop £10.50 × 0.5,0.5,1	5.25	5.25	10.5
	49.35	32.85	58.20

Workbook Activity 19

Answer is C.

		£
Direct labour	4.5 hours × £8.50	38.25
Direct material	1.1 tonnes × £25	27.50
Variable overhead	£378,000/12,000 tonnes	31.50
Marginal cost = Total variable costs per tonne		£97.25

Workbook Activity 20

Answer is D.

Contribution per tonne	=	Selling price – Variable cost
	=	£132 – £97.25
	=	£34.75

Workbook Activity 21

(a) **Blidworth Loam Ltd**

Budgeted operating statement for the year

	Marginal costing format	*Absorption costing format*
Production (tonnes)	12,000	12,000
Sales (tonnes)	11,500	11,500
	£	£
Revenue	1,518,000	1,518,000
Variable costs		
Direct labour (12,000 × 38.25)	459,000	459,000
Direct material (12,000 × 27.50)	330,000	330,000
Variable overhead (12,000 × 31.50)	378,000	378,000
Closing inventory for marginal costing (W1)	(48,625)	
	1,118,375	
Contribution	399,625	
Fixed costs	250,000	250,000
Closing inventory for absorption costing (W2)		(59,042)
Operating profit	149,625	160,042

(b) The difference in profit can be proved as 500 tonnes × £20.833 = £10,417.

Workings

(W1) 500 tonnes × £97.25 = £48,625

(W2) Fixed production overheads are absorbed at £250,000 ÷ 12,000 = £20.833 per tonne
Inventory adjustment = 500 tonnes × (£97.25 + £20.833) = £59,042

4 Cost management

Workbook Activity 10

Transport company

MEMORANDUM

To:	General Manager
From:	Assistant management accountant
Date:	Report on proposal to purchase vehicle cleansing machine

(1, 2) The results of the investment appraisal

I have carried out an appraisal of this proposal using the net present value method. The results of my calculations are shown in the Appendix.

The project generates a positive net present value of £11,995. This means that the wealth of the company would be increased by this amount if the project is undertaken.

(3) A recommendation concerning the proposal

Since the proposal is forecast to result in a positive net present value, I recommend that it should be accepted.

If I can be of any further assistance in this matter, please do not hesitate to contact me.

Appendix: appraisal calculations

The net present value of the cash flows from the project

Year	*Total cash flow*	*Discount factor*	*Present value*
	£		£
0	(80,000)	1.000	(80,000)
1	29,600	0.909	26,906
2	29,200	0.826	24,119
3	28,780	0.751	21,614
4	28,339	0.683	19,356
Net present value			11,995

Workbook Activity 11

MEMORANDUM

To: The divisional accountant

From: Assistant management accountant

Date: 7 December 20X5

Subject: Capital appraisal of new machine

As a result of using discounted cash flow, the net present value of the project is £45,600 and so the proposal appears to be worthwhile. This amount represents the gain to the company in the equivalent of pounds today from carrying out the proposal.

Taking risk into account brings in greater complexities. Although not always so, risk often increases with time. The further into the future are the cash flows, the more uncertain they tend to become.

Recommendation

Given that the proposal has a positive Net Present Value at 25 per cent, it meets the company's requirements for investment proposals. Before finally deciding whether or not to go ahead with the project, further consideration should be given to any risk inherent in such a long period.

Appendix 1 Investment appraisal (£)

End of year	*Cash flow £*	*Discount factor*	*Discounted cash flow*
0	(600,000)	1.000	(600,000)
1	240,000	0.800	192,000
2	240,000	0.640	153,600
3	240,000	0.512	122,880
4	240,000	0.410	98,400
5	240,000	0.328	78,720
Net Present Value			45,600

5 Time series, sampling and index numbers

Workbook Activity 14

Star Fuel

Task 1

Quarter	*Season*	*Trend*	*Absolute variance*	*(a) Forecast (absolute)*	*Percentage variance*	*(b) Forecast (percentage)*
17	A	2,680,000	350,000	3,030,000	115	3,082,000
18	B	2,720,000	250,000	2,970,000	110	2,992,000
19	C	2,760,000	–400,000	2,360,000	85	2,346,000
20	D	2,800,000	–200,000	2,600,000	90	2,520,000

Working

Trend for quarter 17

Trend (y) = 2,000,000 + (40,000 × 17) = 2,680,000

Task 2

Quarter		*Actual*	*Forecast (absolute)*	*Error forecast*	*Forecast (percentage)*	*Error forecast*
17		3,079,500	3,030,000	–49,500	3,082,000	+2,500
18		3,002,400	2,970,000	–32,400	2,992,000	–10,400
19		2,346,500	2,360,000	+13,500	2,346,000	–500
20		2,490,200	2,600,000	+109,800	2,520,000	+29,800

(a) Examining the residual errors from using the two different methods of measuring seasonal variations, the percentage seasonal variation always results in a lower error than the absolute variance. On the basis of the sample of four quarters, the percentage seasonal variation thus appears to be the more accurate method for calculating seasonal variations.

(b)

Quarter	*Season*	*Trend*	*Seasonal variation %*	*Forecast*
21	A	2,840,000	115	3,266,000
22	B	2,880,000	110	3,168,000
23	C	2,920,000	85	2,482,000
24	D	2,960,000	90	2,664,000

Workbook Activity 15

(a) **2001**

	Q1	*Q2*	*Q3*	*Q4*
Actual price per tonne	£40	£44	£64	£76
Seasonal variation	– £4	– £8	+ £4	+ £8
Trend	£44	£52	£60	£68

(b) **2002**

Trend (+ £8 per quarter)	£76	£84	£92	£100
Seasonal variation	– £4	– £8	+ £4	+ £8
Forecast price per tonne	£72	£76	£96	£108

Workbook Activity 16

Revision of standards based on changes in the index

Category of cost	*Current standard*	*Revised standards*			
		Q1	Q2	Q3	Q4
Direct labour hour rate	£7.00	£7.21 (W1)	£7.21	£7.21	£7.21
Raw material cost/tonne	£55.00	£56.38	£56.94	£57.23	£57.23
Fixed overhead recovery rate per hour	£12.50	£12.63	£12.69	£12.75	£12.79

Working

(W1) $£7 \times \frac{108.15}{105.00} = £7.21$

The other numbers are obtained in a similar manner.

6 Standard costing and variance analysis

Workbook Activity 15

AH x AR

2,000 x £10 = £20,000

AH x SR

2,000 x £9.80 = £19,600 Rate variance = £400 A

SH x SR

2,050 x 1 x £9.80 = £20,090 Efficiency variance = £490 F

			£
Budgeted/Standard cost of labour for actual production			20,090
Variances	**F**	**A**	
Direct labour rate		400	
Direct labour efficiency	490		
Total variance	490	400	90
Actual cost of labour for actual production			20,000

Workbook Activity 16

Actual fixed overheads = £39,000

Expenditure variance = £1,000 F

Budgeted fixed overheads = £40,000

Volume variance = £2,000 A

SQ x SR

19,000 x £2 = £38,000

			£
Budgeted/Standard fixed cost for actual production			38,000
Variances	**F**	**A**	
Fixed overhead expenditure	1,000		
Fixed overhead volume		2,000	
Total variance	1,000	2,000	1,000
Actual fixed cost for actual production			39,000

Workbook Activity 17

AH x AR

24,000 x £8 = £192,000

AH x SR

24,000 x £8.50 = £204,000

Rate variance = £12,000 F

SH x SR

400 x 50 x £8.50 = £170,000

Efficiency variance £34,000A

			£
Budgeted/Standard cost of labour for actual production			170,000
Variances	**F**	**A**	
Direct labour rate	12,000		
Direct labour efficiency		34,000	
Total variance	12,000	34,000	22,000
Actual cost of labour for actual production			192,000

Workbook Activity 18

AQ x AP

112,000 x £4 = £448,000

AQ x SP

112,000 x £4.50 = £504,000 Price variance = £56,000 F

SQ x SP

2,100 x 56 x £4.50 = £529,200 Usage variance = £25,200 F

			£
Budgeted/Standard cost of materials for actual production			529,200
Variances	**F**	**A**	
Direct materials price	56,000		
Direct materials usage	25,200		
Total variance	81,200		81,200
Actual cost of materials for actual production			448,000

Workbook Activity 19

Actual fixed overheads = £1,245,000

Expenditure variance = £5,000F

Budgeted fixed overheads = £1,250,000

Volume variance = £45,000 A

SQ x SR

24,100 x £50 = £1,205,000

			£
Budgeted/Standard fixed cost for actual production			1,205,000
Variances	**F**	**A**	
Fixed overhead expenditure	5,000		
Fixed overhead volume		45,000	
Total variance	5,000	45,000	40,000
Actual fixed cost for actual production			1,245,000

Workbook Activity 20

AQ x AP

2,000 x £5 = £10,000

AQ x SP

2,000 x £5.50 = £11,000 Price variance = £1,000 F

SQ x SP

400 x 6 x £5.50 = £13,200 Usage variance = £2,200 F

			£
Budgeted/Standard cost of materials for actual production			13,200
Variances	**F**	**A**	
Direct materials price	1,000		
Direct materials usage	2,200		
Total variance	3,200		3,200
Actual cost of materials for actual production			10,000

Workbook Activity 21 (December 2002)

Task

(a)

(i)	Standard price of material per litre	(£106,250/12,500)	£8.50
(ii)	Actual price of material per litre	(£99,072/11,520)	£8.60
(iii)	Standard litres of material per barrel	(12,500/2,500)	5.00
(iv)	Standard labour rate per hour	(£60,000/10,000)	£6.00
(v)	Standard labour hours per barrel	(10,000/2,500)	4.00

(vi)	Standard machine hours per barrel	(20,000/2,500)	8.00
(vii)	Fixed overheads per budgeted machine hour	(£200,000/20,000)	£10.00
(viii)	Standard absorption cost per barrel	(£366,250/2,500)	£146.50

(b)

(i) Material price variance

Actual price × actual quantity (given)	£99,072
Standard price × actual quantity (£8.50 ×11,520)	£97,920
	£1,152 (A)

(ii) Material usage variance

Standard price × actual quantity (£8.50 × 11,520)	£97,920
Standard price × standard quantity (£8.50 × 5 litres × 2,400)	£102,000
	£4,080 (F)

(iii) Labour rate variance

Actual rate × actual hours (given)	£61,488
Standard rate × actual hours (£6.00 × 10,080)	£60,480
	(£1,008) (A)

(iv)	Labour efficiency variance	
	Standard rate × actual hours	
	(£6.00 × 10,080)	£60,480
	Standard rate × standard hours	
	(£6.00 × 4 × 2,400)	£57,600
		(£2,880) (A)
(v)	Fixed overhead expenditure variance	
	Actual fixed overheads	£185,808
	Budgeted fixed overheads	£200,000
		£14,192 (F)
(vi)	Fixed overhead volume variance	
	Standard rate × budgeted machine hours	
	(£10.00 × 8 × 2,500)	£200,000
	Std rate × actual machine hours produced	
	(£10.00 × 8 × 2,400)	£192,000
		(£8,000) (A)
(vii)	Fixed overhead capacity variance	
	Standard rate × budgeted machine hours	
	(£10.00 × 8 × 2,500)	£200,000
	Standard rate × actual machine hours worked	
	(£10.00 × 18,960)	£189,600
		(£10,400) (A)

(viii) Fixed overhead efficiency variance

Standard rate × actual machine hours worked	
(£10.00 × 18,960)	£189,600
Std rate × actual machine hours produced	
(£10.00 × 8 × 2,400)	£192,000
	£2,400 (F)

Standard costing reconciliation statement week ended 30 November 2002

Standard cost of actual production (£146.50 × 2,400)		£351,600
Material price variance	(1,152) (A)	
Material usage variance	£4,080 (F)	
Labour rate variance	(£1,008) (A)	
Labour efficiency variance	£2,880 (A)	
Fixed overhead expenditure variance	(£14,192) (F)	
Fixed overhead capacity variance	(£10,400) (A)	
Fixed overhead efficiency variance	£2,400 (F)	£5,232 (F)
Actual cost of actual production		£346,368

Workbook Activity 22 (December 2003)

Task

(a) (i) Standard price of fuel per gallon:

£50,400 / 33,600 — £1.50

(ii) Standard fuel usage for 160 flights:

33,600 × 160 / 168 — 32,000 gallons

(iii) Standard hourly rate for pilots:

£67,200 / 1,344 — £50.00

(iv) Standard pilot hours per flight:

1,344 / 168 — 8 hrs

(v) Standard pilot hours for 160 flights:

1,344 × 160 / 168 — 1,280 hrs

Alternative answer: 160 × 8 = 1,280 hrs

(vi) Standard fixed overhead cost per budgeted flying hour:

75,600 / 672 — £112.50

(vii) Standard flying hours per flight:

672/168 — 4 hrs

(viii) Standard flying hours for 160 flights:

672 × 160 / 168 — 640 hrs

Alternative answer: 160 × 4 = 640 hrs

(ix) Standard fixed overhead absorbed by the 160 flights:

640 × £112.5 — £72,000

(x) Standard cost of actual operations:

£193,200 × 160 / 168 — £184,000

(b)	(i)	Fuel price variance:	
		£61,440	
		38,400 x £1.50	£3,840 (A)
	(ii)	Fuel usage variance:	
		38,400 x £1.50	
		32,000 x £1.50	£9,600 (A)
	(iii)	Rate variance for pilots:	
		£79,872	
		1,536 x £50.00	£3,072 (A)
	(iv)	Efficiency variance for pilots:	
		1,536 x £50.00	
		1,280 x £50.00	£12,800 (A)
	(v)	Fixed overhead expenditure variance:	
		£76,200 – £75,600	£600 (A)
	(vi)	Fixed overhead volume variance:	
		£75,600	
		640 x £112.50	£3,600 (A)
	(vii)	Fixed overhead capacity variance:	
		£75,600	
		768 x £112.50	£10,800 (F)
	(viii)	Fixed overhead efficiency variance:	
		768 x £112.50	
		640 x £112.50	£14,400 (A)

(c) Standard Costing Reconciliation Statement – 28 days ended 30 November 2003

	£	£
Standard cost of actual operations		184,000
Fuel price variance	(3,840) (A)	
Fuel usage variance	(9,600) (A)	
Rate variance for pilots	(3,072) (A)	
Efficiency variance for pilots	(12,800) (A)	
Fixed overhead expenditure variance	(600) (A)	
Fixed overhead capacity variance	10,800 (F)	
Fixed overhead efficiency variance	(14,400) (A)	
	(33,512) (A)	
Actual cost of operations		217,512

Task

MEMO

To: Lisa Margoli

From: Accounting Technician

Date: 3 December 2003

Subject: Fixed overheads

Thank you for raising your concerns with me about the fixed overheads for the Alpha City route.

(a) The use of flying hours to absorb the fixed overheads is justified because in the traditional absorption system of selecting a single driver to absorb costs, it is preferable to choose a driver that the fixed costs depend on. In this example, flying hours does influence the level of fixed costs. However, an alternative would be to use the number of passenger journeys as this is the actual product that Econair is selling.

(b) Using flying hours to absorb the fixed overheads results in an apparently illogical capacity variance; the number of flights are below budget (160 rather than 168) and yet the number of flying hours are above budget. This results in a favourable capacity variance. However, if passenger journeys were used to absorb the fixed overheads, the capacity variance will be favourable because more passengers are flown on each journey.

It should be noted that the main cause of the illogical variances is that the standard number of hours per flight appears to be set incorrectly at 4 hours, whereas each journey takes nearly 5 hours. If the standard was revised, the variances would appear more logical.

(c) The original budgeted fixed overheads were simply added together and divided by the number of aircraft. This ignores the fixed costs drivers. For example, the cost of luggage handling and in-flight facilities was included in the total budgeted fixed overheads but only consumed by the flights to Betaland. The flights to Alpha City should not bear these costs. The revised budgeted fixed costs for Alpha City are as follows:

Fixed overhead	*Driver*	*Apportionment*	*Total*
Aircraft maintenance	Flying hours	£116,480 × 672/2912	£26,880
Insurance	Insurance value	£98,020 × 20/100	£19,604
			£46,484

Workbook Activity 23 (June 2004)

Task

(a) (i) Actual price of materials per kg $\frac{£143,000}{27,500}$ = £5.20

(ii) Standard usage of materials for actual production

900 units × 30 kg = 27,000 kgs

(iii) Actual labour rate per hour

$\frac{£26,040}{4,200}$ = £6.20

	(iv)	Standard labour time for actual production		
		900 units × 5 hours		4,500 hours
	(v)	Budgeted production overheads		
		1,000 units × £20	=	£20,000
(b)	(i)	The material price variance		
		Actual price paid for 27,500 kg	=	£143,000
		Standard price 27,500 kg × £5	=	£137,500
		Variance		£5,500 (A)
	(ii)	The material usage variance		
		Actual material used for 900 desks = 27,500 kg x £5		£137,500
		Standard usage for 900 desks = 900 × 30 = 27,000 kg x £5		£135,000
		Variance		£2,500 (A)
	(iii)	The labour rate variance		
		Actual price paid for 4,200 hours	=	£26,040
		Standard price for 4,200 hours × £6	=	£25,200
		Variance		840 (A)
	(iv)	The labour efficiency variance		
		Actual hours producing 900 desks	=	4,200 hours x £6
		Standard hours = 900 × 5 hours	=	4,500 hours x £6
		Variance		£1,800 (F)
	(v)	The fixed overhead expenditure variance		
		£23,000 – £20,000 = £3,000 (A)		
	(vi)	The fixed overhead volume variance		
		5,000 x £4 compared to 4,500 × £4 = £2,000 (A)		
	(vii)	The fixed overhead capacity variance		
		5,000 x £4 compared to 4,200 × £4 = £3,200 (A)		
	(viii)	The fixed overhead efficiency variance		
		4,200 x £4 compared to 4,500 × £4 = £1,200 (F)		

(c) **Operating statement for May 2004**

	£	£	£
Standard absorption cost of actual production (900 × £200)			180,000
	Favourable	*Adverse*	
Material price variance		5,500	
Material usage variance		2,500	
Labour rate variance		840	
Labour efficiency variance	1,800		
Fixed overhead expenditure variance		3,000	
Fixed overhead capacity variance		3,200	
Fixed overhead efficiency variance	1,200		
	3,000	15,040	12,040
Actual absorption cost of actual production			192,040

(d) **MEMO**

To: Sam Thomas

From: Accounting Technician

Date: June 2004

Subject: Operating statement

The operating statement shows the variances that cause the difference between the standard and actual cost of production.

The report would be improved if the variances were reviewed and the cause of the variances identified. In particular, significant adverse variances should receive particular attention. It may be that the standards are out-of-date and should be changed. On the other hand, the variances may reflect inefficiencies that need to be addressed.

The statement should also consider the responsibility of the managers of the departments where the major variances are found. The idea of controllable and uncontrollable costs is relevant here. It may be that some cost variances are not under the control of the managers and the responsibility for these costs needs to be identified.

7 Investigating and reporting variances

Workbook Activity 8 (December 2001)

Task

(a)	(i)	Standard number of compact discs produced per labour hour: 800 CDs/8 labour hours	=	100
	(ii)	Budgeted machine hours of the department: 880 budgeted labour hours/8 labour hours per machine hour	=	110 hours
	(iii)	Budgeted departmental fixed overheads: £33,000 × 880 labour hours/1,320 labour hours	=	£22,000
	(iv)	Actual fixed overheads: £34,500 × 880 labour hours/1,320 labour hours	=	£23,000
	(v)	Standard fixed overhead rate per labour hour: £33,000/1,320 labour hours*	=	£25.00
		*or £22,000/880 labour hours or £200/8 labour hours		
	(vi)	Standard labour hours produced: 96,000 CDs/100 per labour hour	=	960 hours
	(vii)	Actual number of blank CDs issued to production: £20,790/£0.21	=	99,000 blank CDs

	(viii)	Actual cost of actual production including fixed overheads:		
		Labour		£7,252
		Material		£20,790
		Fixed overhead		£23,000
				£51,042
	(ix)	Standard cost of actual production:		
		£416/800 × 96,000	=	£49,920
(b)	(i)	Material price variance:		
		99,000 x £0.21		
		99,000 x £0.20	=	£(990)A
	(ii)	Material usage variance:		
		99,000 x £0.20		
		96,000 x £0.20	=	£(600)A
	(iii)	Labour rate variance:		
		980 x £7.40		
		980 x £7.00	=	£(392)A
	(iv)	Labour efficiency variance:		
		980 x £7.00		
		960 x £7.00	=	£(140)A
	(v)	Fixed overhead expenditure variance:		£
		Actual fixed cost		23,000
		Budgeted fixed cost		22,000
				£(1,000)A
	(vi)	Fixed overhead volume variance:		
		880 x £25		
		960 x £25	=	£2,000 F
	(vii)	Fixed overhead capacity variance:		
		880 x £25		
		980 x £25	=	£2,500 F
	(viii)	Fixed overhead efficiency variance		
		980 x £25		
		960 x £25	=	£(500) A

(c) **Standard costing reconciliation statement – week ended 30 November 2001**

	£
Standard cost of actual production	49,920
Summary of variances:	(990) A
Material price	
Material usage	(600) A
Labour rate	(392) A
Labour efficiency	(140) A
Fixed overhead expenditure	(1,000) A
Fixed overhead volume	2,000 F
	(1,122) A
Actual cost of production	51,042

Task

LETTER

Gransden, Yelling and Co
Accountants and Registered Auditors

5 December 2001

Jamil Baharundin
CD Products Ltd
Anytown

Dear Mr Baharundin

Thank you for your letter and observations regarding the introduction of the new reporting format based on the standing costing technique.

I list my response to your questions below:

(a) **Issues to consider before investigating a variance**

There are two principal factors to consider here:

Cost v benefit.

Is the variance a 'one off' or an early warning of a longer term problem?

A variance may thus be investigated if it:

exceeds a minimum absolute amount

exceeds a minimum percentage amount constitutes an element of a continuing trend is totally unexpected

is considered to be a sign of a longer term problem.

You may decide not to investigate a variance if:

the cause is already known and considered out of management's span of control.

it is considered as 'one off' and will correct itself in the short-run.

(b) **Sub-division of the material usage variance**

For the week ended 30 November 2001, 96,000 CDs were pressed although 99,000 blank CDs were used. Of the 3,000 difference, 1,920 (96,000 × 2%) could be accounted for as scrapped production, leaving 1,080 unaccounted for. The sub-division of the material usage variance is:

Variance arising from scrapped discs (1,920 × £0.20)	£384 A
Variance arising from other reasons (1,080 × £0.20)	£216 A
Material usage variance	£600 A

(c) **Demand for pressing and finishing**

Fixed overheads have simply been apportioned to cost centres on the basis of labour hours and a recovery rate based on labour hours has been pre-determined.

An analysis of the activities reveals that a large proportion of the fixed costs relate to the CD Pressing Department.

As a result the standard costs of the pressing activity have been understated while finishing costs are overstated. If this has been built into selling prices for these activities then it may explain why there is excess demand in the CD Pressing Department.

Budgeted fixed overheads of £30,800 are attributable to pressing and thus the fixed overhead recovery rate for this activity should be £35 (£30,800 ÷ 880) per labour hour and not £25 as the 'blanket rate' suggests.

Yours sincerely
AAT Student

Workbook Activity 9 (December 2000)

(a)	(i)	Standard price of fuel per litre:		
		£497,664/1,244,160	=	£0.40
	(ii)	Standard litres of fuel for 5,760 ferry crossings:		
		1,244,160 × (5,760/6,480)	=	1,105,920 litres
	(iii)	Standard labour rate per hour:		
		£466,560/93,312	=	£5.00
	(iv)	Standard labour hours for 5,760 ferry crossings:		
		93,312 × (5,760/6,480)	=	82,944 hours
	(v)	Standard fixed overhead per budgeted operating hour:		
		£466,560/7,776	=	£60.00
	(vi)	Standard operating hours for 5,760 crossings:		
		5,760 × (7,776/6,480)	=	6,912 hours
	(vii)	Standard fixed overhead cost absorbed by the actual 5,760 ferry crossings:		
		6,912 hours × £60.00	=	£414,720

(b)	(i)	Material price variance:		
		1,232,800 x £0.46		
		1,232,800 x £0.40	=	£(73,968) A
	(ii)	Material usage variance:		
		1,232,800 x £0.40		
		1,105,920 x £0.40	=	£(50,752) A
	(iii)	Labour rate variance:		
		89,856 x £5.25		
		89,856 x £5.00	=	£(22,464) A
	(iv)	Labour efficiency variance:		
		89,856 x £5.00		
		82,944 x £5.00	=	£(34,560)
	(v)	A Fixed overhead expenditure variance:		

	£
Actual fixed overhead	472,440
Budgeted fixed overhead	466,560
Variance	(5,880) A

(vi)	Fixed overhead volume variance:		
	7,776 x £60		
	6,912 x £60	=	£(51,840) A
(vii)	Fixed overhead capacity variance:		
	7,766 x £60		
	7,488 x £60	=	£(17,280) A
(viii)	Fixed overhead capacity variance:		
	7,488 x £60		
	6,912 x £60	=	£(34,560) A

(b) **Travel Ferries Ltd – Reconciliation statement for the year ended 30 November 2000**

F = Favourable

A = Adverse

	£
Standard cost of actual operations (W)	1,271,808
Summary of variances:	(73,968) A
Material price	
Material usage	(50,752) A
Labour rate	(22,464) A
Labour efficiency	(34,560) A
Fixed overhead expenditure	(5,880) A
Fixed overhead volume	(51,840) A
	(239,464)
Actual cost	1,511,272

Working

£1,430,784 × 5,760/6,480 = £1,271,808

Task

MEMO

To: Chief Executive

From: Management Accountant

Date: 6 December 2000

Subject: Explanation of variances

I refer to the concern you have expressed recently regarding the adverse variances in the report on Travel Ferries' operations for the year ended 30 November.

In reply to your comments, I wish to make the following observations concerning:

- further analysis of the material price variance.
- identification of uncontrollable variances.
- controllable variances and their investigation.

(a) **Material price variance (fuel)**

Actual market price was £0.40 × 1.2 = £0.48 per litre.

Actual price paid was £0.46 per litre.

Variance due to other reasons:		
1,232,800 litres x £0.46	=	£24,656 F
1,232,800 litres x £0.48		
The variance due to an invalid standard was:		
1,232,800 litres x £0.48	=	£(98,624) A
1,232,800 litres x £0.40		
Price variance reported		£(73,968) A

(b) The labour efficiency variance is due to the extra time worked due to adverse weather conditions. The additional operating hours resulted in an extra 6,912 labour hours being worked.

This adverse efficiency is not controllable by management since management cannot control the weather.

(c) Controllable variances would include the labour rate variance and the fixed overhead capacity variance. Neither of these can be attributed to adverse conditions.

The capacity variance is adverse as the number of ferry crossings made was well below budget.

Workbook Activity 10 (June 2000)

(a) (i) Budgeted labour hours of production for NGJ Ltd:

Labour hours	*Budgeted hours per unit*	*Budgeted production*	*Budgeted hours*
Basic	6	10,000	60,000
Grand	1	70,000	70,000
Super	1	70,000	70,000
Total budgeted labour hours			200,000

(ii) Standard factory fixed overhead rate per labour hour:
(£600,000/200,000 hours) £3.00

(iii) *Basic* budgeted factory fixed overhead:
(£600,000 × [60,000/200,000]) £180,000
Basic actual factory fixed overhead:
(£630,000 × [60,000/200,000]) £189,000

(iv) Actual material cost per metre:
(£872,298/69,230) £12.60
Actual labour hourly rate:
(£343,735/70,150) £4.90

(v) Standard absorption cost of actual *Basic* production:

Material (£12 × 6 metres × 11,500 *Basics*)	£828,000
Labour (£5 × 6 hours × 11,500 *Basics*)	£345,000
Factory fixed overheads (£3 × 6 hours × 11,500 *Basics*)	£207,000
	£1,380,000

	(vi)	Actual absorption cost of actual *Basic* production:		£872,298
		Material		
		Labour		£343,735
		Factory fixed overheads		£189,000
				£1,405,033
(b)	(i)	Material price variance:		
		69,230 x £12.60		
		69,230 x £12.00	=	£(41,538) A
	(ii)	Material usage variance:		
		69,230 x £12.00		
		69,000 x £12.00	=	£(2,760) A
	(iii)	Labour rate variance:		
		70,150 x £4.90		
		70,150 x £5.00	=	£7,015 F
	(iv)	Labour efficiency variance:		
		70,150 x £5.00		
		69,000 x £5.00	=	£(5,750) A
	(v)	Fixed overhead expenditure variance:		£
		Actual fixed cost		189,000
		Budgeted fixed cost 60,000 x £3		180,000
		Variance		£(9,000) A
	(vi)	Fixed overhead volume variance:		
		60,000 x £3		
		69,000 x £3	=	£27,000 F
	(vii)	Fixed overhead capacity variance:		
		60,000 x £3		
		70,150 x £3	=	£30,450 F
	(viii)	Fixed overhead efficiency variance:		
		70,150 x £3		
		69,000 x £3	=	£(3,450) A

(c) **Standard costing reconciliation statement – year ended 31 May 2000**

		£
Standard cost of actual production		1,380,000
Summary of variances:		
Material price	(41,538) A	
Material usage	(2,760) A	
Labour rate	7,015 F	
Labour efficiency	(5,750) A	
Fixed overhead expenditure	(9,000) A	
Fixed overhead volume	27,000 F	
		(25,033) A
Actual cost of production		1,405,033

F = Favourable
(A) = Adverse

Task

MEMO

To: Basic Product Line Manager

From: Management Accountant

Date: 21 June 2000

Subject: Variances

Further to your comments on the variances relating to Basic production, I wish to make the following observations.

(a) Market price of material per metre during the year was: £12.60 × (100/90) = £14.00

(b) The sub-division of the price variance on further analysis shows a variance arising due to the contracted price being different from the actual price, amounting to: (£14.00 – £12.60) × 69,230 = £96,922 F

Variance arising from other reasons:
(£12.00 – £14.00) × 69,230 £(138,460) A

£(41,538) A

(c) A value adding benefit from the purchasing manager's action not shown in the variances is the continuous supply of material supporting production as a result of the contract.

(d) Overhead recovery based on traditional absorption costing concepts focuses on charging overheads to production rather than seeking to control these overheads.

Activity based costing, however, firstly identifies activities which consume cost and recognises the reason why overheads are incurred.

The technique analyses the fixed costs and identifies cost drivers, the factors which generate cost, together with seeking to control these overheads.

Overhead is then recovered to products using cost driver rates, thus charging overhead to products which cause them to be incurred.

(e) It is clear that £202,000 of the budgeted overhead arose because of the mechanised production of Grand and Super products.

It may also be the case that most of the depreciation charge also relates to machinery used on those products.

As the Basic production only uses a small area of the production facility, much of the rent and rates relate to production driven by the needs of Grand and Super.

It is highly likely that the ABC method would have reduced the overhead attributed to Basic production.

Workbook Activity 11 (December 1999)

Task

(a) **Budget and actual data**

(i) Actual number of meals:

4 meals × 7 days × 648 guests = 18,144

(ii) Standard number of meals:

3 meals × 7 days × 648 guests = 13,608

(iii) Actual hourly rate for catering staff:

$5,280 cost ÷ 1,200 hours = $4.40

(iv)	Standard hours allowed to serve three meals:		
	(648 × 3 meals × 7 days) ÷ 12	=	1,134
(v)	Standard overhead per guest:		
	$38,340 budgeted overheads ÷ 540 budgeted guests	=	$71.00
(vi)	Standard cost of providing for 648 guests:		
	Meals: $3.00 × 13,608 meals	=	$40,824
	Catering staff: $4.00 × 1,134 hours	=	$4,536
	Fixed overheads:		$46,008
	$71.00 standard overhead per guest × 648 guests	=	$91,368

(b) **Variances**

(i)	Material price variance:		
	18,144 x $2.75		
	18,144 x $3.00	=	$4,536 F
(ii)	Material usage variance:		
	18,144 x $3.00		
	13,608 x $3.00	=	$(13,608) A
(iii)	Labour rate variance:		
	1,200 x $4.40		
	1,200 x $4.00	=	$(480) A
(iv)	Labour efficiency variance:		
	1,200 x $4.00		
	1,134 x $4.00	=	$(264) A

(v) Fixed overhead expenditure variance:

	$
Actual fixed costs	37,800
Budgeted fixed costs	38,340
Variance	540 F

(vi) Fixed overhead volume variance:

540 x $71.00

648 x $71.00 = $7,668 F

(c) **Bare Foot Hotel Complex**

Standard costing reconciliation statement – week ended 27 November 1999

	$
Standard cost of providing for guests	91,368
Summary of variances:	4,536 F
Material price variance	
Material usage variance	(13,608) A
Labour rate variance	(480) A
Labour efficiency variance	(264) A
Fixed overhead expenditure variance	540 F
Fixed overhead volume variance	7,668 F
	(1,608) A
Actual cost of providing for guests	92,976

Task

MEMO

To: Alice Groves

From: Assistant Management Accountant

Date: 1 December 1999

Subject: Standard costing reconciliation statement

(a) The labour efficiency variance can be sub-divided into that part due to guests taking, on average, four meals per day and that part due to other underlying efficiency reasons. The detailed analysis is reproduced below:

Standard cost of standard hours – 3 meals per guest (1,134 × $4):	$4,536
Standard cost of standard hours – 4 meals per guest: [(648 ÷ 12) × 4 meals × 7 days] × $4	$6,048
Variance due to guests taking more meals than planned	$(1,512) A
Standard cost of standard hours – 4 meals per guest	$6,048
Standard cost of actual hours (1,200 × $4)	$4,800
Other efficiency variances	$1,248 F

(b) **Fixed overhead capacity and efficiency variances**

Both the capacity and efficiency variances are sub-divisions of the fixed overhead volume variance.

The volume variance measures the amount of under or over-recovery of fixed overhead due to either an increase or decrease in volume; in this case meals served and/or guest days.

The capacity element of this variance considers the increase or decrease in hours worked compared with the hours budgeted or planned and its effect on volume.

The efficiency variance measures the effect of the efficiency of labour on the volume achieved.

In the situation under review the capacity was favourable although the efficiency was adverse. The additional volume was achieved by increasing the hours worked.

(c) The fixed overhead relates to a number of hotel activities, not just catering, and therefore a sub-division of the volume variance would not 'add value' to the reporting of the variances; as such an analysis would be of no use to management.

Workbook Activity 12 (June 1999)

Task

(a) **Calculation of quantities**

(i)	Actual litres used:	
	£338,283 / £40.20	8,415
(ii)	Actual hours worked:	
	£110,330 / £5.90	18,700
(iii)	Standard litres for 1,700 tins of Zed:	
	1,700 × 5 litres	8,500
(iv)	Standard labour hours for 1,700 tins of Zed:	
	1,700 × 10 hours	17,000
(v)	Standard hours of fixed overheads charged to budgeted production:	
	1,750 × 10 hours	17,500
(vi)	Standard hours of fixed overheads charged to actual production:	
	1,700 × 10 hours	17,000

(b) (i) Material price variance:

8,415 x £40.20

8,415 x £40.00 = £(1,683) A

(ii) Material usage variance:

8,415 x £40.00

8,500 x £40.00 = £3,400 F

(iii) Labour rate variance:

18,700 x £5.90

18,700 x £6.00 = £1,870 F

(iv) Labour efficiency variance:

18,700 x £6.00

17,000 x £6.00 = £(10,200) A

(v) Fixed overhead expenditure variance:

	£
Actual fixed cost	410,000
Budgeted fixed cost	420,000
Variance	£10,000

(vi) Fixed overhead volume variance:

17,500 x £24

17,000 x £24 = £(12,000) A

(vii) Fixed overhead capacity variance:

17,500 x £24

18,700 x £24 = £28,800 F

(viii) Fixed overhead efficiency variance:

18,700 x £24

17,000 x £24 = £(40,800) A

(c) **Standard costing reconciliation statement; standard to actual cost – May 1999**

	£
Standard cost of actual production (1,700 tins @ £500)	850,000
Summary of variances:	(1,683) A
Material price	
Material usage	3,400 F
Labour rate	1,870 F
Labour efficiency	(10,200) A
Fixed overhead expenditure	10,000 F
Fixed overhead volume	(12,000) A
	(8,613) A
Actual cost of production	858,613

Task

MEMO

To: Production Director

From: Management Accountant

Date: 16 June 1999

Subject: Material variances

I refer to your observations regarding the material variances shown on my recent standard costing reconciliation statement.

If the standard price of material had been revised to incorporate the index then the price would have been:

£40 × (125.86/124.00) = £40.60 per litre

(a) It is possible, using this additional information, to sub-divide the price variance to that element due to the price increase highlighted in the index and that attributed to the efficiency of the purchasing department:

Revised standard price	£40.60	Revised standard price	£40.60
Original standard price	£40.00	Actual price	£40.20
Difference	£0.60 (A)	Difference	£0.40 (F)
Actual quantity (litres)	8,415	Actual quantity (litres)	8,415
Price variance due to revised price	£5,049 (A)	Price variance due to purchasing	£3,366 (F)

(b) There can be a number of factors which influence the reporting of a favourable usage variance; these include:

(i) incorrect setting of the standard usage

(ii) data errors as when a clerk misreads a figure

(iii) some drums of material containing more than 50 litres resulting in more material being used than recorded as being used

(iv) errors in the automatic weighing system. In May, 8,415 litres of material were used to produce 1,700 tins of Zed. This is equivalent to 4.95 litres per tin. The lowest acceptable error is only 0.5% or 4.975 litres per tin.

This suggests that there might be a problem with the settings of the measuring machine.

8 Performance indicators

Workbook Activity 13

5 x £50,000 = £250,000

ROCE = Operating profit / Capital employed x 100%

20% = Operating profit / £400,000

Operating profit = £80,000

Gross profit margin = Gross profit / Sales revenue x 100%

20% = Gross profit x £1,000,000

Gross profit = £200,000

Current ratio = Current assets / Current liabilities

2 = (Inventory + £120,000) / £200,000

Inventory = £280,000

Receivable days = Receivables / Sales revenue x 365

80 = £400,000 / Sales revenue x 365

Sales revenue = £1,825,000

Value added = Sales revenue – Cost of materials used and bought in services

Value added = £950,000 – £400,000 – £200,000

Value added = £350,000

Payable days = Payables / Cost of sales x 365

30 = Payables / £700,000 x 365

Payables = £57,534

$$\text{Activity ratio} = \frac{1{,}502}{1{,}470} \times 100 = 102.2\%$$

$$\text{Efficiency ratio} = \frac{1{,}502}{1{,}630} \times 100 = 92.1\%$$

$$\text{Capacity ratio} = \frac{1{,}630}{1{,}470} \times 100 = 110.9\%$$

Workbook Activity 14

Stonehill Quarries Ltd

(a) **Return on capital employed**

$$\frac{\text{Net profit before finance costs and tax}}{\text{Total assets} - \text{Current liabilities}} \times 100\%$$

20X2	*20X3*
$\frac{0.95}{4.12} \times 100\%$	$\frac{0.86}{4.47} \times 100\%$
	0.92
= 23.06%	= 19.24%

Asset Revenue

$$\frac{\text{Revenue}}{\text{Total assets} - \text{Current liabilities}}$$

20X2	*20X3*
$\frac{5.38}{4.12}$	$\frac{6.68}{4.47}$
= 1.31 times	= 1.49 times

Net profit before finance costs and tax as a % of revenue

$$\frac{\text{Net profit before finance costs and tax}}{\text{Revenue}} \times 100\%$$

20X2	*20X3*
$\frac{0.95}{5.38} \times 100\%$	$\frac{0.86}{6.68} \times 100\%$
= 17.66%	= 12.87%

Current ratio

Current assets : Current liabilities

20X2	*20X3*
1.47 : 1.12	1.84 : 1.25
= 1.31 : 1	= 1.47 : 1

Acid test

(Current assets – Inventories) : Current liabilities

20X2	*20X3*
1.47 – 0.55) : 1.12	(1.84 – 0.60) : 1.25
= 0.82 : 1	= 0.99 : 1

Receivables collection period

$\frac{\text{Receivables}}{\text{Revenue}} \times 365 \text{ days}$

20X2	*20X3*
$\frac{0.88}{5.38} \times 365$ days	$\frac{1.19}{6.68} \times 365$ days
= 60 times	= 65 times

Payables payment period

$\frac{\text{Trade payables}}{\text{Purchases *}}$

20X2	*20X3*
$\frac{0.66}{3.21} \times 365$ days	$\frac{0.82}{4.32} \times 365$ days
= 75 days	= 69 days

Finished goods inventory in days

$\frac{\text{Inventories (finished goods)}}{\text{Cost of sales}} \times 365 \text{ days}$

20X2	*20X3*
$\frac{0.43}{4.43} \times 365$ days	$\frac{0.45}{5.82} \times 365$ days
= 35 days	= 28 days

Labour cost % of revenue

20X2	*20X3*
$\frac{0.98}{5.38} \times 100\%$	$\frac{1.25}{6.68} \times 100\%$
= 18.22%	= 18.71%

Operating costs % of revenue

20X2

$\frac{4.43}{5.38} \times 100\%$

= 82.34%

20X3

$\frac{5.82}{6.68} \times 100\%$

= 87.13%

Distribution costs % of revenue

20X2

$\frac{0.49}{5.38} \times 100\%$

= 9.11%

20X3

$\frac{0.61}{6.68} \times 100\%$

= 9.13%

Admin costs % of revenue

20X2

$\frac{0.22}{5.38} \times 100\%$

= 4.09%

20X3

$\frac{0.27}{6.68} \times 100\%$

= 4.04%

Value added per '£' of employee costs

Value added:

	20X2	*20X3*
	£m	£m
Revenue	5.38	6.68
Bought in materials and services	3.21	4.32
Value added	2.17	2.36

Value added per '£' of employee costs

20X2

$\frac{2.17}{0.98}$

= £2.21

20X3

$\frac{2.36}{1.25}$

= £1.89

(b) **Return on capital employed**

The company has experienced a significant decline in profitability in 20X3 to a level below that for the sector as a whole. However, a return of 19% may be considered a good level of performance but a further decline may be the sign of longer term problems.

Asset Revenue

The company has increased its volume of sales to net assets ratio, but is not generating the volume experienced by the sector.

Profit margin

One reason for the reduction in the primary ratio (the ROCE) is highlighted here. There has been a significant fall in the profit margin, so although sales volume has increased there has been a reduction in the margin.

The return to sales is now approximately 13% compared with 15% for the sector.

Current ratio and acid test

The company's liquidity is still relatively sound, with the acid test only marginally less than the desired level of 1 : 1 and also the average for the sector.

Liquidity has strengthened in 20X3.

Receivables collection period

The receivables day period has increased and is currently 65 days compared with 60 days average for the sector.

Tighter controls are required here and if the trend continues upward the company may be exposing itself to the incidence of bad debts.

Payables payment period

The company's period is typical of the sector as a whole. There has been a fall in payable days as the company has utilised some of its excess cash flow in this area.

Finished goods inventory in days

The company is holding less than one month's supply of finished inventory. It is not sacrificing liquidity by tying up excess working capital in the form of inventory.

The company's inventory management controls are tighter than those for the sector.

Labour costs % of revenue

There has been a marginal increase here but the ratio is still at an acceptable level of control.

Operating costs % of revenue

There has been a significant increase here which indicates that operating overheads and some other direct costs need tighter controls. It may be that the company has an ageing plant and maintenance charges are on an upward trend.

If these assumptions are not the case, there may have been a significant shift in product mix which can influence product profitability.

An analysis of the above factors needs to be carried out to assess fully the change in this measure of efficiency.

Distribution and admin costs to revenue

These measures are well in line with the sector average and indicate good sound controls in these areas of cost.

Value added per '£' of employee costs

The effectiveness and efficiency of the human asset resource has been offset by the adverse factors highlighted above.

The productivity of labour is now some 3% less than the sector average.

Workbook Activity 15 (June 2001)

Task

(a) **Revenue margin**
(£324,000/£6,480,000) × 100 = 5%

(b) **Return on capital employed**
(£324,000/£1,620,000) × 100 = 20%

(c) **Asset Revenue**
(£6,480,000/£1,620,000) = 4 times

(d) **Average age of Inventory**
(£120,000/£1,080,000) × 12 = 1.33 months

(e) **Average age of Payables** = 2 months
(£180,000/£1,080,000) × 12

(f) **Added value per employee**

Revenue		£6,480,000
Less: Material A10	£1,080,000	
Less: Other material and bought in services	£108,000	£1,188,000
Added value		£5,292,000

Added value per employee (£5,292,000/140) = £37,800

(g) **Wages per production employee**

(£1,296,000/140) = £9,257

(h) **Capacity ratio**

(10,800 Alphas/12,000 Alphas) × 100 = 90%

(i) **Contribution per Alpha**

Selling price per unit (£6,480,000/10,800) = £600

Marginal cost per unit (£2,484,000/10,800) = £230

Contribution per Alpha = £370

Task

(a) **Cost of quality**

Cost of remedial work	£120,000
Inspection costs of A10 goods received	£69,600
Cost of A10 returns	£48,000
Customer support for faulty products	£194,400
Cost of quality	£432,000

(b) **Revised profit**

Revised unit contribution (£370 – £10)		£360
Revised volume		12,000
Revised total contribution (£360 × 12,000)		£4,320,000
Revised fixed costs:		
Existing	£3,672,000	
Less: Saving in cost of quality	£432,000	£3,240,000
Revised profit		£1,080,000

(c) **Increase in cash**

Increase in profit (£1,080,000 – £324,000)	£756,000
Add: Decrease in Inventories	£120,000
Less: Decrease in Payables	(£180,000)
Increase in cash	£696,000

(d) **Revised capital employed***

Net non-current assets	£1,600,000
Cash	£80,000
	£1,680,000

(e) **Revised return on capital employed**

(£1,080,000/£1,680,000) × 100 = 64%

**Alternative answer to (d):*	£1,556,000
Equity (£800,000 + £756,000)	
Loans (£820,000 – £696,000)	£124,000
Revised capital employed	£1,680,000

Workbook Activity 16 (December 2000)

Task

(a)	Gross profit margin:	
	£221,760/£633,600 × 100%	35%
(b)	Net profit margin:	
	£76,032/£633,600 × 100%	12%
(c)	Return on capital employed:	
	£76,032/£95,040 × 100%	80%
(d)	Asset turnover:	
	£633,600/£95,040	6.67 times
(e)	Number of passengers in the year:	
	£633,600/£1	633,600 passengers
(f)	Total cost per mile:	
	(£633,600 – £76,032)/356,400	£1.56
(g)	Number of journeys per day:	
	356,400/(18 miles × 360 days)	55 journeys
(h)	Maintenance cost per mile:	
	£28,512/356,400	£0.08
(i)	Passengers per day:	
	633,600/360	1,760 passengers
(j)	Passengers per journey:	
	1,760/55	32 passengers
(k)	Number of drivers:	
	£142,000/£14,200	10

Task

MEMO

To: Chief Executive

From: Management Accountant

Date: 6 December 2000

Subject: Performance of Travel Bus Ltd

I refer to your observations relating to the performance of Travel Bus Ltd and detail my comments below.

(a) **Relationship between productivity and profitability**

Productivity is the measure of outputs against inputs and is usually a nonfinancial measure.

An example of productivity is output per employee. Increases in productivity do not always lead to an increase in profitability. Profits may fall if finished goods or services rendered are sold at a market price less than previously charged. Cost increases not passed on in increased prices may also adversely affect profitability, even though productivity may have risen.

(b) **Driver productivity**

One measure of driver productivity is miles driven per driver. There has been a reduction in this measure from 40,500 miles per driver in 1999 to 35,640 in 2000. These results do not support the drivers' claims.

(NB: An alternative measure could have been passengers per driver.)

(c) **Reasons for improved profitability**

Both volume and price have increased, passengers per day and per journey have increased together with fare per passenger journey.

These factors have resulted in fixed costs being recovered faster by an increase in contribution.

Volume has increased and may be the effect of the free parking supported by council policy.

(d) **Indicator of passenger satisfaction**

The number of journeys per day has increased from 50 to 55. This indicates that there was a decrease in waiting time between journeys.

The figures provided do not indicate any measure of the punctuality of the service.

(**NB:** Other comments could include the number of passengers having to stand throughout the journey and the catering for disabled passengers.)

(e) **Possible safety indicators**

Maintenance cost per mile is an indicator of safety issues. The maintenance cost per mile has fallen from £0.10 to £0.08 and as the fleet is a further year older the question of safety needs to be reviewed.

One additional safety indicator is the provision of security facilities at both the car park and the bus terminal.

(**NB:** Accidents per year would also be a useful measure.)

Workbook Activity 17 (June 2000)

Task

(a)	Return on capital employed:	10.00%
	($1,188,000/$11,880,000) × 100%	
(b)	Asset turnover:	2.50 times
	$29,700,000/$11,880,000	
(c)	Revenue (or net profit) margin:	4.00%
	$1,188,000/$29,700,000 × 100%	
(d)	Actual number of return flights per year:	2,160
	6 × 360	
(e)	Actual number of return passengers per year:	108,000
	$29,700,000/$275	

(f) Average seat occupancy: 62.50%

108,000/(2,160 × 80) × 100%

(g) Actual number of passenger-miles:

108,000 × 300 32,400,000

(h) Cost per passenger mile:

$28,512,000/32,400,000 miles $0.88

(Total cost = Revenue – profit = $29,700,000 – $1,188,000 = $28,512,000)

Task

MEMO

To: Carol Jones

From: Management Accountant

Date: 21 June 2000

Subject: Competitive advantage

I outline below the forecast performance for SeaAir for the year to 31 May 2001.

(a) Forecast number of passengers:
9 flights × 80 seats × 55.00% occupancy × 360 days = 142,560

(b) Forecast net profit for the year to 31 May 2001:

	$000
Revenue: 142,560 flights × $275	39,204
Fuel and aircraft maintenance: $14,580,000 × 9/6	21,870
Take off and landing fees at Waltonville: $2,160,000 × 9/6	3,240
Aircraft parking at Waltonville: $2,880,000 × 50%	1,440
Depreciation of aircraft	600
Salaries of flight crew: $380,000 + $58,000	438
Home airport costs	8,112
Net profit	3,504

(c) Revised return on capital employed:
($3,504,000/$11,280,000) × 100% 31%
(Net assets: $11,880,000 – $600,000 extra depreciation = $11,280,000)

(d) SeaAir has a competitive advantage as its route to Waltonville is over the sea and therefore cannot be threatened by other rail or road transport. This allows SeaAir to charge an economic fare. Also, with a lower seat occupancy, SeaAir customers may have a better choice of flights.

(e) One major expense which does not add value in the eyes of a customer is the cost of aircraft parking at Waltonville.

Workbook Activity 18 (December 1999)

Task

(a) Return on capital employed:
(£48,000 ÷ £200,000) × 100% = 24%
Scorecard: financial perspective.

(b) Revenue (net profit) margin percentage
(£48,000 ÷ £240,000) × 100% = 20%
Scorecard: financial perspective (and possibly internal perspective as partly measuring unit cost).

(c) Asset turnover:
£240,000 ÷ £200,000 = 1.2 times
Scorecard: internal perspective, demonstrating intensive use of assets and, hence, unit cost

(d) Research and development as percentage of production:
(£15,900 ÷ £53,000) × 100% = 30%
Scorecard: innovation and learning perspective.

(e) Training as percentage of labour costs:
(£5,200 ÷ £26,000) × 100% = 20%
Scorecard: innovation and learning perspective or possibly the internal perspective (TQM).

(f) Average age of finished inventories:
(£13,000 ÷ £52,000) × 12 = 3 months
Scorecard: customer perspective as the greater the amount of finished inventory, the less time customers have to wait for delivery.

Task

Notes on Performance Indicators for the St Nicolas Police Force

To: James Alexander

Prepared by: Financial Analyst

Date: 1 December 1999

The following are my observations on the issues you raised on the performance indicators.

(a) **Calculation of the four indicators currently used by the St Nicolas Police Force**

- Percentage of cash expenditure to allocated funds for the year:
  ($2,910 ÷ $3,000) × 100% = 97%
- Average police hours spent per crime investigated:
  [40,000 ÷ 5,000] = 8 police hours
- Average police hours per crime solved:
  [40,000 ÷ 2,000] = 20 police hours
- Clear-up rate:
  [(2,000 ÷ 5,000) × 100%] = 40%

(b) **Limitations to the clear-up rate**

There may be an element of timing differences. Some crimes solved this year may have been investigated in the previous year.

Not all crimes are investigated.

There is no particular definition of a crime. For example, if a criminal burgles 30 homes, is that one crime or a series of crimes?

(c) **Performance indicators and the balanced scorecard**

(i) The percentage of cash expenditure to allocated funds may be considered inadequate in terms of the financial perspective as it ignores the investment in resources used. It also focuses on only one aspect of performance – keeping within spending limits.

(ii) The clear-up rate may be considered inadequate from the customer perspective as it takes no account of investment in crime prevention. Crime prevented does not feature in the statistics and the public may feel that they are receiving 'added value' from the force if there was less crime with high clear-up rates.

(iii) Hours spent on investigating crime may be a measure of energy invested by the force in attempting to solve crime. It may also be a pointer to inefficient investigatory work.

(iv) Innovation and learning perspective may be satisfied by a number of measures. The force's objectives would include making St Nicolas a safer environment.

Hours invested in crime prevention measured against crime reduction may be considered under this perspective.

The police training and continuing professional development programmes are also relevant here.

Workbook Activity 19 (June 1999)

Task

Performance indicators for ALV (West) Ltd

(a)	Asset turnover:		
	£2,520/£2,100	=	1.2 times
(b)	Net profit margin:		
	(£378/£2,520) × 100	=	15%
(c)	Return on capital employed:		
	£378/£2,100 × 100	=	18%
(d)	Wages per employee:		
	£260,000/20	=	£13,000
(e)	Production labour cost per unit:		
	£260,000/30,000	=	£8.67
(f)	Output per employee:		
	30,000/20	=	1,500 units

(g) Added value:

£2,520,000 – £1,020,000 = £1,500,000

Added value per employee:

£1,500,000/20	=	£75,000

(h) Profit per employee:

£378,000/20	=	£18,900

Task

Report on the Efficiency and Productivity of ALV (East) and ALV (West)

Prepared for: Jill Morgan, Chief Executive

Prepared by: Accounting Technician

Date: 16 June 1999 Introduction

The objective of this report is to define the terms 'productivity' and 'efficiency' and relate these concepts to the divisions within the company.

It then considers performance indicators for these concepts and compares divisional performance, finally deriving further measures of productivity relevant to both divisions.

(a) **The meaning of productivity and efficiency**

These terms are often used to mean the same measure of performance. Both relate to volume of output from a given input, for example, in the quarry industry, output in tonnage per labour hour or employee.

- Productivity is a measure of outputs related to inputs – usually in physical terms.
- Efficiency is usually measured using financial values for inputs and outputs. The value of outputs less value of inputs when measured against resources used is a measure of efficiency.

(b) **Two performance indicators to measure efficiency**

In 'for-profit' organisations, the ultimate tests of efficiency are return on investment and the net return to revenue.

Comparing the two divisions using these measures:

Indicator	*East*	*West*
Return on investment (ROCE)	42%	18%
Net profit margin	20%	15%

East is more efficient than West.

(c) **Two performance indicators to measure productivity**

- Output per employee.
- Value added per employee.

Comparing divisional performance using these measures of productivity, it is clear that West is the division with the higher productivity.

Indicator	*East*	*West*
Output/employee	556 units	1,500 units
Value added/employee	£27,778	£75,000

(d) **An alternative measure of productivity**

Indicator	*East*	*West*
Net non-current assets	£360,000	£2,100,000
Output	10,000 units	30,000 units
Net non-current assets/unit output	£36.00	£70.00

(e) Why productivity and efficiency measures may give different rankings

There are two main factors here which cause these differences in ranking:

- West division has a greater investment in non-current assets and, as the productivity measures indicate, it is relatively new investment.
- East has much older plant; the statement of financial position figures indicate that the plant is 8 years old compared with 2 years in the case of West. The buildings are also of a similar pattern, much older for East than West.

This relatively new investment in West reflects in the higher productivity. Much more up-to-date plant, probably hi-tech, and better plant layout would 'add value' to productive capability.

Likewise, as East's assets are almost written off, their return looks much more favourable. The older capital equipment has a lower depreciation charge which also affects profitability.

Workbook Activity 20 (June 2002)

Task

(a)	Gross profit margin: £2,250,000/£6,000,000 × 100% =	37.5%
(b)	Net profit (or Revenue) margin: £240,000/£6,000,000 × 100% =	4%
(c)	Return on capital employed: £240,000/£3,000,000 × 100% =	8%
(d)	Asset turnover: £6,000,000/£3,000,000 =	2 times
(e)	Average age of receivables: £1,500,000/£6,000,000 × 12 =	3 months
(f)	Research and development/Production: £768,000/£4,800,000 × 100% =	16%
(g)	Training/Production: £576,000/£4,800,000 × 100% =	12%
(h)	Customer support/Revenue: £240,000/£6,000,000 × 100% =	4%
(i)	Returns/Revenue: £300,000/£6,000,000 × 100% =	5%
(j)	Average delay in supplying customers: 6,000/20,000 × 12 =	3.6 months
	(= annual shortfall ÷ annual production) × 12	

Task

(a) **Gross profit margin:**

Internal (since measuring unit cost); financial

(b) **Net profit (or Revenue) margin:**

Internal (since measuring unit cost); financial

(c) **Return on capital employed:**

Financial

(d) **Asset turnover:**

Internal (since measuring the intensive use of assets and, hence, unit cost)

(e) **Average age of receivables:**

Customer (since offering an extra service); financial

(f) **Research and development/Production:**

Innovation and learning

(g) **Training/Production:**

Innovation and learning

(h) **Customer support/Revenue:**

Customer

(i) **Returns/Revenue:**

Internal (since measuring quality); customer

(j) **Average delay in supplying customers:**

Internal; customer

Task

MEMO

To: Finance Director

From: Financial Analyst

Date: 19 June 2002

Subject: Profitability of Hand Power Systems Ltd

(a) **Accounting policies**

(i) **Inventory valuation:** the Inventory has been valued on a last-in, first-out basis This means that the cost of revenue is found by using the latest cost of purchases first and then working backwards through earlier purchases.

As a result, the closing inventory will relate to the cost of even earlier purchases. With decreasing prices, this means that the cost of revenue might be understated and, hence, profit overstated.

(ii) **Depreciation:** the non-current assets originally cost £5,000,000. Assuming straight line depreciation and no residual value, if the annual depreciation is £1,000,000 then the non-current assets are being depreciated over 5 years. If the normal life is 10 years then the effect of this over prudent policy will be to reduce profits.

(b) **Forecast data for the year to 31 May 2003**

(i)	Selling price per computer: £6,000,000/20,000 × (100/120) =	£250
(ii)	Revenue volume: 20,000 × 130% =	26,000
(iii)	Revenue: £250 × 26,000 =	£6,500,000
(iv)	Unit material cost: £3,360,000/24,000 × (140/175) =	£112
(v)	Unit labour cost: £960,000/24,000 × 75% =	£30
(vi)	Production volume:	
	Revenue volume	26,000
	Less opening inventory	5,000
	Production	21,000
(vii)	Forecast cost of production:	
	Materials (21,000 × £112)	£2,352,000
	Labour (21,000 × £30)	£630,000
	Fixed overhead (£480,000 – £160,000)	£320,000
	Cost of production	£3,302,000
(viii)	Forecast cost of revenue:	
	Cost of production	£3,302,000
	Add opening inventory	£1,350,000
	Cost of revenue	£4,652,000
(ix)	Forecast gross profit (£6,500,000 – £4,652,000)	£1,848,000

Workbook Activity 21 (December 2002)

Task

(a)	Operating surplus/fee income	(£35,200/£1,760,000 × 100%)	2%
(b)	Return on net assets	(£35,200/£7,040,000 × 100%)	0.50%
(c)	Average age of receivables	(£440,000/£1,760,000 × 12)	3 months
(d)	Average age of payables	(£96,000/(£128,000 + £160,000) × 12)	4 months
(e)	Number of children in school	(£1,760,000/£22,000)	80
(f)	Occupancy rate of school	(80/100 × 100%)	80%
(g)	Number of teachers	(80 children/4 children per teacher)*	20
(h)	Number of nursing and support staff	(80 children/2 children per member of staff)*	40
(i)	Total cash-based expenses= total expenses – depreciation	= £1,724,800 – £236,800	£1,488,000
(j)	Number of months cash-based expenditure payable	(£62,000/£1,488,000 × 12)	0.5 months
***Alternative answers:**			
	Total teachers' salaries/average salary	(£600,000/£30,000)	20
	Total nursing and support staff salaries/average salary	(£480,000/£12,000)	40

(a) Forecast operating statement – year to 31 August 2003

Fee income	(88 × £22,000)		£1,936,000
Teacher salaries	(22 × £30,000)	£660,000	
Nursing salaries	(44 × £12,000)	£528,000	
Administrative costs (no change)		£120,000	
Power (no change)		£128,000	
Housekeeping (no change)		£160,000	
Depreciation (no change)		£236,800	£1,832,800
			£103,200

(b) Receivables (£1,936,000 × 1½/12) £242,000

(c) Payables ([£128,000 + £160,000] × 2/12) £48,000

(d) Revised carrying amount of non-current assets:

Carrying amount 31 August 2002	£6,634,000
Depreciation year to 31 August 2003	£236,800
Carrying amount 31 August 2003	£6,397,200

(e)

Cash balance 31 August 2002			£62,000
Add:	Operating surplus		£103,200
	Non-cash items (depreciation)		£236,800
	Change in receivables	(£440,000 – £242,000)	£198,000
Less:	Change in payables	(£96,000 – £48,000)	(£48,000)
Cash balance 31 August 2003			£552,000

(f) Capital employed:

Carrying amount of non-current assets 31 August 2003	£6,397,200
Receivables	£242,000
Cash	£552,000
Less: Payables	(£48,000)
Net assets 31 August 2003	£7,143,200

Task

MEMO

To: Carol Jones

From: Management Accountant

Date: 4 December 2002

Subject: Action plan and targets

(a) If the action plan is achieved, the target results will be as follows:

(i) Operating surplus as a percentage of fee income

(£103,200/£1,936,000 × 100%) 5.33%

(ii) Return on net assets

(£103,200/£7,143,200 × 100%) 1.44%

(iii) Cash available after buying new equipment:

Forecast cash balance before buying equipment	£552,000
Less: Cost of new equipment	£400,000
Forecast cash balance after buying new equipment	£152,000

(iv) Number of months cash-based expenses can be paid from the cash balance:

Cash expenses

(£1,832,800 – £236,800 = £1,596,000)

Number of months cash

(£152,000/£1,596,000 × 12)

(b) In all cases, the action plan exceeds the proposed targets.

(c) Productivity measures output from a given input, generally in physical terms. Productivity, however, does not measure the value of that output, efficiency does. Efficiency measures the value of the output from the value of the input.

(d) An example of improved productivity in the current action plan is the more intensive use of the school's land and buildings by increasing the number of children. In financial terms, there has also been an increase in efficiency as both the operating surplus and the return on net assets have improved. Had the extra child places been provided free of charge, productivity would still have increased, but financial efficiency would have fallen.

Workbook Activity 22 (December 2003)

Task

(a)	Selling price per Zeta: £14,400,000/360,000	£40
(b)	Material cost per Zeta: £5,760,000/360,000	£16
(c)	Labour cost per Zeta: £3,600,000/360,000	£10
(d)	Contribution per Zeta: £5,040,000/360,000	£14
(e)	Contribution percentage: £5,040,000/£14,400,000 × 100%	35%
(f)	Net profit (or Revenue) margin: £576,000/£14,400,000 × 100	4%
(g)	Return on capital employed: £576,000/£9,600,000 × 100	6%
(h)	Asset turnover: £14,400,000/£9,600,000	1.5 times
(i)	Average age of receivables in months: £2,400,000/£14,400,000 × 12	2 months
(j)	Average age of inventory in months: £1,440,000/£5,760,000 × 12	3 months
(k)	Average age of payables in months: £1,200,000/£5,760,000 × 12	2.5 months

(l) Added value per employee

Revenue:	£14,400,000	
Material:	(£5,760,000)	
Heat, light and power:	(£720,000)	
Added value:	£7,920,000	
Added value per employee: £7,920,000/180		£44,000

(m) Average delay in completing an order months

Order volume:	390,000	
Revenue volume:	360,000	
Backlog:	30,000	
Average delay: 30,000/360,000 × 12		1 month

(n)	Cost of quality Inspection:	£80,000	
	Reworking:	£40,000	
	Customer support:	£200,000	£320,000

Task

(a)	Forecast demand: 360,000 × 84/70	432,000
	Add backlog	30,000
	Revenue volume (units)	462,000
(b)	Planned revenue volume:	462,000
	less available Inventory of material	90,000
	Purchases (units)	372,000
(c)	Cost of purchases: 372,000 × £16	5,952,000
(d)	Selling price per Zeta: £40 × 171/180	£38
(e)	Revenue: £38 × 462,000	£17,556,000
(f)	Total contribution. As the cost of material remains the same, the contribution is only affected by the selling price.	
	Reduction in selling price: £40 – £38 = £2	
	Revised unit contribution: £14 – £2 = £12	
	Total contribution: £12 × 462,000	£5,544,000
(g)	Fixed costs	
	Existing fixed costs:	£4,464,000
	less cost of quality (80 + 40 + 200) (000s)	£320,000
		£4,144,000
(h)	Profit: £5,544,000 – £4,144,000	£1,400,000

(i)	Net assets	
	Net non-current assets last year:	£6,000,000
	less extra year's depreciation	£1,000,000
	Carrying amount	£5,000,000
	Receivables: £17,556,000 × 2/12 (Revenue × 2 months)	£2,926,000
	Cash (given)	£960,000
	Payables: £5,952 × 1/12 (purchases × 1 mth)	(£496,000)
	Net assets	£8,390,000

(j) Revised NP (or Revenue) margin:

$£1,400/£17,556 \times 100 \left(\frac{\text{Net profit}}{\text{Turnover}}\right)$ 7.9745%

(k) Revised return on capital employed:

$£1,400/£8,390 \times 100 \left(\frac{\text{Net profit}}{\text{Net assets}}\right)$ 16.687%

Workbook Activity 23

Task

(a)

	Actual	*Budget*
Gross profit margin (W1)	16.7%	20.0%
Operating profit margin (W2)	4.2%	8.0%
Return on capital employed (W3)	10.7%	20.0%
Inventory turnover (in months) (W4)	1.3	1.0
Labour capacity ratio (W5)	97.0%	100.0%
Labour efficiency ratio (W6)	96.2%	100.0%

Workings – note that the workings only show the calculation of the actual figure. The budget is calculated in the same way.

1 $\frac{\text{Gross profit}}{\text{Revenue}} = \frac{460,400}{2,750,000}$ = 16.7%

2 $\frac{\text{Operating profit}}{\text{Sales}} = \frac{115,400}{2,750,000}$ = 0.0419 = 4.2%

3 $\frac{\text{Operating profit}}{\text{Net assets}} = \frac{115,400}{1,075,400}$ = 0.1073 = 10.7%

4 Inventory turnover (also called 'Inventory holding period')

$\frac{\text{Closing inventory}}{\text{Cost of sales}} \times 12 = \frac{240,000}{2,289,600}$ = 1.257 = 1.3

5 Labour capacity ratio

$\frac{\text{Actual hours worked}}{\text{Budget hours}} = \frac{58,200}{60,000}$ = 0.97 = 97%

6 Labour efficiency ratio

$\frac{\text{Actual output in standard hours}}{\text{Actual production hours}} = \frac{11,200 \times 5(W)}{58,200}$ = 0.96 = 96%

Working

Standard hours per desk = $\frac{60,000}{12,000}$ = 5 hours

(b)

MEMO

To: Sam Thomas

From: Accounting Technician

Date: June 2004

Subject: Performance indicators

(i) **Gross profit margin**

An increase in the selling price or a reduction in the cost of a desk will result in an increase in the gross margin. At present, however, the company is achieving the budgeted price of £250 per desk and it may not be possible to increase the price. If this is the case, efforts should be made to reduce the cost of production.

(ii) **Operating profit margin**

The operating profit margin will increase if the company can reduce its distribution and administration costs. The actual results are £15,000 below budget, so it may be difficult to make further savings in this area.

(iii) **Return on capital employed**

The return on capital employed will improve if operating profits improve with no increase in capital employed. The measures detailed above will, therefore, have the effect of improving the return.

One could also examine whether an asset disposal programme could be implemented and the proceeds distributed to shareholders. This would have the effect of reducing capital employed and improving the return on capital employed.

(iv) **Inventory turnover**

The current Inventory of desks represents 1.2 months' production. An increase in revenue volumes may lead to a reduction in the number of desks held in inventory and will consequently improve this indicator. Alternatively, the company should examine whether inventory levels can be reduced.

(v) **Labour capacity ratio**

The labour capacity ratio is below budget and probably results from a lower than anticipated demand for desks. Increased Revenue will again improve this ratio.

(vi) **Labour efficiency ratio**

The efficiency ratio is below budget and indicates inefficiencies within the production department. This may be caused by machine breakdowns or poor quality materials that are difficult to work. Workplace training and increased supervision are also likely to lead to improvements in this indicator.

Task

MEMO

To: Sam Thomas
From: Accounting Technician
Date: June 2004
Subject: Value Engineering Production cost of an executive desk

It is clear from the actual results for November that, although the budgeted revenue price has been achieved, the gross margin has not. Value engineering may be employed to examine ways in which production costs may be reduced.

Value engineering is the process of reducing costs by:

- simplifying the product design
- eliminating unnecessary functions in the production process.

Value engineering requires the use of functional analysis which involves the identification of the attributes of the executive desk. Once these are established, a price can be determined for each attribute.

Functional analysis may lead to a change in design and a reduction in the materials required for production. Also, if the product design is simplified, assembly time may be reduced and this will lead to lower labour costs.

PRACTICE ASSESSMENT

1 Practice Assessment Questions

Section 1

Task 1

(a) The following information has been calculated for the production of one Oval:

Expense	*Units*	*Unit cost*
Direct material	10 litres	£7.50
Direct labour	2 hours	£6.00
Fixed overheads		£8.00

Fixed overheads are absorbed on a labour hour basis.

Complete the standard cost card below by filling in the gaps

	Quantity	*Unit cost* £	*Total cost* £
Material			
Labour			
Fixed overheads			
Total			

(b) A publisher uses 2,500,000 sheets of paper to produce 5,000 books. The standard number of sheets used in each book is [ ]

Task 2

A company provides you with the following budget and actual information:

Standard cost information

Output	2,400 litres
Direct material	10 litres @ £7.50 per litre
Direct labour	2 hours @ £6.00 per hour
Fixed overheads	2 hours @ £8.00 per hour

Actual information

Output		2,400 litres
		£
Direct material	24,550 litres	184,616
Direct labour	5,040 hours	30,492
Fixed overheads		38,500

Additional information

- Budgeted fixed overhead for the year is £38,400.
- Overheads are recovered on the basis of direct labour hours.
- Production is anticipated to be evenly spread throughout the year.

Calculate the following cost variances:

	£	F / A
Direct labour rate variance		
Direct labour efficiency variance		
Direct material price variance		
Direct material usage variance		

Task 3

Using the information in task 2, calculate the following variances:

	£	F / A
Fixed overhead expenditure variance		
Fixed overhead capacity variance		
Fixed overhead efficiency variance		

Task 4

Using the information in Task 2 and 3, prepare a statement reconciling the standard cost of actual production to the actual cost for the period.

	£	F / A	£
Standard cost of actual production			
Direct labour rate			
Direct labour efficiency			
Direct material price			
Direct material usage			
Fixed overhead expenditure			
Fixed overhead volume			
Total variance			
Actual costs			
Direct material			
Direct labour			
Fixed overhead			
Actual cost of production			

Task 5

(a) The table below contains the last three months cost per litre for a product.

Jan	*Feb*	*Mar*
Actual price was £6.00	Actual price was £6.00	Actual price was £6.30
Seasonal variation was –10p	Seasonal variation was –15p	Seasonal variation was +10p

The trend in prices is an increase of £ [ ] per month

(b) A company has provided the following information:

	Jan	*Feb*	*March*
Total cost	£15,000	£20,000	£22,320
Total quantity purchased	2,000 m	2,500 m	2,480 m

The cost index for March based upon January being the base period, with an index of 100 is:

A 120

B 124

C 133

D 149

(c) The Production Director has asked for your help. She has been given an equation and information to estimate the cost of asphalt for the coming three months.

The equation is Y = a + bX, where

X is the time period in months

The value for X in May 2011 is 18

Y is the cost of asphalt

The constant "a" is 100 and constant "b" is 2.7.

The cost of asphalt is set on the first day of each month and is not changed during the month.

The expected price of asphalt per tonne for June 2011 is £ [ ]

and for July 2011 is £ [ ]

Task 6

You are an Accounting Technician reporting to the Finance Director of ABC Ltd. You have just produced the following operating statement:

Budgeted costs for actual production			£386,400
	Favourable	*Adverse*	
Direct material price		£400	
Direct material usage		£1,650	
Direct labour rate	£900		
Direct labour efficiency		£1,200	
Fixed overhead expenditure		£5,000	
Fixed overhead capacity	£10,000		
Fixed overhead efficiency		£6,000	
Total variance	£10,900	£14,250	(£3,350)
Actual cost of actual production			£389,750

The Production Director has given you the following information:

- A pay rise for staff is still outstanding;
- Two new operators are being trained;
- 3 machines are reaching the end of their operational lives.

Draft a report to the Finance Director giving one reason for each of the following variances:

(i) direct materials price variance;

(ii) direct materials usage;

(iii) direct labour rate variance;

(iv) direct labour efficiency variance;

(v) fixed overhead expenditure;

(vi) fixed overhead volume.

REPORT

To:

From:

Date:

Subject:

[illegible]

Task 1

[illegible]

Standard cost information

Direct materials	[illegible]	[illegible]
Direct labour	[illegible]	[illegible]
Fixed overheads	[illegible]	[illegible]

Actual information

[illegible]	[illegible]	[illegible]
[illegible]	[illegible]	[illegible]
[illegible]	[illegible]	[illegible]

Additional information

- Budgeted fixed overhead for the year is [illegible]
- Overheads are absorbed on the basis of direct labour hours.
- Production is scheduled to be evenly spread throughout the year.

Calculate the capacity, efficiency and activity ratios.

Capacity ratio	
Efficiency ratio	
Activity ratio	

Task 2

[illegible]

[illegible]	
Selling price	
Fixed overheads	
Labour	
Material	
Inventory levels	

Section 2

Task 1

A company provides you with the following budget and actual information:

Standard cost information

Output	2,400 litres
Direct material	10 litres @ £7.50 per litre
Direct labour	2 hours @ £6.00 per hour
Fixed overheads	2 hours @ £8.00 per hour

Actual information

Output		2,400 litres
		£
Direct material	24,550 litres	184,616
Direct labour	5,040 hours	30,492
Fixed overheads		38,500

Additional information

- Budgeted fixed overhead for the year is £38,400.
- Overheads are recovered on the basis of direct labour hours.
- Production is anticipated to be evenly spread throughout the year.

Calculate the capacity, efficiency and activity ratios:

Capacity ratio	
Efficiency ratio	
Activity ratio	

Task 2

A company is looking to increase its revenue and profits. Current figures (per annum, unless stated otherwise) are as follows:

Revenue volume	10,000 units
Selling price	£2 per unit
Fixed overheads	£5,000
Labour	£0.50 per unit
Material	£0.20 per unit
Inventory levels	Nil

In order to increase revenue to 15,000 units the selling price would need to fall to £1.80 per unit, the variable costs would fall by 10%, and fixed overheads would fall by £2,000.

Extra investment in assets would be required of £50,000 which would be depreciated at 10% per annum.

The total annual change in profit would be:

	Current	*Future*	*Change*
Revenue			
Material			
Labour			
Fixed overhead			
Depreciation			
Additional profit			

The return on the additional investment would be ☐ %.

Concerned that revenue may not reach the 15,000 unit level, the Finance Director would like to know the break even volume.

Fixed costs	£
Contribution per unit	£
Break even volume (units)	

Task 3

Yarrow Limited has discovered that instead of buying a machine outright it could lease it instead. You are required to complete the following tasks to establish whether the company should lease or buy the machine.

The discount factors you will need are shown below:

Year	*Discount factor 10%*	*Year*	*Discount factor 10%*
0	1.000	3	0.751
1	0.909	4	0.683
2	0.826	5	0.621

Calculate the discounted lifecycle cost of purchasing the machine based upon the following:

- purchase price of £700,000;
- annual running costs of £50,000 for the next five years, paid annually in arrears;
- a residual value of £200,000 at the end of the five years.

Year	*0*	*1*	*2*	*3*	*4*	*5*
Cash flow						
DF						
PV						
NPC						

Calculate the discounted lifecycle cost of leasing the machine for five years based upon the total annual costs of £200,000 paid annually in advance.

Year	*0*	*1*	*2*	*3*	*4*
Lease costs					
DF					
PV					
NPC					

Based on the calculations it is best to [ ] the machine, in order to save £ [ ]

Task 4

Duo Ltd owns two factories, A and B, which make and sell furniture to customers' orders. Each factory has its own general manager who is responsible for revenue policy, pricing and purchasing. The forecasts for both factories for the year ending 31 December 20XY are shown below.

Income Statement extract for the year ending 31 December 20XY

	Factory A	*Factory B*
	£000	£000
Turnover	2,200	2,850
Materials	660	784
Direct labour	440	448
Fixed production overheads	220	420
Cost of sales	1,320	1,652
Gross profit	880	1,198
Sales and distribution costs	(520)	(640)
Administration costs	(210)	(250)
Operating profit	150	308

Statement of Financial Position extract at 31 December 20XY

	£000	£000
Non-current assets	1,255	7,410
Inventory	120	142
Receivables	183	238
Cash	2	10
Payables	(60)	(100)
Net assets	1,500	7,700

Other data

Units produced and sold	22,000	30,000
Budgeted labour hours	75,000	85,000

The following information is also relevant:

- Inventories comprise **raw materials** for both factories.
- Inventory will remain unchanged throughout the year.
- The amount for trade payables relates only to purchases of inventory.
- Factory A has a capacity of 70,000 labour hours and Factory B 140,000 labour hours.
- Sales and distribution costs are variable with revenue from each factory.
- Administration costs are fixed.

The following performance indicators have been calculated:

Performance Indicator	*Factory A*	*Factory B*
(a) Gross profit margin	40.0%	42.0%
(b) Operating profit margin	6.8%	10.8%
(c) Return on capital employed	10.0%	4.0%
(d) Inventory turnover in months	2.2	2.2
(e) Age of payables in months	1.1	1.5
(f) Age of receivables in months	1.0	1.0
(g) Labour capacity ratio	107.1%	60.7%

When she received the performance indicators, your Managing Director called a meeting to discuss future manufacturing strategy. Several changes were proposed including the following:

From the Managing Director:

"I propose that we close Factory A and transfer its business to Factory B."

From the General Manager of Factory A:

"I estimate that 60% of Factory A's output is sold locally. If we close Factory A, this business will be lost. Also, the closure costs will be £250,000. Surely, the General Manager of Factory B should be looking to increase revenue from his facility."

From the General Manager of Factory B:

"Given the current poor economic climate, I think it would be wrong to plan an increase in our revenue. Taking on 40% of Factory A's revenue would lead to an increase in our fixed production overheads and administration costs. I estimate that production overheads would increase by £100,000 and administration costs by £60,000. In addition, all sales and distribution costs will rise in line with turnover."

From the Finance Director:

"If we close Factory A, we will centralise purchasing. I have carried out some research and we can move to just-in-time manufacture. If we rationalise our supplier base, we can save 5% in our total material costs and remove the need to hold raw material inventories."

(a) Prepare a revised Income Statement for Factory B, assuming Factory A is closed.

	£000
Revenue	
Materials	
Direct labour	
Fixed production overheads	
Cost of sales	
Gross profit	
Sales and distribution costs	
Administration costs	
Operating Profit	

(b) Using appropriate financial data and performance indicators, write a memo to the Board of Directors on whether to proceed with the closure of Factory A.

As the basis for your decision, your memo should include:

(i) a brief comparison of the performance of Factory B before and after closure of Factory A;

(ii) a brief comparison of the company's performance before and after closure of Factory A.

MEMO

To:

From:

Date:

Subject:

PRACTICE ASSESSMENT ANSWERS

2 Practice Assessment Answers

Section 1

Task 1

(a)

	Quantity	*Unit cost* £	*Total cost* £
Material	10	7.50	75.00
Labour	2	6.00	12.00
Fixed overheads	2	8.00	16.00
Total			103.00

(b) 2,500,000 / 5,000 = **500**

Task 2

	£	*F / A*
Direct labour rate variance AQ x AP = 5,040 x AP = £30,492 AQ x SP = 5,040 x £6 = £30,240	252	A
Direct labour efficiency variance AQ x SP = 5,040 x £6 = £30,240 SQ x SP = 2,400 x 2 x £6 = £28,200	1,440	A
Direct material price variance AQ x AP = 24,550 x AP = £184,616 AQ x SP = 24,550 x £7.50 = £184,125	491	A
Direct material usage variance. AQ x SP = 24,550 x £7.50 = £184,125 SQ x SP = 2,400 x 10 x ££7.50 = £180,000	4,125	A

Task 3

	£	F / A
Fixed overhead expenditure variance Actual = £38,500 Budget = £38,400 (2,400 x 2 x £8)	100	A
Fixed overhead capacity variance Budget = £38,400 (4,800 x £8) AH x SP = 5,040 x £8 = £40,320	1,920	F
Fixed overhead efficiency variance AH x SP = 5,040 x £8 = £40,320 SH x SR = 2,400 x 2 x £8 = £38,400	1,920	A

Task 4

	£	F / A	£
Standard cost of actual production (W1)			247,200
Direct labour rate	252	A	
Direct labour efficiency	1,440	A	
Direct material price	491	A	
Direct material usage	4,125	A	
Fixed overhead expenditure	100	A	
Fixed overhead volume	NIL	N/A	
Total variance	6,408	A	6,408
Actual costs			
Direct material	184,616		
Direct labour	30,492		
Fixed overhead	38,500		
Actual cost of production			253,608

(W1) (£75 + £12 + £16) x 2,400 = £247,200

Task 5

(a)

Jan	*Feb*	*Mar*
Actual price was £6.00	Actual price was £6.00	Actual price was £6.30
Seasonal variation was –10p	Seasonal variation was –15p	Seasonal variation was 10p
Trend £6.10	Trend £6.15	Trend £6.20

The trend in prices is an increase of £0.05 per month.

(b) **A**

	Jan	*Feb*	*March*
Total cost	£15,000	£20,000	£22,320
Total quantity purchased	2,000 m	2,500 m	2,480 m
Cost per m	£7.50	£8.00	£9.00
Index	100		£9.00 / £7.50 x 100 = **120**

(c) The equation is Y = a + bX, where the value for X in May 2011 is 18

The constant "a" is 100 and constant "b" is 2.7.

Y = 100 + (2.7 x 19) = 151.3 (June)

Y = 100 + (2.7 x 20) = 154.0 (July)

Task 6

To: Finance Director	Subject: Reason for variances
From: Accounting Technician	Date: December 20XY

(i) Material price variance – Adverse

The company must have paid a higher price for its materials than it expected, perhaps due to general price increases (inflation), or a shortage in supply where high demand can push prices up.

(ii) Material usage variance – Adverse

The machines which are reaching the end of their operational life may not be working accurately and causing wastage of the material. Another reason could be that the trainees are making mistakes causing the wastage.

(iii) Direct labour rate variance – Favourable

The actual rate paid to staff must be lower than the standard. This could be due to the standard having been set to take account of the pay rise which has not yet happened. Alternatively, the two new operators may be on lower wages until they are more experienced and they may lower the average wage rate.

(iv) Direct labour efficiency variance – Adverse

This could be due to the training of the 2 new staff which not only reduces their efficiency but also the efficiency of the other operators training them.

(v) Fixed overhead expenditure variance – Averse

The actual bills for fixed overheads (such as rent) at the end of the period must total more than the budgeted figure anticipated at the beginning of the period.

(vi) Fixed overhead volume variance – Favourable

The volume variance is the sum of the capacity and efficiency variance .i.e. £10,000F + £6,000A = £4,000F. This will have arisen due to the actual number of units produced being greater than the budgeted number. This means that the company has over-absorbed its fixed overhead.

Section 2

Task 1

Capacity ratio = $\frac{\text{Actual hours worked}}{\text{Budgeted hours}} \times 100\%$ $= \frac{5,040}{4,800} \times 100\%$	105%
Efficiency ratio = $\frac{\text{Standard hours produced}}{\text{Actual hours worked}} \times$ 100% $= \frac{(2,400 \times 2)}{5,040} \times 100\%$ $= \frac{4,800}{5,040} \times 100\%$	95.2%
Activity ratio = $\frac{\text{Standard hours produced}}{\text{Budgeted hours}} \times$ 100% $= \frac{4,800}{4,800} \times 100\%$	100%

Task 2

	Current	*Future*	*Change*
Revenue	20,000	27,000	7,000
Material	(2,000)	(2,700)	(700)
Labour	(5,000)	(6,750)	(1,750)
Fixed overhead	(5,000)	(3,000)	2,000
Depreciation	Nil	(5,000)	(5,000)
Additional profit			1,550

The return on the additional investment would be **3.1 %.** (1,550 / 50,000 x 100)

Fixed costs (3,000 + 5,000)	£8,000
Contribution per unit (1.80 – 0.18 – 0.45)	£1.17
Break even volume (units)	6,838

Task 3

Year	*0*	*1*	*2*	*3*	*4*	*5*
Cash flow	(700,000)	(50,000)	(50,000)	(50,000)	(50,000)	150,000
DF	1	0.909	0.826	0.751	0.683	0.621
PV	(700,000)	(45,450)	(41,300)	(37,550)	(34,150)	93,150
NPC	(765,300)					

Year	*0*	*1*	*2*	*3*	*4*
Lease costs	(200,000)	(200,000)	(200,000)	(200,000)	(200,000)
DF	1	0.909	0.826	0.751	0.683
PV	(200,000)	(181,800)	(165,200)	(150,200)	(136,600)
NPC	(833,800)				

Based on the calculations it is best to **BUY** the machine, in order to save **£68,500.**

Task 4

(a) Revised Income Statement for Factory B, assuming Factory A is closed.

	£000
Revenue	3,730.0
Materials	995.6
Direct labour	624.0
Fixed production overheads	520.0
Cost of sales	2139.6
Gross profit	1,590.4
Sales and distribution costs	837.6
Administration costs	310.0
Operating Profit	442.8

Workings:

		£000
Revenue	(40% × 2,200) + 2,850	3,730.0
Materials	95% × [(40% × 660) + 784]	995.6
Direct labour	(40% × 440) + 448	624.0
Fixed production overheads	420 + 100	520.0
Sales and distribution costs	(640/2,850) × 3,730	837.6
Administration costs	250 + 60	310.0

MEMO

To: Board of Directors
From: Accounting Technician
Date: December 20XY
Subject: Manufacturing Strategy

The revised operating statement for Factory B indicates that an operating profit of £442,800 can be made if Factory A closes. This compares with an operating profit for Factory B of £308,000 before closure of Factory A. This profit is based on a number of assumptions which include:

1 40% of revenue from Factory A being transferred to Factory B with the same sales prices and direct costs achieved by Factory A

2 an estimate that fixed production and administration costs will increase by no more than £160,000 in total for Factory B

3 achievement of a 5% reduction in material costs from adopting just-in-time manufacture.

A comparison of performance indicators for Factory B before and after closure of Factory A would indicate an improved performance for Factory B. For example, the operating profit margin increases from 10.8% (308 / 2,850 x 100%) to 11.9% (442.8 / 3,370 x 100%) and the capacity ratio from 60.7% (given) to 82.1% (60% of A 75,000 hrs lost = 45,000 hrs lost. Therefore, 30,000 A + 85,000 B = 115,000 hrs of 140,000 hrs available in factory B = 82.1%). However, from the company's perspective, it should analyse the consolidated performance of both factories pre-closure with the performance of Factory B after the closure of Factory A.

It is important to note that without closure of Factory A, the saving of 5% on material costs would still be available to the company. This saving would amount to £72,200 ((£660,000 + £784,000) x 5%) and would increase the combined operating profits from Factories A and B to £530,200 (£150,000 + £308,000 + £72,200). In addition, the company would not incur closure costs of £250,000. Overall, in the short term the company will achieve greater profits from continuing to operate both factories.

Glossary

Term	Description
Absorption costing	Stock units are valued at variable cost plus fixed production overheads.
Activity based costing	A more accurate method of charging costs to cost units than absorption costing.
Attainable standard	A standard that can be achieved in reasonably good conditions.
Balanced scorecard	An approach to performance measurement that recognises that the business must be successful from several perspectives, not just in earning short-term profits.
Basic standard	A standard that is fixed historically and not changed.
Benchmarking	Comparison of the performance of one's own business with the performance of competitors, in order to identify areas of improvement.
Breakeven point	The level of activity required to make no profit and no loss.
Capital expenditure	Expenditure on the purchase or improvement of fixed assets, appearing in the balance sheet.
Contribution	Sales revenue less variable cost of sales.
Cost absorption	The charging of overhead costs to cost units.
Cost accounting	The analysis of costs and revenues to provide useful information to assist the management accounting function.
Cost allocation	The charging of overhead costs to the specific cost centre that incurred them.

Term	Description
Cost apportionment	The splitting of shared overhead costs between relevant cost centres using an appropriate basis.
Cost centre	A location, function, activity or item of equipment in respect of which costs are accumulated.
Cost of quality	The difference between the actual cost of producing, selling and supporting the company's products, and the equivalent cost if there were no failures during production or usage.
Cost reduction	A process to drive down the unit cost of products without reducing their suitability for the use intended.
Cost unit	An individual unit of product or service for which costs can be separately ascertained.
Cost-volume-profit (CVP) analysis	Analysis of the effects of changes of volume on contribution and profit.
Depreciation	An annual internal charge to the profit and loss account that spreads the net cost of a fixed asset over the number of years of its useful life.
Direct costs	Costs that can be related directly to a cost unit.
Direct expenses	Expenses that can be related specifically to a cost centre.
Discounted cash flow	An investment appraisal technique which discounts future cash flows to a present value.
Effectiveness	The degree to which an objective or target is met.
Efficiency	The relationship between inputs and the outputs achieved.
Expenses	Items of expenditure that are not labour or materials related.
Financial accounting	The production of an historic record of transactions presented in a standard format for use by parties external to the business.
Fixed costs	Costs that vary with time, not activity level.
Ideal standard	A standard that can only be achieved in perfect conditions.

Term	Description
Idle time	Paid for, but non-productive, hours.
Index numbers	A method of assessing growth by allocating an index number of 100 to a base figure in a series, and converting all other figures in the series to an index number using the formula: $\text{Index} = \frac{\text{Current years figure}}{\text{Base year figure}} \times 100$
Indirect cost	Other costs. Also called overheads.
Interdependence of variances	The fact that different variances may be linked by a common cause.
Investigation of variances	Examining the causes of variances with a view to introducing controls.
Key factor analysis	The technique of allocating resources between products according to contribution per unit of resource.
Limiting factor	The resource whose shortage limits the entire capacity of the business operation. Also known as the key factor.
Management accounting	The generation, presentation and interpretation of historic, budgeted and forecast information for management for the purposes of planning, control and decision-making.
Management information system (MIS)	A system providing managers at all levels of a business with the information that they need to carry out their roles.
Marginal costing	Costing system under which stocks are measured at their marginal (Variable) cost only. All fixed costs are written off as incurred.
Margin of safety	The amount by which the level of activity can fall below budget before a loss is made.
Over/under absorption (recovery)	Where the amount of overhead absorbed into cost units, using the pre-determined absorption rate, is more/less than the overheads actually incurred.

Term	Description
PEST analysis	Analysis of the political, economic, social and technological environment facing an organisation.
Population	The entire set of data from which a sample is selected.
Present value	The value at today's date of an amount of cash received/paid at some time in the future, taking account of the compound interest earned over the relevant period.
Primary data	Data gathered expressly for the purpose in hand.
Productivity	The efficiency of resource usage (particularly labour) and often measured in non-financial terms.
Random sampling	Sampling method in which every item in the population has an equal chance of being selected.
Revenue expenditure	Expenditure on goods and services that will be charged to the profit and loss account.
Sampling	Investigating less than 100% of the items in a population, in order to draw a conclusion about the population.
Secondary apportionment	The re-apportionment of service cost centres' overhead costs to production cost centres.
Secondary data	Data gathered for a purpose other than the purpose in hand.
Semi-variable costs	Costs with both a fixed and variable element.
Significance of variances	Assessing the importance of variances with a view to investigation, typically by expressing the variance as a percentage of the standard amount.
Standard cost	The planned unit cost of the products, components or services produced in a period.
SWOT analysis	Analysis of an organisations strengths, weaknesses, opportunities and threats.

Term	Description
Time series	A set of values recorded for some variable over a period of time.
Total absorption costing	Costing system under which stocks are measured at their total production cost (including fixed production overheads).
Total quality management	A business philosophy dedicated to a continuous improvement in quality, efficiency and effectiveness.
Trend	The general direction in which a time series is going, once the short-term variations have been eliminated.
Usage	The quantity of items required for sale (in the case of goods for resale) or production (in the case of components or raw materials) in a given period.
Variable costs	Costs that vary in direct proportion to the level of activity.
Variance	The difference between a planned, budgeted or standard cost and the actual cost incurred.

INDEX

A

Absorption, 53, 56
Activity ratio, 381
Activity-based costing (ABC), 69
Additive model, 165
Allocation, 52
Apportionment, 52
Appraisal costs, 396
Asset turnover, 354
Attainable (expected) standards, 203

B

Balanced scorecard, 398
Basic standards, 203
Batch costs, 30
Benchmarking, 405
Breakeven analysis, 92

C

Capacity ratio, 381
Capacity variance, 226
Closure of a business segment, 373
Cluster sampling, 174
Contribution, 89
Cost accounting, 24
Cost centres, 31
Cost classification, 33
Cost control, 403
Cost drivers, 70
Cost pools, 70
Cost reduction, 403
Cost units, 28
Cost-volume-profit (CVP) analysis, 91
Critical success factors (CSFs), 399
Current ratio, 358
Cyclical variations, 147

D

Direct costs, 34

E

Effectiveness, 347, 381
Efficiency, 347
Efficiency ratio, 381
Efficiency variance, 226

F

Failure costs, 395
Financial accounting, 2
Fixed costs, 37
Fixed overhead expenditure variance, 224
Fixed overhead volume variance, 225
Flexibility, 387
Forecasting, 9

G

Gearing, 380
Gross profit margin, 355

H

High/low method, 41

I

Ideal standards, 202
Idle time, 220
Index numbers, 175
Indirect costs, 34
Innovation, 386
Interdependence of variances, 295
Inventory holding period (inventory days), 359

Investigation of variances, 289
Investment centres, 32

J

Job costs, 30
Journal entries, 244

K

Key performance indicators, 399

L

Labour efficiency variance, 218
Labour rate variance, 217
Lifecycle costing, 132
Limiting factor analysis, 97
Limiting factors, 372
Linear regression, 159
Liquidity, 358

M

Management accounting, 2
Management information systems (MIS), 3
Margin of safety, 93
Marginal costing, 81, 236, 283
Materials price variance, 211
Materials usage variance, 212
Mechanisation, 373
Moving averages, 149
Multiplicative model, 170
Multi-stage sampling, 173

N

Net present cost, 129
Net present value (NPV), 122
Net terminal cost, 129
Non-random sampling methods, 174

O

Overhead, 51

P

Performance indicator, 347, 387, 428
Prevention costs, 396
Product lifecycle, 133
Productivity, 381, 390
Profit centres, 32
Profit margin, 353
Profitability, 391

Q

Qualitative performance indicators, 347
Quality circles, 395
Quality of service, 386, 393
Quality-related costs, 395
Quantitative performance indicators, 347
Quick ratio, 358
Quota sampling, 174

R

Random sampling, 173
Random variations, 148
Ratio analysis, 348
Reconciliations, 276
Resource utilisation, 386, 391
Responsibility accounting, 295
Return on capital employed (ROCE), 351

S

Scattergraph, 148
Seasonal variations, 147, 164
Semi-variable (mixed) costs, 38
Standard cost, 198
Standard cost card, 208
Standard costing, 198
Stepped costs, 38
Stratified sampling, 173
Systematic sampling, 173

T

Target costing, 404
Time series analysis, 146
Total quality management (TQM), 394
Trade payables payment period (trade payable days), 360
Trade receivables collection period (trade receivable days), 359
Trend, 147

U

Unit costs, 386, 390

V

Value added, 383
Value engineering, 404
Value enhancement, 403, 404
Variable costs, 36
Variance analysis, 208

W

What if? Analysis, 368